Leckie
the education publisher
for Scotland

UPDATED FOR THE REVISED EXAM!

N5 & Higher PSYCHOLOGY

STUDENT BOOK

N5 & Higher PSYCHOLOGY STUDENT BOOK

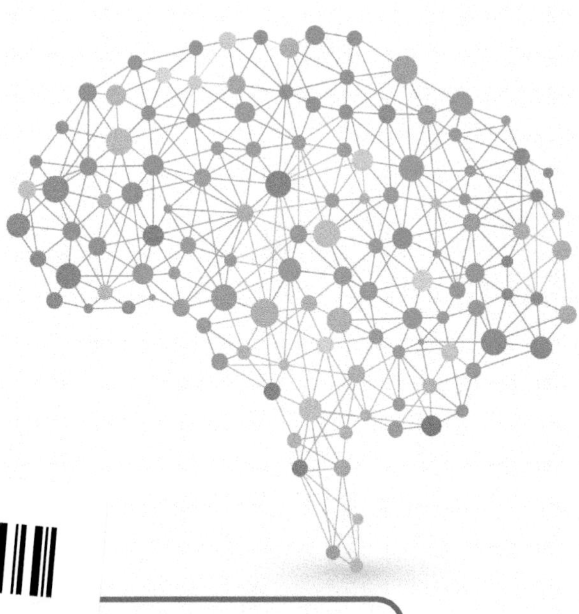

onathan Firth

Introduction

1 Introduction to Psychology

What this book covers

This textbook aims to help you develop the knowledge and skills needed to excel in your National 5 or Higher coursework and exam. Don't worry if you have never studied Psychology before – most people on this course are beginners, even at Higher level. If you are fortunate enough to be able to study National 5 one year followed by Higher the next year, then this textbook can be used for both years of study.

What is Psychology?

A common and reasonable question is to ask what the study of Psychology is all about. In fact, you have asked psychological questions before – though perhaps you didn't realise it – whenever you have considered why someone behaves the way they do. If you have an idea about how people are affected by their parents or their friends, or why people get addicted to drugs, or what attracts one person to another, then you have the beginnings of a psychological theory or hypothesis. As a science, though, a theory is not enough in Psychology – we also need evidence. An important part of this subject is the research needed to find factual evidence about human behaviour.

It is worth dispelling a couple of myths before you start:

Myth: Psychology is all about mental illness. In fact, this is just one of a number of areas of study – and it is just as important to study what makes people happy and successful. In addition, only a small proportion of psychologists work as therapists. Some other psychology careers include sports psychology, forensic psychology, educational psychology, research, and teaching.

Myth: Psychology is all about the brain. Studying the brain is not the same as studying the human mind. The study of the brain as an organ is known as neuroscience, and is a branch of biology. There are many important overlaps between the two, but the bulk of psychology does not involve looking at brains.

Myth: Psychology is all common sense. Psychology is based on the scientific method and regardless of what people *believe* to be true we need factual research evidence. Sometimes the evidence fits with what we consider common sense but sometimes it does not – many findings throughout the history of the subject have been highly unexpected.

Psychology involves the study of people's actions ('behaviour') and the thought processes in their minds, and is therefore often referred to as *the science of the mind and behaviour.* Have a look at the chapter headings in this book to get more of an idea about of the kind of areas that we study – though in fact, any type of behaviour can be (and probably is) studied by psychologists.

Structure of the course

In what order should the chapters be read? You may find that your school or college tackles the topics in a different order from the way they are presented in this textbook. Your teachers or lecturers will have chosen how to teach the course based on their knowledge and experience of the subject, and the chapters in this book can be used in more or less any order – though this chapter should be read first as an introduction, and it would be helpful to read chapter 8 (Research) before moving on to chapter 9 (the Assignment).

Generally speaking, you will cover one of the option topics in chapters 3 to 6 and one of the option topics in chapters 11 to 14; everything else is mandatory. Therefore, the following chapters, or at least part of them, should be studied by all learners at both National 5 and Higher:

- Sleep (chapter 2)
- Research (chapter 8)
- The Assignment (chapter 9)
- Conformity (chapter 10)

All of these have differences depending on the level, and there is advice throughout the book to help you identify which part of the topics you need to focus on.

All Higher option topics are included. The National 5 course includes a choice of two option topics for each unit, and although this book provides popular choices it is possible that your school or college will choose a different topic. Refer to the Key Skills section (see chapter 7) to ensure that you understand how to tackle exam questions in any topic, and look out for further support materials on the Leckie and Leckie website.

Top tip

SQA documents can be changed. ALWAYS check the most recent version of key course documents.

Top tip

Discuss exam format and assessment standards with your teacher or lecturer.

Top tip

Familiarise yourself with the format of SQA's specimen question paper.

Thinking psychologically

This course will help you to think psychologically and scientifically – a mindset that you can apply to your everyday life. Using psychological knowledge to improve your own life and other people's wellbeing in the real world is called **psychological literacy.** To get the most out of this course, don't just focus on preparing for your exam, but tackle the subject more widely – read current articles about psychology online, or in student magazines. Try to make connections between psychology and the real life situations that you are interested in.

You may feel confident enough to tackle some books related to psychology, too. The following are very easy reads and ideal places to start. All are available as ebooks, or try asking your librarian:

- *What the Dog Saw* by Malcolm Gladwell
- *The Man who Mistook his Wife for a Hat and Other Clinical Tales* by Oliver Sacks
- *The Naked Ape* by Desmond Morris
- *Mindset: How You Can Fulfil Your Potential* by Carol Dweck
- *Elephants on Acid: and Other Bizarre Experiments* by Alex Boese
- *Night School: Wake Up to the Power of Sleep* by Richard Wiseman
- *They F*** You Up: How to Survive Family Life* by Oliver James

If tackling these books seems daunting, remember that academic and popular science books are not novels, so you don't need to read them from cover to cover! Read the start, dip in to whichever chapters sound relevant, and skip bits that are of less interest.

Eating and thinking are examples of behaviours

Laughing is a response to the stimulus of a joke

? Discussion point

Do you understand what is meant by a stimulus and a response? Can you think of another example?

Introduction to the approaches

Why do we behave the way we do? Most issues in psychology are based on this fundamental question. Psychologists try to explain why we act the way we do and why we think the way we do. They try to explain all kinds of **behaviour**. In psychology, the word behaviour can be used very broadly and refer to all kinds of human actions. Shouting, eating, kissing, thinking or picking your nose – all of these are examples of behaviours.

Of course, behaviours usually don't happen for no reason, but are the reaction to something, such as when someone is rude to you and you get angry. Two other psychological terms are useful here – a **stimulus** is a very general word that means anything from the environment which impacts on an individual. This could be anything from a person smiling at you, to hearing music, to an uncomfortable seat. Essentially, a stimulus is anything that can be detected by your senses (Watson, 1913). It is a neutral word, which does not imply that anything good or bad is happening; the plural is 'stimuli'. For example, '*...the stimulus in this experiment was a serious of short noises played through headphones...*' A **response** is another general word meaning any action or biological reaction (i.e. any *behaviour*) that results from a stimulus. If someone tells you a joke and you laugh, the joke is a stimulus and the laughter is a response.

As well as actions, psychologists are of course interested in **the mind**. Psychology would like to explain why people have particular ideas, moods and attitudes, and how these things connect to behaviour. A general term for all of the activities of the mind is our **thought processes**.

Fundamentally, we are interested in thought processes, but the main thing we can observe is behaviour. The two things are linked and sometimes very hard to separate, and both are very much studied. Psychology is therefore often referred to as *the science of the mind and behaviour*.

Scientific explanations

In everyday life, people use many ways of trying to explain why behaviours occur, but most explanations are not very systematic. We might rely on assumptions, and our explanations are likely to be affected by prejudices and by the viewpoint of our particular culture. We may observe a stimulus and a response, and jump to a conclusion that the two must be directly connected.

For example, how would you explain it if someone commits a crime? Look at the following example:

Rob's case

Rob was 14. His teacher shouted at him, and he was sent to stand outside the classroom. Instead of staying there, he ran out of school, picked up a stone, and smashed the window of a shop.

Our everyday explanations might look at the event at school that made Rob angry and prompted him to act that way. We might also think of Rob's parents and other role models, or say that he had something in his basic character that made him more at ease breaking rules than most people are. These explanations might have an element of truth, but they are not scientific explanations that have been tested or that rule out other variables.

In contrast, psychologists try to explain behaviour by studying it scientifically. They conduct experiments, often keeping conditions constant and changing just a single thing, to see what effect it has on behaviour. This is called an experiment and it is a key part of the scientific method. You will learn more about **research methods** in chapter 8.

Different approaches to psychology

The history of psychology has been dominated by conflicting explanations for behaviour and thought processes. These are called **approaches** to psychology. A key skill throughout the topics of this course will be to analyse different theories which are based upon these approaches.

For any behaviour, there is more than one explanation for why it occurred. As the evidence we have may not be complete, there can be a scientific debate as to how best to explain the available evidence. Just as geologists might study rock samples and debate processes such as glaciation, so, too, psychologists try to make sense of the available evidence and draw conclusions.

What is more important – parental upbringing or the social group that we join?

Make the link

...between the nature-nurture debate in Psychology and in other subjects such as Modern Studies.

The nature-nurture debate

A good example of different approaches is the well-known **nature-nurture debate**. In the previous section, a *nature* explanation would say that Rob is basically a bad person, perhaps with genes that made him more likely to commit an aggressive act. A *nurture* explanation would focus on Rob's upbringing, and look at the influence of his parents as well as social pressure from his friends in order to understand why he committed the act of vandalism.

Psychologists have been arguing both sides of the nature-nurture debate for years, but the choice is now seen as over-simplistic, as it has become clear that both nature and nurture can influence behaviour. Also, it is important to separate out different aspects of nature or nurture. For example, on the nurture side, what is more important – parental upbringing or the social group that we join?

What is an approach?

An approach is a particular way of looking at psychology and it involves certain key beliefs about human behaviour and the human mind. It can include:

- Particular types of theories: for example, some approaches prefer logical flow charts, some have highly mathematical theories and others prefer general concepts.
- Particular methods of study: whether researchers in the approach prefer experiments, surveys, case studies, etc.
- Particular areas of study: approaches tend to link to particular topics. However, as you will see during this course, topics can be explained using more than one approach, and psychologists do not often agree on which approach is the most useful.

One viewpoint says that our brain is directly controlling what we do

Several approaches

The psychological approaches are more detailed and sophisticated explanations of behaviour. The short explanations that follow summarise eight major ways of explaining behaviour in a simplified form:

- Due to the brain. One viewpoint says that our brain is directly controlling what we do and that our brain chemistry determines how we react to things.
- Due to upbringing. The person's personality and tendencies throughout life are shaped by our early experiences, for example, by strict/loving parents.
- Due to hidden emotions and thoughts that we are not even aware of (in the 'unconscious' parts of the mind).

- Conscious decision making and/or information processing. A person has a set of beliefs and knowledge that allows them to decide what to do. This perspective thinks our behaviour is based on rational choices.
- Due to learning, and the good or bad outcomes of interactions. The person has associated good outcomes with certain behaviours and now does those things more (and vice-versa for bad outcomes).
- As a product of our genes and evolution. Some psychologists think that behaviours are determined mainly by genetics, and that these genes evolved through natural selection because they helped our ancestors to survive.
- Human nature. Although people are basically good at heart, most people are not truly themselves because they have been treated badly in life and do not make the most of themselves.
- Culture and society. We learn how to behave from the people around us, and can be 'programmed' by our society. What we consider 'normal' depends strongly on our culture.

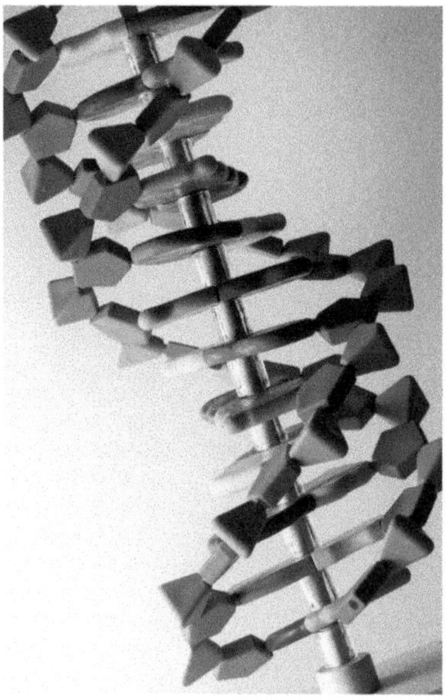

Some psychologists think that behaviours are determined mainly by genetics

Discuss how these explanations can apply to some human behaviours such as the following:

- why people get angry when they are insulted
- why some people work hard and others do not
- why many people are afraid of harmless spiders
- why people have bad habits like biting their nails
- why someone dislikes a particular food.

Top tip

Note how most of these approaches are based on either nature or nurture, but focus on a specific aspect.

Feedback on discussion

In principle, any of the approaches can be used to explain any of the behaviours. The examples below show two fairly straightforward possibilities for each one, but well done if you considered other combinations.

How can nail biting be explained by the approaches?

- Getting angry when insulted
  Hidden emotions: threats to self-esteem may lead to a defensive reaction that we do not consciously understand. Genes and evolution: in our evolutionary past, it may have been advantageous to try to achieve higher status, and therefore to react aggressively to insults.
- Why some people work hard and others do not
  Upbringing: parental behaviour may play a role, with parents as role models. Human nature: some people may be fulfilling their full potential, while others have unfulfilled potential due to negative life circumstances.
- Why many people are afraid of harmless spiders
  Genes and evolution: in our evolutionary past, these animals (or similar ones) might have presented much more of a threat than they do today. Learning: we may have had a bad and upsetting experience, for example having seen someone else scream at a spider.

! Syllabus note

Approaches are the basis of theories throughout the course. You won't be asked about approaches in the exam, but you will use this knowledge when explaining theories.

- Why people have habits
  The brain: certain brain areas give us a sense of reward/pleasure from our habits. Hidden emotions: habits such as nail biting may relate to unconscious emotions from childhood such as wanting to be fed as a baby.
- Why someone dislikes a particular food
  Culture and society: we tend to like what is normal to us, and foods that are unfamiliar for our culture may seem strange or unappealing. Conscious decision-making: we may have a belief that a particular food is dangerous or unhealthy, and have therefore decided not to eat it.

Key concepts

- Behaviour
- Stimulus
- Response
- The mind
- Thought processes
- Research methods
- Approach
- Nature-nurture debate

Activities

1. Look at the eight short explanations on pages 8–9 again. Can you use them to explain a more complex behaviour, such as why Rob committed an act of violence? How about explaining why people fall in love or what job they choose to do? You may need to use a combination of approaches for this. Take some notes and report them back to fellow students or write a blog post with your ideas.
2. Discuss the optional approaches with classmates and your teacher/lecturer, and make sure you know which topics you will be studying, and which approaches you should apply to each topic.

Sample answer for Rob's case

Rob's parents may have been very strict

- Brain: some violent killers have been shown to have brain abnormalities – it is possible (though unlikely) that Rob has this kind of abnormality.
- Upbringing: Rob's parents may have encouraged aggression in some way such as by being aggressive role models, or alternatively they may have been very strict and he may be rebelling.
- Hidden emotions: Rob may be directing the anger he feels towards his teacher/peers/parents at an easier target by breaking the window.
- Decision making: Rob may have rationally decided it would be a waste of time to stand outside the classroom, and he would rather have some fun.
- Learning: perhaps Rob has done this in the past and has been rewarded by attention and special treatment, or just by the thrill of breaking things.
- Genes: humans, especially males, have a history of violence. Rob has inherited genes for anger and aggression.
- Human nature: Rob could be a good person but he is constantly getting a hard time from parents and teachers and perhaps being bullied too. Until he is in a warmer and more accepting environment, he can't be his true, creative self.
- Culture: Rob has grown up seeing violence all around him and on TV and he has learned that it is an appropriate response to dealing with problems. Also, he may be a member of an aggressive subculture such as a gang or be experiencing peer pressure that encourages him to appear as a rebel.

The biological approach

The **biological approach** tries to explain behaviour in terms of the biological processes within our bodies, especially the brain, our genes and chemicals such as hormones and neurotransmitters. For example, researchers into aggression who take a biological approach to psychology have tried to explain aggressive behaviour in terms of hormones such as testosterone, or in terms of parts of the brain that regulate emotion. This contrasts with researchers from other approaches who have tried to explain aggressive behaviour in terms of parenting and life experiences.

This approach uses an understanding of the human body to explain behaviour. There are four key biological processes that the approach focuses on:

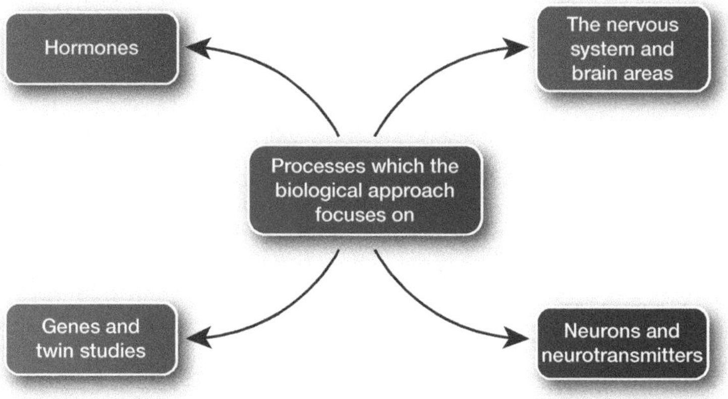

Top tip

Hormones play a role in a great many areas of Psychology. In particular, the topics of Sleep, Depression, Stress, Relationships and Aggression all focus on the effect of hormones on behaviour.

The biological approach explains aggressive behaviour in terms of hormones such as testosterone (see chapter 14)

The nervous system and brain areas

A key aim of this approach is to understand the links between the **nervous system** and psychological processes. The nervous system is the network of nerve cells around your body, including the brain, the spinal cord, and all of the nerves that connect the brain and spinal cord to your organs, muscles and sense organs. In particular, the nervous system divides into two main branches – the central nervous system and the peripheral nervous system, each of which can be further divided up:

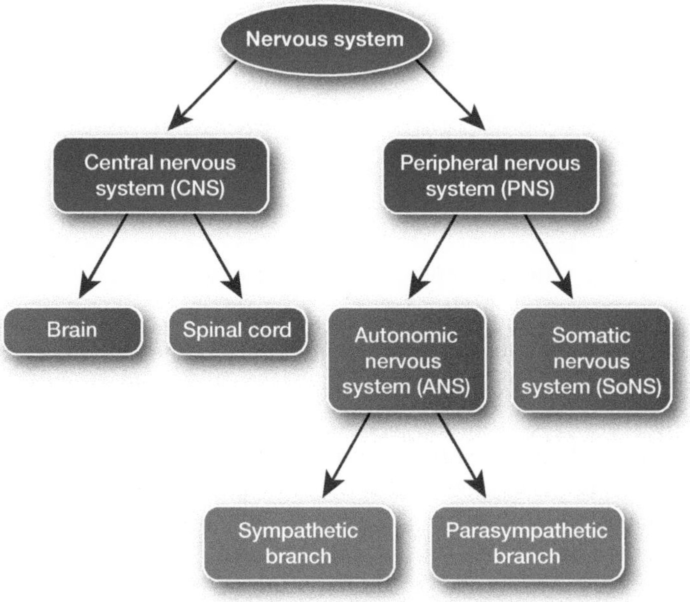

The central nervous system is comprised of **the brain** and spinal cord, and of particular interest to psychology is the brain – the largest and most complex part of the nervous system. Biological psychologists believe that all thoughts and behaviour ultimately depend on brain function. More complex thought processes are thought to take place in the outermost part of the brain, the cerebral cortex, and in particular, the outer layers of the cerebral cortex – the **neocortex**. This is the main part that you can see if you look at a picture of the outside of a human brain. The neocortex is proportionately smaller in other mammals and does not exist at all in fish or insects. It is often shown as comprising four main areas called lobes – the frontal, parietal, occipital and temporal lobes, though it is actually one continuous layer of cells:

> **Top tip**
>
> The neocortex is composed of the six outer layers of the cerebral cortex. There are other layers underneath it that are called the allocortex. However, psychologists tend to be more interested in the neocortex, as most of our advanced psychological abilities are processed there. '*Neo*' means 'new' – it is the most recently evolved part of the brain.

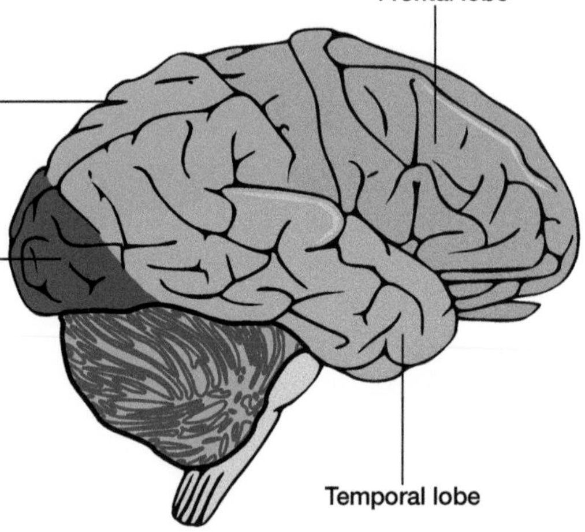

The brain

While biological psychologists believe that the brain and nervous system are responsible for our behaviour, it is difficult to know exactly what area(s) of the brain are involved in any particular behaviour or thought process. It has been a major aim of the biological approach to find out the functions of different areas of the brain. The idea that particular brain areas each have a specific function is called **localisation**.

In the early days of medical anatomy, the brain was a mystery; unlike other parts of the body, it is impossible to guess the function of a brain area simply by looking at it. A breakthrough came in the 1800s when surgeon Paul Broca studied a patient who had lost the ability of speech, but still understood language and had nothing physically wrong with his mouth or throat. Examining the patient's brain *post mortem*, Broca found that a small area of the frontal lobe was missing. Broca realised that this area must be vitally important for speech production; it became known as 'Broca's area'.

The brain studied by Broca, at the Dupuytren museum in Paris

Since the 1800s, many further cases have been studied and researchers have found out about the function of many areas of the brain, and new techniques have been developed. Towards the back of the neocortex, for example, a huge area processes information from the eyes in order to perceive different shapes and textures. Also important is the frontal lobe, which is essential for planning and decision making, and the **limbic system**, where our emotions are processed. Loss of any of these key areas due to brain damage could have dramatic effects, making us lose key thought processes or emotions.

Throughout the 20th century, new techniques were developed that allowed researchers to study individuals who had suffered brain damage, as well as healthy individuals. Two interesting techniques include:

Electrical stimulation

Researcher Wilder Penfield was an expert on the structure of the brain. He performed surgery on damaged brain areas of patients with severe epilepsy to try to stop electrical activity spreading from these areas throughout the cerebral cortex. Penfield's aim was to surgically remove this damaged area in order to stop the seizures from occurring. In order to do so with minimum harm to the patient, Penfield used an electrical probe that stimulated areas of the exposed brain on the operating table, while the patient was still conscious. Remarkably, patients reported vivid sensations and thoughts coming to mind when particular areas of their brain were electrically stimulated. One patient famously said, 'I smell burnt toast!' These medical investigations suggested that particular areas of the brain may be responsible for very specific psychological functions.

A Canadian stamp celebrating Wilder Penfield

Brain scans

Viewing the activity of a living brain is much easier nowadays due to the invention of brain scans. One of the most useful types, the **fMRI scan** (functional magnetic resonance imaging), involves measuring the activity of different brain areas by scanning for oxygen use using an electromagnet. Tiny changes in the brain's oxygen use can be detected and analysed using the scanner's computer. This is very useful to psychologists because it gives a picture of brain activity as someone is doing a task – if someone is reading, for example, visual and verbal areas would be 'lit up' on the scan because those areas are active and therefore using more oxygen.

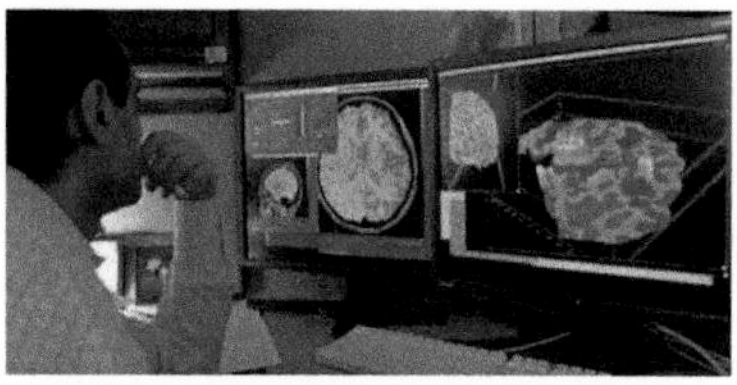

An fMRI scan of the brain

Another useful brain scan is called an electroencephalogram or EEG. This doesn't give a image of what the brain looks like, but instead measures the electrical activity of the brain i.e. the 'brain waves'. This is an essential tool when studying sleep patterns.

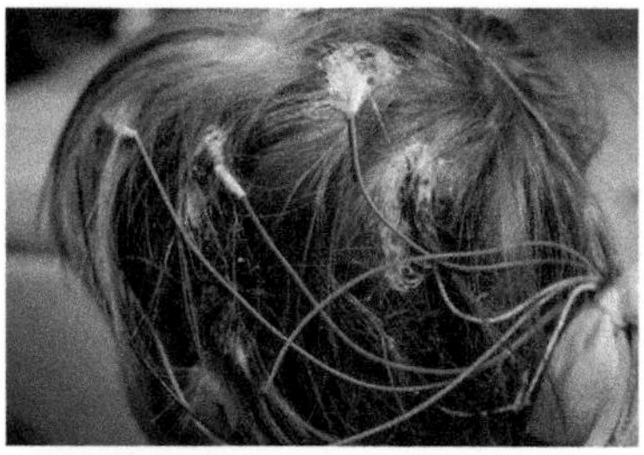

EEG electrodes

With this new technology, biological psychologists are starting to find out more about how the brain controls behaviour and which brain areas are responsible for cognitive functions such as language, memory and intelligence.

Key study: Raine *et al.* (1997): study of brain abnormalities in murderers

Aim: *The study aimed to find out whether there are differences in the brains of people who commit violent crimes.*

Method: *This was a quasi-experiment. One group of participants consisted of 41 people (39 male, two female) who had been charged with murder and had pled not guilty on the grounds of insanity, then been referred for brain scans. They were compared with a control group of 41 people with no convictions.*

Findings: *The brain scans of the people that had been charged with murder showed a lower level of activity in the prefrontal cortex, as well as in the corpus callosum – the area of fibres that connects the two sides of the brain – than the people with no convictions. They also found that the murderers had more asymmetric brain function, with one side more active than the other in several areas.*

Evaluation: *This study provided an interesting perspective on how serious crimes may be linked to reduced brain function. However, we cannot be sure why these brain differences existed, and it is certainly not possible to determine a cause-and-effect relationship between brain abnormalities and murder – for example, we can't scan everyone's brain and determine who is going to commit a murder! Brain scans are useful but it is not always clear what a lower level of brain activity actually means. Also, murder is a varied crime, and it is hard to generalise to all murderers, or to people who commit other crimes.*

Top tip

Test your own ability to sketch a brain and label the main areas. What do you know about localisation of function in each of these areas?

Dr Adrian Raine showing a 3D MRI scan of a murderer's brain

Neurons and neurotransmitters

The human brain is composed of billions of individual brain cells and biological psychologists have become aware of the importance of the way these cells communicate with each other and interact. The most important cells are called neurons – these are the cells that process information and control behaviour.

Top tip

The Raine *et al.* (1997) study could also be used as research evidence in the Aggression topic.

In the late 1940s, Donald Hebb proposed a major theory of the biological approach. He suggested that when we learn things, neurons in our brains are changed, with synapses between these cells being strengthened or new ones forming (Hebb, 1949). At the time, microscopes were not advanced enough to study the connections between neurons, and so nobody could check whether Hebb was correct. However, since that time, the electron microscope has been invented, and the general principle of Hebb's idea has been supported by later research – neurons do change their structure through experience (Kandel & Hawkins, 1992).

Neurotransmitters are messenger chemicals that are released into the gap between two neurons, called the **synapse**. Drugs can interfere with this process, as can be easily observed any time someone you know consumes a psychoactive drug such as alcohol – alcohol and other drugs work by interfering with or mimicking neurotransmitters in the synapses of a person's brain.

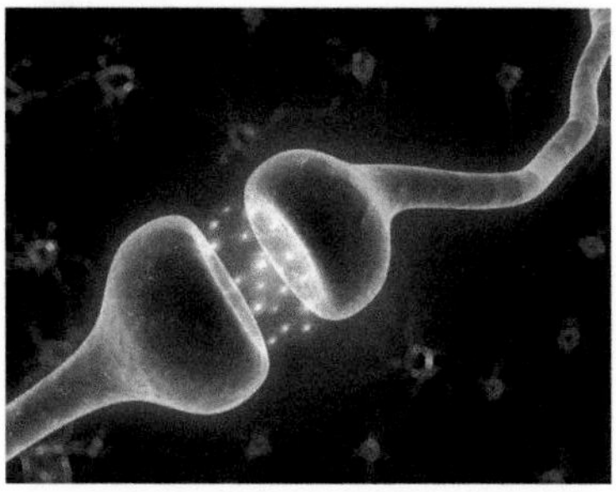

An artist's impression of a synapse

It is really important to have a basic understanding of how brain cells communicate. It will help you to understand medical treatments and the effects of drugs in the other topics. Also, this is an efficient thing to learn – all neurons work in essentially the same way – so learn about one, and you will understand billions.

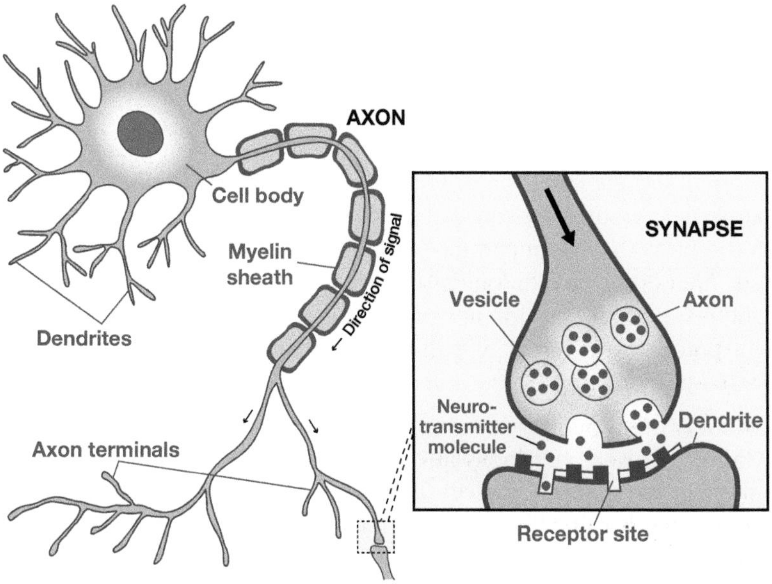

Neuron and synapse

Make the link

...with the action of anti-depressants on the brain, explained in chapter 4.

Hormones

A **hormone** is a chemical that is released by a gland in the body that can affect our organs, including the brain. We have often heard the moody behaviour of friends and family members, particularly adolescents, described in terms of 'hormones'. Is this idea based on reality – do hormones affect our behaviour and moods?

Some hormone levels change as we enter puberty, and several major mental illnesses also first appear at this stage of life – for example, the eating disorder *anorexia nervosa* tends to be diagnosed at around age 14. Depression is found in children, but from puberty onwards it is more common in females. Angold *et al.* (1999) concluded that this difference was best explained in terms of hormonal changes.

Make the link

...with the role of the hormone melatonin in sleep – see chapter 2.

Hormones can affect our behaviour throughout life, usually in a helpful way – in fact, they play an essential role in governing mood, sleep, sexual arousal and many other functions. The hormone melatonin is released at night to help us start to feel sleepy as it gets darker, while stress hormones are an important part of how we react to threats.

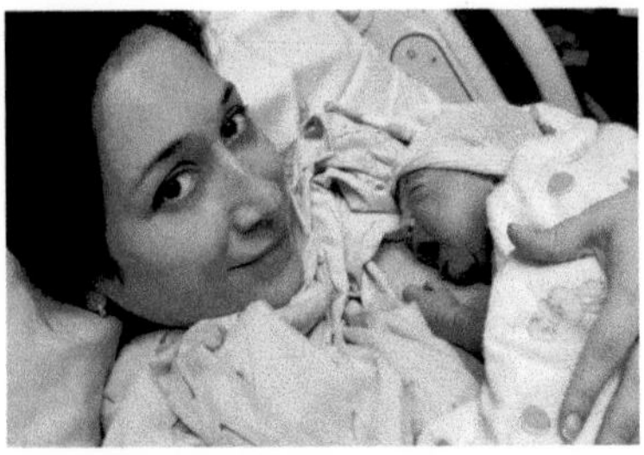

Oxytocin is released in large amounts when a woman gives birth, promoting an immediate strong emotional bond

One hormone has an especially positive effect – **oxytocin**, sometimes called the 'love hormone' is essential for bonding. It is released in large amounts when a woman gives birth, promoting an immediate strong emotional bond to be formed with the new baby (Gordon *et al.*, 2010). The same hormone also plays a large role in romantic relationships later in life, being released during attraction and helping to maintain fidelity (Scheele *et al.*, 2012; see chapter 13). The biological approach, therefore, tries to explain a range of processes from mental illness to falling in love in terms of hormones.

Genes and twin studies

In every human cell, there is a set of **chromosomes**, made of DNA, which control the development and behaviour of that cell. Each chromosome is made up of a number of functional units called **genes**. Each gene can control the development of proteins and therefore has an effect on how that cell works. Just as your genes can influence your physical appearance, for example, by making your skin and eyes a particular colour, it appears that the genes that control the development of the nervous system can have an effect on psychological processes too. Numerous psychological disorders are associated with genetic factors – both depression and schizophrenia are more likely to occur if a parent or identical twin has the disorder (e.g. McGuffin *et al.*, 1996 – see chapter 5).

Twin studies are used to examine the effects of genes on behaviour

One way of studying the effect of genes on behaviour is the **twin study**, where the researcher looks at one or more sets of identical twins. If one twin has a psychological disorder or an exceptional talent, what are the chances that the other twin has it as well? Of course, twins may have had a very similar upbringing to each other, and therefore, it is not just their genes that are similar – their environment is, too. One way around this is to compare identical twins (who share 100% of their genes) with fraternal twins (who share approximately 50%, the same as any brother or sister). Numerous research studies have suggested that identical twins tend to share more characteristics, as evidenced by a greater level of similarity between identical than non-identical twins in areas such as intelligence, personality and the chance of having a mental illness.

? Discussion point

What is meant by '*et al.*' in research? Why is it used? (See p.382 for feedback.)

Evaluation of the biological approach

It is usually an oversimplification to link a psychological process to a single brain area. Researchers are increasingly linking psychological functions to pathways involving several brain areas and the connections between them. In addition, there are individual differences in brain structure, and the brain can reprogramme itself through experience (Doidge, 2007).

Although Kandel and Hawkins (1992) found support for Hebbian learning, they also found it to be oversimplified, as there are other mechanisms by which brain cells strengthen their connections, not just the strengthening of a synapse. More recent research by Sheffield and Dombeck (2015) suggested that dendrites and cell body might be active at different times, which goes against the traditional biological theory of how cells communicate and form memories.

Stress in childhood could determine whether a gene is expressed

The biological approach explains disorders such as depression and attention deficit hyperactivity disorder (ADHD) in terms of genes and disordered brain chemistry. However, Brown and Harris (1978) researched social factors in depression (e.g. unemployment) and found that working class women were five times as likely to be depressed as middle-class women, while prevalence of depression is much higher in the USA (17%) compared to Japan (3%). ADHD is rarely diagnosed in France. These findings suggest that biological factors cannot explain psychological disorders and that culture and society must play a role too.

Genes can be influenced by our surroundings and upbringing – they can be 'switched on and off'. Whether they are **expressed** or not can depend on what happens in our environment. It is therefore impossible to predict how a person will act just by studying their genes. Stress in childhood is one possible environmental influence that could determine whether a gene is expressed (Raj & van Oudenaarden, 2008). The study of gene expression is known as **epigenetics**.

Top tip

Neuron or neurone? Either spelling is fine, although 'neuron' is more common in research. As with other aspects of style where there is an optional spelling, it is best to pick one and stick with it! There is no difference in pronunciation either.

Make the link

With biological explanations of depression, discussed in chapter 4.

Make the link

With the role of epigenetics in aggression, discussed in chapter 14.

Top tip

The principles of the biological approach can be used to help with evaluation in several topics throughout this course. For example, the concept of epigenetics can be used to help criticise any theory which suggests that a trait or problem is mainly determined by a person's genes.

Top tip

Summarise the main areas of this approach onto an index card. Write evaluation points on the back.

Key concepts

- Biological approach
- Nervous system
- The brain
- Neocortex
- Localisation
- Limbic system
- fMRI scan
- EEG
- Synapse
- Hormone
- Oxytocin
- Chromosomes
- Twin study
- Expression (of genes)

Questions

1. What is the technical name for a brain cell?

2. What is the name for the part of the nervous system that includes the brain and spinal cord?

3. What area of the frontal lobe plays a key role in speech?

4. What particular psychological process is associated with the limbic system?

5. Which hormone plays an important role in love, trust and bonding?

6. Name two psychological disorders that show considerable changes after puberty.

7. What is the name for the type of body part that releases hormones?

8. What is the name for the functional part of a chromosome?

9. What does it mean if a gene is not 'expressed'?

10. What does *et al.* stand for in a research citation?

Activities

1. Draw a labelled diagram of both the brain and a neuron. Label all parts of the neuron. Label as many brain areas as you can and write a short description of what each one does. It doesn't need to be a work of art – just try to make it clear.

2. Make your labelled diagram of the brain into a mini-poster. You could focus on a particular part of the brain or certain parts, e.g. the lobes, or brain parts related to language. Put your mini-poster up in your study space or classroom.

The psychoanalytic approach

The **psychoanalytic approach** (also called 'psychodynamic') emphasises the role of the **unconscious** mind in human behaviour, and states that childhood and interactions with our parents can shape personality. It was founded by Sigmund Freud, an Austrian doctor who came to believe that many physical illnesses had psychological causes. He thought that a large part of the mind was hidden to us, and that it would require his talking therapy – **psychoanalysis** – for people to uncover and deal with the hidden conflicts in their minds. Freud made extensive use of case studies of individuals rather than experiments, and made a huge contribution to the development of psychotherapy.

'...we come to the conclusion, from working with hysterical patients and other neurotics, that they have not fully succeeded in repressing the idea to which the incompatible wish is attached. They have, indeed, driven it out of consciousness and out of memory, and apparently saved themselves a great amount of psychic pain, but in the unconscious the suppressed wish still exists...'

Source: Freud (1910, p.189)

! Syllabus note

Although largely historical, the psychoanalytic approach provides a useful perspective on why we have dreams (see chapter 2) and can be applied to many other topics as well. For example, the concept of defence mechanisms is helpful when analysing relationships, memory and prejudice, among other areas.

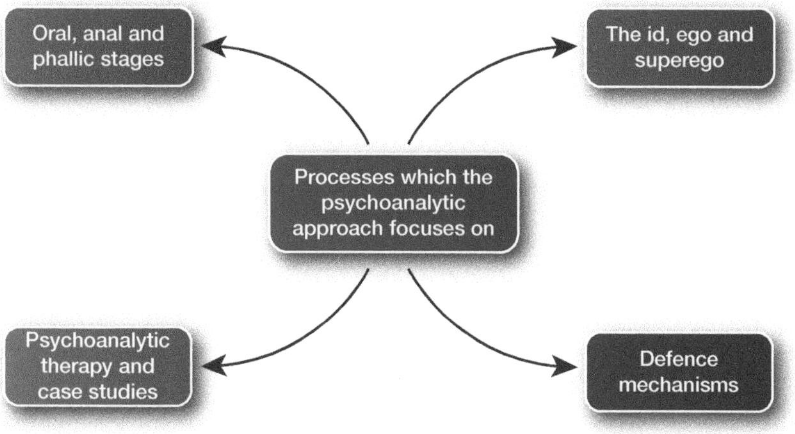

Sigmund Freud

The id, ego and superego

Freud initially thought that the mind was divided into two parts – the conscious and unconscious. However, in his later writings, he explained that there are three main parts to the mind: the **id**, the **ego** and the **superego** (Freud, 1933):

- The id is the unconscious mind. It is the first to develop during childhood. Its motivations are simple and it desires pleasure and gratification. Like a very young child, the id does not understand rules or consequences. Nevertheless, it provides energy for the other parts of the mind, via the libido.
- The ego is the conscious mind – the part you are aware of and that controls all of our rational thoughts.
- The superego is partly conscious and partly unconscious. It is our awareness of society's rules, and therefore provides us with a moral sense of right and wrong. If we do things that our superego does not approve of, then we get a feeling of guilt.

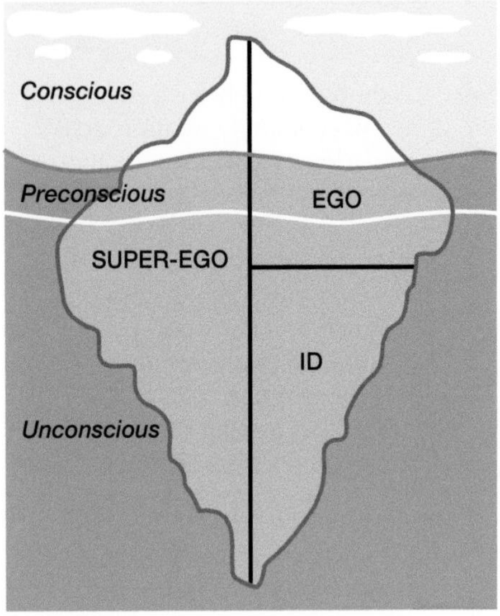

The ego/superego/id iceberg

Freud thought that the id (unconscious) was the source of energy and drives. One of the most important of these was the drive to obtain pleasure, and he called this the **libido**. Libido can be thought of as our sex drive, but is perhaps better seen more generally as 'desire'. Freud thought that even in childhood the libido motivates behaviour, although not in the same way as for adults (Freud, 1910).

Psychological problems can arise from **conflicts** between the conscious and unconscious. The rational ego may be urging a person to do one thing, but the irrational id is prompting them to do something different. Like an iceberg, the largest and most powerful part of the mind – the unconscious – was thought to be beneath the surface. The term **preconscious** is used to mean things that are not conscious at the time – that is, we are not thinking about them – but they could become conscious (Freud, 1933). Our memories fall into this category.

? Discussion point

Do you agree that people are sometimes motivated by thoughts, feelings or memories that they are unaware of? Have you ever done something and been unsure why you did it?

Oral, anal and phallic stages

Freud developed a controversial theory of how people's minds develop through childhood. He thought that just as adults get physical pleasure from sex, so children get pleasure from their bodies too, but from different body parts. He thought that a baby derives pleasure from its mouth (being fed) and called the associated period of development the **oral stage**. He also thought that toddlers get pleasure from controlling bladder and bowel movements when going to the toilet/potty. This was called the **anal stage**.

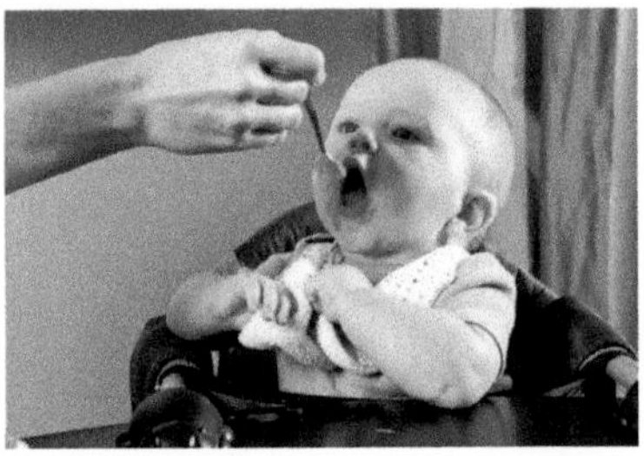

This theory was not just about explaining behaviour during breast-feeding or toilet training – Freud thought that these stages had an important influence on later personality, too. He explained that some people develop a **fixation** in these stages, leading to effects on their personality later in life. Fixation might result from getting too little stimulation during these stages, or from being harshly punished, such as a child being strictly told off for having an accident during toilet training. The idea of people having an 'anal personality' derives from this idea – an *anally retentive* personality is fussy and strict, with an obsession with neatness. Someone with an 'oral personality' may habitually bite their nails, smoke or overeat.

Someone with an 'oral personality' may be a smoker

Perhaps more important still was Freud's view of what happened next. Inspired by a dream that he had about his own mother, Freud stated that boys at around the age of five move into the **phallic stage**, and develop the **Oedipus complex**, where they become romantically attached to their mother as an idealised role model of the opposite sex (Freud, 1910, see box). The boy then feels guilt and fears being punished by his father. Freud's case study of **little Hans** (see chapter 2) is a key example of this stage from his research – Hans was afraid of horses, but Freud thought that in fact, he was afraid of his father. Therefore, Hans was seen as an example of the Oedipus complex.

The Oedipus and Electra complexes

The Oedipus complex is named after a legend from Ancient Greece – Oedipus was the son of the king and queen of the ancient Greek city of Thebes. It was prophesied that he would kill his father and marry his mother, so his father abandoned Oedipus on a hillside to die. However he was rescued and grew up to be a young man, unaware that he was really a prince. When he returned to Thebes, he fought and killed the king, and married the widowed queen, thus fulfilling the prophecy.

The Electra complex is named after Electra, daughter of the legendary King Agamemnon. According to Homer's *Iliad*, Agamemnon was the king who led an alliance of Greek armies to attack and besiege the city of Troy, after a Trojan prince abducted his brother's wife Helen. After he returned from the 10-year war, his own wife had remarried, and she and her new husband plotted to kill him. However, his daughter Electra plotted to murder her mother in revenge.

A painting of Oedipus with his daughter, Antigone

It may be obvious that this part of Freud's theory cannot be applied directly to girls; psychoanalyst C.G. Jung (1961) later developed the idea of the **Electra complex** to suggest that a similar process of falling in love with the father happens to girls (see box above).

Freud said that this stage is resolved when the child appeases the same-sex parent by copying their behaviour, and therefore, at this stage, the boy starts to behave in a more traditionally masculine way and girls adopt traditionally feminine behaviours, such as the clothes that they choose to wear and the activities they are interested in (Freud, 1933).

Defence mechanisms

Freud believed that the ego tries to defend itself by distorting reality. According to this approach, a lot of problematic or disturbed behaviour may be caused by the **defence mechanisms** that the mind uses. Freud believed that some uncomfortable thoughts are a threat to the ego, so they are repressed – pushed out of the conscious mind and into the unconscious. This concept of **repression** is one of the most important defence mechanisms.

In another famous case, Freud's patient, **Anna O**, suffered from paralysis on her right side, and felt nausea when eating or drinking. She also spoke in bizarre strings of apparently unconnected words, and at times seemed unable to understand people. Freud and his colleague Breuer believed that her discomfort with drinking stemmed from a repressed memory of a dog drinking from her water glass. Freud claimed that when the repressed memory was made conscious through therapy, the problem was solved (Freud, 1910). However, later researchers suggested that Anna suffered from a form of epilepsy worsened by drug dependence, making any attempt to generalise from her case problematic (Orr-Andrawes, 1987).

Sigmund and Anna Freud

Sometimes thoughts and memories are thought to have been repressed, meaning that they have apparently been forgotten, but in reality have been pushed out of the ego and into the id because they are too painful or disturbing.

Sigmund Freud's daughter, Anna Freud, was also a prominent psychologist. She wrote a book entitled *The Ego and the Mechanisms of Defence* that expanded on her father's idea of repression, and established defence mechanisms as a key concept in the approach; some of the terms have become part of everyday speech. As well as repression, five major defence mechanisms you should be aware of are as follows:

Regression	Not to be confused with repression, regression means acting in a more childlike way. This links to Freud's theory of psychosexual development – comfort is found in a more childlike state rather than the threatening and conflict-filled present. Examples could include sucking your thumb/biting your nails or chewing on things when anxious, having a childish tantrum or just curling up in your bedroom like a young child might do.
Denial	This is when people distort reality, typically by stating that something is less of a problem than it is. They may ignore the risks of behaviour such as smoking or unprotected sex, or fool themselves into believing that their behaviour is normal or harmless.
Displacement	This is where it would cause anxiety or simply be impossible to direct our emotions towards their true target, so instead we begin to focus the same emotion on another, more accessible target. Examples could be feeling very angry with a strict parent but being too afraid to say so, and so bullying another child instead. Little Hans was thought to have displaced his fear of his father onto horses. Romantic attraction can also be displaced.
Projection	This is where we claim that our feelings belong to someone else. Have you ever heard someone say '*I think my friend is worried about her exams*' or claim that a friend is attracted to someone? Projection could include negative feelings about ourselves. '*You think I'm stupid, don't you?*'
Reaction formation	This is when someone's behaviour is the opposite of their true feelings. For example, if someone is attracted to another person, they may be rude and hurtful instead of showing affection. Similarly, sexual desires may be warded off by exaggerated disgust towards sexuality. The behaviour is as far as possible from their true feelings, so that the ego does not have to consciously accept the true feelings that cause anxiety.

Psychoanalytic therapy and case studies

Arguably, this approach's most lasting influence has been on therapy. Sigmund Freud's approach of listening to patients and analysing what they say has influenced how therapists work today. Many people still work as psychoanalytic therapists, and it is possible to receive psychoanalytic therapy for mental health problems either privately or on the NHS. What is more, even those who do not consider themselves psychoanalysts have been influenced, directly or indirectly, by Freud's methods and ideas.

? Discussion point

What happens if two people simultaneously *project* their feelings onto each other?!

In the early days of psychoanalysis, Freud used the technique of **dream analysis**, believing that dreams reveal unconscious thoughts and motivations (you will learn more about his theories of dreams in chapter 2). As time went on, Freud found **free association** to be a more reliable technique (Freud, 1910). This involves letting the patients speak in an uninterrupted stream of ideas, with one idea leading to the next. Freud felt that this allowed ideas from the unconscious to be revealed. Free association also aimed to strengthen the ego and help patients to develop a clearer idea of reality, and to make the pressure from the superego more humane and less focused on punishment and guilt (Nelson-Jones, 2000). During sessions, the therapist would stay relatively quiet and take notes while the client did most of the talking. Freud's preference was for patients to lie on a couch, not looking at the therapist.

Psychoanalytic therapy

This approach also became well known for using the **case study method**. A case study involves the in-depth study of one person, usually over many weeks or months (it is 'longitudinal'). It gathers a lot of data, and typically involves a range of techniques such as interviews, observations, personality tests and brain scans. It is an ideal technique for unique cases, such as people with unexplained mental illnesses or brain damage. You can read more about this research method in chapter 8.

Freud studied the dreams of his individual patients, for example in the case of Hans, mentioned above (see chapter 2 for more information).

Evaluation

Although it was once central to psychology, the influence of the psychoanalytic approach has decreased in recent years; many current university degrees in psychology now only teach it as a historical perspective. However, it is still an important approach to therapy and has been used to explain phobias (see chapter 3).

The concept of the unconscious mind and the idea that we may be unaware of the reasons behind some of our motivations has returned to popularity. However, many of Freud's theories of the mind are controversial and even 100 years on there is a lack of research evidence to support them. Psychoanalytic theory as a whole is too vague and broad to be testable, and can therefore be called unscientific, though some of the mini-theories within it such as repression can and have been tested (Fisher and Greenberg, 1996).

Top tip

Summarise the main areas of this approach onto an index card. Write evaluation points on the back.

Defence mechanisms are still a useful concept in therapy (Krauss Whitbourne, 2011), although there are various explanations for why people display these behaviours. Key terms such as 'denial' and 'projection' are still widely used.

Key concepts

- Psychoanalytic approach
- Psychoanalysis
- Id
- Ego
- Superego
- Libido
- Conflicts
- Preconscious
- Oral stage
- Anal stage
- Fixation
- Phallic stage
- Oedipus complex
- Electra complex
- Little Hans
- Anna O
- Defence mechanisms
- Repression
- Regression
- Denial
- Displacement (psychoanalytic)
- Projection
- Reaction formation
- Dream analysis
- Free association
- Case study (research method)

Questions

1. Which part of the mind is entirely unconscious?
2. What object was used as an analogy for the fact that much of the mind is beneath the surface?
3. During which stage does an infant get pleasure from using the toilet, according to this approach?
4. What was the main psychological problem of 'little Hans' that his father reported to Freud?
5. What is the name given to the complex experienced by little boys who love their mother and fear their father?
6. Which defence mechanism involves refusing to accept reality such as risky behaviour being a problem?
7. Which defence mechanism involves acting in the opposite way to your own feelings?
8. Which defence mechanism involves saying that someone else is feeling something, when you are actually feeling it yourself?
9. What became the main technique used in psychoanalytic therapy?
10. Give one feature of the case study method.

Activities

1. Working with another student, write a short fictional dialogue that demonstrates one or more of the defence mechanisms. Then read it out to the class and see if they can figure out which mechanism is at work.
2. Look out for examples of defence mechanisms over the next few days, and report them back to class; for ethical reasons, you **must not** use real names if you are discussing the behaviour of friends or family during class.

The cognitive approach

The **cognitive approach** seeks to explain atypical behaviours in terms of knowledge, beliefs and thought processes. A key concept in the approach is that between every stimulus and response, there is a set of psychological processes, called **mediators**, that can affect the way an individual responds.

Two key examples of mediators are memory and perception:

Memory: the process of taking in relevant information, storing it, and then recalling it when required.

Perception: the process of using information from the senses in order to establish a coherent understanding of external events.

! Syllabus note

Theories linked to the cognitive approach are found throughout modern psychology. You will encounter one or more cognitive theories or concepts in nearly every topic on this course.

Illusions are a great example of how perception relies on beliefs. When looking at the famous Leeper's Lady illusion, for example, some interpret the face as a young woman looking away, and some as an older woman looking downwards. Expectations and experience affect what we see. This demonstrates the importance of mental processes in making sense of our surroundings – our experience of the world is constructed in the brain according to our own unique set of cognitive processes.

The Leeper's Lady illusion

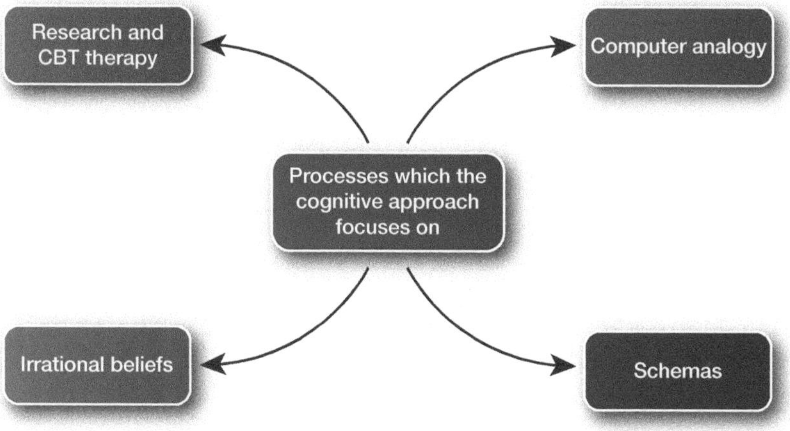

The computer analogy

The cognitive approach started to become the dominant viewpoint in psychology at around about the same time as computer science was taking off. Researchers inevitably began to make comparisons between human cognitive processes and the information processing done by a computer. This **computer analogy** dominated the early days of cognitive psychology and researchers began to ask – would it be possible to develop a computer that could think like a person?

Top tip

Discuss the Leeper's Lady illusion with classmates. Do you know any other illusions? Try to explain the illusions if other people are finding them hard to see or understand.

If you study the Higher option topic of Memory, you will notice many similarities in the way human memory is described and terms that are used in computing. For example, researchers talk about:

- storage
- code/encoding
- processing

However, some researchers have rejected this comparison as over-simplistic. For example, Bruner (1992) stated that the mind and a computer are fundamentally different because a computer does not try to make sense of stimuli. It is important in his view that the cognitive approach focuses on *meaningful* processing.

? Discussion point

What similarities are there between the human mind and a computer? What about differences?

The computer analogy dominated the early days of cognitive psychology

Schemas

A **schema** means a set of ideas, or a pattern of thought about a particular concept or situation. The key idea is that information is not stored separately, but is linked together with other relevant information. We may have a schema for a school building, for example, which will be drawn from our direct experience of school buildings, as well as buildings that we have seen or read about. The result is a concept that includes the typical or average features. A **script** is similar to a schema, but it concerns what to do or say in a social situation. Most situations involve scripted behaviour, for example, meeting someone for the first time, sitting down to do an exam or going into a job interview (Fayol & Monteil, 1988).

Schemas play a role when it comes to jokes or stories. If someone tells a joke which begins *'a man walked into a bar…'* this deliberately activates the schemas for a typical man and a typical bar. Of course, each person will have slightly different schemas for both of these things – because everyone has different experiences, everyone's schemas will be different. However, it is very likely that your schemas will be similar to those of other people with a similar upbringing, and someone from a different culture from yourself will have very different schemas (Bartlett, 1932 – see key study).

Key study: Bartlett's (1932) schema research

Aim: *Sir Frederic Bartlett, working at Cambridge University, was one of the first British researchers to study memory and thought processes. His approach was very different to other early cognitive psychologists in that he studied memory using meaningful material such as folk stories and pictures.*

Sir Frederic Bartlett receives the Queen's Medal

Method: *Bartlett showed participants images and stories that were from an unfamiliar culture. They then had to recall these items, sometimes over a series of recollections. His most famous task involved a Native American folk story called 'War of the Ghosts':*

One night two young men from Egulac went down to the river to hunt seals and while they were there it became foggy and calm. Then they heard war-cries, and they thought: 'Maybe this is a war-party'. They escaped to the shore, and hid behind a log. Now canoes came up, and they heard the noise of paddles, and saw one canoe coming up to them. There were five men in the canoe, and they said:

'What do you think? We wish to take you along. We are going up the river to make war on the people.'

One of the young men said, 'I have no arrows.'

'Arrows are in the canoe,' they said.

'I will not go along. I might be killed. My relatives do not know where I have gone. But you,' he said, turning to the other, 'may go with them.'

So one of the young men went, but the other returned home. And the warriors went on up the river to a town on the other side of Kalama. The people came down to the water and they began to fight, and many were killed. But presently the young man heard one of the warriors say, 'Quick, let us go home: that Indian has been hit.' Now he thought: 'Oh, they are ghosts.' He did not feel sick, but they said he had been shot.

So the canoes went back to Egulac and the young man went ashore to his house and made a fire. And he told everybody and said: 'Behold I accompanied the ghosts, and we went to fight. Many of our fellows were killed, and many of those who attacked us were killed. They said I was hit, and I did not feel sick.'

He told it all, and then he became quiet. When the sun rose he fell down. Something black came out of his mouth. His face

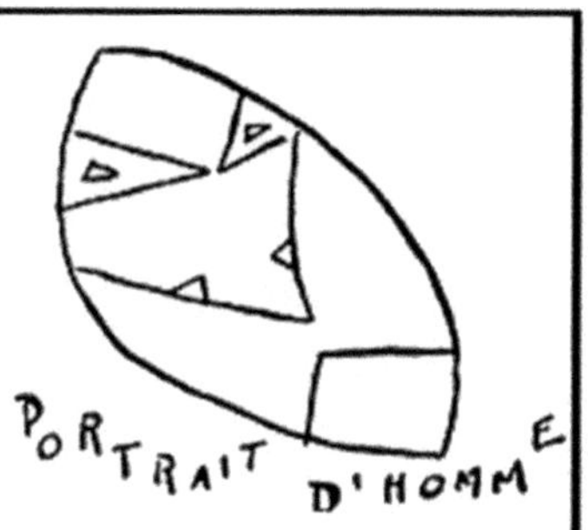

Picture 1: Original drawing

Picture 2: Reproduction of original

Picture 3: Reproduction of picture 2

Picture 4: Reproduction of picture 3

Picture 5: Reproduction of picture 4 (everything from memory)

Image from another of Barlett's studies, showing how drawings of faces changed as different people attempted to copy the previous version

became contorted. The people jumped up and cried. He was dead.

Findings: *Bartlett reported that people change information as they try to recall it. The distortions that occurred when his participants recalled images could be dramatic.*

Bartlett observed several key distortions when participants recalled the 'War of the Ghosts' story:

- *Preservation of detached detail: remembering single unusual items out of context.*
- *Simplification: stories became more basic.*
- *Subtraction: removing elements that didn't fit the participants' culture.*
- *Transformation: things were changed to make them seem more familiar.*

He concluded that we refer to schemas if we are unsure about certain details, and memories are therefore a mixture of what has actually happened, and assumptions which fill in the gaps in our recollections. When doing his tasks, participants had tried to make sense of the story – but struggled because it came from a different culture. Bartlett called this attempt 'effort after meaning' – and considered it to be a key factor in memory distortions.

Evaluation: *This was one of the earliest demonstrations of the importance of schemas. A strength of the study is that it used real world stimuli such as stories, and it was therefore high in mundane realism. However, a weakness is that we very rarely come across information that is totally unfamiliar.*

Top tip

If you are studying the option topic of Memory, Bartlett's (1932) study can be used as evidence for long-term memory.

Another early cognitive theorist who helped to develop the concept of schemas was Jean Piaget. Piaget was interested in cognitive development, which means how our cognitive abilities develop through childhood. In particular, he believed that a child's thinking is fundamentally different from that of adults.

Piaget studied his own children as they grew older and realised that their schemas became more complex and sophisticated over time. Piaget thought that schemas develop through two key processes.

- **Assimilation** means fitting new information to an existing schema, for example, seeing an unfamiliar type of dog and categorising it as a dog.
- **Accommodation** means changing the schema. For example, a young child at first may think that a zebra is a 'stripy horse', but then realise that it is a different animal. This results in two separate schemas – a horse schema and a zebra schema.

Jean Piaget

Piaget also realised that young children try to solve problems differently from adults, sometimes leading to errors. For example, a pre-school child will focus on just one element of a problem and ignore other equally important elements. Piaget called this **centration**. A classic demonstration of centration involves showing a child two glasses of different shapes, one tall and thin and the other short and wide. Most children below the age of seven fail to realise that a tall glass of water contains the same amount as a shorter, wider glass, even if they see the water poured from one glass into the other. They reason that the taller glass is 'bigger' and therefore contains more. They centre just on one feature – the height of the glass – and therefore fail to judge its volume accurately.

Irrational beliefs

The traditional philosophical view of the human mind was that it was rational. Although Freud recognised that irrational thought processes can affect us, he considered these to be childlike unconscious forces, while the ego was seen as rational (see previous section). Piaget thought that errors were made by children and that we get gradually more rational – his theories didn't focus on errors made by adults.

Is there more water in the tall glass?

However, later cognitive psychologists have identified several ways in which human thought processes are biased or **irrational**. One basis for this is that we are guided by **beliefs** about the world, and that these beliefs may at times be wrong and harmful. For example, Ellis (2003) states that a lot of anxiety can arise from distorted beliefs such as:

Personalisation: a tendency to relate all events to oneself. For example, if someone doesn't talk to you in the corridor, personalisation would be thinking *'she must be in a bad mood with me'* rather than, for example, *'she must be busy and distracted'*.

Overgeneralisation: taking one thing and applying it to many or all situations. For example, upon failing a test, a student may overgeneralise and think, *'I'm useless at everything'*.

Make the link

...with Ellis's explanation of depression (see chapter 4).

Selective abstraction: tendency to focus on one small part of an event or series of events. For example, after a date that went well overall, the person may focus on one thing that went wrong (for example, maybe they tripped and felt clumsy) and ignore all the positive events, therefore remembering it as having been a really bad evening.

Humans don't actually work everything out like a computer, but instead rely on simplistic assumptions. These help the mind to save on limited mental resources such as attention. Tversky and Kahneman (1974) found that when shown the possible outcome of six coin tosses, people judged H-T-H-T-T-H as being more likely than H-H-H-T-T-T, even though each has exactly the same probability of happening. Essentially people's behaviour is not always rational, but is instead often guided by intuition.

Tversky and Kahneman argued that humans use simple rules to guide their behaviour, called **heuristics** (or 'rules of thumb'). One heuristic is called the **availability heuristic**, and it states that if asked how common something is, we judge it based on how easy it is to think of examples. This is often a good strategy – but also leads to major mistakes. Examples might come to mind more easily due to personal prejudices or obsessions, or simply because we have come across those examples more recently. On those occasions, the availability heuristic will bias us to give an inaccurate response.

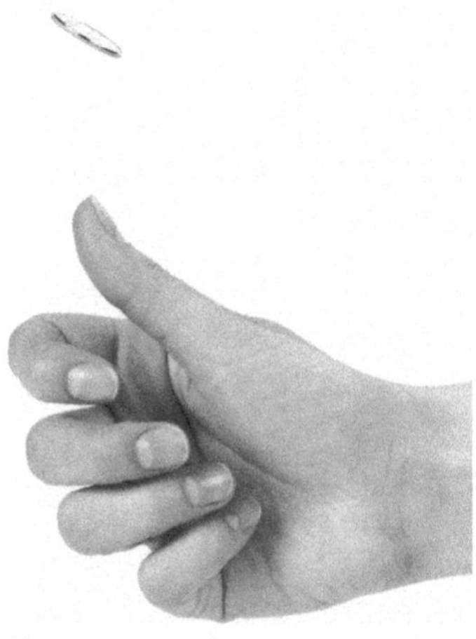

The outcome of a coin toss is always 50:50!

Research and CBT therapy

The cognitive approach is known for its use of **experiments**. An experiment is a controlled study, where one thing is changed and everything else is kept constant. For example, researchers might conduct an experiment into the effects of noise on people's ability to solve problems – two groups of people might solve problems, one with background noise and one in silence. Everything else would be the same, for example, the amount of time allowed. Such experiments tend to be done in controlled conditions such as university laboratories. As the cognitive approach focuses on thought processes, experiments tend to be done on people rather than animals.

A lot of anxiety can arise from distorted beliefs

? Discussion point

Do these distortions seem more or less realistic/relevant to you than the defence mechanisms of the psychoanalytic approach? Are they similar? Should both be used to explain human behaviour?

Questionnaires are also widely used, for example, to ask people about their beliefs and attitudes (see chapter 8 for more on these methods).

According to this approach, if thinking can be changed then so can behaviour. The idea that irrational beliefs can influence feelings (rather than the other way round) is known as cognitive primacy. If a person's thinking about stress is changed, for example, then they will become less stressed. If their perceptions about eating and about their own weight change, then they may stop having an eating disorder. There have been various forms of cognitive therapy over the years, but currently the most popular and widespread form is **cognitive behavioural therapy (CBT)**. It is a very structured form of therapy, where the therapist will challenge beliefs that seem unjustified or irrational. There are also behavioural tasks that the patient should do between sessions, such as trying out new behaviours. CBT is explained in more detail in chapter 3.

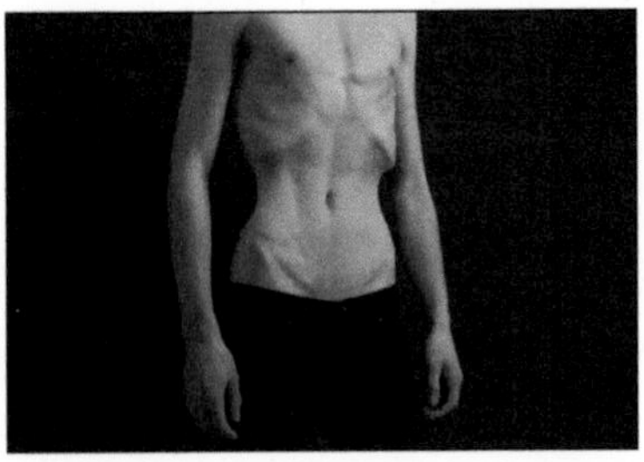

CBT might be used to help someone with an eating disorder

Top tip

Summarise the main areas of this approach onto an index card. Write evaluation points on the back.

Evaluation

The cognitive approach is hugely influential and its models of thought processes and decision making have influenced therapy and treatment methods. Ideas such as heuristics and schemas have influenced areas as diverse as memory, stress and prejudice, as you will see when you tackle the option topics in this course.

The approach is supported by a large body of experimental findings showing that thought processes are not always logical and can be distorted, such as the work of Tversky and Kahneman (1974). However, much of the research is based in the laboratory. In particular, research into the key cognitive areas of memory and perception has tended to be very artificial.

The approach assumes that thought processes cause people to have negative feelings and behaviours, but thoughts may sometimes be the result rather than the cause of conditions such as stress and depression (Schachter & Singer, 1962).

Research on cognitive processes has tended to ignore the underlying brain processes involved. This is changing, however, as brain scanning technology improves.

Questions

1. What is meant by a mediator?
2. Complete: studying the mind as an information processor is part of the _______ analogy.
3. Why did Bruner criticise the emphasis on information processing?
4. What is a schema?
5. What is a script?
6. Which early researcher studied cognitive development in children?
7. What is meant by centration?
8. Which cognitive distortion concerns relating events to oneself?
9. What is selective abstraction?
10. What is the main form of cognitive therapy called?

Key concepts

- Cognitive approach
- Mediators
- Illusions
- Computer analogy
- Schema
- Script
- Assimilation
- Accommodation
- Centration
- Irrational beliefs
- Beliefs
- Personalisation
- Overgeneralisation
- Selective abstraction
- Heuristic
- Availability heuristic
- Experiment (research method)
- Questionnaires (research method)
- CBT – cognitive behavioural therapy

Activities

1. Find more illusions, in books or online. Choose one illusion and then make an A3-sized poster showing both the illusion and your explanation of how it works. These can then be used to decorate your classroom, corridor or study space. Alternatively, make a short PowerPoint of illusions and show it to your class.
2. Think of examples for each of the cognitive distortions from your own life experiences. (If you note them down, do not use real names.)
3. Divide an A4 page into four sections and in each section write a one paragraph summary of the following:
   - computer analogy
   - schemas
   - irrational beliefs
   - CBT.

The behaviourist approach

The **behaviourist approach** was founded by American psychologist John Watson (1878–1958), through his article, 'Psychology as the BehaviouristViews it' (Watson, 1913). Inspired by the work of Russian physiologist Ivan Pavlov and drawing on his own laboratory work at John Hopkins University in Baltimore, Watson proposed that the main aim of psychology should be to be able to predict and control behaviour. He argued that this could be achieved using carefully designed and controlled experiments and that psychology should be entirely an objective, scientific discipline.

! Syllabus note

Theories based on the behaviourist approach play a major role in the National 5 topic Phobias, but you will encounter them in many other contexts – not least the rewards and punishments that exist in education!

Watson disliked a lot of the work being done in psychology at the time, considering it too subjective. In being more scientific, Watson said, it was necessary to study psychology in terms of learned behaviour and the formation of associations between stimuli and responses, and to avoid subjective mental terms: *'I believe we can write a psychology [and] never use the terms consciousness, mental states, mind, content, introspectively verifiable, imagery and the like'* (Watson 1913: 160).

John Watson

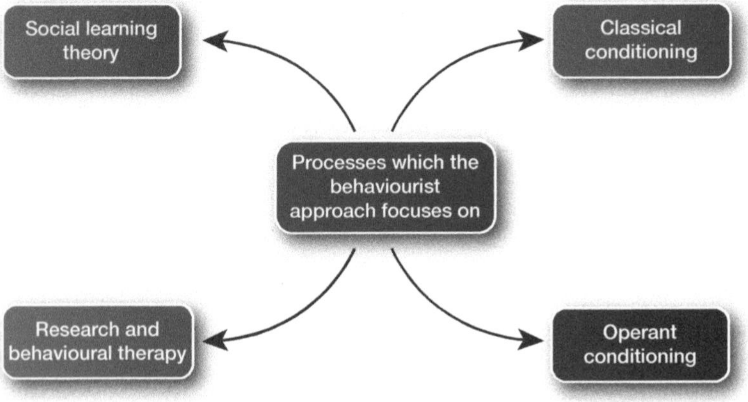

Classical conditioning

The first major theory in the behaviourist approach is **classical conditioning**, which means learning an **association** between two stimuli. This occurs when one stimulus already produces a response, for example, a snake or a spider that causes us to feel fear, or a slice of cake that causes our mouths to water. Behaviourists call this the unconditioned stimulus. The other stimulus is neutral – it does not cause a reaction, for example, a light flashing on or a tone playing.

The key to classical conditioning is that the unconditioned and neutral stimulus are repeatedly paired together. In real life, this might happen by accident, but behaviourist psychologists generally test it under controlled conditions in a laboratory. After time, the neutral stimulus starts to cause the same response as the unconditioned stimulus. An association has therefore been learned – the individual has been *conditioned* to respond to a previously neutral event.

? Discussion point

Has anybody in your class used the principle of classical conditioning to train a pet?

Russian biologist Ivan Pavlov was the first to experimentally describe classical conditioning – he observed it in his laboratory dogs and discovered it largely by accident. When studying the digestive systems of the dogs in his lab, Pavlov realised that the animals learned to react to hearing the lab assistant's footsteps before they were fed – they produced saliva in their mouths before they were given any food. The animals had learned to associate the food with the sound of the footsteps.

Pavlov then carried out an experiment to test this more systematically. A bell was sounded for a dog to hear. A few seconds later, food (meat powder) was presented so that the dog salivated and ate. This procedure, pairing together the bell and the food, was repeated several times. Finally, the bell was sounded but no food was produced. It was observed that the dog now salivated in response to the bell alone – a learned association. Pavlov had experimentally demonstrated classical conditioning.

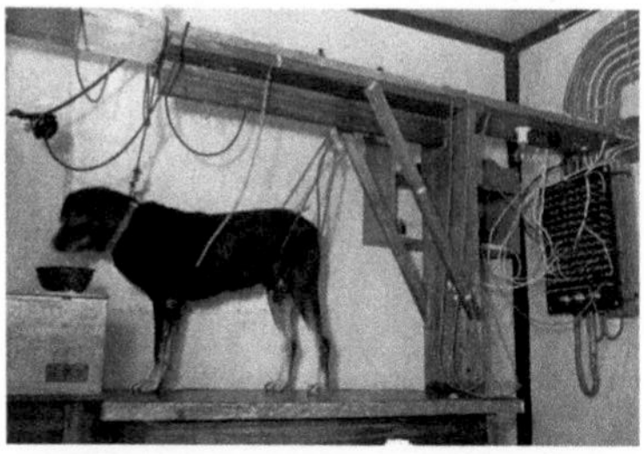
A dog in one of Pavlov's experiments

Pavlov became famous for his discovery. Other psychologists such as Watson began to wonder if this basic form of learning might be the basis for all of our actions. Later researchers have confirmed that classical conditioning occurs in a huge range of organisms, from humans to sea slugs (Kandel & Hawkins, 1992).

The following abbreviations are used to describe stimuli and responses in classical conditioning:

US	Unconditioned stimulus
UR	Unconditioned response
CS	Conditioned stimulus
CR	Conditioned response

Now he fears even Santa Claus

Little Albert

Key study: Watson and Rayner (1920): the study of 'little Albert'

Aim: *Watson and Rayner (1920) wanted to show that fear could be learned in a human child through classical conditioning, in just the same way that Pavlov's dogs had learned an association.*

Method: *The study was conducted on an 11-month-old child nicknamed 'little Albert'. They gave the child animals such as a white rat to look at, and hit an iron bar behind his head with a hammer to make a loud unpleasant noise, causing him to become frightened and cry.*

Findings: *The child soon learned to associate fear with the rat and he cried as soon as he saw it. This effect generalised to other small animals such as a rabbit. The way Albert was conditioned is similar in principle to Pavlov's research on dogs – learning occurred by an association being formed between two things.*

Evaluation: *This was an important demonstration of classical conditioning in humans, though highly unethical – an infant was deliberately made to cry and feel frightened.*

Operant conditioning

A related theory of learning is **operant conditioning**. The key difference between this and classical conditioning is that rather than an association being formed between two stimuli, the person behaves in some way first, and this is then followed by a consequence. The individual then associates the behaviour with the consequence. If the consequence is pleasant, the person is more likely to repeat the behaviour.

B.F. Skinner with a rat in a 'Skinner box'

Operant conditioning was first described by Jerzy Konorsky, but it was the American researcher B.F. Skinner who fully developed the concept. He used the term **operant** to apply to anything that modified the likelihood of a behaviour to be repeated. Skinner's early experiments were carried out with animals such as rats. The rat would be placed in a closed box – now known as a **Skinner box** (see left) – and its behaviour would be observed. Eventually, the rat's normal exploration would take it close to a bar, and when it placed its front paws on the bar, a pellet of food would be delivered. The rat would now be attracted to that part of the box and return there to repeat the process again. According to Skinner, the food is a reinforcer, and the bar pressing will continue as long as it is reinforced by food.

Operant conditioning can be a gradual process, with behaviours getting stronger or weaker over time. This strengthening of habits through rewards is known as **reinforcement**. According to Skinner, a reinforcer is an outcome which increases frequency of a behaviour – in other words, a reward, while a **punishment** reduces behaviour. Reinforcement could involve something good being given, such as a food pellet to the rat in a Skinner box, or something unpleasant being removed, such as loud noise being switched off. These are called **positive reinforcement** and **negative reinforcement** respectively:

Positive reinforcement: something pleasant is given	Example: a food reward
Negative reinforcement: something unpleasant is removed	Example: a noise being switched off

Skinner (1938) stated that without a reinforcer, the behaviour would reduce in strength. However, a behaviour would reduce more quickly after a bad outcome, for instance, a punishment. Reinforcers and punishers are both types of operants, that is, outcomes. However, punishments cannot permanently stop a behaviour because the *lack* of a response cannot be reinforced (Catania, 1992).

Social learning theory

People do not just learn things directly through their own experience – they can also learn from observing others. For example, if you see someone else try a trick on their bike and then fall off and injure themselves, you will probably avoid trying it yourself. In the behaviourist approach, **social learning theory** explains learning from the experiences of others. We can learn from observation and from seeing others being rewarded and punished. In this sense, social learning can be like an indirect form of operant conditioning.

The most famous research study into learning through observation was conducted by Albert Bandura, who studied how aggression is learned. He believed that learning depends on its social context, and often takes place via **modelling** of a behaviour by another person, such as a parent or teacher. He conducted a study where children observed adults hitting a doll. Afterwards, the children observed the adult being rewarded, punished, or neither (no consequences). The children showed significantly more aggression after observing the adult being rewarded (Bandura, 1965). This work has been applied to the study of media violence (see the Higher topic of Aggression – chapter 14).

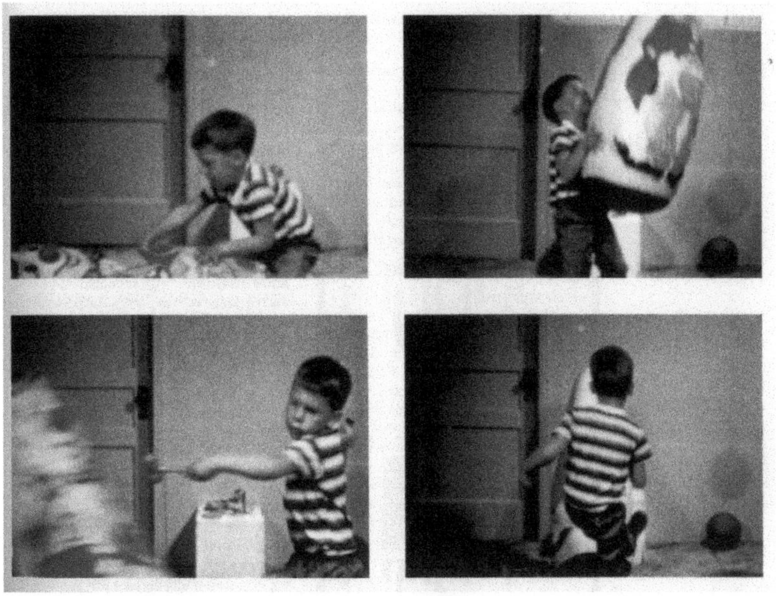

A child in Bandura's study

? Discussion point

Think of examples of positive and negative reinforcements in the classroom or at home as you were growing up. Did teachers and parents always reward good behaviour? Could bad behaviour have been accidentally reinforced?

Albert Bandura, with a photo from his study

Make the link

...to your knowledge of Media Studies.

? Discussion point

Why do you think behaviourist researchers did so many studies on animals and children, rather than on adults?

Research and behavioural therapy

Research in the behaviourist approach is largely based on objective science. There is an emphasis on lab experiments, most of which involved direct observation of behaviour, because researchers in this approach do not focus on mental processes. In contrast to the cognitive approach, a lot of the research is done on animals rather than humans.

How does a baby learn what the word for 'cup' is?

Evaluation

This approach has been criticised for relying on laboratory experiments with animals, as generalising the results of these studies to humans may not be valid. Although Watson viewed animal and human behaviour as being a continuous scale of complexity with humans at the upper end, many researchers feel that humans should be the main objects of study in psychology.

The two types of conditioning are useful in explaining many types of learning, but too simplistic to fully explain all human behaviour. According to Skinner (1957), babies learn language through conditioning. For example, if an infant sees a cup and hears an adult say the word 'cup', it forms an association between the two. Then, if the child tries to say the word, it will be rewarded by a *'well done'* from its carers, reinforcing the action (operant conditioning). However, linguist Noam Chomsky criticised Skinner's theory of language learning (Chomsky, 1959). He believed that babies develop mental rules of grammar, and use these to form sentences. For example, in English, the child learns that to make a verb past tense, it needs to add an *'-ed'* ending. Without having learned all the exceptions to this rule, it over-applies the rules, making mistakes such as *'I eated'* or *'I forgetted'*. These mistakes are significant, as the infant never hears them from adults, so it cannot be imitating them or learning them through classical conditioning.

Wolfgang Köhler

It's not clear that animals always learn just through conditioning, either. When studying learning in an ape called Sultan, researcher Wolfgang Köhler (1925, cited in Glassman, 2000) observed that the ape appeared to think through a problem as a whole, and show insight. Sultan was inside a cage, and was given a stick that was too short to reach a banana that Köhler had placed outside the cage. Sultan then moved to the back of his cage and stared at the sticks for some time. Then, without any need for practice or reinforcement, he suddenly picked up the smaller stick, used it to pull the longer stick towards him, and then used the longer stick to reach the fruit. Sultan seemed to have had a moment of insight, unrelated to simple operant conditioning or trial and error.

Questions

1. True or false: Pavlov's experiment with the dogs is an example of operant conditioning.
2. Which type of conditioning was demonstrated in the study of little Albert?
3. What is the name for the strengthening of a behaviour through repeated rewards?
4. Which leads to the weakening of a behaviour – negative reinforcement, or punishment?
5. Which type of conditioning is also called 'learning by association'?
6. True or false: behaviourists focus on thought processes that we cannot see or measure.
7. True or false: the behaviourist approach is also called 'stimulus-response' psychology?
8. What is the name of the apparatus that Skinner used to study rats and birds?
9. Which behaviourism-influenced theory suggested that we can learn through observation, not just directly through our experiences?
10. Did other researchers accept Skinner's behaviourist explanation of how language is learned?

Key concepts

- Behaviourist approach
- Classical conditioning
- Association
- Operant conditioning
- Reinforcement
- Punishment
- Skinner box
- Positive reinforcement
- Negative reinforcement
- Social learning theory
- Modelling
- Operant

Sultan riding a bicyle, from the Berliner Illustrierte Zeitung *magazine*

Top tip

Summarise the main areas of this approach onto an index card. Write evaluation points on the back.

Activities

1. Complete the gap-fill text:

   Behaviourism is based around two theories of learning – classical and ________ conditioning. Classical conditioning involves associations being formed between a response/ behaviour and a stimulus that is initially ________ (has no effect on the animal). The process of classical conditioning involves an unconditioned stimulus (US) and an unconditioned response (___) being associated together, after which the stimulus is termed the conditioned stimulus (___) and the response is termed the ________ ________ (CR). Operant conditioning means that behaviours increase or decrease in strength or frequency because they have a good or bad outcome. ________ conditioning is based around reinforcement and punishment. Actions increase if they are followed by positive or negative __________. Actions decrease if they are followed by positive or negative punishment. Positive means that something happens or is given. Negative means that something does not happen or is taken away. Classical and operant conditioning contribute a great deal to our understanding of human and animal behaviour. The behaviourist approach is very objective and uses the __________ method rigorously in order to support its conclusions. However, it is important to realise that not every behaviour is conditioned. Behaviourism cannot explain all behaviours in humans (or even in animals). __________ development in humans, for example, and creative behaviour cannot be accounted for solely by behaviourist explanations.

2. Think of an example from your life of when an animal has learned a new behaviour. Now try to explain it in terms of classical and operant conditioning. Write some notes, and then try to explain it to a classmate. Do you think conditioning is enough, or has the animal shown intelligent thought?

3. Write the full terms beside the abbreviations below and give an example for each one, which could be drawn from the examples you have discussed.

US: ________	UR: ________
Example:	Example:
CS: ________	CR: ________
Example:	Example:

The evolutionary approach

The **evolutionary approach** to psychology states that human behaviour is best explained in terms of the **evolution** of our species over time. It has links to the biological approach, because it also emphasises the importance of genetics, but rather than explaining behaviour in terms of physical processes within the body, evolutionary psychologists are more interested in understanding what life was like for humans in the past, and how this affects our behaviour today. The way that genes and other structures affect our behaviour could be considered the *'how'* questions – how do genes affect behaviour? How do hormones affect mood? Whereas, evolutionary psychologists are more interested in the *'why'* questions – why do we have a stress response? Why do people typically form long-term romantic relationships? Why do people feel anxious if they are different from their peers? According to this approach, the answers to these questions come from understanding human evolution.

> **! Syllabus note**
>
> The evolutionary approach can be linked to any topic but it plays a particularly major role in the topics of Sleep, Stress, Social Relationships and Aggression.

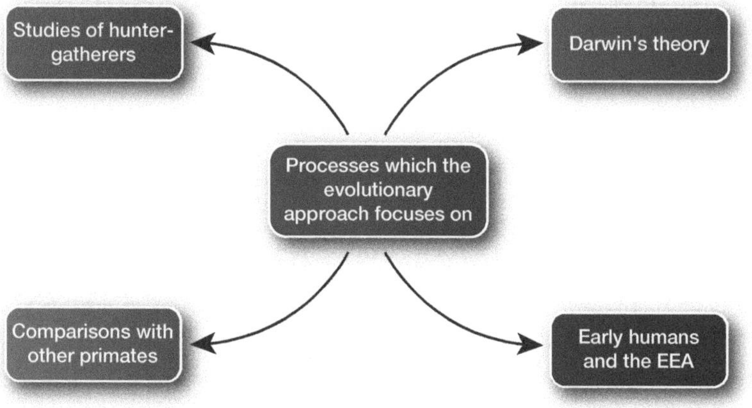

> **Top tip**
>
> There are links between this approach and the biological approach, as both refer to genetics.

Darwin's theory

Darwin's key insight was that as successful characteristics were passed on from parents to offspring, then, over time, an entire species could change, with characteristics that aided survival in their environment becoming more common. As the environment changes, so characteristics will change too. This principle of selection by the environment is called **natural selection**.

Humans, therefore, have evolved the way we have because – according to the principle of natural selection – certain characteristics made our ancestors more likely to survive. Why do we walk upright on two legs? Why are our brains much larger than those of other apes? These characteristics must have given our ancestors a survival advantage, according to the theory.

The same reasoning can be applied to behavioural and psychological characteristics, such as language, love and aggression. This is more controversial, as our behaviours are shaped not just by our genes but by learning, upbringing and culture.

> **Top tip**
>
> The evolutionary approach has many similarities with ethology, which you will encounter if you study the option topic Aggression. The key difference is that ethologists mainly study non-human animals in their natural habitats, while evolutionary psychologists focus more on human behaviour, using evidence from fossils and from various human societies. Ethology could be considered a minor approach in its own right.

Early humans and the EEA

Charles Darwin

A Darwin's Finch (also known as the Galapagos Finch or Geospizinae)

A model of the face of an adult female Homo erectus on display at the Smithsonian Museum of Natural History in Washington, D.C.

As with other species, humans evolved gradually in response to changes in our environment. Groups of early monkeys and apes changed according to environmental conditions just as the finches Darwin studied on the Galapagos Islands did, with certain characteristics proving to be more successful. As early apes moved around and separated into different groups, they found different environmental conditions. Over a long period of time, the different conditions prompted different characteristics to evolve through natural selection, resulting in separate species of ape.

Of greatest interest is how early humans separated from chimpanzees and other apes. It is likely that a common ancestor of both humans and chimps lived around 7 million years ago. This does not mean that modern chimps are our ancestors! However, it appears that humans have changed a lot during this time, while chimpanzees – probably because their rainforest environment has not changed much – have remained fairly similar to our common ancestors.

The development of modern humans was gradual, and several species of **hominins** – that is, early humans – existed and then died out. **Australopithecus** was chimp-like in appearance but walked upright, and lived in Africa between 2 and 4 million years ago. **Homo erectus** was another major species that spread around the world and had a greater ability to build and use tools. The earliest fossil evidence dates from 1.9 million years ago, and the most recent specimens lived 143,000 years ago (Smithsonian, 2015).

Our own species of anatomically modern humans – technically called **Homo sapiens** – is thought to have evolved around 300,000 years ago in south-western Africa and eventually spread around the rest of the world via the Middle East (note that Homo erectus was still in existence when our Homo sapiens ancestors spread around the world).

Evolution is driven by the environment – characteristics that will help a species to survive depend on the environment that it is in. For example, characteristics that help animals to survive in an ocean are different from the characteristics that are useful in a desert. The **environment of evolutionary adaptiveness** (EEA) means the environment in which human ancestors are thought to have lived for most of our recent evolution. It is thought that modern humans evolved largely in a savannah (grassland) environment.

For most of this time, people lived in small tribal groups, hunting animals and gathering berries and roots, catching fish, etc. People made or used temporary shelters such as tents made out of animal skins, and moved around according to the seasons and the movement of animals that they hunted. These were the conditions in which we evolved. In comparison, it is only in the last 12,000 years or fewer that humans have developed agriculture and lived in settled villages and towns. Truly 'modern life' – with cars, computers, phones, modern houses, etc. – has existed for a tiny fraction of humans' time on earth.

As it formed by far the larger part of our evolutionary development, evolutionary psychologists attempt to explain psychological phenomena and problems with reference to the EEA. For example, stress and mental illness may be caused partly because we experience things that didn't exist in our EEA, such as money, exams, and junk food.

It appears that our early ancestors stopped living in rainforests. There is no way of knowing for certain why our ancestors stopped living in rainforest environments and began to live on the savannah – it may possibly relate to changes in climate, or gradual migration. Undoubtedly though, according to natural selection, the changed environment had an effect on the characteristics most useful for survival.

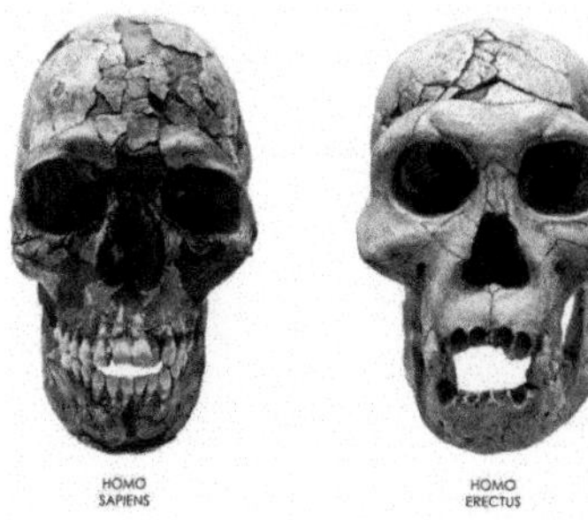

Skulls of Homo sapiens and Homo erectus

Frequently asked questions about evolution

Q: Isn't evolution just a theory?
A: It is a theory. As discussed in chapter 8, what this means is that it is the best explanation scientists have for the many factual observations that have been made. Scientific theories can never be proved – they are always our closest estimate and they are gradually improved and refined over time. There is a wealth of evidence that supports the general principles of Darwinian evolution, but some details are still a matter of debate.

Q: How does this explain the origin of life?
A: It doesn't. The theory of evolution is an explanation of how species change over time, and does not aim to explain how life originated on Earth. There are several other theories that attempt to explain how the first life forms appeared.

Q: I find it hard to believe that we evolved from monkeys.
A: Darwin's contemporaries mocked him for suggesting that we evolved from primates (although he was not the first to suggest this – just the first to explain how it happened). The fact that a theory seems hard to believe at first glance is not a reason to reject it; for centuries, most humans refused to believe that the Earth revolved around the Sun.

Q: Does this mean that I shouldn't believe in God?
A: It's up to you what you believe. Scientific theories attempt to explain the physical world and the creatures in it, using natural rather than supernatural explanations. Many scientists do believe in god(s) and/or follow religions. However, it is fair to say that the theory of evolution does not fit with a *literal* interpretation of some religious texts.

It is thought that chimpanzees are our nearest relatives

Dunbar concluded that the maximum functional group size for humans is approximately 150

? Discussion point

Can we figure out the ideal human group size from studying other primates? Do you believe that 150 is the ideal group size, and if so, what does that mean for the size of schools, companies, or the neighbourhoods that we live in?

The San people of the Kalahari

Comparisons with other species

Another aspect of the evolutionary approach involves the study of other, closely related species such as the primates (apes and monkeys). The idea is to find out more about what our nearest relatives are capable of, and therefore draw conclusions about the earliest human ancestors. As chimpanzees and bonobos (pygmy chimps) are our nearest relatives, they tend to be the most studied.

One fundamental question is why humans and other primates have evolved relatively large brains compared to other mammals. In answering that question, it might be possible to explain why humans have exceptionally large brains and high intelligence. Two main possibilities are that:

1. A large brain is necessary to deal with a complex environment in terms of survival or feeding. For example, carnivores tend to have larger brains than herbivores.

OR

2. A large brain is necessary to deal with a large social group. With more individuals in the social group, each person requires more resources to deal with interaction, and maintaining relationships.

Byrne and Corp (2004) found a correlation between levels of social deception in different primate species and the size of their brains – in particular, their neocortex – lending support to the second theory. Similarly, Dunbar (1992) studied the ratio of group size to neocortex size of various primates, and concluded a maximum functional group size for humans of approximately 150 (see chapter 13).

Comparisons with hunter-gatherers

Until around 12,000 years ago there was no agriculture at all, and all humans around the world lived as **hunter-gatherers**. As agricultural technology spread from one community to another, humans developed techniques for storing, planting and harvesting crops and for managing livestock and keeping them safe from predators. With the birth of agriculture, humans had regular surpluses of food for the first time, and began to trade.

However, there are many groups of people around the world who still live as hunter-gatherers. Some move from one area to another in search of food and other resources, while others live in settled communities but forage and hunt for food rather than farming (Rowley-Conwy, 2001). Examples include the Inuit of the Arctic, the San people of the Kalahari, and the Pirahã people of the Amazon rainforest. From the point of view of the evolutionary approach, studying hunter-gatherers provides an interesting demonstration of how people behave without modern technology. These societies may be the closest thing we have to being able to observe the conditions in which humans evolved.

Dunbar's theory about group size (see previous section) has been compared to the size of groups in contemporary hunter-gatherers, and it was found that many modern hunter-gatherer tribes average around 150 individuals (Dunbar, 1993). This supports the idea that the social pressures of a larger group are too cognitively demanding, and that evolution has set an upper limit of group size beyond which the costs start to outweigh the benefits.

Evaluation of the evolutionary approach

This area of study is based on sparse fossil evidence, and theories about exactly how and when the various species of early hominids evolved are still being debated. For example, if a new Homo erectus fossil was discovered, it could change our understanding of exactly where and when these hominins lived. However, over time, a gradually clearer picture is emerging.

A Homo erectus fossil brow

The evolutionary approach has been accused of justifying disparities between the sexes, such as men working and women looking after children. Similarly, there is an ethical debate over the study of how unethical behaviours such as murder and rape might have evolved. In response, evolutionary psychologists call such criticisms the **naturalistic fallacy**, stating that just because something *did* happen in evolution, doesn't mean that it *should* happen in contemporary society.

Pinker (1994) has criticised comparisons with other species, suggesting that little if anything can be concluded from comparing humans to other apes. Chimpanzees are our near relatives, sharing many physical characteristics, but humans have unique characteristics such as language, which shows that some of our most important psychological characteristics have evolved very recently.

Top tip

Summarise the main areas of this approach onto an index card. Write evaluation points on the back.

Questions

1. Who came up with the theory of evolution by natural selection?
2. How long have humans existed?
3. Are humans a type of ape?
4. Are apes and monkeys the same?
5. Did we evolve in the rainforest?
6. How long is it since agriculture was developed?
7. What does EEA stand for?
8. What is a hunter-gatherer?
9. How large is an ideal human group, according to Dunbar?
10. Give two evaluation points that relate to this approach.

Key concepts

- Evolution
- Natural selection
- Hominins
- Australopithecus
- Homo erectus
- Homo sapiens
- Environment of evolutionary adaptiveness (EEA)
- Hunter-gatherer
- Naturalistic fallacy

Activities

Australopithecus first evolve
Chimp-like hominins that walked upright and lived in Africa.
First cities
The earliest complex urban civilisations developed.
Modern humans first evolve
The first humans who were anatomically the same as ourselves.
Beginning of the most recent glacial period (or 'ice age')
The earth cooled and huge ice sheets spread across temperate areas, leading to a major drop in sea levels.
Neanderthals died out
Neanderthals were a species of hominin that lived alongside modern humans, but then became extinct.
Homo erectus first evolve
Early humans who spread around the world and were able to build and use tools.
Agriculture
Humans began to grow crops and keep livestock rather than hunting and gathering food.
The 'missing link'
The last common ancestor of both chimpanzees and humans.

1. Label the events marked on the cards on a timeline as to when they occurred. (See p.382 for feedback on this activity.)
2. Describe one human behaviour or problem, and think about how it may have been affected by evolution. Conduct some research to find out what scientists have said about this issue. Present this issue and your findings to your class.

Two further approaches: humanist and sociocultural

The five approaches described so far are not the only approaches in psychology, but they are the most well-known and influential, and the easiest to apply to the topics covered in this book. The psychoanalytic and behaviourist approaches dominated psychology in the early-mid 20th century, while nowadays the cognitive, evolutionary and biological approaches are more popular.

The following two approaches are less prominent, but studying them will help you to understand psychology more fully. The humanist approach has had a major impact on therapies for psychological problems and disorders, and could provide further evidence if you are studying the Depression topic. The sociocultural approach is also relevant to depression, and has influenced many of the ideas that you will study in the Social Behaviour unit.

The humanist approach

The **humanist approach** suggests that human nature is essentially positive and that people do bad things or are mentally ill because society stops them from fulfilling their potential. This approach, therefore, contrasts with the psychoanalytic view of an irrational and violent human nature. The humanist approach is still very popular in therapy, but its key ideas do not feature strongly in other major areas of psychology research, perhaps because they are seen as rather vague and simplistic.

Hierarchy of needs

The **hierarchy of needs** is a humanist theory that humans have a series of needs, where more basic ones need to be satisfied before higher-level ones can. Abraham Maslow (1943) presented this in the form of a pyramid-shaped diagram:

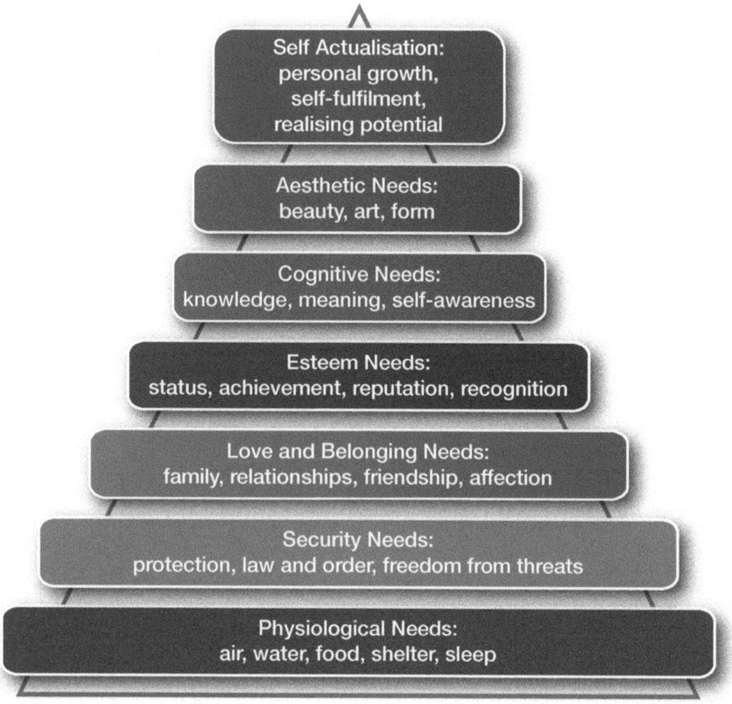

Maslow's hierarchy of needs

Notice that things like a love of learning (cognitive needs) and appreciation of art (aesthetic needs) are impossible to achieve unless the individual has first satisfied their safety, belonging and esteem needs. For example, a child is unlikely to care about learning if they are being rejected by their peers. At the top of the hierarchy is what humanist theorists saw as the pinnacle of human development – **self actualisation**. Maslow believed that only a few people ever achieve this, and cited Albert Einstein and Abraham Lincoln as examples of people who did.

Albert Einstein – he may have been 'self actualised'

Humanist therapy

On the surface, humanist therapy can resemble psychoanalysis – a discussion between the client and therapist, usually on a one-to-one basis. However, it is **client-centred**, which means that rather than being directed by the therapist, the client must make the main choices. Carl Rogers (1961) viewed counselling and therapy as a relationship between client and therapist, and stated that for it to be successful, the client must choose to improve. Meanwhile the therapist should provide a supportive environment, which involves showing **empathy** with the client's problems, and being honest about their own feelings.

Key traits of a successful humanist therapist	
Empathy	Showing concern for the client
Congruence	Being honest about their own feelings
Unconditional positive regard	Always being unconditionally positive and accepting

The sociocultural approach

The **sociocultural approach** suggests that all human behaviour is fundamentally programmed by society. According to this research, our behaviour cannot be understood separately from the social context in which it occurs. It is associated with the topics of social psychology, such as Conformity and Prejudice, but as an approach or perspective it applies to all areas of human behaviour. The fundamental assumption is that behaviour can be very strongly affected by the society and culture that we live in, and that we tend to adopt the beliefs and values of that culture. Most early 20th century psychology largely ignored culture, but later researchers began to realise the important influence that society has on behaviour.

Top tip

The sociocultural approach tends not to use lab experiments. According to this perspective, it is pointless to study behaviour away from its social context.

Individualistic versus collectivist cultures

A **culture** means a set of shared values. According to this approach, everyone is influenced in some way or other by the values of their culture. Inside any culture (e.g. Scottish) there can be many smaller cultures known as **subcultures**, some of which are easily identified – students, punks – and others that are less obvious.

! Syllabus note

The concept of culture plays an important role in all of the Social Behaviour topics, and the concept of culturally-biased research can be used as an evaluation point for many different theories and studies.

One important cultural difference is the contrast between **individualist cultures** and **collectivist cultures**. Some human cultures including most Central American and Southeast Asian countries have been described as collectivist, meaning that they place great value on family success and group harmony. The wants of the individual are considered a lower priority than the needs of the group in these cultures. Other parts of the world – notably North America, most of Western Europe, and Australia – are described as individualist cultures. This means that the success of the individual is paramount. There is a lot of competitiveness in individualist cultures and family/community tend to be a lower priority.

Make the link

...with conformity and obedience – see chapter 10.

Smith and Bond (1993) found higher **conformity** levels in collectivist societies in comparison to individualist societies, perhaps because an emphasis on group harmony makes people more inclined to conform to the behaviour of others around them.

Features of individualistic cultures	Features of collectivist cultures
Personal success is important	Group or family success is important
Competition is prevalent	Cooperation is prevalent
People are encouraged to do things their own way	People are encouraged to do things according to traditions
People fear failure	People fear social rejection

People are encouraged to do things their own way in individualistic cultures

Family success is important in collectivist cultures

American students are commonly used as participants for social psychology studies

Culturally biased research

A major issue in the sociocultural approach is the level of **cultural bias** in mainstream research. Smith and Bond (1993) studied the references in the most popular North American social psychology textbook, and they found that 94% of the first-named authors cited were based in North America.

A similar problem relates to the nature of the participants in much of this research. Out of convenience, many researchers test their own students. Sears (1986) found that in published social psychology research studies between 1980 and 1985, 54% used American psychology students as participants, and a further 21% used other American students. Additionally, only 29% of studies were conducted in a natural social habitat. This situation has resulted in a huge number of major studies and theories being based on a group of people that are different from the broader population in important ways, according to Sears (1986):

- They are more egocentric.
- They have a stronger need for peer approval.
- They are more likely to be compliant to authority.

This is an especially important issue in the study of human social behaviour. The sociocultural approach would argue that many major ideas and conclusions in Psychology are biased.

Summary and evaluation

- The **humanist approach** sees humans as essentially good and creative, but constrained by society.
- The hierarchy of needs is Maslow's theory of the progression people have to go through in order to reach the stage of self-actualisation.
- Rogers suggested that therapists must be congruent, empathic, and show unconditional positive regard for clients.
- The **sociocultural** approach suggests that human behaviour can only be explained in its social context.
- The sociocultural approach suggests that most research is culturally biased because of the over-use of American students as participants.
- There is major cultural distinction between individualist versus collectivist cultures, which can affect many behaviours.

Activities

1. Research one of these approaches in more depth. If you are up for the challenge, exploring one of the other approaches to psychology is a great exercise in independent learning. Each approach is a piece of the overall puzzle in terms of understanding human behaviour as a whole. Nowadays, it is rare for a psychologist to fully endorse one approach and dismiss all others; instead, they refer to several according to what is most appropriate. Especially as a student, it is premature to dismiss any particular approach to psychology until you have fully understood its strengths and weaknesses.
2. Check back to the task at the start of this chapter. Which approaches do the simple explanations there link to?

Key concepts

- Humanist approach
- Hierarchy of needs
- Self actualisation
- Client-centred therapy
- Empathy
- Sociocultural approach
- Sociology
- Culture
- Subculture
- Individualist culture
- Collectivist culture
- Conformity
- Cultural bias

End of topic project

Individually or in a group, your task is to find out more about one of the key researchers who influenced the approaches to psychology and make a presentation in some form.

You need to select:

- A researcher or theorist. A historical figure is the obvious choice, for example Hebb, Freud, Watson, Piaget, Ellis, Darwin or Rogers, but a modern researcher is also fine provided you can explain how they contributed to one of the approaches.
- A method of presentation. There are many suitable choices here – essay, poster, blog post, PowerPoint. The following shows how one of the many fun 'fake Facebook' sites could be used to present information about behaviourist researcher Ivan Pavlov:

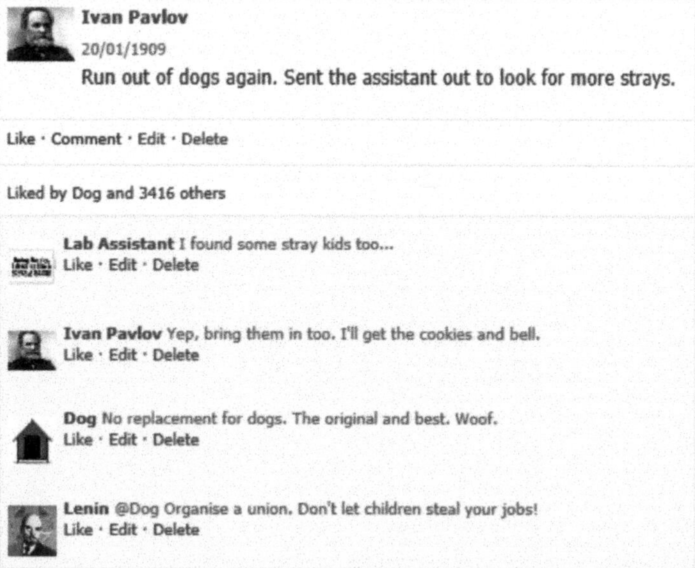

If possible, find out if you can get together with other classes in your school or college, or even among several different schools/colleges to present your work. You may be both informed and inspired by what others produce! If this isn't practical, you could post your project responses as blog posts, and invite other Higher/National 5 students to write their reactions as comments.

Individual behaviour

2 Sleep and dreams

For the topic of Sleep, you should be able to explain

- Biological processes in sleep.
- Explanations of dreaming and the processes that occur when we dream.
- Theories of sleep and dreams.
- Research evidence relevant to the topic.
- Factors that affect sleep.

You need to develop the following skills:

- Explaining concepts and processes relevant to sleep.
- Explaining, evaluating and analysing theories and research relevant to sleep.
- Using research evidence to back up your explanations of human behaviour.
- Applying your understanding of sleep to real situations.

! Syllabus note

Sleep is a mandatory topic in both Higher and National 5 Psychology. This chapter will provide the key information for both courses. Your teacher or lecturer will be able to guide you to the sections most relevant to the exam you are sitting.

What is the purpose of sleep?

Sleep can be defined as a state of reduced conscious awareness during which the body is less active and less responsive to the outside world. We spend a quarter or more of our lives asleep. What is the purpose of this behaviour? And why do we have dreams? Do they mean something, or are they just a by-product of brain processes that occur during sleep? These are the issues which will be covered in this chapter.

The biology of sleep

Sleep stages

As part of the scientific method (see chapter 8), researchers make controlled observations of behaviour. This is difficult to do when people are sleeping, but one way of gathering evidence is to use a **polysomnography** – a study of a sleeping individual which records multiple physical changes in the brain and body. An important part of this is a brain monitor called an **electroencephalogram**, or **EEG**. This measures the brain's electrical activity, displaying it on a screen or printout. A polysomnography also measures other bodily activity such as eye movements and heart rate.

It is important to realise that the nature of sleep changes through the night. When we sleep, the brain goes through five **sleep stages**. In stages 1–4, the body goes gradually into a deeper sleep, becoming harder to wake. The change from one stage to the next can be observed by the size and speed of electrical brainwaves that show up on the EEG in a polysomnography. Stages 3–4 have large, slow waves called **delta waves**, and these two stages in particular are sometimes called **slow-wave sleep**.

In the fifth stage, **REM sleep**, the brain becomes much more active and we start to have dreams. The body is physically tense, and temporarily paralysed so that we cannot move. This type of sleep is found in all vertebrate animals and it may well be the case that some other animals have dreams, too. REM stands for 'rapid eye movement' because the eyes show bursts of quick movements even though the eyelids remain closed. Because this stage is so different from the others, the first four stages are often called **non-REM sleep** (or nREM).

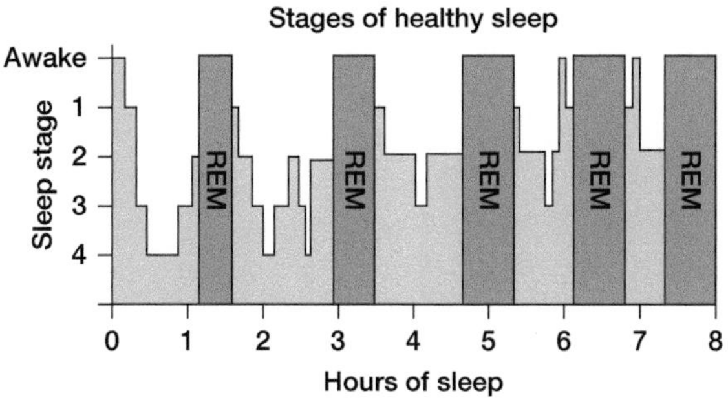

Sleep stages graph

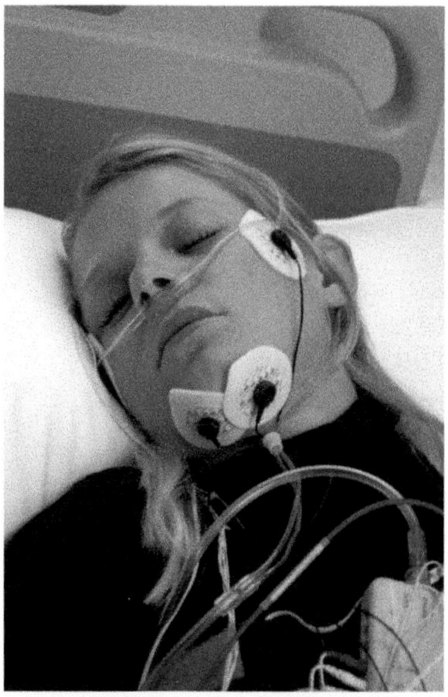

A woman being monitored as part of a sleep study

? Discussion point

Have you observed an animal, such as a pet, which appears to be dreaming?

So what actually happens to you in the different stages? Each stage has its own features:

Stage 1	This is the stage between wakefulness and sleep. You are easily woken in this stage and you can still hear noise around you such as talking or music playing. Your eyes are shut but occasionally flicker open. To put it in everyday language, you are 'drifting off'.
Stage 2	This stage begins after about 10 minutes. You now become less responsive to the environment and are sleeping soundly. However, if woken, you might not realise that you have been asleep. Sharp spikes of electrical activity called **sleep spindles** occur in the brain; some researchers think that these keep you from waking up at this stage (Halasz *et al.*, 1985).
Stage 3	After 25 minutes, you enter stage 3. The EEG begins to show some delta waves and the number of these gradually increases. You are now very unresponsive to the environment and would be hard to wake up.
Stage 4	There is no dramatic change to mark the start of stage 4. The sleep just gets gradually deeper, and delta waves become more common until they dominate the EEG recordings. Now only loud noise or shaking could wake you up, and you would be groggy and disorientated.
REM sleep	About 90 minutes on, a dramatic change occurs. The EEG pattern suddenly becomes very mixed in comparison to the slow regular delta waves of before. Your eyes will be rapidly moving from side to side beneath the eyelids. However, the rest of the body does not move – it is temporarily paralysed. If woken at this stage, you will be much less groggy – and will almost certainly report having been dreaming. All of us, therefore, dream every night, several times per night.

Sleep begins in stage 1 and progresses through stages 2–4 before entering REM sleep. Once REM sleep is over, the body usually returns to stage 2 sleep. This process is usually repeated four or five times per night (Carlson, 1998).

> **Top tip**
>
> Sleep stages 1–4 are sometimes referred to as N1, N2, N3 and N4. It is also fairly common for researchers to refer to N3 and N4 as a single stage, and therefore to say that there are three nREM sleep stages overall.

Key study: Dement and Kleitman's (1957) study of REM sleep

Aim: *Dement and Kleitman aimed to find the link between dreams and sleep stages. In particular, they wanted to know the function of REM sleep and whether eye movements during REM sleep were connected to the content of dreams.*

Method: *In their study, they used nine adults (seven male, two female) who came to a sleep laboratory for a polysomnography. The participants had been told to avoid alcohol and caffeine during the day. The participants slept in the sleep laboratory and were woken several times during the night by the researchers. They were asked if they had been dreaming, and if so, what their dream had been about and how long it had lasted.*

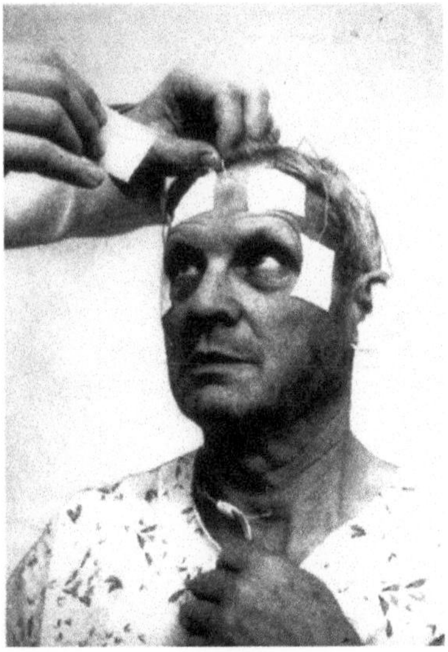

Nathaniel Kleitman taking part in one of his own sleep studies

Findings: *Dement and Kleitman found that participants were much more likely to say that they had been dreaming if woken during REM sleep, doing so on almost 80% of wakings, compared to around 9% if woken during nREM sleep. They also said that their dream had been shorter if they were woken five minutes after the start of the REM phase, compared to being woken 15 minutes after it started.*

In terms of eye movements, these did appear to link to what participants had been dreaming about. A participant who had been making left-to-right movements of the eyes reported a dream about people throwing tomatoes at each other, for example. After each waking, participants generally got back to sleep inside five minutes.

Evaluation: *This study used a small sample, and its artificial setting – including frequent wakings – may have affected the quality of their sleep or the content of their dreams. Nevertheless, this was strong evidence that REM sleep is dream sleep, which has been supported by subsequent research. It is harder to generalise the findings linking dream content to eye movements as each dream was different. Another limitation is that the study focused on adults, and the results can't be generalised to children.*

> **Top tip**
>
> Ensure that you know which research studies are mandatory and which are optional for your exam.

> **Top tip**
>
> Summarise the key sections of research studies – aim, method, findings and evaluation – onto four index cards, one for each section. Use these to test yourself periodically.

Circadian rhythms

Our body has a way of keeping track of time that we call our **body clock** (or 'circadian clock'). This controls **circadian rhythms** – the body's natural processes that vary over a 24-hour cycle. The most obvious examples of circadian rhythms are the **sleep/wake cycle** and our appetite for food. Other things also vary across 24 hours, such as body temperature and hormone levels.

Biological psychologists have identified a particular part of the brain which controls circadian rhythms – an area of the **hypothalamus** called the **suprachiasmatic nucleus (SCN)**. The SCN gets information from nerve cells in the eyes about whether it is light or dark, allowing the brain to know when it is time to sleep.

One of the main functions of the SCN is to control the release of **melatonin**, a hormone which makes us feel sleepy. The SCN sends a message to the pineal gland, and this gland releases the hormone. In all animals, melatonin is released when it gets dark. It is therefore usually released into the bloodstream in the evening when the sun goes down and it gets dark.

The sleep hormone melatonin is released in all animals when it gets dark. In nocturnal animals, this prompts them to wake and become active

The release of melatonin makes a person start to feel tired and eventually fall asleep. However, it doesn't act instantly. Usually melatonin will start to be released in the early evening. Melatonin levels peak in the middle of the night and then start to fall back down towards daytime levels.

Adenosine

In addition to the role of melatonin in making us sleepy, a chemical called **adenosine** builds up in our neurons during the day as a natural by-product of the brain's activities (Benington & Heller, 1995). This also causes us to feel tired and fatigued. When we sleep, this build-up is cleared, and the adenosine gets replaced by energy in the form of glycogen.

The effects of adenosine help to explain the way caffeine can interfere with sleep. Caffeine blocks adenosine receptors in neurons, making the body less responsive to the build-up of adenosine and reducing feelings of tiredness (see the final section of this chapter for more about factors that affect sleep).

> **Top tip**
>
> Nocturnal animals also release melatonin when it gets dark, but it functions to wake them up rather than make them feel sleepy.

> **Top tip**
>
> You could remember the SCN as having the same abbreviation as 'Scottish candidate number'!

Zeitgebers

As mentioned above, the SCN triggers the release of melatonin when it gets dark. However, to an extent the body is able to keep track of time without any external sensory information such as darkness. Internal cues to the body clock – known as **endogenous cues** – are the reason that we maintain a 24-hour schedule of feeling wakeful/tired even if travelling to other countries where the time is different. This means that even if we stayed in total darkness for a long period of time, we would still maintain an approximately 24-hour bodily cycle, releasing melatonin once a day.

> **Top tip**
>
> Light affects the SCN, the SCN controls the pineal gland, and the pineal gland releases melatonin.

This concept was put to the test by French researcher Michel Siffre, who slept in a cave in the Alps in perpetual darkness for several weeks. In a test monitored by NASA, it was found that his circadian rhythms maintained a cycle of just over 24 hours. This had the effect that his day/night cycle shifted forward by a few minutes each day. It can be concluded that the brain is able to maintain an approximately 24-hour cycle due to endogenous cues, but it requires **exogenous (external) cues** to maintain its body clock more precisely.

When we are exposed to normal conditions, the brain avoids this gradual shift of the circadian rhythm because of exogenous cues, in particular light and dark. **Zeitgeber** – a German word meaning 'time-giver' – is another name for the exogenous cues that help the brain to know what time it is. Light and darkness are both zeitgebers, telling our brain that it is time to sleep or wake up.

In our evolutionary past, we would start to feel sleepy as the day got late and it got darker. Nowadays, of course, we use artificial lights and often stay awake (or get up) when it is dark outside. Recently, researchers have realised that artificial light can disturb our circadian rhythms and affect the quality of sleep (see the final section of this chapter).

Are you an owl or a lark?

Individual differences in circadian rhythms

You have probably heard people describe themselves as 'not a morning person' and there appear to be genuine biological differences, with some people more prone to early waking and early bedtimes than others (Phillips, 2009). Such differences are largely genetic. Sleep researchers sometimes call the early risers 'larks' and the late risers 'night owls', although the technical name for this difference is your **chronotype**.

Only around 25% of people are true night owls; this group tend to do better at logical tasks in the evening and creative tasks in the morning, while most people are the opposite (Pink, 2018). As society is largely set up to suit people who prefer early starts, there can be a tendency for people with late chronotypes (night owls) to be at a disadvantage. This can affect academic performance, sports and many other aspects of life. Guthrie *et al.* (1995) found that larks got better grades, particularly in classes which took place earlier in the day.

However, sleep patterns also depend on our environment and our culture. Until the 1800s, it was common to get up mid-way through sleep, sometimes to do some work or visit neighbours, write letters or to have sex – so the idea of having a single period of sleep that begins well after dusk may be very much a modern phenomenon (Ekirch, 2006). What's more, if people are not exposed to extended artificial light but instead to just 10 hours of light per day, they revert to having two four-hour blocks of sleep separated by one hour awake (Wehr, 1992). An eight-hour block of sleep may therefore reflect our bodies' adaptation to modern life – and to electric lighting.

There are variations in how much sleep people need. Most seem to need around seven to eight hours per night to function well but there are individual differences, and this also changes over the lifespan. Babies and young children need much more sleep and the amount reduces right through into old age. A few people function well on six hours of sleep or less (Van Dongen *et al.*, 2005) but most people who get such a small amount of sleep are accumulating a **sleep debt** – a lack of sleep that they have to 'pay back' by oversleeping on other nights, such as at the weekend.

In a study of over 3,000 teenagers, Wolfson and Carskadon (1998) found that students who got a longer night's sleep on a regular basis obtained higher grades. The mean amount of sleep reported among their sample of 13 to 17 year olds was seven hours and 20 minutes, and they stated that: *'undoubtedly, most adolescents require more'* (p.885). This suggests that the brain needs a full night's sleep to consolidate new learning (an idea that is discussed in more detail later in this chapter). A limitation of the study is that it did not follow participants longitudinally, to find the long-term effects of lower levels of sleep on each participant.

A study found that pupils who sleep more regularly get better grades

There are also important changes in the timing of sleep during adolescence. Regardless of their general tendency towards early or late bedtimes, a person's body clock shifts gradually later until their mid-teens and then starts to get earlier again. This means that regardless of whether you consider yourself a lark or an owl, your preferred bedtimes and wake times are likely to be later in your late teens than at any other point during your life. Because of this, some schools have experimented with a later start time for senior pupils!

Polyphasic sleep

Most people in the UK sleep in a single block of time, for example eight hours every day. However many people elsewhere in the world – as well as most other great ape species – break their sleeping time up, with a main block and a shorter nap or siesta.

Some people have tried taking this further by breaking their sleep time into three or more naps. This can reduce the overall amount time spent sleeping, but is difficult to adjust to and doesn't fit well around conventional work or study schedules! This 'polyphasic sleep' could form the topic of an interesting essay or blog post.

The role of the brain

The brain controls all of our behaviour and sleep is no different. You have already seen several ways in which the brain is involved in sleep. These include:

- The SCN triggers the release of melatonin when it receives information that suggests it is getting dark.
- The SCN also controls our internal (endogenous) body clock, causing us to maintain circadian rhythms on an approximately 24-hour cycle, even if there are no zeitgebers or when we are travelling across time zones.
- Adenosine builds up in our neurons as a natural by-product of the brain's daily activities, leading us to feel fatigued later in the day.
- The brain cycles through REM and non-REM sleep during the night. Non-REM sleep can be divided into separate stages, each with its own characteristic electrical activity in the brain, for example the delta waves found in stages 3 and 4. These can be measured using an EEG brain scan.
- Sleep is also important for the brain to stay in good health and to consolidate new memories that have been learned.

Top tip

There is a lot of new biological terminology in this section. Test yourself on the terms, and then ask a classmate or family member to test you.

Key concepts

- Sleep
- Body clock
- Circadian rhythms
- Sleep/wake cycle
- Chronotype
- Sleep debt
- Polysomnography
- Electroencephalogram (EEG)
- Sleep stages
- Delta waves
- Slow-wave sleep
- REM sleep
- Non-REM sleep
- Sleep spindles
- SCN – suprachiasmatic nucleus
- Hypothalamus
- Melatonin
- Adenosine
- Endogenous cues
- Exogenous cues
- Zeitgeber

Questions

1. What is the general term for sleep that is *not* REM sleep?
2. What term is given to the body's 24-hour rhythms such as the sleep/wake cycle?
3. What does an EEG measure during sleep?
4. How many sleep stages does the average person go through in total, in an entire night's sleep?
5. According to Dement and Kleitman (1957), what happens during REM sleep?
6. What does 'zeitgeber' literally mean?
7. What part of the brain contains the suprachiasmatic nucleus (SCN)?
8. What hormone triggers us to feel sleepy and fall asleep?
9. What chemical builds up in our brain cells during the day?
10. At what point in the lifespan does the body clock shift to its latest pattern in terms of bedtimes and wake times?

Activities

1. Delta waves are shown on an EEG during deep sleep. Find out about other brain waves: alpha, beta, theta and gamma. Print out a picture of how these look on an EEG recording.
2. List at least five concepts relating to the biology of sleep. (You can use the 'key concepts' box to help you.)

   Now connect the concepts in a 'concept map' diagram, like the one found here: www.jonathanfirth.co.uk/maps. You should label logical connections between the concepts, such as 'is part of', 'depends on' and 'follows after'. For example, REM sleep would be labelled as one of the sleep stages, while the release of melatonin could be shown to be dependent on the action of the SCN. You could make a final version of your diagram as a poster, adding images where relevant.

The restoration theory of sleep

The previous section has explained some of the biological processes that occur during sleep. But what is sleep for – what adaptive purpose does it serve? This section looks at a major theory of sleep which focuses on the idea that sleep is necessary to restore and repair the body or brain, in the context of the broader evolutionary explanations of sleep.

The theory

Sleep appears to be universal among complex animals – it has been observed in species ranging from humans to fruit flies (Abel *et al.*, 2013). We know that for evolutionary reasons, sleep must fulfil an essential function, or at least have fulfilled an essential function in our evolutionary past – if it wasn't useful, animals would not do it, because any competing animal that did not sleep would have a survival advantage.

One major possibility is that sleep is necessary for **bodily restoration**, for the body to rest and recover from exertions.

The restoration theory of sleep states that the main function of sleep is as a period of down time to allow repair and maintenance, in much the same way that shutting down a factory could allow machines to be checked and repairs to be made. This theory, best summarised by Oswald (1966), states that all animals sleep because it allows the body – and the brain – to carry out essential repair tasks.

Possible **restoration** functions that the body might need to do during sleep include:

- repairing minor injuries, such as to skin or muscles
- removal of waste chemicals in the muscles
- replenishing neurotransmitters and/or energy in the brain.

Top tip

Put these three restoration functions on an index card for revision.

The rationale behind this theory is that a period of physical inactivity might be essential, or at least very helpful, for this restoration to happen. Sleep causes the body to be relatively inactive – repair functions may be more successful during inactivity as no further damage is being done to body tissues, or because fewer toxins/waste products are being produced.

Sleep may help injuries to heal

Horne found that sleep deprivation did not affect the participants' athletic ability

Evidence

The restoration theory found support in a study by Shapiro *et al.* (1981). In a study of runners, it was found that their sleep lasted on average 90 minutes longer than usual over the two nights following an ultramarathon. In particular, it was non-REM sleep which lengthened, rising from 25% to 45% of total sleep. This supports the idea that the body needs more sleep time to repair itself when it has experienced a lot of minor injuries or damage.

However, Horne (1978) reported that sleep deprivation did not interfere with participants' ability to play sport. Nor did it make them ill. It seems that sleep is not essential for physical functioning, at least in the short-term.

Body or brain?

? Discussion point

Can you think of any other experiments that could be done to test the effect of sleep on restoration?

It may be important to distinguish between restoration of the body and restoration of the brain. Hobson (2005) disagrees with the idea that bodily restoration is the purpose of sleep. He states that sleep is entirely for the brain, noting that bodily restoration could be achieved by simply resting.

Horne and Harley (1988) believe that a warming of the brain during exercise led to longer sleep in the Shapiro *et al.* study (see above), not wear and tear to the body. To test this, they heated people's faces and heads using a hairdryer! Four out of their six participants were then found to have a longer period of non-REM sleep. This finding goes against the idea that sleep is needed to repair the body but it could be the case that repair of the brain is its key function. Alternatively, perhaps some activities like exercise interfere with other brain functions, such as memory consolidation, and the brain then needs to catch up on these by having a longer period of sleep.

Adam and Oswald (1983) believed that both brain and body are restored by sleep, though during different sleep stages. They suggested that REM sleep is essential for **brain restoration**. During this stage, neurons can grow and be repaired, and neurotransmitters can be replenished. In their view, slow-wave sleep (that is, non-REM sleep stages 3 and 4) is essential for bodily restoration.

To support their argument, Adam and Oswald (1983) drew on several pieces of evidence, including:

- Hospital patients who have had spinal operations or have taken drug overdoses engage in longer periods of REM sleep, supporting the idea that this stage is essential for repairing the brain and other parts of the nervous system.
- The level of neurotransmitters in the brain reduces during the day, supporting the idea that it needs to be replenished at night.

Top tip

Adam and Oswald (1983) argued that REM sleep is for brain restoration while non-REM sleep is for bodily restoration.

Evaluation

Restoration is not the only possible explanation for why all animals sleep. An alternative idea is that it gives animals a survival advantage by helping them to save energy by keeping them inactive when they are not gathering food, or keeping them out of danger. This fits with the finding that carnivores sleep more than herbivores (Siegel, 2005), as carnivores generally have fewer enemies and spend less time gathering food. However, it can't explain why animals completely lose conscious awareness during sleep, which is not a survival advantage. This makes restoration theory a stronger evolutionary explanation.

Bodily restoration also struggles to explain why sleep would have evolved. As Rasch and Born (2013) argue:

[restoration] could be likewise achieved in a state of quiet wakefulness and would not explain the loss of consciousness and responsiveness to external threats during sleep. These prominent features of sleep strongly speak for the notion that sleep is mainly 'for the brain'.

Source: Rasch & Born (2013, p. 613)

Brain restoration, on the other hand, might only be possible if the brain is essentially 'switched off' during the process. This makes it a stronger explanation than bodily restoration.

Sleep probably has multiple functions and the fact that restoration happens during sleep doesn't mean that this is sleep's only function, or even its main one. It has become widely accepted that REM sleep and non-REM sleep have different functions from each other (Siegel, 2005). It is therefore probably over simplistic to suggest that sleep is just about restoration. Another key function that takes place during sleep is the processing of information and consolidation of new memories. This will be discussed in the next section.

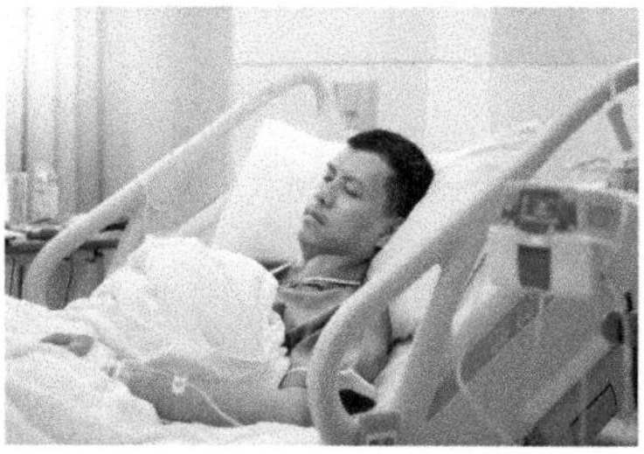

Sleep may have other functions, besides restoration

For humans, it is clear that sleeping too little seems to result in poorer performance and an increased chance of accidents. This supports the restoration theory (Coren, 1998), although again, these findings say more about brain restoration than bodily restoration – body function appears to be more or less normal after sleep deprivation, as found by Horne (1978).

It's unclear whether the increased REM sleep after brain injury is due to restoration, or if it has another cause. For example, key processes such as consolidating memories may take longer if the brain has been injured, thus increasing the length of this stage.

Key concepts

- Bodily restoration
- Restoration
- Brain restoration

Questions

1. According to the restoration theory, why do organisms sleep – to repair damage or to hide from predators?
2. Describe an alternative to restoration theory, which explains sleep in terms of its evolutionary benefits.
3. Name three key repair processes which can occur during sleep.
4. Why would sleeping be a good time for the body to repair itself?
5. What type of sleep lasted longer in runners after a race, in the Shapiro *et al.* (1981) study?
6. What did Horne and Harley (1988) find when they heated participants' heads with a hairdryer?
7. How did Adam and Oswald (1983) divide up the possible restoration functions of REM sleep and non-REM sleep?
8. What evidence did Adam and Oswald (1983) give to support their view?
9. Did Rasch and Born (2013) believe that sleep was mainly for the brain or mainly for the body?
10. Do all animals sleep for a similar length of time?

Activities

1. Discuss possible ways that you could do an experiment into restoration theory. How could you measure growth hormones, restoration of wear and tear, physical restoration in nerve cells, such as replenishing energy and neurotransmitters in the brain? Consider the ethics involved!
2. Find out how long some common animals sleep for and make a chart or a poster. Try to find out about species differences in both REM sleep and non-REM sleep, and about when species sleep. Are there any animals that particularly surprise you?

Explanations of dreams

Psychoanalytic explanation of dreams

You will remember that the psychoanalytic approach (also called the 'psychodynamic approach') to psychology explains processes in terms of the unconscious mind (see chapter 1). It states that the id is your unconscious, while the ego is your conscious mind. During sleep, the id becomes dominant, and the id's main motivation is pleasure.

Although this approach to psychology is largely historical and often seen as unscientific, it was certainly influential in the study of **dreams**. According to Freud's classic work *On the Interpretation of Dreams* (1900), dreams reveal our unconscious wishes and fantasies. Freud believed that dreams involve **wish fulfilment** – we dream about what we want, especially about wishes that have been thwarted in real life.

Freud believed that dreams involve wish fulfilment

Psychoanalysts believe that only some thoughts are truly inaccessible. There are others which we may be unaware of at a particular moment but which can become conscious if we make the effort. These are our **preconscious** thoughts. Most memories about ourselves and our lives are therefore preconscious. The contents of our dreams are also in the preconscious. This suggests that it is possible to remember and explain the content of your dreams.

Freud also thought that dreams contain a series of **symbols**, with the true meaning of the dream hidden from the conscious mind. In particular, anything which is disturbing or embarrassing can be hidden by the unconscious mind using a symbolic image. These symbols may be based on the psychosexual obsessions of the person's psychological stage of development.

Freud believed that a dream about a storm was a sign that the person was experiencing emotional turmoil

Two important terms to be aware of are the **manifest content** and the **latent content** of the dream. The manifest content is what is apparent on the surface – what the dream appears to be about. However, this aspect of dream content is seen by the psychoanalytic approach as being just a symbol of something else. The latent content is what (according to this approach) the dream is really about – its hidden meaning. For example:

Manifest content	Latent content
School	Learning or being judged
A storm	Emotional turmoil
Teeth falling out	Worries or lack of control
Pregnancy	A new aspect of the self

Top tip

The use of symbols in dreams can be seen as another example of a defence mechanism used by the mind (see below, and chapter 1).

Therefore, understanding a dream involves a process of interpretation of the manifest content in order to reveal the latent content and therefore the true meaning.

Top tip

Ensure that you can distinguish between what is meant by latent and manifest content of dreams. It's a good idea to prepare a simple example of each that you could give in an exam answer.

Make the link

...between the different explanations of dreams and the psychological approaches covered in the introduction of this book.

Discussion point

Do you think that our dreams have hidden meanings? Have you ever tried to analyse a dream or had someone else do it for you?

A sleep study could involve a dream diary

In addition, Freud thought that several processes occur which distort the true meaning of the dream, making the content harder to understand. Two of these processes are:

- **Condensation**. This is where several ideas or symbols in the dream get merged together.
- **Secondary elaboration**. This is the dreamer's own interpretation which occurs after waking, or things that they add when telling the dream. This makes it harder for an analyst to recognise the latent content.

The psychoanalytic approach is known for the case study method, which for studies of sleep could involve interviews and dream diaries used to record individual patients' experiences (see chapter 8 for more on this method). One of the best examples of this is Freud's case study of little Hans (see key study), in which the interpretation of Hans's dreams was crucial. Key features of the method that can be seen in this context include:

- The study is in-depth and longitudinal. It took over a year to study and analyse Hans's case.
- Qualitative data was gathered. In this case, this came via Hans's father, who had informally questioned Hans about the dreams.
- It tends to focus on unusual cases. Here, it was a case of phobia.

Role of defence mechanisms

In chapter 1, we looked at psychoanalytic defence mechanisms such as repression and denial. Several of these can be seen in the psychoanalytic theory of dreams. For example:

1. Repression involves putting unwanted thoughts or dark secrets, often with sexual content, from the conscious ego into the unconscious id. Repression is a major cause of dreams, according to this theory. Repressed desires are kept out of the mind while we are awake, but they return during dreams in a hidden form.
2. Secondary elaboration could involve hiding the more embarrassing aspects of a dream when the dreamer interprets it upon waking. This is a type of defence mechanism, and could also involve denial or reaction formation.
3. Displacement may occur within the dream. This is where something unimportant is brought to prominence, in order to shift attention away from what is really important. It plays a similar psychological role to replacing repressed feelings with symbols, and makes it harder for a therapist to uncover the latent content. Symbols are also a form of ego defence.

Key study: Freud's case study of 'little Hans'

Aim: *Freud wanted to provide evidence of his controversial Oedipus complex (see chapter 1), a theory that suggests that children go through a stage of development where they fear their same-sex parent and have a childish romantic love for their opposite-sex* *parent. When he was approached by a friend, Herr Graf, whose son suffered from a severe phobia of horses, Freud decided to see if the boy's behaviour fitted his theory.*

Method: *Freud's study was a case study, although it was unusual compared to modern case studies in that he did not study the patient, 'little Hans', directly, but instead exchanged letters with Herr Graf, discussing the boy's behaviour, and in particular, his phobia of horses. This was more problematic at the time than it would be today because horses were an everyday sight on city streets in the early 1900s.*

Findings: *Freud was very interested to hear about Hans's dreams and fantasies, because he thought that these were evidence of unconscious processes. Hans had three key dreams.*

- In one, he dreamed that he was married to his mother and they had their own family. This was interpreted by Freud as showing Hans's romantic desire for his mother.
- In another dream, a crumpled giraffe was being squashed by a large giraffe. The giraffes were in his parents' bed. Freud said that this dream showed Hans's fear and hostility towards his father.
- In a third dream a plumber came to the house and removed Hans's penis, replacing it with a larger one. Freud said that this showed Hans's desire to be a grown up man and marry his mother, as well as linking to the penis obsession of the phallic stage of development.

Hans also had certain fantasies and dreams about peeing. He was caught playing with his penis and his mother threatened to have the doctor cut it off! This provoked some anxiety.

Overall, Freud concluded that Hans's dreams, fears and fantasies were evidence for his Oedipus complex. The horses represented his father who Hans unconsciously feared, while the dreams indicated love for his mother.

Evaluation: *The case of Hans had many of the strengths of case studies, including detailed unstructured interviews and going into the case in depth. However, it is possible that Freud and Hans's father distorted the evidence to fit the theory and there could be other explanations for Hans's dreams. Hans, whose real name was Herbert, found out about the study in adulthood and claimed that he had no recollection of the dreams and fantasies described in Freud's research, or of fearing horses. The study is also limited in that no controlled observations were made of Hans's behaviour. It is hard to generalise from one patient in a case study – in this case, Hans's issues do not prove that all boys fear their fathers.*

Freud with 'little Hans'

Evaluation

A strength of the psychoanalytic approach is its impact in terms of popular understanding of dreams. It has had a major effect on society, in particular in terms of the idea that dreams have hidden meanings. Freud also helped to move forward the scientific study of dreams by

Carl Jung

? Discussion point

Do you think, as Freud did, that Hans's behaviour and fantasies were relatively normal for his stage of development?

? Discussion point

Why do you think abbreviated names or fake names are sometimes used to describe patients in research?

stating that dreams have a psychological meaning, rather than (as was widely thought prior to his work) predicting the future. However, his work relies too heavily on case studies such as that of Hans. The findings of such studies are hard to generalise to other people.

Psychoanalysts do not all agree on how to interpret dreams. In particular, Freud and Jung took different approaches. Jung (1964) disagreed with Freud's method of interpreting dreams and said that a dream's symbols are unique to the individual and cannot have a general meaning. He also stated that dreams should only be interpreted on the basis of what actually appears in the dream, and not translated by the therapist. So, for example, he would not say that a dream about giraffes was actually a dream about your parents.

Another obvious challenge for Freud's idea of wish fulfilment is that many dreams are unpleasant. The approach struggles to give a satisfactory explanation of nightmares. More broadly, there is a lack of scientific evidence that dreams have a hidden meaning at all. Later theories (see below) think that the content of our dreams may have a more mundane explanation.

Biological explanation of dreams

As with other aspects of sleep, the processes that occur when we have dreams can be explained biologically. As we have seen in the previous section, dreaming occurs in one of the stages of sleep – REM sleep. Rather than look for the meaning of dreams, biological psychologists think that dreams are largely the result of a side effect of brain activity during sleep, and are therefore meaningless. This contrasts greatly with Freud's ideas!

The **activation-synthesis** hypothesis devised by Hobson and McCarley (1977) states that dreams result from neurons firing randomly in a brain area called the pons. These then send messages to the neocortex. The neocortex tries to make sense of the messages, creatively making up narratives that fit with the random signals that it is receiving, and these form dreams. The 'activation' refers to the firing of neurons in the pons, while 'synthesis' refers to the cortex putting this information together into a dream that makes sense.

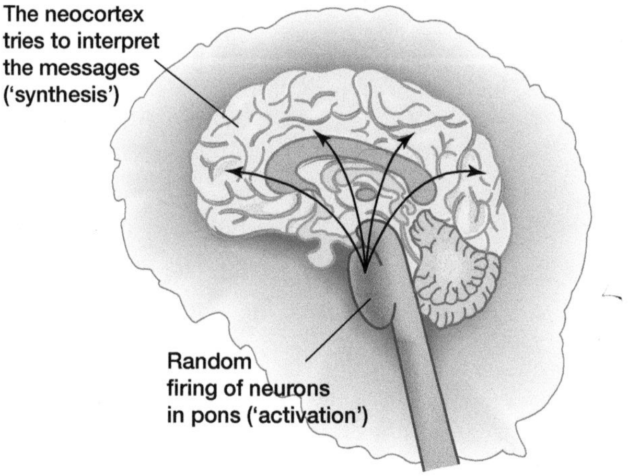
The neocortex tries to interpret the messages ('synthesis')
Random firing of neurons in pons ('activation')

The activation-synthesis hypothesis

Evaluation

The biological explanation of dreams is supported by both theory and evidence. However, the theory doesn't entirely explain why we dream about particular things.

Even if the activation of brain areas is not as random as it seems, this biological perspective can still hold. For example, if the reason that certain brain areas become active is because they are being repaired or because memories are being consolidated during sleep (see the theories in the next section), the processes of activation and synthesis could still happen.

However, most people do not find it satisfying to say that their dreams are entirely random, and the biological explanation struggles to explain some facts, such as that 70% of dreams make sense to the dreamer and that experiences from the previous day tend to appear during dreams (Domhoff *et al.*, 2005).

Some researchers believe that the main function of dreams is the reorganisation of memories

Top tip

Sleep's role in problem solving could link to incubation – the idea that creative insights can occur over a period of time when we stop thinking about a problem. Some artists and scientists claim to have had creative ideas during dreams.

Cognitive explanation of dreams

The cognitive approach to psychology explains behaviour in terms of beliefs and schemas, and sees the mind as an information processor (see chapter 1). One key cognitive idea is that the purpose of sleep and dreams is to facilitate **information processing**, for example by consolidating memories and helping with **problem solving**.

This perspective states that the brain reorganises memories during sleep and that dreams occur as a by-product of this process, as various memories are strengthened or changed. This view of dreams has similarities to the activation-synthesis theory in that both see dream content as a by-product of other processes, with no deeper meaning. However, rather than being random, the memories that are strengthened or forgotten will depend upon what has been recently learned, and on their importance to the individual.

Top tip

The cognitive approach has the potential to be combined with the biological approach, when knowledge of cognitive functions is combined with an understanding of the underlying biological processes. This field is known as cognitive neuroscience.

In 1983, researchers Francis Crick and Graeme Mitchison famously wrote:

'We dream in order to forget.'

Source: Crick and Mitchison (1983)

They devised a key cognitive theory of dreaming known as the **reorganisation** theory. It suggests that the main function of dreams is to make the most of our ability to store memories. Crick and Mitchison believed that our brain's storage capacity is limited, and that some memories are therefore deleted overnight in order to use storage space more efficiently.

> **? Discussion point**
>
> What did Crick and Mitchison mean by *'we dream in order to forget'*?

The theory is based on the concept of **reverse learning**, meaning that learning can be undone during REM sleep. They believed that dreams are just a side effect of a decluttering process that takes place in the brain – the neocortex becomes overloaded with information during the day, and that during REM sleep, unwanted memories are deleted in order to improve organisation and make space. As these unconnected memories and ideas are activated, a random selection of thoughts and memories form into a dream.

Francis Crick – who first became famous for his research into the structure of DNA

Crick and Mitchison believed that there are two main categories of memories:

- **Adaptive memories**: things that will be useful for us to retain.
- **Parasitic memories**: useless or harmful memories that waste resources.

They believed that the brain benefits from reverse learning of parasitic memories and that this is the purpose of REM sleep. As well as taking up space, these memories were thought to lead to obsessions and compulsive behaviour. Therefore, the theory states that the purpose of sleep is to make us think and act more efficiently.

Research evidence

To support their theory, Crick and Mitchison refer to other species that lack REM sleep – the echidna and two species of dolphin. These animals also have larger brains than might be expected for their overall body size. The researchers conclude that the 'pruning' of memories during REM sleep allows the brain to be smaller and more efficient in other species.

Certain species of dolphin do not dream; the large size of their brains could suggest that the 'pruning' of memories during REM sleep allows the human brain to be smaller

The researchers have also run **neural network** computer models of learning. In these, they have found that memories are easily overloaded but that this can be reduced using reverse learning. They also found that the computer models acted in highly repetitive ways – which they compared to obsessive behaviour in humans – and had 'hallucinations' based on old information that had not been deleted.

However, numerous studies have shown that rather than clearing space, sleep actually tends to strengthen our memories. Walker *et al.* (2003) used a finger-tapping task to study the role of sleep in learning new memories. They found that sleep helps the memories to be reliably encoded, and that recalling an item the following day reactivates the memory, allowing a skill (such as playing a musical instrument) to be refined. Even a nap can be beneficial – Mednick *et al.* (2003) found that for a perception task, the same benefit was found after a 90-minute nap (containing all sleep stages) as after a full night's sleep. This idea has been supported by research into infants – Seehagen *et al.* (2015) found that when babies were learning a new action, those who had taken a nap showed a better recall of the skill than those who had not. Sleep therefore facilitates information processing.

Rasch and Born (2013) note three major pieces of evidence against Crick and Mitchison's reorganisation theory:

1. People who were asked to suppress (i.e. try to forget) memories prior to a period of sleep actually remembered them better than a control group who stayed awake.
2. Creative thinking can be improved by sleep, indicating that key information is well remembered and better organised after sleeping.
3. Patients with post-traumatic stress disorder (PTSD) often suffer repetitive nightmares. Far from being associated with deleting bad memories, these nightmares seem to make the disorder worse.

There is also good evidence that the brain has an effectively unlimited storage capacity for memories (for example Bjork, 2011), a finding which goes against the idea that it is necessary to delete files in order to make space.

Stickgold (2009) has investigated the processes by which memories develop during sleep. According to his research, sleep can be of benefit to every type of memory, but he suggests that people who have a medium (rather than strong or weak) memory trace gain the biggest benefit.

Evaluation

In general, the cognitive approach to dreaming suggests that dreams are largely meaningless. This is similar to biological explanations. It also helps to explain content of the dreams – we are more likely to dream about recent memories. This approach therefore predicts that there will be links between what we think about during the day and what appears in our dreams, an idea called the **continuity hypothesis of dreams**. For example, if you have been speaking to a visiting family member that you rarely see, that person may then appear in your dream.

A strength of the reorganisational theory is that it gives a clear theory about why REM sleep could be important. By making memory more efficient, Crick and Mitchison (1983) argue that better use is made of the available space in the brain. The theory is also consistent with some of the biological evidence about what happens during sleep, such as the activation-synthesis theory.

However, a major weakness of the theory is that it is based on computer models of memory, and lacks research support on human participants. Nowadays, researchers increasingly agree that sleep is essential to strengthen and consolidate memories, and that it does not delete memories. Research on dolphins also cannot be reliably generalised to humans.

Sleep helps skills such as playing a musical instrument to be refined

A study showed that a nap helped babies to recall new skills

? Discussion point

Why do you think babies sleep much more than adults do?

? Discussion point

Have you ever tried having a 'power nap' or otherwise napping during the day? Do you find it helpful?

Top tip

Running computer simulations of thought processes is a typical method used as part of the cognitive approach to psychology. Reorganisation theory is an excellent example of the cognitive approach, as it links to the computer analogy.

? Discussion point

Have you ever dreamt about someone shortly after meeting them for the first time or after spending time with them during the day?

Top tip

List the ways in which sleep links to memory, information processing, problem solving or creativity.

Reorganisational theory does not explain why dreams have a narrative (a story). Our dreams appear to make sense the majority of the time (Domhoff *et al.*, 2006) and this doesn't seem to fit well with the idea that random memories are being activated and destroyed.

Overall, the reorganisation theory in its original form does not have much support nowadays, but the broader idea that sleep is *important* for cognitive abilities such as memory is widely accepted.

An alternative cognitive view from Domhoff (2011) focuses more on the subjective meaning of the dreams, and the beliefs and culture of the dreamer. In his view, a dream is what happens when the mind does not have any other task to do. He draws comparisons between the dream and waking experiences such as daydreams, saying that they are very similar in content and that both reflect our schemas and our cultural beliefs. Supporting this idea, Domhoff notes that hunter-gatherer cultures dream more about animals than do people in industrialised countries.

Key concepts

- Dreams
- Wish fulfilment
- Preconscious
- Symbols
- Manifest content
- Latent content
- Condensation
- Secondary elaboration
- Activation-synthesis
- Reorganisation
- Reverse learning
- Adaptive memories
- Parasitic memories
- Neural network
- Continuity hypothesis of dreams
- Information processing
- Problem solving

Questions

1. Which term means the true meaning of dreams according to Freud's theory, manifest content or latent content?

2. In little Hans's dreams, which animal represented his parents, according to Freud?

3. What term means combining more than one idea or fantasy into a dream symbol?

4. How does the psychoanalytic approach differ from other approaches to explain dream meanings?

5. What is the term for the biological theory that dreams are due to random firing of neurons in the pons?

6. What is the continuity hypothesis?

7. What can reverse learning do to a memory according to Crick and Mitchison's (1983) theory?

8. Why are parasitic memories deleted according to Crick and Mitchison (1983)?

9. What computer-based evidence was given in support of the reorganisational theory?

10. Do other researchers agree that sleep causes forgetting?

Activities

1. Which of these approaches to explaining dreams makes most sense to you? Discuss this question in a pair or group OR write a response to it in your notebook or blog.
2. Write down the events of one of your dreams. Underline any key events, people or objects. Now have a look at a dream dictionary (either a book, or an online version) and try to find out what this manifest content might actually mean (i.e. what latent content it represents). Does it make sense to you?

Factors that affect sleep quality

Although scientists do not fully agree on the purpose of sleep, it is clear that good, regular sleep plays an important role in memory, health and other issues.

We know that sleep is essential – so what happens when you don't sleep at all? One famous case of **sleep deprivation** involved Peter Tripp, a New York DJ who stayed awake for 200 hours in aid of charity, while broadcasting from a booth in Times Square and being regularly tested by psychologists. His case shows how dramatic the effects of sleep loss can be:

Peter Tripp during the 'wakeathon'

He looked weary but no radio listener or casual onlooker could imagine the truth of his experience. It resembled a medieval torture... By 100 hours, only halfway, he had reached an inexorable turning point. Now he could only perform one or two of the daily battery of tests. Tests requiring attention or minimal mental agility had become unbearable to him and the psychologists testing him. As one later recalled, 'Here was a competent New York disc jockey trying vainly to find his way through the alphabet.' By 170 hours the tests were torture. A simple algebraic problem that Tripp had earlier solved with ease took such superhuman effort that he was frightened, and his agonised attempts to perform were painful to watch.

Loss of concentration and mental agility were not the worst, however. By 110 hours there were signs of delirium. As one of the doctors recalled, 'We didn't know much about it at the time because he couldn't tell us.' From his later statements, his curious utterances and behaviour at the time, it became clear. Tripp's visual world had grown grotesque. A doctor walked into the booth in a tweed suit that Tripp saw as a suit of furry worms. A nurse appeared to drip saliva. A scientist's tie kept jumping. This was frightening, hard to explain, and sometimes Tripp grew angry wondering if this were a bona fide experiment or a masquerade. Around 120 hours, he opened a bureau drawer in the hotel and rushed out calling for help. It appeared to be spurting flames. Tripp thought the blaze has been set deliberately to

In England there are over 10 million prescriptions per year for sleeping pills

? Discussion point

Have you ever suffered from insomnia or hypersomnia?

test him. In order to explain to himself these hallucinations – which appeared quite real – he concocted rationalisations resembling the delusions of psychotic patients.

Source: Lindzey et al. *(1978: 172–173)*

Clearly, reduced sleep can be harmful to our mental health. Poor sleep can affect our mood and functioning. It can make it unsafe to drive due to reduced attention levels, and over the longer term it can cause mental health problems, in particular depression.

Difficulties sleeping can also be harmful to physical health – poor sleep has been linked to coronary heart disease, digestive illnesses and reproductive problems (Czeisler *et al.*, 1990).

Factors that make it harder to sleep can lead to **insomnia** – a condition which literally means an inability to get to sleep or stay asleep. This may lead to a knock-on effect of extreme sleepiness the following day, when sufferers may fall asleep uncontrollably and at unpredictable times. Excessive sleepiness is known as **hypersomnia**.

Insomnia is often treated using drugs. In particular, most **sleeping pills** are from a class of hypnotic-sedative drugs which are often effective in terms of making people feel sleepy, but due to problems with side effects and addiction they are not recommended for long-term use. Often they fail to tackle the cause of the insomnia, which may be environmental. Stress can also make it harder to sleep.

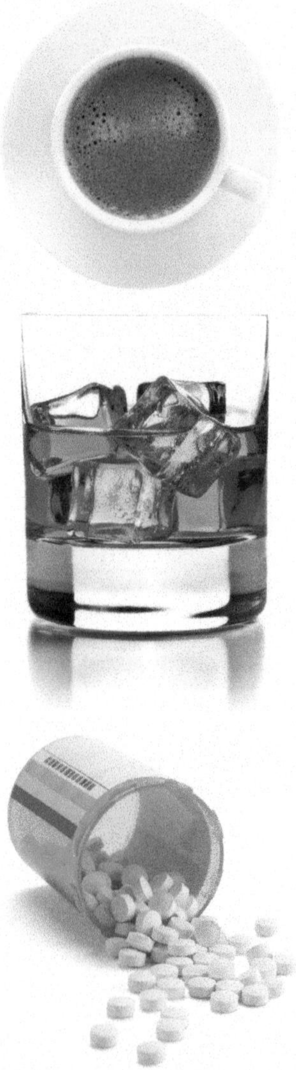

Drugs can affect sleep

Drugs

One factor that can affect sleep is the use of recreational or prescription **drugs**. **Stimulant** drugs have the effect of making people more alert or keeping them awake and can reduce the quality of sleep.

One example of a stimulant is **caffeine**. This is the world's most popular psychoactive drug and it is present in food and drinks such as coffee, tea, chocolate and most energy drinks. It can also be taken in tablet form. People drink coffee to keep them alert, but taking it in the evening can make it harder to get to sleep. Many people don't realise that it can take over five hours for the level of caffeine in the blood just to drop to half of the level it was at after taking the caffeine (Statland & Demas, 1980). The effects of caffeine are due to its ability to block adenosine receptors (see the first section of this chapter). This means that the natural tendency to become fatigued later in the day has less of an effect. Other than its effect on sleep, caffeine is considered a relatively safe drug.

Amphetamine (often called 'speed') is another stimulant – although it is a class B illegal drug, it is widely used for socialising and by some workers on long overnight shifts.

Alcohol – technically a type of drug – can also affect sleep, usually making people feel more sleepy. Many people like to drink alcohol in the evenings to help them get to sleep, but alcohol changes the proportions of REM and non-REM sleep. However, tolerance to alcohol develops quickly, resulting in normal patterns of sleep for healthy people consuming moderate amounts of alcohol (Roehrs &

Roth, 2001). Therefore, it is unlikely to be of any long-term benefit in the treatment of insomnia and can lead to more frequent wakings.

Prescription drugs can interfere with sleep patterns as an undesired side effect, either by making it harder for us to sleep or by making us drowsy. Some drugs such as anti-histamines (taken for allergies) come in 'non-drowsy' versions.

Light

As mentioned in the first section of this chapter, artificial light and screens can affect the release of melatonin. If the SCN fails to keep track of day and night due to bright artificial lights acting as zeitgebers, it may release melatonin at the wrong time, or fail to release it when we do want to sleep. Some people need to take **melatonin supplements** to help them sleep.

In particular, light from some types of low-energy lightbulb and from phone or computer screens can be problematic. This is because the light contains a large proportion of blue wavelengths, which can have a stronger effect in suppressing sleep (Santhi *et al.*, 2012). In particular they suppress or delay the production of melatonin.

Chang *et al.* (2015) studied the bedtime use of tablets and eReaders which emit light. They found that participants in their study released less melatonin, took longer to get to sleep, had less REM sleep during the night and were less alert in the morning. This research suggests that it can be highly problematic to look at screens in the hour or so before trying to go to sleep, and that even people who don't suffer from insomnia could experience poorer sleep quality. Combined with the role of sleep in memory consolidation discussed in the previous section, this research has caused concern among educators.

Artificial light can affect the release of melatonin

Shift work and jet lag

Jobs involving **shift work** – where people work at varying times of the day or night – can also affect sleep. The problem arises because during a night shift the individual's circadian rhythms are telling the body that it should be sleeping, but they have to stay awake. Then, when trying to catch up on sleep during the day, they may find it hard to fall asleep or to sleep soundly. In severe cases, a person with ongoing insomnia due to shift work can be diagnosed with a sleep disorder.

? Discussion point

Think of practical ways that you could reduce your exposure to screens and artificial lighting during the period of time immediately before you want to go to sleep.

Jet lag can cause a similar problem in the short-term. This occurs when people travel to a different time zone by plane, for example, going from Scotland to North America on holiday. The SCN takes time to adjust to a different time zone and the person may feel sleepy during the day and find it hard to get to sleep at night. This is because the SCN still causes melatonin to be released when it is evening in the old time zone, due to the body's endogenous cues (see the first section of this chapter). This can lead to insomnia at night and hypersomnia during the day. Melatonin supplements can help travellers adjust to a new time zone and avoid jet lag (Wagner, 1999).

As researched by Czeisler and colleagues (see key study), **light therapy** can be a very useful treatment for shift work. If scheduled effectively, the person's circadian rhythms can reset to the desired time schedule. The application of strong light acts as a zeitgeber, affecting the SCN.

Key study: Czeisler *et al.*'s (1990) study of shift work

Aim: *This study aimed to find a routine, including light exposure, which would help nightshift workers fully adapt to daytime sleeping. Nightshifts are associated with poor sleep and health problems but previous research had shown that the presence of light or darkness regulates the circadian rhythms and it can 'reset' the suprachiasmatic nucleus by up to 12 hours.*

Method: *The timing of exposure to light appears to be important, and therefore the researchers designed a schedule of light exposure to help nightshift workers. The study was carried out on eight healthy men in their 20s, none of whom had regularly worked a nightshift. Each came to the researchers' lab at 23:45 for six days of 'shifts' that involved staying awake, doing cognitive tests and reporting their own alertness and mood. Otherwise, they were free to do their own work. Men in the experimental group only were exposed to very bright light during the nightshift (12,000 'lumens' of brightness, compared to the approximately 150 lumens of normal artificial room lighting).*

Findings: *Biological measures such as body temperature showed that the experimental group had had their circadian rhythms adjusted forward by over nine hours, while the control group were unchanged. Both subjective assessments of alertness and performance on cognitive tests were similarly shifted. It appeared that among the experimental group only, their body clock had shifted from day to night due to the bright light exposure.*

Evaluation: *A strength of the study is that the light/dark schedule made allowances for the fact that night workers are typically exposed to natural light on their way home from work each morning – a problem of some other studies. In addition, the time difference between the mean low-point of body temperature of the control versus experimental group was huge, and statistically very unlikely to have occurred by chance. Conversely, the sample was very small, and contained only men, making it harder to generalise the results. Several extraneous variables were not fully controlled; for example, when they ate breakfast or how much time they slept for.*

Shift workers are at risk of developing a sleep disorder

After a long trip travellers may experience jet lag

Light therapy can be an effective treatment for sleep disorders

Charles Czeisler

Parasomnias

A **parasomnia** means a sleep problem or disorder that is not connected with the amount of sleep a person gets (which means they are not suffering from insomnia or hypersomnia) but relates to abnormal behaviours while sleeping.

Night terrors is a form of parasomnia that is relatively common among young children. During deep sleep, the individual sits up or screams and appears terrified. They may look awake but they are quite unaware of their surroundings and cannot be reasoned with. Their eyes may be open, but they show no sign of recognising people or their surroundings and they may lash out if people try to comfort them.

Night terrors are not the same thing as nightmares – they do not occur during REM sleep – but they are linked to sleepwalking (see below). Although distressing, night terrors are usually brief – the individual may calm down and go back to sleep, or wake up and be disoriented. They typically have no memory of the incident the next day. It can be caused by being over-tired during the day, by stress or a traumatic incident, or by minor illnesses. Night terrors are much more common in children but can continue into adolescence or even adulthood.

Similar to night terrors, an individual who is **sleepwalking** is unresponsive to their surroundings and cannot hear people who are talking to them. They may engage in common/routine everyday behaviour such as walking around the house, getting dressed, eating or going to the toilet. This can cause problems especially in unfamiliar environments, as the sleeper may urinate somewhere inappropriate or eat something harmful.

Sleepwalking is usually harmless, but steps may be taken to ensure sleepwalkers do not injure themselves; in some cases the person may leave the house and put themselves at considerable risk, for example a patient woke up on a high cliff, unable to remember how he got there (Wilson & Nutt, 2013).

Sleepwalkers may engage in everyday behaviour such as eating

Key concepts

- Sleep deprivation
- Sleep disorder
- Insomnia
- Hypersomnia
- Parasomnia
- Sleeping pills
- Melatonin supplements
- Shift work
- Jet lag
- Light therapy
- Drugs
- Stimulant
- Caffeine
- Amphetamine

Questions

1. Name one example of a mental or physical problem which can result from or be more likely due to poor sleep.
2. Name one example of a hallucination suffered by Peter Tripp during his sleep deprivation 'wakeathon'.
3. Give two examples of drugs that make people less likely to get to sleep.
4. What natural process does caffeine interfere with?
5. Why can looking at a screen before bed be problematic?
6. What is meant by jet lag?
7. For how long did Czeisler *et al.* study their participants?
8. What variables were changed for the experimental group in the Czeisler *et al.* study?
9. What is a parasomnia?
10. What are melatonin supplements used for?

Activities

1. Complete the following table:

Factor in sleep	Effect	How it impacts on sleep

2. Research another case study of sleep deprivation, or a sleep disorder other than insomnia. Explain the findings to a fellow student or to your class. Are there any overlaps with the effects of drugs or jet lag on sleep?

End of topic project

- Working together with other students if possible, conduct a survey to find out the sleep habits of other learners. You could look at issues such as:
  - time of going to bed
  - time of getting up
  - whether people have a sleep debt that they make up at weekends
  - how long it takes people to go to sleep
  - attitudes to being sleep deprived.
- If you like, this could be conducted as a quasi- or natural experiment (see chapter 8) comparing, for example, larks versus owls or older versus younger students, and some aspect of their sleep habits, or the effect of sleep timing/duration on score in a memory task. Or you could simply survey sleep habits more widely and calculate percentages of responses to these questions.
- Discuss the details of your methodology with your teacher or lecturer before you begin.
- Write up your findings. Look up relevant research, and include at least one background study to support your conclusions.

End of topic specimen exam questions

National 5

1. Briefly explain one finding from the Dement and Kleitman (1957) study of sleep. — 2 marks
2. Describe what is meant by REM sleep and non-REM sleep. — 4 marks
3. According to the psychoanalytic approach in psychology, what is the difference between the manifest content of a dream and the latent content of a dream? — 4 marks
4. Explain Oswald's (1966) restoration theory of sleep. — 6 marks
5. Explain one strength and one weakness of Freud's (1909) study of 'little Hans'. — 4 marks

Higher

1. Explain two biological processes that occur during sleep. — 8 marks
2. Analyse the reorganisation theory of sleep and dreams. — 12 marks
3. Explain the different factors that can affect sleep. Refer to research evidence in your answer. — 20 marks

Top tip

Ask your teacher or lecturer about the mark allocation for each topic, and ensure you refer to and try to answer the SQA's specimen question paper.

3 Phobias

For the topic of Phobias, you should be able to explain:

- What is meant by a phobia.
- The characteristics of specific phobias, social anxiety disorder and agoraphobia.
- The role of genetic inheritance in phobias.
- The two-process model of phobias.
- Therapies for phobias, including systematic desensitisation and social skills training.

You need to develop the following skills:

- Explaining the different theories of phobias.
- Describing research that links to the theories of phobias.
- Explaining strengths and weaknesses of research studies.
- Explaining strengths and weaknesses of therapies.

! Syllabus note

Phobias is a topic in the Individual Behaviour unit in National 5 Psychology. Higher students should instead study one of the following option topics: Depression (chapter 4) OR Memory (chapter 5) OR Stress (chapter 6).

Most of us have noticed or experienced a **phobia** in some way – whether our own, or that of another person. We may be aware of others having strange and irrational fears of certain types of animals, or avoiding certain situations. The study of 'little Hans' in chapter 2 also demonstrated an example of a phobia (of horses). What exactly causes this type of behaviour, and what is its purpose? This chapter will look at psychological explanations of why people have phobias and how they are treated.

What is a phobia?

Psychological problems

The study of phobias is part of an area of psychology known as psychopathology. 'Psyche' means the mind and 'pathology' means the study of illness or suffering, so the term psychopathology literally means the study of psychological or mental illness. The kind of questions asked in this area of psychology include:

- Why do some people do things that harm themselves or others?
- Why do some people feel very unhappy?
- Why might people hear voices in their head?
- Why might people obsessively fear things that appear to be harmless?

Explaining and treating psychological problems has been one of the biggest concerns of psychologists throughout the history of the subject. As you know, there are different approaches to explaining human behaviour (see chapter 1), and they play a role in this topic. You will see how different theories have tried to explain phobias either in terms of biology and evolution, or in terms of the behaviourist approach and its theories of conditioning.

It might strike you that a phobia is not a psychological **disorder** – many people have one or more phobias and would nevertheless be considered entirely normal and mentally healthy. This relates to a broader discussion of what mental health actually is. When someone is physically ill, we wouldn't say that they are an ill person, but rather that they are a person who has an illness that needs to be treated. In a similar way, we might say that a person with a severe phobia has a problem which could benefit from treatment. They may have other problems too, or this might be their only psychological concern.

A particular group of psychologists – clinical psychologists – study the behaviours and thought processes which affect a person's mental health, and help to identify solutions. In doing so, they may work together with doctors and psychiatrists.

What is abnormality?

It would be unsatisfactory for psychologists to decide what was mentally healthy and what was not, simply on the basis of what seemed normal to them. However, this is exactly what happened in the past! Nowadays, we try to find objective ways of defining what is normal and what is not. In particular, psychologists focus on the criteria of **harm** and **distress**:

- Is the behaviour causing the individual distress?
- Is the behaviour harming the individual, or affecting their ability to fully enjoy their life?

> **Top tip**
>
> These two criteria – distress and harm – can help us to distinguish a phobia from a 'normal' fear.

Defining normality on the basis of 'distress' means saying that something is psychologically **abnormal** or problematic if the person themselves is feeling anxious, unhappy or scared because of the behaviour.

Harm could mean the person hurting others or themselves, but it also includes anything that prevents a person from leading a normal life – from functioning fully as a healthy human being. This could include being willing to take part in everyday situations and being able to hold down a job. Things which stop an individual from functioning are called maladaptive behaviours. A phobia may make it difficult to function, for example due to avoiding any situation that may trigger their fear(s).

Defining phobia

Phobias form part of a group of disorders called **anxiety disorders**. The experience of **anxiety** is an emotional response to potential risks, worries and fears. It is something that we all experience from time to time, but anxiety disorders relate to extreme levels of anxiety.

The way phobias have been defined reflects the need for an objective definition that reflects distress and harm. The **DSM-5** is the American Psychiatric Association's manual for diagnosing disorders, and it states that in a phobia, the person's level of fear is out of proportion to the risk posed, and interferes with everyday life (APA, 2013). For example, being very afraid of flying insects is often out of proportion to any risk they pose, while refusing to ever go to a park or garden for fear of seeing a bee would interfere with everyday life.

Often, a phobia will be linked to having had an **aversive experience** at some point – a frightening event that triggered or worsened the fear. For example, a person with a phobia of insects, as described above, may have been stung by a bee at some point. Of course, other people may experience similar aversive experiences and *not* develop a phobia. The major theories about why people develop phobias are discussed later in this chapter.

Symptoms of a phobia

Like any psychological problem or disorder, a phobia can be described in terms of a set of **symptoms**. For a phobia, these are focused on two key things:

- **anxiety** about the feared stimulus
- **avoidance** of the feared stimulus.

Top tip

Summarise the symptoms of a phobia on an index card for revision.

The most obvious symptom is that the individual has a deep and persistent aversion to the object or situation, resulting in anxiety linked to the individual thinking and worrying about the object of their phobia. In extreme cases, when exposed to the stimulus accidentally (for example when a person with a phobia of clowns unexpectedly sees a clown), this can lead to a **panic attack**.

The anxiety/panic in turn will typically have multiple physical symptoms, such as:

- raised heart rate
- sweating
- nausea.

The fear of public speaking is a social phobia

The other major symptom is that the person tries to avoid the feared object or situation, often at a certain cost or risk in terms of their everyday life. For example, someone who is afraid of thunder and lightning may avoid going outside, particularly in the summer months. Someone who is afraid of injections may avoid necessary medical treatment. Someone who is afraid of public speaking may avoid applying for a promotion at work because they think they may be asked to give a presentation.

Example

A real-world example of the impact of the **avoidance** aspect of a phobia on someone's professional life is that of the Dutch footballer Dennis Bergkamp. Bergkamp was a star player for Arsenal Football Club for many years, during which time the team played many Champions League matches against sides in mainland Europe. However, Bergkamp had a phobia of plane travel, and therefore refused to fly overseas with the rest of the squad. This led to him missing key matches, though for some closer fixtures he travelled by car instead. His phobia appears to have been stimulated by having been on a flight during which the plane's engine cut out (BBC, 2002).

A fear of flying is a good example of an irrational fear. Although there are certain risks, the risk of accident or death from a plane crash is statistically very low – lower than that for travel by car. Bergkamp's case shows how a phobia can impact on some aspects of everyday life, while the person still functions at a very high level in other aspects (in this case, in terms of his sports performance).

Questions

1. What two criteria can help clinical psychologists to decide objectively if a person has a problem?
2. To what group of disorders do phobias belong?
3. How might an aversive experience link to having a phobia?
4. What is meant by a behaviour being 'maladaptive'?
5. What is DSM-5?
6. What are the two key symptoms of any phobia?
7. People with phobias try hard to keep away from situations or places where they might encounter the feared stimulus. What is this behaviour called?
8. Why might avoidance behaviour cause problems?
9. What is a panic attack?
10. In what situation might a person with a phobia have a panic attack?

Key concepts

- Phobia
- Disorder
- Abnormal
- Distress
- Harm
- DSM-5
- Aversive experience
- Symptoms
- Anxiety disorders
- Anxiety
- Avoidance
- Panic attack

Activities

1. What is normal? Discuss with a group or write a short description of how we can reasonably distinguish between normal and abnormal – in terms of fears and other behaviour.
2. Find out about another case of a famous person who suffers/suffered from a phobia. Did it disrupt their life or career? Take some basic notes, and be prepared to share this information with the rest of your class.

Types of phobias

Specific phobias

Phobias are common psychological problems and are also very varied, as there are many different things of which we can be phobic. Some of the most common and obvious examples are called **specific phobias**, which means having a phobia of a specific stimulus such as an object, an animal or a form of travel. Examples include phobias of snakes, spiders, clowns, flying or blood.

As discussed above, experiencing the feared stimulus – or the immediate prospect of experiencing it – tends to result in an acute stress reaction or panic attack. The person may think about the stimulus excessively and try to avoid it.

Specific phobias are irrational fears of objects and situations, such as spiders or plane travel

Specific phobias are sometimes categorised into different groups. Most of the things that people tend to have specific phobias of fall into one of the following categories:

- Animals, e.g. dogs, worms, spiders
- Medical, e.g. blood, injections, infection
- Environmental, e.g. heights, enclosed spaces, water
- Travel/situational, e.g. flying.

Specific phobias tend to last for at least six months and can be lifelong. In any given year, between 6% and 9% of the population of Europe and North America suffers from a specific phobia severe enough to be diagnosed (APA, 2013).

Social anxiety disorder

A person may have a social phobia, which is similar to a specific phobia but which relates to one or more social situations. These include situations where multiple other people are present, and particularly where a person might be the focus of some attention, such as speaking in public, eating in public, or mingling at a party. The fear tends to relate more to how other people might react than to the situation or action itself. For example, the phobic person might be happy to eat alone but not to eat in public.

The DSM-5 diagnosis of such problems does not classify them as specific phobias but as **social anxiety disorder**. The key psychological feature of this disorder is that the person is highly concerned with how they will be viewed by others, and that they worry about presenting themselves positively. They fear that despite wanting to make a good impression, they will be unable to do so. They also tend to obsess over perceived past mistakes they have made in social settings. There is an extreme fear of embarrassment, out of proportion to the likelihood that the person would actually be laughed at or humiliated.

Social anxiety disorder can also relate to situations such as meeting new people or speaking to an authority figure. The disorder can lead to a person avoiding these situations because they are overwhelmed by anxiety, or feel fear/panic at the prospect. This can affect a person in the workplace.

Most psychologists would consider social anxiety to be different from simply being introverted, which tends to be seen as a personality trait. An introvert may prefer to avoid parties and social gatherings, but doesn't necessarily fear them or worry about them. Social anxiety disorder does overlap with other psychological problems, in particular depression or other anxiety disorders. In other words, if you have one of those problems, you are statistically more likely to have social anxiety disorder as well.

Social anxiety could relate to workplace situations

As many as 8% of the population suffer from social anxiety disorder at any given time (Stein *et al.*, 1994). As with specific phobias, social anxiety disorder tends to last over a long time period. How common the disorder is varies in different parts of the world, ranging from 2% to 7% of the population in a given year.

Agorapobia

Agoraphobia is an extreme fear of going outside alone, or of being in crowded or enclosed public places. The fear is out of proportion to the risk of harm in any of these situations.

Typically the sufferer experiences an intense anxiety that can lead to a panic attack when they go outside. This situation may be worsened by their own worries or by a belief that they are going to have a panic attack.

Having experienced panic on one or more occasions tends to lead to a strong avoidance behaviour, with the agoraphobic individual unwilling to go out in case this happens again.

Agoraphobia can cause a lot of problems for sufferers. They may, in effect, be housebound due to being highly unwilling to go out alone, so it can interfere with their ability to work, study or socialise. However, it's not always the case that an agoraphobic individual is entirely unable to go outside. They may be able to go out in certain circumstances, such as when accompanied, when travelling by car, or if they are sure that there will be very few strangers around.

A person with agoraphobia could find themselves housebound due to being averse to going out alone

Every year, around 1.7% of adults and adolescents have a diagnosis of agoraphobia and it is twice as common among women. It can be triggered by a highly stressful incident such as an attack or mugging.

The term agoraphobia comes from the Greek word *agora*, meaning marketplace. Although it may seem to have a lot in common with specific phobias such as the fear of flying, it is usually considered to be an anxiety disorder in its own right, rather than a form of specific phobia. It is more connected to feelings of anxiety and panic than the fear of a specific stimulus or event.

Key concepts

- Specific phobias
- Social anxiety disorder
- Agoraphobia

Questions

1. What is the general name for a phobia of a particular type of thing, such as blood or spiders?
2. Give an example of an environmental specific phobia.
3. How common are specific phobias?
4. True or false: specific phobias only last for a short time.
5. What is the official DSM-5 diagnosis for a person who has a phobia of a social situation?
6. Give an example of a social situation which may cause fear or anxiety.
7. What is the particular worry that tends to characterise all social situations that cause anxiety?
8. What might happen to a person with agoraphobia if they go outside alone?
9. Are all agoraphobia sufferers entirely housebound?
10. Which gender experiences a higher rate of agoraphobia?

GO! Activities

1. In a group, discuss what problems the following phobias could cause in terms of your relationships, work/studies and everyday life:
   - fear of air travel
   - fear of heights
   - fear of public speaking
   - fear of cats.
2. Draw a 3×3 grid in your notes. In the top row, write down the three types of phobia described in this section. In the rows below, write down at least two important facts about each type of phobia. At first, do your best to do this without checking your notes. Afterwards, go back over the section above to see if there is anything important that you missed.

Genetic explanations of phobias

As mentioned earlier, an aversive experience can trigger a phobia in some individuals while very similar experiences fail to do so in other people. Why is this the case? Why don't we all react in the same way to a frightening situation in early childhood?

Genetics is one possible explanation. Genetic differences may lead to some people being more likely to develop a phobia than others; in other words, they are predisposed to develop a phobia, or are more vulnerable to doing so. This could be related to their specific family history, and be passed on from parent to child. Alternatively, it may link to evolved, species-specific characteristics.

Heritability

It is difficult to clearly establish the role of genes in phobias. This is because alongside their genetic differences, everyone's life experiences are different, making it hard to untangle the roles of nature and nurture (see chapter 1). People only share half of their genes with each parent, causing further difficulties in discovering whether traits can be passed on from parent to child.

One useful type of evidence comes from twin studies. These are research studies which aim to find out the extent to which disorders are at least partly genetic, by studying **identical twins** and comparing them with **fraternal twins**. True identical twins, also called **monozygotic** or MZ twins, are born with the same set of genes, whereas fraternal twins, also called **dizygotic** or DZ twins, are no more closely related than any other siblings.

For example, a score on any kind of test can be compared between the twins to see if there is a strong or a weak correlation. If there tends to be a higher correlation between identical twins than fraternal twins, this suggests that genes play a role.

Distel *et al.* (2008) conducted a large-scale twin study with over 5,000 participants in order to find out about the role of genes in phobias. They focused on medical specific phobias, social anxiety and agoraphobia. The study used the 'fear questionnaire', which has five questions about each of the three types of phobia (15 questions in all). Comparisons were made between older (25+) and younger (16–24) participants in the study. They also compared the twins to their other siblings, and to their spouses (if they were married). The results showed that:

- Women had higher levels of self-reported phobias of all three types, except for the medical phobias among the older age group.
- There were relatively few age differences overall – levels of phobias stayed steady across different ages.
- There was no difference in the level of phobias between non-identical (DZ) twins and their other siblings.
- The correlation of questionnaire scores between pairs of identical (MZ) twins was more than twice as large as that for non-identical (DZ) twins, suggesting that genetics play a role in phobias.

Overall, the researchers concluded that genetics play a significant but not overwhelming role in developing a phobia. A strength of the Distel *et al.* study is that it used a very large sample, and that it compared different age groups. The study also helped to establish that genetic factors are not due to 'assortive mating', that is, people with phobias tending to have children with other people who also have phobias (something that would make the genetic effect look bigger than it actually was).

However, the Distel *et al.* study didn't use samples of people who had been diagnosed with phobias by experts, and instead relied on questionnaires. This is a weakness of the study. In addition, the study didn't look at some of the most common phobias, for example fears of small animals. Also, the presence of a correlation between genetic relatedness and phobias does not prove that the genes directly cause phobias.

Evolutionary explanations

Twin studies might tell us about how phobias are linked to our genetic characteristics, but they don't tell us why we have these genes. What evolutionary processes involved in **genetic inheritance** might have made it an advantage for our species to develop fears that cause distress and harm our everyday functioning?

As with other areas of the evolutionary approach (see chapter 1), researchers have tried to establish the advantage of developing a phobia. One possibility is that it is an effective and relatively rapid way of learning to avoid a danger, and may therefore lead to a survival advantage in some circumstances. For example, for most animals in their natural habitats, quickly learning to fear snakes will be a safer strategy than learning by trial and error. It's also worth noting that evolution is a slow process, so many of the problems associated with phobias relate to characteristics that evolved thousands or millions of years ago. For example, fearing large groups of strangers may have been advantageous in the past, but may cause problems in the modern world.

On this basis, evolutionary psychologists have suggested that humans and other animals may be **genetically prepared** to fear certain things which would have been dangerous in our ancient past (Seligman, 1971). This would help to explain why we so easily learn phobias of things like spiders, snakes, dogs, heights or blood – any of which could have been associated with risks in our evolutionary past. In contrast, it's uncommon to have a phobia of more modern threats that our ancestors would never have experienced, such as guns, electricity or cars.

? Discussion point

If we only have phobias of things that were dangerous to our ancestors, why are some people afraid of travelling by aeroplane?

To investigate this theory, Cook and Mineka (1989) conducted a study on rhesus monkeys. First, they recorded a video of an adult monkey reacting in fear. Then they edited the video to make it appear as if the adult was frightened of a toy snake, or of another stimulus such as a toy rabbit. Finally, they showed the different versions of the video to a baby monkey. It was found that baby monkeys easily learned to fear the snake, but did not learn to fear the toy rabbit (see key study).

What exactly are we predisposed to fear? Bennet-Levy and Marteau (1984) conducted a study where people were shown images of insects and other animals. They found that uglier animals were more fear-inducing. The researchers concluded that what made an animal ugly was how alien-looking it was compared to humans. Other mammals – with which we share many characteristics such as number of eyes and number of limbs – tended to be viewed as attractive, and not fear-inducing. Species with very different features to mammals, such as tentacles, multiple eyes or multiple legs, tended to be viewed as ugly and frightening, as were animals that were slimy or moved suddenly.

Key study: Cook and Mineka (1989): Can monkeys learn to fear any type of animal?

Aim: *People tend to develop phobias of things which could have been dangerous for our ancestors, such as snakes, spiders or heights. In contrast, it seems to be much rarer to have a phobia of things which have only recently presented a danger. It may be the case that evolution has prepared us to easily learn a fear of certain types of things and not others. Cook and Mineka (1989) aimed to test the idea of evolutionary 'preparedness' to learn a fear.*

Method: *The researchers edited a video of an adult monkey reacting with fear to make it look like it was afraid of either a toy snake or a toy rabbit. This video was then shown to groups of young monkeys.*

Findings: *When the young monkeys then had to collect food from an enclosure containing the toy snake, they took longer than normal to do so (they were more fearful and wary), but there was no increase in time when the toy rabbit was present in place of the toy snake. It appeared that a monkey can easily learn a fear through observation if the object is relevant in terms of evolutionary risk, like a snake, but not if it is irrelevant, like a rabbit.*

Evaluation: *Cook and Mineka's (1989) research into infant monkeys fits with the everyday observation that a fear of things like snakes and spiders is common, and suggests that this is the case because during much of our evolution, it has been an advantage to learn to fear these animals. However, as with other experiments on animals, it is difficult to generalise the results of the research to humans. It's possible that the monkeys had not actually learned a phobia of the toy snake but were being more cautious due to uncertainty. There are also ethical issues with the study. It can be argued that teaching a young monkey to have a phobia is cruel, and exposes them to stress.*

Can young monkeys learn fears from their parents?

Inheritance of fearful memories

As noted above, evolution is a slow process, and the explanation for why we are more likely to develop a fear of snakes and other potentially dangerous stimuli probably lies in the distant past of our species.

However, recent research on mice has provided initial evidence that a fear can be inherited much more directly – from parent to child. In a study by Dias and Ressler (2014), male mice were taught to fear a certain chemical smell by associating it with unpleasant electric shocks. Unsurprisingly, the animals maintained this fear and continued to show avoidance behaviour towards the smell at a later time. Much more surprisingly, the offspring of these mice later showed fear of the same smell. Despite never having smelled the particular chemical used in the study, both children and grandchildren of the experimental animals were more likely to shudder when exposed to it. This included offspring who had not spent any time with their father, and therefore couldn't have learned anxiety from him directly, for example though imitation.

In the study by Dias and Ressler, mice were taught to fear a chemical smell

The Dias and Ressler study seems to show that some forms of emotional memories can be inherited across generations – a finding that goes against the mainstream biological view of how both learning and evolution work (see chapter 1). If the same were true for humans, it would pose interesting questions about whether stress or anxiety in a parent could lead to their children (or subsequent generations) being more prone to phobias and other anxiety disorders. It would also help to explain the cycles of risk seen in families where multiple generations have experienced addictions or mental illness.

Human fears tend to involve a lot of thought processes – worries, obsessions and so on – that are unlikely to take place in mice

However, it is important to be cautious when drawing conclusions from these findings. It is hard to generalise from mice to humans, and also hard to generalise from a learned fear of a smell to the experience of phobias and social anxiety. Human fears tend to involve a lot of thought processes – worries, obsessions and so on – that are unlikely to take place in mice.

Perhaps most problematically, Dias and Ressler have not yet established a biological mechanism that would allow a fear to be genetically transmitted from father to child via the DNA in a sperm cell. Nevertheless, it remains an interesting area for future research.

Questions

1. What basic debate in psychology is linked to the difficulty in establishing whether a person's phobia is influenced by their genes?
2. What two types of twins are compared in a 'twin study'?
3. What three types of phobia were covered by the 'fear questionnaire' used by Distel *et al.* (2008)?
4. What did Distel *et al.* (2008) conclude regarding the genetic basis of fears?
5. What is meant by being 'genetically prepared' to learn a fear?
6. True or false: Cook and Mineka (1989) showed that all baby monkeys are afraid of snakes.
7. From the results of the Cook and Mineka research study (1989), can we be sure that the baby monkeys had actually learned a phobia?
8. In Dias and Ressler's (2014) study on mice, what did the offspring show fear of?
9. Did the Dias and Ressler (2014) study support the mainstream biological view of how learning and inheritance work?
10. Give a limitation of the Dias and Ressler (2014) study.

Key concepts

- Genetics
- Genetic inheritance
- Identical/monozygotic twins
- Fraternal/dizygotic twins
- Genetically prepared

Activities

1. Working in pairs where possible, list strengths and weaknesses of three research studies from this section of the chapter. Do any of them share the same strengths and weaknesses? How many of these evaluation points link to the methodology used?

Behaviourist explanations of phobias

Classical conditioning

As you may remember from chapter 1, the behaviourist approach to psychology explains human behaviour in terms of learning, and places little or no emphasis on thought processes.

A major concept from this approach is **classical conditioning**, which is learning via association. This is where people learn to associate two stimuli together – one of which is neutral and one of which provokes a reaction. The best-known example of this comes from Ivan Pavlov's experiments, which showed that dogs could learn to react to a previously neutral sound, such as a bell, when it was repeatedly paired with something pleasant, such as food.

Music may be associated with pleasant experiences via a process of classical conditioning

The behaviourist approach explains fears and anxieties in terms of classical conditioning. American researcher John Watson was one of the founders of this approach and, together with his colleague Rosalie Rayner, he demonstrated that a human infant could learn a phobia: an 11-month-old child, 'Albert', learned to fear an animal that he initially did not react to, simply by associating it with a fear-inducing noise (Watson & Rayner, 1920; see chapter 1 for a fuller description of the study). The Dias and Ressler (2014) study (see previous section) used a similar principle in teaching mice to fear a smell.

Pupils may form emotional associations with school via classical conditioning

Similarly, anxiety and panic could be learned through classical conditioning (Mowrer, 1939). If an individual repeatedly experiences anxiety-provoking situations, for example in a school classroom, then they may start to associate the initially neutral stimulus (the classroom) with fear. After that, simply entering that place could cause anxiety or even a panic attack. A study by Di Gallo and Parry-Jones (1996) found that around 20% of people who had experienced a car accident later developed a phobia of car travel, and were particularly averse to travelling at high speeds.

Operant conditioning

Another major idea associated with the behaviourist approach is **operant conditioning**, which states that the frequency or strength of a behaviour can be modified depending on its outcome. If actions have a pleasant outcome, the behaviour will increase. If they have an unpleasant outcome, the behaviour will decrease. This idea was developed by several researchers but is most strongly associated with the work of B.F. Skinner. He explained that a behaviour will be weakened or become less frequent if it is punished, and it will be strengthened or become more frequent if it is reinforced. A reinforcer doesn't need to be a direct reward – it could involve something unpleasant being removed. This is called **negative reinforcement** (see page p. 34–35).

Negative reinforcement is a useful concept when explaining the avoidance behaviour seen in phobias. According to the behaviourist approach, the phobic individual is anxious about the stimulus and they avoid the stimulus in some way. The result of this action is that their anxiety reduces. They have experienced negative reinforcement – by taking away the feared stimulus, the behaviour (in this case, the avoidance) is strengthened, meaning it will be even more likely to occur in future. In the Di Gallo and Parry-Jones study (see above), this could mean that if people avoided travelling by car after their accident, this would only serve to strengthen the phobia. (The same could be said of Dennis Bergkamp – see page 81.)

Example

Lauren is scared of dogs and is very anxious about visiting her friend who has a pet dog. She goes to the friend's front door and hears the dog begin to bark. She feels terrible anxiety, and decides to leave without ringing the doorbell. She hurries away down the street. Lauren has avoided the feared stimulus, and by no longer being close to the dog or hearing it bark, the avoidance has been strengthened via negative reinforcement.

Two-process model

What happens when classical and operant conditioning combine? According to Mowrer (1947), they can work together to form and then reinforce a phobia. This theory of phobias is called the **two-process model**:

1. The acquisition of a new phobia occurs via classical conditioning, in the same way it happened in the case of 'little Albert' (Watson & Rayner, 1920), except that it happens by chance in the real world. The person sees the initially neutral stimulus while they are anxious or fearful, or the stimulus directly causes pain and fear due to an aversive experience, such as being stung, bitten or attacked.
2. The newly formed fear is then maintained and strengthened via operant conditioning. The person feels better and more relaxed every time they avoid the stimulus. This acts as a reward – strengthening the fear. At the same time, approaching or thinking about the feared stimulus causes anxiety, and this acts as a punishment.

Key study: Mowrer's (1960) study of the two-process model

Aim: *Mowrer wanted to produce evidence of the two-process model which he had previously presented. This was a model of how phobias develop via classical conditioning, and are maintained and strengthened via operant conditioning.*

Method: *The researcher first trained rats to fear a buzzer by pairing it repeatedly with an electric shock. This procedure had previously been used by Ivan Pavlov, among others. After repeated trials, the rats would show a fear response to the buzzer alone. Mowrer then trained the rats to jump over a barrier. When they did so, they avoided the electric shocks.*

Findings: *The rats learned to jump the barrier to avoid the electric shock. This maintained their fear of the buzzer. Mowrer concluded that the initial fear had been learned through classical conditioning and the avoidance behaviour which maintained the fear had been learned through operant conditioning. This supported the two-process model.*

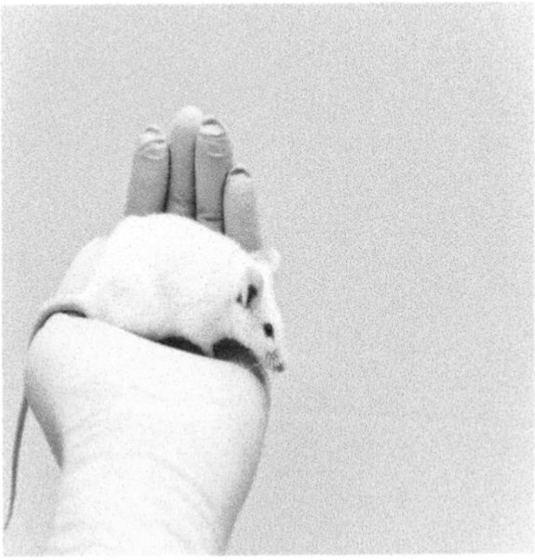

Mowrer's study was conducted on laboratory rats

Evaluation: *Mowrer's study was unethical, as it exposed rats to fear and pain. It is also – as with any study of rats – difficult to generalise their avoidance behaviour to phobias in humans. On the positive side, this was a well-controlled laboratory experiment. It was the most direct test of the two-process model of its time. Despite its ethical problems, the findings had potential to inform treatments for phobias, thereby helping to relieve suffering.*

Observational learning

Phobias could be learned from other people or the media via observational learning

As you may recall from chapter 1, the early behaviourist theories have been developed to include social learning theory, based on the work of Bandura and others. The key idea here is that people don't need to learn something directly. They can engage in **observational learning** – learning by watching what happens to other people. The monkeys in Cook and Mineka's (1989) study showed observational learning, with the young monkeys learning from viewing a video of an adult (see previous section of this chapter).

In the case of a phobia, observational learning would occur by observing an aversive experience happening to someone else, such as seeing them undergoing a painful medical procedure or being bitten by an animal. The fear, learned from other people, could then be reinforced as described by the two-process model.

Bandura *et al.* (1963) also found that observational learning can occur through the media, such as watching TV, with an effect which is almost as strong as observation in real life (see chapter 1). This means that phobias could potentially be learned from watching TV shows or horror movies.

Evaluation

A strength of behaviourist explanations of phobias is that the key theories of conditioning have been demonstrated in controlled laboratory experiments of animals, and these findings can, in principle, be applied to almost every type of human behaviour or disorder. The two-process model presents a plausible explanation of phobias which can apply to nearly every type of fear. Although it predates social learning theory, this can easily be added to the model, increasing the number of situations to which it applies.

However, a major weakness is that this approach to psychology ignores people's thoughts and feelings. The avoidance behaviour that might be demonstrated by a rat in an experiment is treated as being basically the same thing as a human phobia. In reality, we know that phobias involve a lot of anxiety and other thought processes. People have the ability to worry about the future – something that may not occur to the same degree in laboratory animals. The development of a phobia may depend to some degree on how a person mentally categorises an aversive experience, and how likely they feel it is to happen again in future. Social anxiety disorder is based on people's irrational worries and fears, rather than on having had multiple aversive experiences.

The behaviourist approach also treats everyone as if they are same. It does not allow for genetic differences in behaviour or personality, and therefore cannot explain why some people are more susceptible than others to developing disorders.

Questions

1. Which psychological approach is the two-process model based on?
2. Which behaviourist theory involves learning by association?
3. Which behaviourist theory involves learning by reward and punishment?
4. Watson and Rayner (1920) demonstrated how classical conditioning could be used to learn a fear. Who was the participant of their study?
5. How might a fear be learned by classical conditioning in everyday life?
6. According to the two-process model, how is a phobia maintained and strengthened?
7. What type of conditioning is typically experienced during avoidance behaviour?
8. What were the two processes as shown in Mowrer's (1960) study?
9. How might a child learn a phobia from their parent?
10. Name a major weakness of behaviourist theories of phobias.

Key concepts

- Classical conditioning
- Operant conditioning
- Two-process model
- Observational learning
- Negative reinforcement

Activities

1. In the case of Lauren and her phobia of dogs (see page 91), how do you think she developed her fear in the first place? Write a short description/explanation or piece of creative writing, drawing on your understanding of classical conditioning and/or social learning.
2. The behaviourist approach is known for avoiding any explanations based on people's thoughts or feelings – instead, it focuses entirely on behaviour that can be observed. Behaviourists also conducted a lot of research on animals. Why might this be an issue with phobias? Would behaviourists use questionnaires that ask people about how much they fear something, or prompt them to remember what caused it? Would they be interested in someone's childhood history? Discuss the implications with a group.

Therapies for phobias

Systematic desensitisation

Some of the key therapies for phobias are based on the behaviourist approach. Even though that approach is now considered too simplistic to explain all aspects of behaviour, the phobia therapies based on it have been found to be effective.

One such technique is **flooding** (also called exposure therapy), which suggests that a fearful stimulus should be presented at its worst so that the person reacts very strongly to it. An example of this would be taking an agoraphobic person to a public place. The person would, of course, react with extreme anxiety, but the therapist would use relaxation techniques to gradually replace the anxiety with a state of calm. Through classical conditioning, a new association between the stimulus and a feeling of calm would be learned. This can be effective, but it can also be highly stressful in the early stages.

A less traumatic option is to build up gradually to exposure via **systematic desensitisation (SD)**. Developed by Wolpe (1958), the technique involves working with a client to draw up a 'hierarchy of fears' – a list of fearful situations from the least feared to the most feared. The idea is to move through each one, gradually getting used to it via a laboratory simulation or exposure to the real thing. Again, classical conditioning would lead to the feeling of anxiety being replaced with a feeling of calm.

An experimental demonstration of this was conducted by Lang and Lazovik (1963), using students who were phobic of snakes. One group of 12 was given SD and worked through numerous sessions with a therapist. They developed a fear hierarchy and then worked through it using relaxation techniques. Another 12 students formed a control group. Before and after the therapy sessions, each participant was taken in to a room with a snake in a tank and asked to approach as close as they could, and touch or hold the snake, if possible. They were ranked on how close they were willing to go, and the results were therefore a direct test of their observable behaviour, rather than a subjective statement of their fear level. The researchers found that, on average, the group who had experienced SD moved significantly closer on the second test, and seven out of twelve were willing to hold or touch the snake. The control group showed no change on the second test.

Systematic desensitisation can be used to treat a phobia of snakes

CBT and social skills training

Cognitive behavioural therapy (CBT) is a **psychotherapy** which aims to tackle irrational thought processes, and to help develop more positive behaviours. It is currently one of the most popular treatments for a range of psychological disorders. It was first developed for depression and then found to be effective for anxiety disorders. As mentioned in chapter 2, it is also used for some sleep disorders.

CBT focuses on dealing with the symptoms/behaviours in the here and now, rather than talking about the past or trying to uncover unconscious fears. It draws on both the behaviourist and the cognitive approach to psychology:

- Cognitive aspects focus on a rational discussion of the client's beliefs.
- Behaviourist techniques such as flooding are often incorporated alongside the talking therapy.

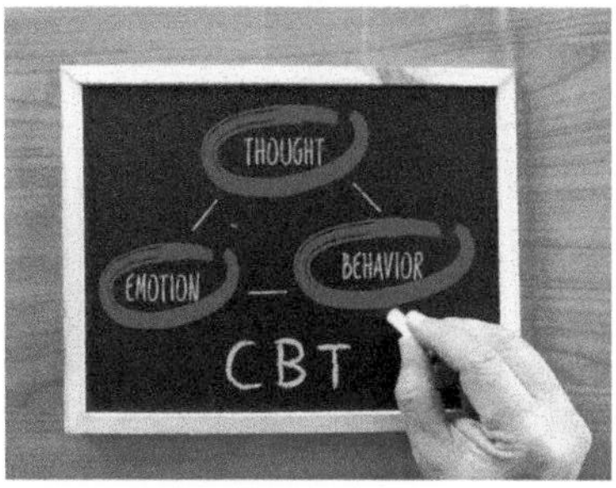

CBT has become a widely used therapy for phobias

Many disorders, including phobias, feature some irrational or harmful thinking and beliefs. CBT therapists discuss a client's beliefs and try to get them to see things more rationally. This process is called **cognitive restructuring**.

Social skills training can be used as a therapy on its own or as part of CBT. As the name suggests, it involves teaching clients social skills, including how to interact more confidently and how to read social cues from others. It is used for several disorders and problems, including social anxiety disorder.

A study by Wlazlo *et al.* (1990) compared the use of flooding and social skills training with office workers who were suffering from social anxiety. The flooding involved putting them into regular group sessions, despite their feeling anxious in this setting. The social skills training involved an office-based training programme. According to self-report three months later and at a two-and-a-half year follow up, both programmes led to significant improvements in both social anxiety and related issues such as mood.

Social skills training could help people with workplace situations

Other therapies

The use of drugs as therapy for psychological disorders is called **chemotherapy**. It involves administering drugs to people who have been diagnosed with disorders. The biological approach to psychology argues that thoughts and behaviour are based on the interaction of neurons in the brain (see chapter 1), and therefore drugs which affect the brain could improve disorders such as phobias.

Chemotherapy is a quick and easy method of treatment and in the UK it is usually cost-free to the patient. However, it is rarely seen as the best choice for treating phobias. Occasionally, if the anxiety is severe, anti-anxiety drugs or anti-depressants may be prescribed as a short-term measure while therapy is undertaken. This is particularly true for people with social phobias or agoraphobia.

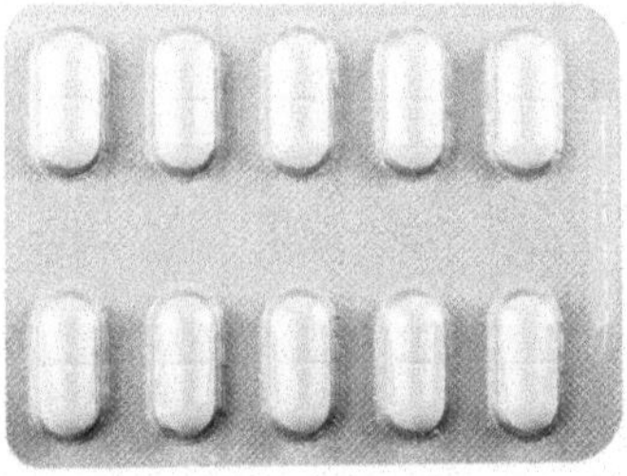

Drugs can be used to treat psychological disorders

Evaluation of therapies

Nowadays pure behavioural therapy is rare, but the techniques are used as part of CBT, and are therefore among the tools available to therapists treating anxiety disorders including panic disorder. It is potentially very useful for phobias, as it tackles beliefs and helps to establish more positive habits. Major strengths of CBT are that it is fast and effective. It is the preferred form of psychotherapy through the NHS in Britain today, and is also widely used in the USA. Unlike drugs, there are few risky side effects. However, as with any psychotherapy, there is a time and cost involved in paying a therapist. Social skills training is useful for social anxiety disorder, but does not tend to be used for specific phobias or for agoraphobia.

A possible weakness of both SD and CBT is that they fail to tackle the root cause of the problem. Psychoanalysts such as Freud believed that surface behaviours – the symptoms of phobias – do not necessarily tell us the cause of a disorder. Instead – like the manifest content in a dream – they are just symbols that cover the true, deeper cause. This could mean that treating the symptoms of a phobia fails to address the underlying problem. However, there is a lack of scientific evidence to prove that phobias hide deeper, unconscious fears, and many patients have been successfully treated using behavioural therapies.

Questions

1. What is meant by psychotherapy?
2. On what theory is flooding based?
3. What problems can occur with flooding?
4. What list is created for SD?
5. Do SD sessions start with the most- or the least-feared item on the list?
6. What does 'CBT' stand for?
7. Does CBT tackle behaviours, irrational thoughts, or both?
8. Name any two disorders or conditions that might be treated using social skills training.
9. What is chemotherapy?
10. Give one evaluation point relating to SD or social skills training.

Key concepts

- Psychotherapy
- Chemotherapy
- Flooding
- Systematic desensitisation (SD)
- Cognitive behavioural therapy (CBT)
- Cognitive restructuring
- Social skills training

Activities

1. Using a specific phobia that interests you, create a systematic desensitisation hierarchy of fears. This should show a set of situations – at least eight – with the least fearful situation at the top of the list and the most fearful situation at the bottom. Now think of how you could work through these in a therapy session. Remember that the sessions could be simulations – they could involve pictures or videos, rather than the real feared stimulus.
2. In pairs, create two short descriptions of fictional characters with specific phobias, social anxiety disorder or agoraphobia – they could be based on famous people but not on your fellow students! Then act out a therapy session for each character – using CBT for one character and SD for the other. (Focus on one session, not the entire hierarchy of fears.) If possible, try to record the therapy sessions and get feedback from your class.

End of topic project

Create a poster or presentation about one example of a phobia. You should include:

- the type of phobia/fear
- a specific example, where relevant (such as an animal or social situation)
- an example patient (don't use someone that you know – the example should be invented or come from a textbook/website)
- at least one explanation/theory of why the phobia might occur
- at least one example of a possible treatment.

Note that psychology researchers and professionals often use posters to present research findings at conferences. Look out for poster competitions for psychology students, too!

Steps:

1. Check your choice with your teacher.
2. Find some sources to research the condition, such as books or websites.
3. Take notes. Include:
   - key features/symptoms
   - description of the patient or case
   - treatments used.
4. Compile your research into a suitable presentation.

End of topic specimen exam questions

1. Describe what is meant by a phobia. — 2 marks
2. Describe the characteristics of one type of phobia. — 3 marks
3. Look at the following scenario and explain two of the possible causes of Naveen's phobia. — 6 marks

   Naveen was stung by a wasp when she was five. Since then, she has been very afraid of wasps and almost as afraid of other flying insects.
4. Describe and explain one treatment for phobias. — 4 marks

4 Depression

For the topic of Depression, you should be able to explain:

- Biological explanations of depression.
- Biological treatments for depression.
- Beck's cognitive theory.
- Research evidence relevant to the topic.

You need to develop the following skills:

- Explaining concepts and processes relevant to depression.
- Explaining, analysing and evaluating psychological theories and research evidence relevant to depression.
- Using research evidence to back up your explanations of human behaviour.
- Applying your understanding of depression to real situations.

What is depression?

Depression typically relates to a severely low, unhappy mood and a loss of interest in one's usual activities. It is part of a broader area known as psychopathology; that is, the study of mental illness.

Although usually a sign of major depressive disorder, a depressed mood can indicate other psychological disorders, too. Sometimes, depression is mild or short-lived, and does not indicate a disorder at all. This chapter will look at the characteristics of disorders and how they are defined, explanations of why they occur and different approaches to treating them.

If you have not previously studied National 5 Psychology, it would be useful to look at the closely related topic of Phobias (see chapter 3) to get an introduction to how psychologists study and explain mental health problems.

! Syllabus note

Depression is a topic in the Individual Behaviour unit in Higher Psychology. National 5 students should instead study the option topic Phobias (chapter 3).

Top tip

If you or someone you know is suffering from depression, you should seek advice from a doctor. This chapter is intended for study purposes only and does not constitute medical advice.

Defining psychological disorders

The big problem with identifying whether someone has a psychological disorder or not is that it is very hard to define which thoughts, feelings or behaviours are normal, and which are abnormal or problematic. Although we may have our own ideas about what is normal and what is not, these are subjective – they depend on an individual's point of view. They also tend to draw on social norms – a society's ideas of what is normal and acceptable and what is not – and these change

Social norms vary over time – in the past it would have been considered abnormal for a woman to want to leave her husband

over time and between cultures. As such, they can't form the basis of a scientific diagnosis.

Instead, psychologists try to use objective ways of defining what is normal and what is not. One way is to focus on the criteria of harm and distress:

- Is the behaviour or feeling causing the individual distress?
- Is the behaviour or feeling harming the individual and/or those around them?

Abnormal behaviour can be defined as that which causes an individual harm or distress

Defining abnormality based on 'distress' means saying that something is psychologically abnormal if the person themselves is feeling stressed, unhappy or scared because of the behaviour. This is, after all, the basis on which someone is likely to seek medical or psychological help. It usefully applies to many disorders such as anxiety, sleep disorders and depression.

Defining abnormality on the basis of 'harm' includes direct forms of harm, such as self-harm, failing to take care of one's own health or hygiene, or attempting suicide. It also includes the harm an individual may cause to other people. The degree or frequency of a harmful behaviour is important in determining the severity of a behaviour – if someone gambles all their money away once per year this might be concerning but is unlikely to require any further action, while if it happens every day there is a clear need of intervention. One occurrence of a behaviour is called an **episode**.

One episode of gambling would probably not be cause for any action

A broader view of harm is that it includes anything that prevents a person from leading a normal life, that is, from functioning fully as a healthy human being. This could include being able to keep yourself clean and fed, having positive relationships, being able to concentrate on everyday tasks and being able to hold down a job. Things that stop an individual from functioning are called **maladaptive** behaviours. Literally, this means 'badly adapted' to living.

Unfortunately, this brings up the issue of social norms and subjectivity again. If someone wants to spend all of their time alone, is this a personal choice or should a psychologist try to change this behaviour on the basis that the individual is not fully functioning? What if the behaviour brings the individual comfort? These are difficult ethical choices that must be made by mental health professionals, usually working in teams and in collaboration with family members.

Lying awake for several hours would be statistically extreme

Finally, the extremity of a problem plays a role in trying to define what is normal and what is not. For example, if most people take 15 minutes to get to sleep then it would be statistically extreme to lie awake for two hours. As the British Psychological Society (2011) put it, most mental distress is on a spectrum with 'normal' experience. The behaviour itself – for example, lying awake – may not be maladaptive, but the problem is the degree, frequency or duration.

This explanation is helpful when a patient's own view of their own distress is considered too subjective. Psychologists can use extremity compared to the general population as an objective way of determining whether there is a problem or not.

The DSM-5

The **DSM-5** is a manual for diagnosing psychological disorders. 'DSM' stands for 'diagnostic and statistical manual' and the current version is the fifth edition (the first one came out in 1952 and the most recent was published in 2013).

This manual aims to help professionals such as psychiatrists and clinical psychologists make objective decisions when diagnosing people with disorders like depression and phobias.

Drawing on the issues surrounding maladaptiveness and harm discussed above, the DSM states what it considers to be a psychological disorder (and what is not) as follows:

'A mental disorder is a syndrome characterized by clinically significant disturbance in an individual's cognition, emotion regulation, or behaviour ... Mental disorders are usually associated with significant distress in social, occupational, or other important activities. An expectable or culturally approved response to a common stressor or loss, such as the death of a loved one, is not a mental disorder...'

Source: American Psychiatric Association (2013, p.20)

It may be clear from the above that even though it attempts to be objective, the DSM cannot avoid social norms having a role to play in whether professional psychologists consider a behaviour normal or not, as the quote above implies that:

- A disorder is a disturbance in functioning.
- Socially acceptable behaviours in response to life events are excluded, for example, grieving.

Diagnosing a disorder using DSM depends on behaviours and feelings, which will often be self-reported by the individual. The manual uses lists of behaviours – which in this context are called **symptoms** – and defines whether someone has a disorder in terms of how many symptoms they show and for how long. The reason for having such criteria is that they help to make diagnosis reliable rather than being subjective and culturally biased. In other words, different psychologists would give the same diagnosis to the same patient.

The DSM-5 lists 271 different psychological disorders categorised into groups such as mood disorders and eating disorders.

One general criticism is that the DSM's lists of symptoms focuses too much on surface behaviours and not enough on causes. It lacks any explanation of why certain disorders can lead to particular symptoms/behaviours.

Another general criticism is that by relying on symptoms, people are 'pigeon holed' into categories. In reality, mental illness is not always

? Discussion point

Are we biased in what we consider harmful or risky behaviour? One researcher, David Nutt, stated that horse riding is statistically more dangerous than taking the drug ecstasy, but society considers it more socially acceptable. He also highlighted base jumping, hang gliding and motorcycling as risky but socially acceptable pastimes (Nutt, 2009). Should we ban behaviours based on their risk of harm or allow people to choose?

Base jumping is very risky, but is socially acceptable

The DSM helps professionals to make objective diagnoses

The DSM-5

Top tip

Diagnosis with the DSM-5 is based on what symptoms are shown and for how long.

Make the link

Sleep disorders (see chapter 2) are often diagnosed using the DSM-5.

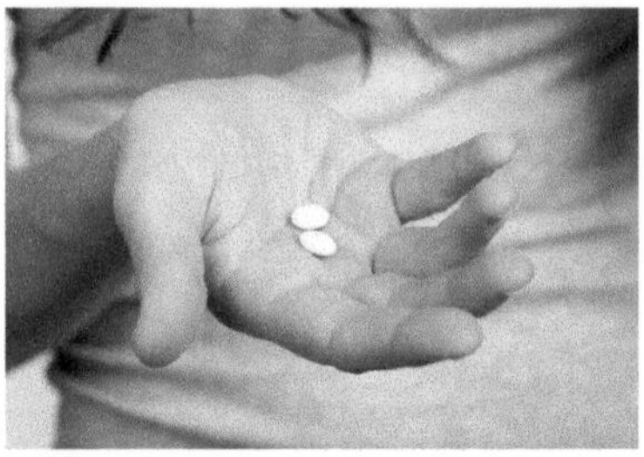

Some people believe that the organisation that produces the DSM is too closely linked to the drug companies

so neat – a person may have some of the symptoms of one disorder and some of the symptoms of another and their symptoms may change in different surroundings (Dalal and Sivakumar, 2009).

Regarding the latest version of the DSM, the DSM-5, there have been a number of further criticisms, including:

- It has 'medicalised' normal experiences such as grief.
- The organisation that produces the DSM is too closely linked to the drug companies that profit from diagnosis.
- There are an increased number of disorders listed in the DSM compared to previous versions.

This has led to accusations that more behaviours are considered to be signs of psychological problems than ever before and continually changing the diagnostic criteria leads to confusion. However, there are positives to recognising new disorders – such changes generally result from research and can lead to better awareness and treatment that is more consistent. One example is self-harm; previously considered a symptom of numerous disorders, it is now treated as a separate disorder: 'non-suicidal self-injury'.

Characteristics of major depressive disorder

Major depressive disorder (also called depression, major depression or unipolar depression) is a mood disorder categorised by the DSM-5. In order to be diagnosed, individuals must show at least one of two key symptoms – low mood or loss of interest in usual activities – on a daily basis for at least two weeks, as well as three other symptoms from the following list:

- difficulties in sleeping
- loss of energy/lethargic, or agitated
- change in body weight
- feelings of worthlessness and guilt
- difficulty in concentrating
- thoughts of death or suicide.

A person with depression may experience a loss of energy

Major depression has a massive and increasing impact on public health and wellbeing. It is projected to become the second biggest cause of years lost to disability worldwide (Murray & Lopez, 1997). A study of Dutch and Australian adults Kruijshaar et al. (2005) suggest that when allowing for bias in reporting such as people misremembering symptoms, 20% to 30% of people have at least one episode of major depression during their lifetime. Patel (2001) notes that culture, sex and income factors can all have a major impact on whether it affects people, with women more likely to be diagnosed than men. Finally, it should be noted that a percentage of the most severely depressed individuals commit suicide, making it one of the most dangerous psychological problems.

Characteristics of persistent depressive disorder

Another diagnosis described in DSM-5 is **persistent depressive disorder** (**PDD**, also known as dysthymia or chronic depression). The key difference between PDD and major depression is its duration and severity. Major depression is characterised by shorter, more severe episodes, while PDD is long-lasting but less severe. In diagnostic terms, a patient could be diagnosed with PDD even if they show fewer symptoms than would be required for a diagnosis of major depression, but they must show the symptoms for longer (two years or more).

Characteristics of bipolar mood disorder

It's important to be able to distinguish both major depression and PDD from another disorder known as **bipolar mood disorder** (formerly called 'manic-depression'). This is a rarer condition where individuals experience a cycle of extremely low and high moods. In other words, they can be depressed at some points (during which time they will exhibit characteristics similar to major depression or PDD) but this is interspersed with periods of high energy and excitement.

When their mood and activity is abnormally high, this is known as a manic state, usually featuring an intense but unfounded excitement, unrealistic plans and risky behaviour. People with depression usually suffer from feelings of mental fatigue but when experiencing a manic episode a person will show an extremely high level of physical and mental energy.

It may sound like a good thing to be in an excited and happy mood, and it is certainly more pleasant for the individual than experiencing depression, but behaviour in this state can be harmful to the self or others. It can be associated with risky or irresponsible behaviour, for example quitting one's job without a realistic alternative.

Key concepts

- Psychopathology
- Mental illness
- Normality
- Abnormality
- Subjective
- Social norm
- Objective
- Harm
- Distress
- Episode
- Maladaptive
- DSM-5
- Symptoms
- Major depressive disorder
- Persistent depressive disorder (PDD)
- Bipolar mood disorder

Questions

1. Why can't we allow psychologists to decide what seems normal based only on their own opinion?
2. Give an example of a maladaptive behaviour.
3. On what basis does DSM suggest that disorders should be diagnosed? Mention two main things.
4. Name three groups of disorder described by the DSM-5.
5. Give one criticism of the DSM-5.
6. According to Kruijshaar *et al.* (2005), how many people experience at least one episode of depression during their lifetime?
7. True or false: lack of energy can be a symptom of major depression.
8. For how long would a person have to show symptoms of major depression in order to be diagnosed, according to DSM-5 criteria?
9. Are the symptoms of PDD different to those of major depression?
10. What symptom makes bipolar mood disorder different to other forms of depression?

GO! Activities

1. Take some time to think about the social norms in your society. These should be things that are not required by law, but which you are expected to do by other people and/or it would be considered weird not to do (a few examples: wearing a coat on a cold day; being quiet during a speech or lecture; eating solid food). What would it be like if these 'normal' things were considered abnormal?
2. Take some time to investigate the system for describing disorders, the DSM-5. Find out about one of the reasons that it has been criticised. Try to find counter arguments as well. Report these back to your class or group.

Biological explanations of depression

The role of neurochemistry

The biological explanation of depression focuses on biological processes within the brain and, in particular, on neurotransmitters and how they function. It is an example of the biological approach to psychology (see chapter 1). **Neurotransmitter imbalance theory** is the idea that the level of one or more type of neurotransmitter is either too low or too high when someone has a disorder, and that this results in the symptoms of the disorder. The theory makes an analogy with bodily illnesses such as diabetes, which have a biological cause. This idea is fundamental to mainstream psychiatry and clinical psychology today and is the basis of most drug treatments for depression and for many other disorders.

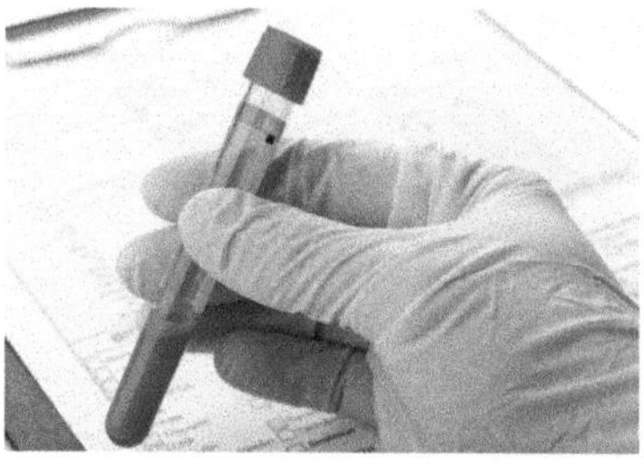
The level of serotonin in the blood can be measured

In major depressive disorder, the approach focuses on the role of the neurotransmitter **serotonin** (also called '5-hydroxytryptamine', or '5-HT'). Serotonin is a neurotransmitter that is produced in the brain and plays a role in mood. It is thought to be at a lower level in depressed patients.

Chemically, serotonin is a monoamine, as are certain other neurotransmitters. The accidental discovery that drugs which reduce levels of monoamines also trigger depression led to the **monoamine hypothesis**. This states that depression is caused by low levels of monoamine neurotransmitters and that the beneficial effects of antidepressants result from raising levels of the same neurotransmitters (Fišar, 2016). It is hard to measure serotonin levels in the living brain but blood levels can be measured and they are generally lower in depressed individuals, supporting the monoamine hypothesis.

> **Top tip**
>
> The monoamine hypothesis is a more specific example of the broader neurotransmitter imbalance theory. It relates to depression rather than to psychological disorders in general.

A major implication of the monoamine hypothesis and its predictions about levels of serotonin in depression is that most treatments for depression aim to increase levels of serotonin in the brain in some way (see below), although some also tackle other monoamine neurotransmitters.

Hormones

Hormones are chemical messengers used by the body. They can trigger feelings of stress, fatigue, aggression or sexual desire. If you have already studied the topic of Sleep, you will be aware that a hormone called melatonin can cause people to feel sleepy.

It is probably already well known to you that hormones can be associated with mood. Hormones associated with puberty affect both mood and behaviour in the early teenage years, while premenstrual syndrome (PMS) is a common mood disturbance associated with the menstrual cycle, leading to increased irritability, anger, crying or anxiety.

The thyroid is a gland in the neck which produces hormones. These **thyroid hormones** affect the rate at which the body uses energy, and can therefore lead to people feeling tired or energetic. Thyroid hormones can play a role in developing depression. However, it's also

Mood can fluctuate after childbirth

important for a psychologist or psychiatrist to establish that depression-like symptoms are not caused by a thyroid disorder in order to avoid a misdiagnosis.

Other hormones can affect mood, too. Shortly after childbirth, the majority of women experience the 'baby blues' – a short-lived depressive state featuring mood swings and tearfulness. It is likely that the baby blues are linked to hormonal shifts as the mother's hormone levels (particularly of oestrogen and progesterone) return to normal levels.

A more severe and prolonged condition called postpartum depression (or 'postnatal depression') is a mood disorder where depression begins after childbirth, usually within one month of the birth. This condition affects around 15% of women (Pearlstein *et al.*, 2009). It may be that the hormonal changes associated with childbirth also play a role in this disorder. However, there are many other possible explanations and it's notable that fathers can also be diagnosed with postpartum depression. Disrupted sleep associated with having a new baby may trigger depression in some individuals, and the stress associated with parenting and life changes could also play a role. All in all, the causes of postpartum depression are currently not fully understood.

Make the link

...with the study of hormones within the topic of Sleep, or the topic of Aggression.

The diathesis-stress model

As you have seen, there are important biological influences on depression, but it is also important that we do not ignore the role of life events. To what extent do people become depressed because of biological factors, and how much is it down to problems and stress that they experience? The **diathesis-stress** model states that it is a combination of the two. Certain people are more prone to depression than others but whether they actually develop it or not will depend on life stress.

An analogy is that in a hurricane, some houses are blown over and others are not. They all experience the same stress (the hurricane) but some succumb to that stress and others are able to stand up to it.

During a hurricane some buildings are blown down whilst others stay standing

- Diathesis: a predisposition in someone's biology or thought processes that makes them more vulnerable to a psychological problem such as depression.
- Stress: life events involving suffering, injury or trauma that make depression more likely to develop.

Often, the diathesis is assumed to be a genetic predisposition to develop a disorder. According to diathesis-stress, even two people with exactly the same genes may have different mental health outcomes. This means that if you possess genes that put you at risk of depression, life experiences will be a crucial factor in whether you actually develop the disorder or not.

The biological approach also conducts twin studies, trying to find out the extent to which disorders are at least partly genetic. One such study was conducted by McGuffin *et al.* (1996; see key study), who found that for depressed patients who had a twin brother/sister, their sibling was much more likely to also have depression if they were an identical twin than if they were non-identical. Such research supports the idea of a strong genetic component in disorders but the differences between twins are consistent with the diathesis-stress model.

Twin studies can be used to investigate the extent to which a disorder is genetic

Key study: McGuffin *et al.* (1996): twin study of depression

Peter McGuffin

Aim: *The researchers wanted to find evidence for the idea that depression has a genetic component.*

Method: *This was a twin study. The researchers studied the UK hospital records of patients with depression and identified 177 patients who had twins. They then contacted their twins, and assessed them to see whether they met the diagnostic criteria for depression too. They also tested each pair to determine whether they were monozygotic (identical) or dizygotic (fraternal) twins.*

Findings: *In twin studies, concordance means the extent to which both twins have the same trait – in this case, depression. Using a statistical technique called probandwise concordance, the researchers found a concordance rate of 46% for monozygotic (identical) twins, compared to 20% for the dizygotic twins. These rates represent the estimated risk that an individual person in either of these groups would develop depression if they had a depressive twin.*

Evaluation: *This study provides evidence that genetic factors play a role in depression but, clearly, some environmental stressors must play a role too, as there was not a 100% concordance rate even among the identical twins. As such, the study supports the diathesis-stress model of depression. However, it is possible that any effect of genetics on depression is indirect. For example, identical twins are more likely to have similar personalities than non-identical twins, even when raised apart (Tellegen et al., 1988) and it is known that personality traits, such as neuroticism, can affect depression (Duggan et al., 1990). Therefore, it is possible that other variables are involved, rather than there being a gene that directly contributes to depression.*

Evaluation of biological explanations

The idea that a psychological disorder is a medical problem caused by neurotransmitters in the brain is prevalent in our culture. It removes blame from patients and it has been largely welcomed as a way of removing stigma by seeing a psychological disorder as 'just an illness'. However, there is very little direct evidence of chemical imbalances in the brain – and any such imbalances could be seen as the effect rather than the cause of psychological problems. Viewing depression and other disorders in entirely biological terms fails to take account of the important social processes that contribute (British Psychological Society, 2011). The emphasis on biology can lead to missed opportunities for intervening in social problems that affect an individual's mental health (Horwitz, 2007).

The diathesis-stress model combines elements of the different approaches to psychology in a way that has been helpful for various disorders. In the case of schizophrenia – another serious psychological disorder – Zubin and Spring (1977) concluded that it develops via a combination of having a high vulnerability to the disorder and experiencing a high level of life stress. Sleep disorders can also be explained in terms of diathesis-stress, as not everyone who experiences factors that harm sleep quality (such as artificial light or irregular shift patterns) goes on to develop a sleep disorder.

The genes related to being tall do not necessarily cause a person to be good at basketball!

However, it remains unclear what constitutes a predisposition to develop a psychological disorder. The 'diathesis' could include several things – most obviously a genetic element, as described in the previous section. However, it could also involve being mentally less resilient. This could be due to the person's personality, their thought processes or a lack of social support.

Twin studies have demonstrated a link between genetic relatedness and the chances of developing depression or another disorder. However, it can't be concluded that genes cause these disorders. By analogy, there is a correlation between having genes related to being tall and being successful at basketball. That does not mean that these genes cause you to have better basketball skills. Joseph (2012, p.65) notes that the genes that supposedly cause disorders have not been found and he criticises *'the failure to seriously consider the possibility that presumed genes do not exist'.*

Make the link

...with the topic of Sleep and with genetic factors in Aggression.

Biological treatments for depression

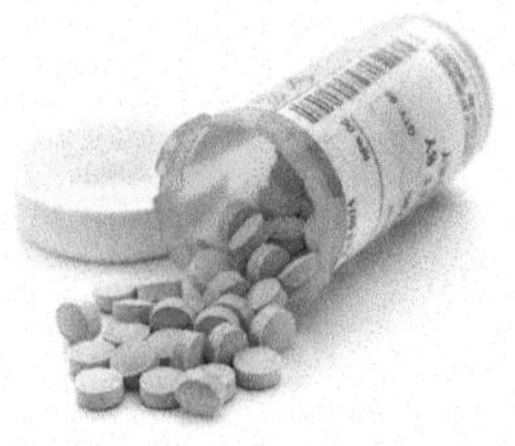

Drugs may be used to treat psychological disorders

The use of drugs as a therapy for a psychological disorder or medical issue is called chemotherapy. Drawing on the monoamine hypothesis of depression and the broader neurotransmitter imbalance theory, a huge range of psychiatric medicines have been developed. They all work in slightly different ways but the principles are similar – they are absorbed into the bloodstream and travel into the brain, where they influence the communication between brain cells at synapses (see chapter 1). This could include mimicking or blocking a neurotransmitter.

For most patients, drug therapy is a quick and easy method, and in the UK, it is usually cost-free to the patient. However, it is costly for the NHS, and some experts have criticised the pharmaceutical companies that develop the drugs for hiding the results of drug trials and promoting expensive new drugs that are little better than previous versions (Goldacre, 2012).

Drugs can provide relief but they do not work equally for all patients and tend to have negative side effects. Drugs could also be viewed as a way of reducing the symptoms of a disorder, rather than tackling the cause.

Some of the main drug therapies and other biological treatments for depression are as follows.

Many drugs have negative side effects

SSRIs

SSRIs (selective serotonin reuptake inhibitors) are a type of drug frequently prescribed for major depression, as well as other disorders such as anxiety and eating disorders. They include the drug fluoxetine (which is also known by its trade name 'Prozac'). They work by reducing brain cells' ability to re-uptake (i.e. reabsorb) serotonin, which causes more of this neurotransmitter to be available in the brain. This is thought to boost the activity of brain areas that are important to mood.

SSRIs are considered to have relatively mild side effects compared to some other psychiatric drugs. However, they tend to cause nausea, can interfere with sleep and can lead to people feeling agitated. They have been linked to sexual dysfunction and in rare cases they can trigger suicidal thoughts or other erratic behaviour. Most of the side effects improve within a few weeks (NHS, 2018).

> **Top tip**
>
> Drug side effects are specific to the patient – two people may have a very different reaction to the same antidepressant. The drugs may also work better for some people than others in terms of improving the symptoms of depression.

SNRIs

SNRIs (serotonin-norepinephrine reuptake inhibitors) are another very widely used form of antidepressant. They were developed more recently than SSRIs and are slightly less specific in their action, as they tackle not just serotonin but also norepinephrine (also known as noradrenaline), another monoamine neurotransmitter that is thought to play a role in mood.

SNRIs have similar side effects to SSRIs and are also similar in terms of how effective they are at treating major depression. (A review by Papakostas *et al.*, 2007, found them to be marginally more effective.) Some forms of SNRIs are also used to treat other disorders such as anxiety, ADHD and chronic pain. Their effect on norepinephrine challenges the popular view that serotonin alone is responsible for depression.

Tricyclics

Tricyclics are another class of antidepressant drugs. They were a popular choice to treat major depression for many decades but have largely been replaced by SSRIs and SNRIs as the first choice of

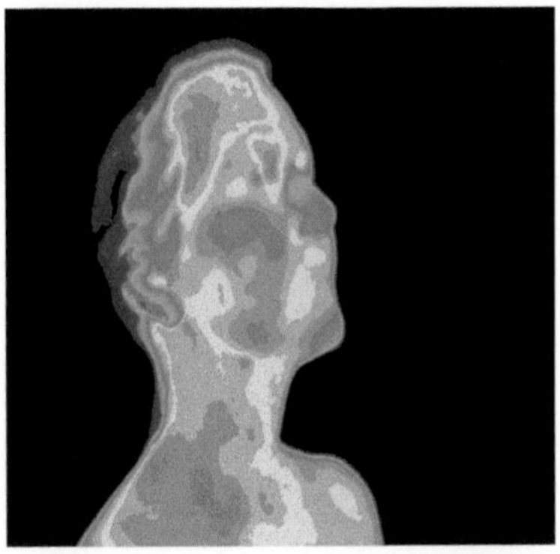

Some antidepressant drugs can affect body temperature

Top tip

If you are asked to analyse types of anti-depressant, a good way to pick up marks would be to compare them to each other. You could also analyse the assumptions and supporting evidence.

Make the link

...with the National 5 topic of Phobias.

treatment. A review of the evidence by Anderson (2000) concluded that although tricyclics and SSRIs/SNRIs were similar in terms of effectiveness, tricyclics have worse side effects. This means that patients are more likely to stop taking them. The more common side effects of tricyclics include blurry vision, constipation, memory impairments and increased body temperature (Gelder *et al.*, 2005). Nowadays, they are most often prescribed to patients for whom SSRIs have not worked.

MAOIs

Monoamine oxidase inhibitors (MAOIs) are another older type of antidepressant drugs. They are now more often used for anxiety disorders or bipolar mood disorder than for major depressive disorder.

As the name suggests, MAOIs work by inhibiting (i.e. blocking or reducing) a hormone called monoamine oxidase. Monoamine oxidase clears excess serotonin from the brain, along with other neurotransmitters such as norepinephrine and dopamine. Inhibiting monoamine oxidase therefore increases the level of these chemicals available in the brain.

As with tricyclics, MAOIs are most commonly used with patients who have not responded to SSRIs. They are less specific than SSRIs because they affect several neurotransmitters, not just serotonin. The main side effect is a risk of high blood pressure, which can be dangerous for some patients. MAOIs also interact dangerously with some other drugs, including recreational drugs.

A newer generation of MAOIs, known as **RIMAs (reversible inhibitors of monoamine oxidase A)**, has been developed in recent years. These are thought to have fewer side effects and to be similar to SSRIs in terms of efficacy, although more research is still needed. They are currently more widely used for social phobias than for depression.

Electro-convulsive therapy

In severe cases of major depression where there is a suicide risk to the patient, **electroconvulsive therapy (ECT)** may be used. ECT is not a drug – it is a form of therapy which involves giving a 70–150 volt electric shock to one or both sides of the head. This can affect blood flow, particularly to the frontal lobe.

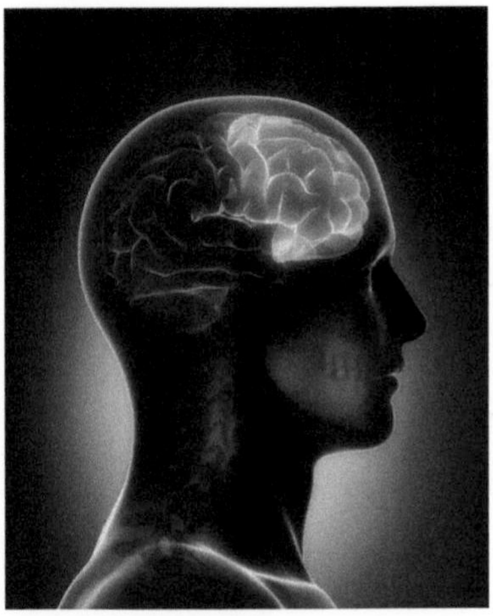

ECT can affect blood flow in the frontal lobe of the brain

The treatment induces a seizure in an anaesthetised patient and is typically given to in-patients within a psychiatric hospital. The treatment is usually given 2–3 times a week for around four weeks.

Compared to chemotherapy, ECT is an invasive form of treatment, as patients typically suffer some distress and disorientation at the time of the therapy. More seriously, they may experience memory loss over the longer term. It is a controversial choice of treatment, not least because it can be administered against a patient's will if he or she is detained under the Mental Health Act. Given the dangers of suicide for people with extreme depression, some psychologists feel that the risks and ethical problems associated with the treatment are justified.

Questions

1. What is the name of the broader biological theory which states that disorders are due to neurotransmitter levels?
2. Which neurotransmitter is thought to play a role in depression?
3. Which hormones are associated with depression?
4. What is meant by the 'diathesis' element of the diathesis-stress theory?
5. What was the difference in the depression concordance rates between identical and fraternal twins in the McGuffin *et al.* (1996) study?
6. Why did the BPS (2011) and Horwitz (2007) object to focusing entirely on biological processes in disorders?
7. What is meant by chemotherapy?
8. What are the most commonly used types of antidepressant drugs for major depression today?
9. What is different about RIMAs, the newer generation of MAOIs?
10. What is the most serious side effect of ECT?

Key concepts

- Neurotransmitter imbalance theory
- Monoamine hypothesis
- Serotonin
- Diathesis-stress
- Thyroid hormones
- SSRIs (selective serotonin reuptake inhibitors)
- SNRIs (serotonin norepinephrine reuptake inhibitors)
- Tricyclics
- MAOIs (monoamine oxidase inhibitors)
- RIMAs (reversible inhibitors of monoamine oxidase A)
- Electroconvulsive Therapy (ECT)

GO! Activities

1. Another disorder which features depression and may have biological causes is SAD – seasonal affective disorder. Find out more about this condition. Can it be attributed to hormones or neurotransmitters, or are there other possible explanations? Could the diathesis-stress model help provide an explanation?
2. The way that psychological problems have been explained and treated has changed throughout history. Find out about a historical explanation or treatment and write a blog post about it and/or give a short verbal explanation to your class.

Cognitive explanations of depression

Beck's cognitive triad

According to the cognitive approach to psychology, the way we think is based partly on schemas – groups of concepts that make up our knowledge of the world (see chapter 1). These schemas affect the way we feel, and people's emotional reactions are often based more on their thought processes about events than on the events themselves. This approach states that we should explain and treat disorders such as depression on the basis of thoughts and beliefs, rather than by trying to alter brain chemistry directly.

According to Beck, how we think about events is more important than the events themselves

Why, then, are some people depressed while others are not? Cognitive researcher Aaron Beck, one of the developers of cognitive behavioural therapy (CBT), stated that depressed people have negative beliefs about three key things (Beck, 1976):

- themselves
- the world
- the future.

For example, they may believe that they are a bad person, that the world is unfair and that nothing is going to improve. These negative beliefs need to be tackled in order to change a person's mood or behaviour. Beck called these beliefs the negative **cognitive triad**.

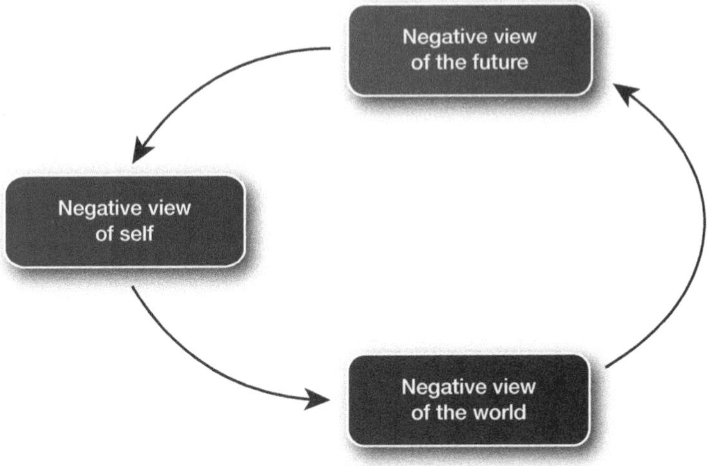

The negative cognitive triad

Negative self-schemas

Beck also believed that the way depressed people think is biased, particularly when it comes to thinking about themselves. This relates to some of the irrational thoughts discussed in chapter 1, such as:

- personalisation – unduly relating all events to oneself
- overgeneralisation – thinking that an event will apply to all situations
- selective abstraction – focusing on only one aspect of an event

Top tip

Think of real examples of each of these forms of irrational thinking, and add them to your notes.

According to the cognitive approach to psychology, it is not uncommon for people to have such flaws in their thinking but someone who is depressed has learned a pattern of negative distortions in their thinking (whereas someone else might distort events in a more positive way).

These negative patterns of thought are based on **negative self-schemas** – sets of harmful beliefs, thoughts and feelings that a depressed person has about themselves. Many of these beliefs will have been learned early in life, perhaps by being told they were a bad person by teachers or parents. These self-schemas continue to change and develop through the lifespan. For example, a depressed individual may think things such as:

- I am useless.
- This problem is all my fault.
- I did this really badly.

Schemas are very resilient cognitive structures, as they are based on multiple interconnected pieces of information as well as on feelings. A good example of the resilience of a schema is a prejudiced belief. It is very difficult to persuade a prejudiced person that they are mistaken. In a similar way, it is difficult to persuade a depressed individual that they are being too hard on themselves, or that their perception of events is unduly negative.

Resilient people have positive expectations, which help them to deal with challenges

Later, Beck said that schemas could combine into a broader 'mode' that includes feelings, motivation and behaviour (Nelson-Jones, 2000). For example, someone may have a failure mode which leads to self-defeating habits, gloomy feelings and assumptions that they will never be successful.

In contrast, people who can be described as resilient have a positive set of schemas and habits, for example high expectations about the future. This helps them to adapt to changes and results in lower stress.

Make the link

...with the topic of Prejudice.

Faulty information processing

Like Beck, Albert Ellis believed that it was necessary to tackle problematic cognitions through therapy in order to treat depression. He argued that an activating event (A) is followed by a belief about that event (B), and then followed by emotional consequences (C). This became known as his **ABC model** (Ellis & Grieger, 1977):

Activating Event >> **B**elief >> Emotional **C**onsequence

He thought that beliefs fundamentally affect a person's emotional responses to life, but also that many of these beliefs are irrational. In other words, we engage in **faulty information processing** – the way a person takes in new information and thinks about it is flawed. Many people have a tendency to overgeneralise pessimistically in their thought processes – leading to self-defeating core beliefs, each phrased as something we 'must' do; each of these has a range of emotional and behavioural consequences (Ellis, 2003):

Belief	Example of emotion/behaviour
I must do well and win approval or else I am a bad person.	Anxiety/lack of assertiveness
Other people must behave well or else they deserve to be punished.	Anger/intolerance
Things must be easy, without any discomfort or danger, or else I cannot enjoy life.	Fear/procrastination

CBT

Both Ellis and Beck contributed to the development of therapies. As mentioned in chapter 1, one of the most popular treatments for psychological problems nowadays is **cognitive behavioural therapy (CBT)**, a psychotherapy that aims to tackle irrational thought processes, including negative self-schemas and the negative cognitive triad.

CBT was first developed for depression and then found to be effective for anxiety disorders and some sleep disorders. It focuses on dealing with the symptoms/behaviours in the here-and-now, rather than talking about parents and childhood.

CBT aims to tackle irrational thought processes

CBT draws on both the behaviourist and the cognitive approach to psychology:

- Cognitive aspects focus on a rational discussion of the client's beliefs.
- Behaviourist techniques can be incorporated.

According to Ellis's view, irrational beliefs mediate our response to situations. Therefore, the CBT therapist discusses the client's beliefs and tries to get them to see things more rationally. This process is called **cognitive restructuring**. In a CBT session, the therapist and client sit on chairs facing each other, rather like a business meeting. Typically, the therapist runs through an agenda at the start. There is no free association or analysis of dreams – the conversation focuses on specific problem situations, for example, family or work conflicts. CBT therapists make use of numerical rating scales to get a quick assessment of how their client felt about specific situations.

Key study: The Treatment of Adolescents with Depression (TADS) study by the National Institute of Mental Health (March *et al.*, 2007)

Aim: *The aim of the study was to test the effectiveness of major treatments for depression in teenagers, in order to help tackle this harmful and common disorder.*

At the time, SSRI antidepressants had been passed as safe to use for children and adolescents by the Food and Drug Administration (FDA) in the USA, but it was unclear whether they were as effective as other treatment options and how severe the side effects were likely to be. This study aimed to provide objective evidence as to whether the benefits of antidepressants outweighed the risks for this age group.

Method: *The study was a drug trial, involving a comparison of four groups:*

- *antidepressant drug*
- *CBT*
- *both antidepressant and CBT*
- *control group (placebo pill).*

The participants were 439 school pupils aged 12 to 17 from various parts of the USA. The antidepressant used was fluoxetine, a common type of SSRI.

Findings: *It was found that antidepressants led to a bigger improvement than CBT after 12 weeks (61% versus 44% were 'much improved'), but after 18 weeks CBT had essentially caught up (65% for antidepressants versus 62% for CBT). Both therapies were better than a placebo. The longer the treatment went on, the better the CBT group did. The best outcomes came from a combination of both antidepressants and CBT, at least in the short to medium term. However, the drugs led to negative side effects, including new suicidal thoughts, which were not found in the CBT or control groups. Overall this study showed that antidepressants were the most effective choice in the short term but over longer timescales CBT was preferable due to its equivalent efficacy without side effects.*

Evaluation: *This study was longitudinal and conducted on a large scale with several hundred participants. It made a carefully controlled comparison of four main clinical interventions. In terms of location, it is a strength that it included students from many schools, but they were all based in the USA, which makes it harder to generalise the findings internationally. It was limited in that it did not include psychoanalysis or other major types of therapy/counselling.*

Evaluation

One of the strengths of cognitive theories of depression is that they attempt to get to the root of the problem by looking at thoughts and beliefs, rather than focusing on symptoms. However, it's possible that low mood causes some negative thought processes and beliefs, rather than these thoughts causing the low mood. Irrational beliefs are found among the healthy population, and it is hard to establish that beliefs cause disorders.

Together, the work of Ellis and Beck has been widely applied in the use of CBT. The popularity and success of this therapy lends some support to the theoretical ideas behind the cognitive approach.

CBT is widely used because it is seen as fast and effective. It is the main choice of psychotherapy on the NHS nowadays, as well as in the USA.

The Treatment of Adolescents with Depression (TADS) study (see key study) compared CBT along with chemotherapy, a combination of both and a control condition. The best and fastest outcomes were found for people who had both CBT and drugs. However, CBT alone has the advantage that there are no risky side effects though as with any psychotherapy, there are costs in terms of both time and money when employing a therapist.

Key concepts

- Cognitive triad
- Negative self-schemas
- Faulty information processing
- ABC model
- Cognitive behavioural therapy (CBT)

Questions

1. What three negative beliefs are included in Beck's 'negative cognitive triad'?
2. Give an example of a negative thought about the self.
3. Are negative self-schemas easy to change?
4. Give an example of a distorted 'must' belief, as described by Ellis (2003).
5. What does CBT stand for?
6. True or false: CBT therapists often use agendas and numerical rating scales during sessions.
7. What term is given to the CBT technique of discussing a client's irrational beliefs to help them to see things more rationally?
8. What did the TADS study (2007) find?
9. Which therapy works best in the long term according to TADS?
10. Is it easy to establish that thoughts cause disorders?

Activities

1. In your notes, write two or more examples of an activating event/belief/emotional consequence.
2. Think of a famous person who seems exceptionally negative about themselves (or, alternatively, exceptionally positive and arrogant). What kind of self-schemas might that person have? Write some examples of the kind of things they appear to believe. Discuss with a classmate what life experiences may have contributed to these beliefs.

End of topic project

Create a poster or presentation about a treatment for depression that interests you. Possible topics include:

- any type of antidepressant
- any type of CBT or similar cognitive therapy
- alternatives to CBT, such as psychoanalytic therapy.

Note that psychology researchers and professionals often use posters to present research findings at conferences. Look out for poster competitions for psychology students, too!

Steps:

1. Check your choice with your teacher.
2. Find some sources to research the condition, such as books or websites on psychopathology. There are some suggested sources in chapter 9.
3. Take notes. Include:
   - key features/side effects
   - explanations of how the treatment was developed
   - how popular and/or successful it is.
4. Compile your research into a presentation.

End of topic specimen exam questions

1.	Explain the features of major depressive disorder and persistent depressive disorder.	8 marks
2.	Analyse the diathesis-stress model of depression.	8 marks
3.	Evaluate the use of SSRIs and SNRIs.	8 marks
4.	Analyse cognitive theories and treatments for depression.	15 marks

5 Memory

For the topic of Memory, you should be able to explain:

- The multi-store model of memory.
- The working memory model.
- Causes of forgetting.
- Research evidence relevant to the topic.

You need to develop the following skills:

- Explaining concepts and processes relevant to memory.
- Explaining, analysing and evaluating psychological theories and research evidence relevant to memory.
- Using research evidence to back up your explanations of human behaviour.
- Applying your understanding of memory to real situations.

! Syllabus note

Memory is a topic in the Individual Behaviour unit in Higher Psychology. National 5 students should instead study the option topic Phobias (chapter 3).

Our memories give us a sense of who we are

Make the link

With stages of sleep, as discussed in chapter 2.

The nature of memory

Memory is part of what makes us human. Without our memories of years gone by, each of us would be unable to function and would have very little sense of who we are as a person. Without the ability to hold information in memory while we are working on it, we would be incapable of completing anything but the simplest of tasks.

Various types of memory are discussed in this chapter but regardless of which type of memory is being studied, a logical set of processes must take place. First, information must enter a memory store. Then it must remain there for a period of time until it is needed or until it can be moved to another store. Finally, it must be retrieved from the store and used – or moved to another store. These three processes are usually called **encoding**, **storage** and **retrieval**.

Storage of a memory may sound like a simple and passive process – like putting something in a drawer until needed – but it is not. In fact, researchers have increasingly found that memory is an active process and new memories must be **consolidated** – strengthened and made permanent – in order to be retained. Sleep appears to be important in this process; according to Rasch and Born (2013), slow-wave sleep (sleep stages 3–4) helps to consolidate new information into long-term memories, while REM sleep stabilises these memories. Walker *et al.* (2003) found that unbroken sleep is vital to the brain processes involved in procedural memories being consolidated.

Memory stores

It is important to understand the basic structure of human memory and to be familiar with certain widely discussed concepts. The first distinction to consider is the difference between **short-term memory (STM)** and **long-term memory (LTM)**. The idea that there are two different memory stores is a very old one in psychology. However, the terms are not used very consistently in everyday speech. Research into these two stores will be discussed throughout the chapter.

The storage of a memory is not like putting something in drawer until it is needed!

Sensory memory

Researchers have also described a very brief store which holds information when it first reaches our senses – **sensory memory (SM)**. It allows things that we see and hear to be retained long enough for us to focus our attention and begin to think about them. It can be defined as a *'vivid memory for the qualities of a sensation such as a sound or a visual image'* (Cowan, 1988). There are actually a set of several different sensory stores, one for each of the senses. Sperling (1960) investigated visual sensory memory and concluded that it that lasts for half a second or less.

A good example of using SM occurs when a person speaks to you and you are not paying attention. If you switch your attention within a couple of seconds and try to focus on what they were saying, you still retain a sensory trace of the words (allowing you to pretend you were listening!). Similarly, visual information can be retained by sensory memory for long enough to connect and make sense of incoming information.

Make the link

...with the topic of Sleep.

? Discussion point

Can you think of examples of different types of memories? Are all types of memories learned and forgotten in similar ways and over similar timescales?

Even if you are not listening you will retain a sensory trace of what someone said for a couple of seconds

Short-term or working memory

If a person studies something and then forgets it a few days later, they may explain it as having only been in 'short-term memory (STM)'. However, in psychology, the term STM refers to much more immediate uses of memory, such as reading a phone number from a website and then holding it in mind for a few seconds before dialling it, or holding a few numbers and steps in mind while solving a maths problem.

In addition, researchers have increasingly come to accept that this memory system is not only responsible for storage, but also for processing information (Cowan, 2017). As such, it is typically called **working memory (WM)**. Working memory can store a short list of items, but it can also use and manipulate information – either new information or information that is being recalled from long-term memory. It is essentially a kind of workspace for the mind.

WM is limited in its duration and can therefore be considered a temporary, rather than a permanent, memory store. Information can fade very quickly if we cease to use it or we get distracted. However, information can be retained in WM for as long as we are using it or focusing on it in some way. For example, we don't forget the key aspects of a maths problem midway through solving it, but we might forget someone's name around thirty seconds after they are introduced to us if we have been talking about something else following the introduction.

WM is also limited in size. It can only hold a few words or numbers at a time. Miller (1956) studied people's ability to retain lists of items, and found that no matter what type of item is stored (lists of words, digits etc.), people could only hold between five and nine items. This became known as the *'magic number, seven plus or minus two'*. This observation can be easily tested, although more recent researchers have found that the limitation is not the number of items but how long they take to say: the capacity of WM is a phrase or group of items that can be spoken in around one-and-a-half to two seconds (Baddeley *et al.*, 1975; see key study on page 129) Cowan (1988) has argued that for unrelated items which can't be rehearsed as a verbal list, the capacity of WM is reduced to a maximum of three or four separate items.

Traditionally, it was assumed that WM only uses acoustically encoded information, that is, it processes items on the basis of their sound (Baddeley, 1966). If a person is given visual information such as a set of pictures to remember they will typically transform them to verbal information and then hold the words based on their sound. However, when people are prevented from using acoustic encoding they can take in items visually (Murray, 1968), so the store must include a visual element too. Indeed, the use of verbal and visual information at the same time is essential to most everyday tasks, such as reading or having a conversation while driving. The different parts of WM are explained in one of the main theories in this chapter: the working memory model (see page 127).

Top tip

If you are asked about short-term memory in the exam, it is fine to talk about working memory as well. Make sure you are clear that short-term memory is an older term that only covers one of the functions (immediate recall of a list) of working memory.

Long-term memory

Unlike working memory, long-term memory (LTM) is a permanent memory store: information encoded to LTM can last a lifetime. It can also be encoded and used straight away, and there is no obvious limit to how much can be stored. That is to say, it doesn't have the same sort of limits to capacity and duration that characterise working memory.

LTM and WM also store information in different ways. While WM is good at remembering lists and at processing verbal and visual items, LTM appears to function more effectively when processing meaningful, factual information, such as the difference between a van and a lorry, or which city is the capital city of a country. This was neatly demonstrated in an experiment by Baddeley (1966) in which he gave participants words to remember which either sounded similar (such as 'cap', 'cab', 'can', 'ban') or had similar meanings (such as 'large', 'big', 'huge', 'giant'). Over a short timescale, participants tended to make errors in remembering the words with similar sounds, showing that WM tends to store words using **acoustic encoding**. However, after a delay of ten minutes or more, participants made many errors with the list of words with similar meanings. This shows that in long-term memory, information tends to be encoded and stored on the basis of its meaning. This meaningful processing is termed **semantic encoding**.

Remembering things such as the capitals of countries depends on semantic LTM

LTM can store other types of information as well as the meanings of words. Remembering the events of your life, such as what you did yesterday evening, is known as episodic LTM (in contrast to semantic LTM). We know that long-term memory must also store some visual and sound-based information. We are able to remember music and what our acquaintances look like, showing that we can retain acoustic and visual information over the long term. Indeed, learning visual and verbal information simultaneously leads to better recall – a phenomenon known as **dual coding**, and one that you can put to use in your studies Additionally, physical skills and procedures such a riding a bike, drawing or playing a musical instrument are permanently stored in

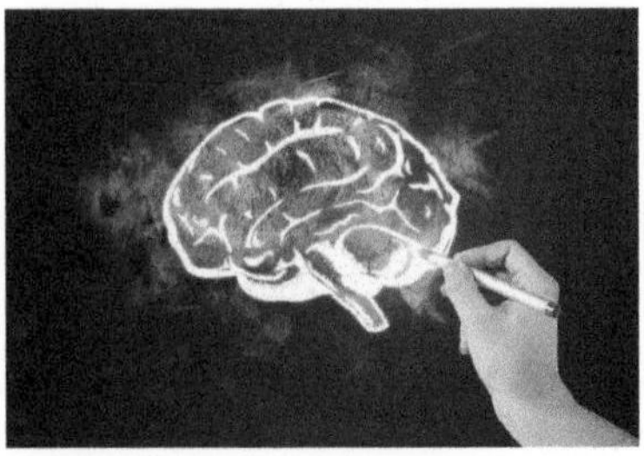

Adding images or sketches to your written notes is an example of dual coding

memory. These sorts of memories are called procedural LTM, and are thought to rely on different brain areas than episodic and semantic LTM.

LTM is sometimes compared to a storehouse, filing cabinet or a computer hard drive. The implication is that its function is purely storage. Items are placed there during learning and remain, separate and relatively unchanged, until we later try to remember them. LTM is certainly very good at storage – its capacity is effectively unlimited (your memory never gets full!). However, in practice, memories are not separate and are stored in such a way that they are both connected to one another and subject to change and distortion over time. As Anderson (1984, p.5) puts it, *'memory is not a basket of facts'*.

Instead, memories are interconnected sets of knowledge, or **schemas**. New learning isn't stored separately (as might happen with a computer) but is interpreted and linked to existing knowledge. As you have seen in chapter 1, Bartlett showed that memories could be distorted to make them more like our expectations, subtracting elements that don't fit. These interconnected long-term memories can even play a role in solving short-term problems, demonstrating that they do not sit inertly in storage until we choose to actively retrieve them (Ericsson & Kintsch, 1995).

As our schemas are influenced by culture and expectations, people should remember things better if they are consistent with a schema. The schema can also be used to make predictions and fill in gaps in knowledge. This is exactly what was found by memory researchers Brewer and Treyens (1981) who studied recall of objects in an office scene (see right). However, in a similar study, Pezdek *et al.* (1989) directly compared schema-consistent and schema inconsistent items, and found that the *inconsistent* items were better recalled. They concluded that this is due to more attention being given to items that seem surprising or unusual during the process of encoding. Either way, it is apparent that memory for objects is influenced by expectations from our schemas.

The lab used in Brewer and Treyens' experiment

Name of store	Capacity	Duration	Main type of encoding	Role of visual and verbal encoding
Working memory (WM) (or short-term memory/ short-term store)	Limited to four discrete items or a list lasting one-and-a-half to two seconds	Information can be retained while still in use but otherwise fades after 30 seconds or less	Acoustic, but depends on the information being processed	Processes visual and verbal information simultaneously in many everyday tasks
Sensory memory	large - all information reaching the senses at any given time	Very brief - two seconds or less.	multiple, one for each sense.	visual information fades more rapidly than verbal.
Long-term memory (LTM)	Unlimited	Effectively unlimited, but subject to forgetting	Semantic (meaningful information), but other modalities can also be retained	Dual coding makes it easier to memorise new information

Memory stores

Key concepts

- STM – short-term memory
- LTM – long-term memory
- Encoding
- Storage
- Retrieval
- Sensory memory
- WM – working memory
- Acoustic encoding
- Semantic encoding
- Dual coding
- Schema

Make the link

...to the role of schemas in the topic of Prejudice.

Questions

1. What three processes can be used to describe any form of memory?
2. Is forming a new memory a simple and passive process?
3. How long does visual sensory memory last?
4. How many types of sensory memory are there?
5. What was the traditional view of how much information working memory can hold?
6. What is thought nowadays about the capacity limit of working memory?
7. Is working memory a temporary or permanent store?
8. Does working memory only hold acoustic information?
9. What type of LTM retains information about life events?
10. Besides storing information, what else can a schema do?

Activities

1. On your own, or with a partner, make a list of at least ten everyday activities where you make use of memory. (You will find that nearly everything involves memory in some way) Now go through the list, identifying the roles of different memory stores described in this section, such as sensory memory, WM and LTM. Think about the role of schemas, too.
2. Draw a blank version of the table on page 121 in your notes. Now close the textbook and try to fill in the details from memory. If you get stuck, refer back to the book. This 'retrieval practice' will help the details to stick in your memory (see chapter 7).

The multi-store model

Atkinson and Shiffrin (1968) provided the best-known theory of how sensory memory, working memory and LTM work together. They said that memory stores function in a linear (one-way) process, with each store acting as the gateway to the next store. Their model is known as the multi-store model of memory (MSM; alternatively, the 'modal model' or 'Atkinson-Shiffrin model').

The stores in the model are the ones that have already been described in this chapter. Atkinson and Shiffrin named these the 'sensory register', 'short-term store' and 'long-term store', but the meaning is the same. For consistency, and to reflect modern research terminology, this chapter will refer to them as sensory memory, WM and LTM.

The function of the sensory memory store may be to hold information for a brief period of time until you are able to focus your attention on it. After this has happened, the new information moves to the more long-lasting memory stores – working memory or long-term memory (see below). This makes evolutionary sense – people can't take in everything simultaneously and we must be able to switch attention in the case of threats, or so that we don't miss vital information. It also fits with what cognitive psychologists know about the limited capacity of mental processes (see chapter 1).

? Discussion point

Can you think of any other examples of sensory memory in action?

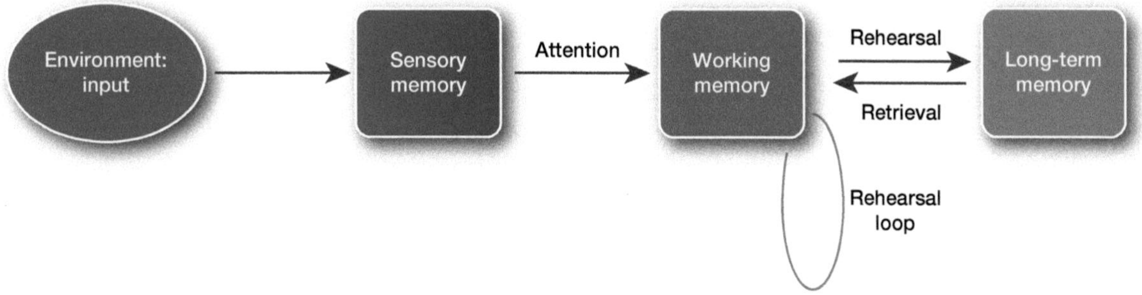

The multi-store model

Connection between stores in the MSM

One of the main contributions of the MSM was to provide an explanation of how the three key memory stores are connected together. According to the model, information coming in through the senses is placed briefly in sensory memory, which is shown to have multiple sub-stores (at least five). If **attention** is paid to information, it travels from there into WM. Attention is therefore a critical process – without it, nothing is ever processed or permanently stored.

In addition, sensory memory has a larger capacity than working memory, but fades very quickly. This means that a lot of information will fade before it can be successfully transferred to working memory. Working memory is a bottleneck in terms of taking in new information.

The longer an item is held in working memory, the better chance it has of being encoded to LTM, thereby forming a permanent memory trace. However, as discussed in the previous section, the capacity of WM is limited and information tends to be rapidly forgotten. The multi-store

Top tip

Note that several key elements in memory come in threes – three processes, three types of long-term memory, three stores in the MSM. Can you find any more?

model showed that people can hold information in WM for longer using a process called **maintenance rehearsal** – essentially, this means saying things repeatedly to yourself in your mind (also called 'rote rehearsal').

Maintenance rehearsal also results in information staying in WM for longer and being processed for longer, so the process plays a key role in encoding the information to LTM. A major prediction of the model is that information will be better remembered in the long term if it is maintained for as long as possible in the WM.

When information is retrieved from LTM it travels back to WM in order to be used. Information can also be lost from all three stores via forgetting. It is lost from WM in a process known as **decay** (see final section of this chapter), where the limited duration of the store leads to forgetting in around fifteen seconds. Decay occurs even more rapidly in SM.

You can hold information in WM for longer by rehearsing it – for example repeatedly saying a phone number aloud

Top tip

When explaining the MSM, ensure that you discuss the key processes of attention and maintenance rehearsal.

? Discussion point

Do you agree that holding/rehearsing things in your WM is a good way of encoding things to LTM? Think of your own experience of trying to memorise things, such as words in a foreign language, lines for a play, a shopping list or instructions for a task at work. How did you manage to do it?

What is the best way to memorise lines for a play?

Evaluation of the MSM

Supporting the model, there is good evidence of separate short-term and long-term stores. The serial position effect (see key study) supports this idea, and neurological evidence from brain scans suggests that these two stores involve different brain areas. Case studies of patients with brain damage to one of the stores but not both such as H.M. (see final section of this chapter) have supported the idea that there are two separate systems in different parts of the brain.

The **primacy effect** is a reliable finding from the recall of lists, where items from the start of a list are better remembered in comparison to the items in the middle. The **recency effect** is where later items are better remembered than the middle items. According to the MSM, the primacy effect occurs because early items are rehearsed and then encoded into LTM, but by the middle of the list there are too many items to rehearse (see key study). The recency effect occurs due to the final few items still being in WM when the list is recalled, but due to its limited capacity, the middle items are lost. This supports the idea of two main separate memory stores, WM and LTM. These two effects together are also called the serial position effect.

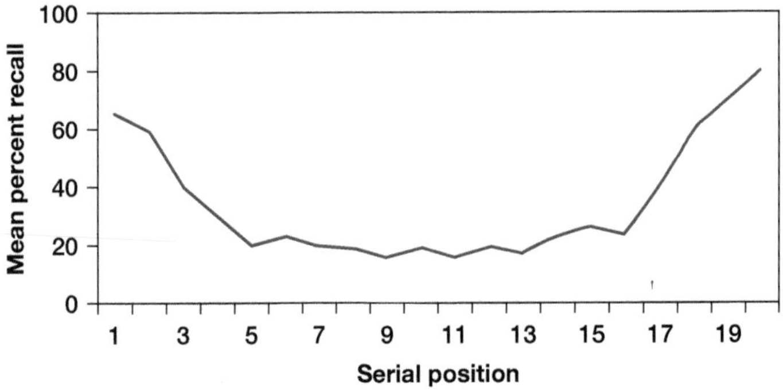

The serial position effect

Supporting this explanation of the primacy and recency effects, Glanzer and Cunitz (1966) conducted an experiment where they slowed down or speeded up the presentation of a list. With a faster list, there is less time to rehearse the first few items, and this led to a smaller primacy effect. Craik (1970) found that the recency effect disappears after a delay, supporting the idea that it is based on immediate recall from WM.

However, brain-damaged patients also present some problems for the model. Some patients with damaged rehearsal abilities are able to function in everyday jobs (Baddeley, 2012). This suggests that WM must be more complex than the model assumes.

The model is over-simplistic. Although the researchers did begin to recognise that short-term store is a form of 'working memory' and may have multiple components (Atkinson & Shiffrin, 1968, p.92–93), they didn't allow for attention playing an ongoing role in selecting, maintaining and processing tasks within working memory, something accepted by most researchers today (Cowan, 2017). They view memory stores as quite passive, and researchers have increasingly accepted that memory is an active process where people try to fill gaps and make sense of information.

Holding/rehearsing info does not guarantee that it is permanently stored in LTM. What is done with the information is more important than how long it is processed for – Craik and Tulving (1975) showed that information was better recalled if questions were asked about its meaning (e.g. 'is it a type of animal?'), rather than about its appearance (e.g. 'is it in capital letters?'), showing that meaningless maintenance rehearsal is not the best way of encoding information to LTM. They developed a theory around the idea that meaningful information is processed more deeply, and called it 'levels of processing' (see activity 3, on p.127).

Overall, MSM is a useful general overview of the structure of memory; however, it lacks detail and there are several more recent research findings that it cannot account for.

Items at the top of a list are usually better remembered than things further down

? Discussion point

What implications does the serial position effect have for your study habits?

Top tip

You could investigate the serial position effect for your assignment.

Key study: Murdock (1962): The serial position effect

Aim: *This study aimed to show that memory has more than one process. It used different lengths of list, and aimed to find out whether poorer recall of items at the beginning or end of a list was due to the amount of information presented, in line with the concept of WM being limited to seven items.*

Methodology: *Murdock gave participants lists of random words to remember and compared the chance of each word being recalled with its position in the list. The shortest lists were 10 items long and the longest lists were 40 items long.*

Findings: *The study found that words at the start of the list were better remembered than those in the middle. This is known as the primacy effect. Words at the end of the list were also better remembered – this is called the recency effect. Overall, these effects are known as the serial position effect. The findings of this study fit well with Atkinson and Shiffrin's (1968) multi-store model. The primacy effect can be explained in terms of easier rehearsal into LTM when there are fewer items to process, while* *the recency effect could be due to the limited capacity of WM – the last few items are retained and immediately recalled. A key finding was that the serial position effect was found regardless of the length of the list that was read out.*

Evaluation: *This was an important and influential study, and one that has been successfully replicated. It played a role in the development of the MSM and other theories. However, there are some limitations. It used random lists of words, meaning that it lacks mundane realism – it didn't use realistic, everyday tasks. It also didn't test items other than lists of words, such as pictures or sentences. As such, the items were not very meaningful to participants. It only looked at immediate, temporary storage, and didn't follow up memory for the items over the longer term, something that might have had more relevance to everyday life.*

Key concepts

- Multi-store model (MSM)
- Attention
- Maintenance rehearsal
- Primacy effect
- Recency effect
- Serial-position effect

Questions

1. How many sensory stores are there, according to the multi-store model?
2. What factor affects whether information is transferred from sensory memory to working memory, according the multi-store model?
3. Which has a larger capacity – sensory memory or working memory?
4. What process affects whether a stimulus is transferred from SM to WM?
5. What process can cause information to be held in working memory for longer?
6. According to the multi-store model, can new information go directly into LTM, without moving through working memory first?
7. What is the name of the effect whereby items at the beginning and end of a list are better remembered?
8. Why is the primacy effect thought to occur, and what might reduce or eliminate it?
9. Name two studies which investigated the serial position effect.
10. Do studies of brain damage support the MSM?

Activities

1. On one side of a page or piece of paper, draw a simple diagram of the multi-store model, showing the boxes linking together. Now, without referring to your notes and textbook, fill in the names of the stores and the processes that link them together.
2. On the other side of your page, write the following headings:
   - attention
   - maintenance rehearsal
   - forgetting
   - retrieval
   - practical example of the MSM in action.

   Write an explanation under each heading. Your response to both tasks can form the basis of a detailed essay answer on the multi-store model.
3. Find out more about the idea of *levels of processing*. This is a separate theory of memory, which could be used in answers on this area of the topic. The concept of meaningful information being more reliably encoded to LTM could be useful for your studies as well – it suggests that re-reading your notes is a bad study strategy but that generating questions and summarising notes would be much more effective (see also chapter 7 for advice on this).

The working memory model

Origins of the model

As the cognitive approach became dominant in the 1960s and researchers started to compare memory to the information processing of a computer, the multi-store model of memory became popular (Baddeley, 2012). However, it became clear that while useful as a general overview, the MSM could not explain the details of how we process everyday tasks such as writing, answering questions and following directions, in part because it was rooted in lab-based experiments with verbal information.

In the early 1970s, researchers Alan Baddeley and Graham Hitch tried to combine key facts about WM into a new model. They wanted to replace the MSM and other older theories, which they saw as limited and inaccurate. In doing so, they developed the **working memory model** (WMM; Baddeley & Hitch, 1974).

In particular, they focused on the way that WM is used as a flexible, active store with which we carry out numerous tasks on a day-to-day basis, such as holding a conversation, playing a game or following a map. Although they weren't the first to use the term 'working memory' instead of 'short-term memory', their work led to the term becoming more widely used and generally accepted. Their research developed the idea that WM is not just a memory store but also a system that can process information and solve problems. Their theory is known as the working memory model.

WM is used as a flexible, active store for everyday tasks such as following a map

Structure of WM

Baddeley and Hitch (1974) proposed a model with a central component called the **central executive (CE)**, which controls the other parts of the model. It is based on the attention we are able to allocate to a task, to different parts of the same task or to several tasks simultaneously.

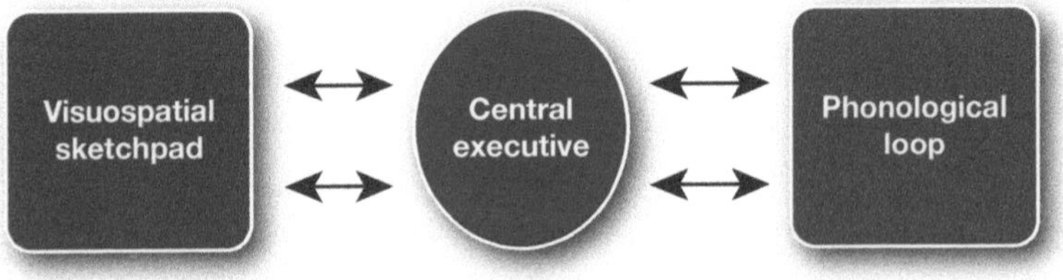

The original working memory model

? Discussion point

Can you imagine using these different parts of working memory as you try out a task? Baddeley suggests that you can experience working memory in action if you mentally walk around a flat or house and count how many windows it has. Take a moment to try this. Can you do it? Most people generate an image in their mind, and imagine moving from room to room.

The other major parts of the model were known as **slave systems**, because they were controlled by the CE. The original version of the model, shown above, included two slave systems processing different types of information. The **visuospatial sketchpad** processes visual tasks, and the **phonological loop** processes verbal information. In the windows task (see sidebar), the central executive forms a plan to tackle the problem, the visuospatial sketchpad allows you to picture the rooms in your mind and the phonological loop maintains and adds to the numbers. The CE also oversees the whole process to check that all the processes are running correctly.

Multi-tasking

The existence of two slave systems allowed for two different tasks to be completed at once, if enough attention is available. Of course, our attention is limited. Dividing attention between more than one task is called **multi-tasking** and it tends to result in both tasks being done poorly, especially if either task is complicated.

Inspired by research that had been done into brain-damaged individuals, Baddeley and colleagues gave ordinary participants tasks designed to use elements of WM, and told them to perform other tasks at the same time. These became known as **dual-task studies**. In one such study, Baddeley *et al.* (1973) asked participants to trace a 'hollow letter F' with a pointer at the same time as doing a verbal task. The two tasks could be done simultaneously without any deficit to either task. However, when participants tried to do two visual tasks at the same time, performance dropped significantly. The researchers concluded that a verbal and a spatial task can be done at the same time without much interference, as they involve separate slave systems.

Multi-tasking tends to result in each task being done poorly

Key features of the model

The WMM takes a very different view of short-term memory to the MSM – it sees it as an active processor rather than a store, that is, a system that is used to carry out day-to-day tasks rather than just hold information for a short time.

Just as MSM makes certain assumptions about how the memory stores work, there are key features of working memory according to this model. These are open to being tested and debated. They include:

- Processing time is based on real time to do tasks. For example, how long it takes to say a sentence in your head is equal to the time it would take to say it aloud. Doing a join-the-dots task in your head takes as long as it would take to do it with a pen.
- Attention is limited. Two tasks can be done simultaneously if they rely on different slave systems. However, complex and novel tasks will use up more attention from the CE, causing everything to run more slowly.

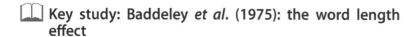

? Discussion point

Think of an activity that involves doing more than one thing at once, such as driving while having a conversation. What happens if one of the tasks suddenly becomes more difficult, for example, having to deal with an accident or diversion on the road ahead of you? (See p.382 for feedback.)

Key study: Baddeley *et al.* (1975): the word length effect

Aim: *In this study, Baddeley* et al. *looked for evidence of one of the key principles of the WM model – that processing something in your head (e.g. rehearsing a word) is done in real-time, that is, it takes the same amount of time as it would to actually say the word.*

Method: *The study tested recall of lists of words by giving people groups of five words which were either short (e.g. 'book') or long (e.g. 'university'). Participants were asked to recall the first three letters each time.*

Findings: *The researchers found that rather than being simply limited to seven items, the number of words that could be held in WM depended on the length of the word – the longer the words, the fewer people could retain. They concluded that memory span is inversely related to word length; this became known as the* ***word length effect****. It was concluded that the phonological loop has a time-limited capacity based on around two seconds of pronunciation time. This fits the WMM assumption that tasks generally take the same amount of time to process in working memory as they would take to do in real life. In contrast, the findings go against the MSM, which states that we can rehearse approximately seven items.*

Evaluation: *The research was useful in that it helped to distinguish between the two main models of memory, supporting the WMM over the MSM. As a lab experiment, it was well controlled, though rather artificial. The findings have been supported by several other studies, including research that found that bilingual speakers of English and Welsh had a shorter digit span in Welsh, in which it takes slightly longer to pronounce the numbers (Ellis and Hennelly, 1980).*

Top tip

The word length effect is evidence *against* the MSM and evidence *for* the WMM. Therefore, it can be used as part of your evaluation of either model.

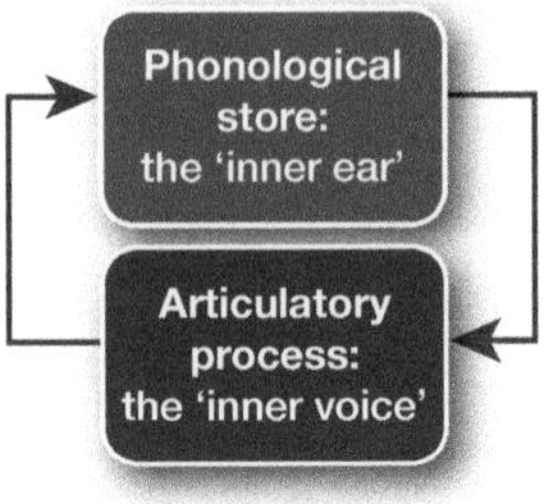

Phonological loop

The working memory model has been continually changed and improved. One of the earliest changes came when Baddeley and colleagues realised that the ability to understand words must be separate from the ability to rehearse them. This was because some brain-damaged individuals could do one of these things but not the other. Therefore, they altered the theory to show the phonological loop as having two parts:

- The articulatory process. This is a rehearsal loop – the 'inner voice' when you say or rehearse words inside your head.
- The phonological store. This is responsible for brief storage/comprehension of sounds. It is nicknamed the 'inner ear'.

Another problem with the original version of the model was that it did not provide a clear explanation of how stimuli from different parts can be combined and linked with LTM. Baddeley therefore proposed a third slave system, the **episodic buffer** (Baddeley, 2000). This is seen as the mind's way of combining a mixture of sights and sounds into a coherent 'episode' that can then be encoded into episodic LTM.

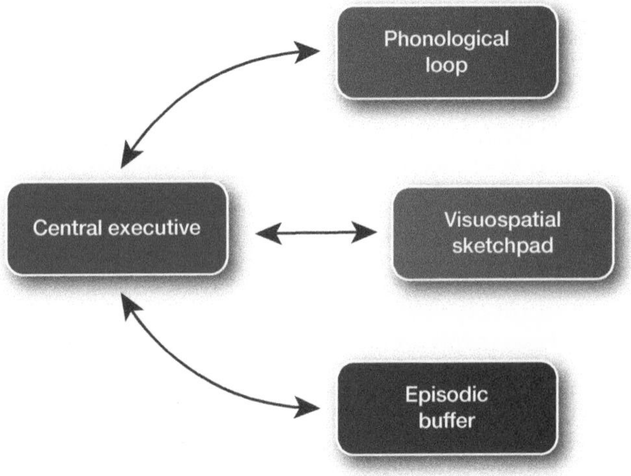

Current working memory model

Features of the WMM	• Proposed by Baddeley and Hitch in 1974. • Emphasises active processing – does not see WM as a passive store of information. • Describes the part of our mind that we use for day-to-day tasks and problem solving. • States that we can do more than one task at once if attention from CE is sufficient. • Time to process tasks in the mind is equivalent to real time taken to do tasks.
Elements of the WMM	• Phonological loop: slave system that processes sounds and language. • Visuospatial sketchpad: slave system that processes images and spatial tasks. • Episodic buffer: slave system that combines stimuli into coherent events. • Articulatory process: part of phonological loop; rehearses words and sounds. Limited to 2 seconds pronunciation time. • Central executive: based on attention and controls all slave systems. • Phonological store: part of the phonological loop; allows us to comprehend the sounds of words.

Evaluation

The model explains certain key facts about WM, for example the word length effect, that were not explained by earlier theories. The word length effect supports the idea that processing of tasks is based on the real-world time to do the tasks, for example, to pronounce words.

Unlike other models, it can be used to explain our ability to keep track of a 'to do' list – prospective memory. According to this view, the CE, as the system for attention, would keep track of whether there are any tasks to be done at any given time. However not every researcher agrees with this view – some believe that prospective memories come to mind without us having to constantly pay a small amount of attention to them (Marsh *et al.*, 2005)

A weakness of the model is that the function and capacity of the CE is unclear: we don't know how much it can hold, how it manages to be modality-free or even if there is only one CE (Eysenck, 1986, argued that it might not be a unitary store). This is one area where a clearer understanding of the biology of working memory might be helpful in order to explain how our system for attention can link to slave systems based on vision, language, episodic memory and possibly others.

Theories need to change over time to take account of new evidence and this model has been able to integrate a large number of newer findings, mainly by making changes to the original model. It has also been used for real-world tasks – the phonological loop is thought to be essential for language acquisition (Baddeley, 2012) and a deficit in the phonological store has been linked to disorders of language development (Gathercole & Baddeley, 1990).

? Discussion point

Question: Why is this called a model? What is the difference between a theory and a model? (See p.382 for feedback.)

The phonological loop is thought to be essential for language acquisition

Key concepts

- Working memory model (WMM)
- Attention
- Central executive (CE)
- Slave system
- Visuospatial sketchpad
- Phonological loop
- Multi-tasking
- Dual-task studies
- Word length effect
- Articulatory process
- Phonological store
- Episodic buffer

Questions

1. What did the working memory model aim to do better than previous models of memory?
2. What is the central component of the working memory model called?
3. What general term did Baddeley and Hitch (1974) use to describe the other key systems of the working memory model?
4. What effect did the study by Baddeley *et al.* (1975) show?
5. What term means doing more than one task at a time?
6. Which part of WM deals with verbal information?
7. True or false: the working memory model states that processing time in WM is equivalent to the real time it would take to do a task.
8. What slave system was added to the model and explains how information can be combined into coherent episodes?
9. What part of the WMM is least well understood?
10. Has the working memory model helped to explain performance on real tasks?

Activities

1. Would the following mainly require use of the central executive, phonological loop or visuospatial sketchpad? Would any of them require more than one of the systems to work together?
   - Counting to 100
   - Parking your car
   - Doing a maze
   - Singing
   - Composing a poem
   - Listening to speech
2. Take a moment to design an experiment on multi-tasking (you don't need to actually carry it out). Perhaps it could be a comparison of how well males and females multi-task. What two (or more) tasks would you use, and how would you measure success on the tasks? What things would you need to keep constant between your two groups?

Forgetting

We have all had the experience of forgetting something important – a person's name, or a fact that we want to learn for an exam, perhaps. There is some debate about why information is lost from memory. This section looks the main psychological explanations of forgetting. It is important to bear in mind the three main memory stores discussed in the first section of this chapter, and consider that these stores may lose information for different reasons.

Trace Decay

One theory of forgetting is that information (the trace) simply fades away over time (it decays). This is known as **trace decay** theory. It is a common experience in everyday life – something can quickly leave our minds, such as when a person tells you their name and just a minute later you find that you can't recall it.

Some memories rapidly fade from our minds

Decay applies particularly to sensory and working memory, and follows from the idea that these stores have a very limited duration. If the length of time something can stay in the stores is limited, then at some point it must decay and be forgotten. Sensory memory is thought to be limited to a couple of seconds at most. The duration of working memory is also very brief if the person does not make use of maintenance rehearsal.

Peterson and Peterson (1959) tested this theory in working memory by showing 'trigrams' of letters (such 'TBX') to participants who then had to count backwards from a number in 3s (for example, '567, 564, 561...') to distract them. The results suggest that information typically decays within less than 30 seconds. This may seem very rapid but it is something that most of us will have experienced – think about opening a cupboard or walking in to a room to get something, only to find that you have forgotten what you were looking for!

Decay is harder to demonstrate in LTM, in part because so much information is stored that it becomes hard to know whether things have truly been forgotten, or have just become harder to retrieve. Atkinson and Shiffrin (1968) thought that LTM forgetting was at least partly due to decay. However, Bjork (1994) argues that items are not forgotten but simply lose retrieval strength, meaning that they become harder to locate in long-term memory.

Interestingly, students tend not to allow for the decay of memory when they are studying. Koriat *et al.* (2004) found that although people accepted the principle of forgetting via decay, they didn't allow for it when they predicted how much information they would remember after a period of time. It appears that when we are studying, we can greatly underestimate the role of forgetting (or at least, of information becoming less accessible).

Top tip

In the Koriat et al study, estimates of how many words people would forget after ten minutes were the same as estimates of how many would be forgotten after a year!

Evaluation

Decay is a more appropriate explanation of forgetting for WM than for LTM. Research studies have demonstrated rapid and large-scale forgetting over brief timescales. Sensory memory is also thought to fade or decay very quickly. However, studies such as Peterson and Peterson (1959) have tended to use arbitrary and meaningless information. It may be that something significant, or which could be linked to LTM schemas, would not decay as quickly. The Peterson and Peterson research does not rule out displacement (see below) from the numbers in the distraction task and, overall, it's very difficult to distinguish between the roles of decay and displacement.

It is widely assumed that memories decay from LTM over time but the alternative view that they simply become less accessible is also popular. It's important to distinguish between LTM forgetting and failure to learn. Rather than having been forgotten, some things (perhaps some ideas studied during your classes) were never properly learned in the first place. This could be because the information was presented too rapidly to process in WM, was not practised soon enough or because it was never fully understood or linked to schemas.

Displacement

Working memory has a limited capacity (Baddeley *et al.*, 1975; Miller, 1956). If it is viewed as a store with a limited amount of space (whether this is seen in terms of the number of items or the pronunciation time), then new information coming in must push out or displace existing information. Forgetting by pushing information out is known as **displacement**. You can think of it as like trying to squeeze items into a full suitcase and other things popping out.

> **Make the link**
>
> ...with variables as part of research in psychology (see chapter 8).

Waugh and Norman (1965) conducted a study to compare the roles of decay and displacement:

- Student participants were read a list of 16 numbers. The last digit in the list was a repeat of an earlier number and was called the 'probe' digit. Participants had to attempt to recall the number which came after the probe in the list. (For example, '2, 4, 6, 7, 8, 1, 8, 3, 7, 5, 4, 9, 1, 5, 8, 6', followed by 3 as the probe digit. The number to be recalled would be 7.)
- The researchers varied how many distracting numbers occurred between the probe and the recall attempt. For example, if the probe was at the start of the list there were more items between it and the recall attempt than if it was near the end of the list.
- They also varied how quickly the numbers were read. Reading the list more quickly should leave less time for decay – so more displacement can occur in the same amount of time. This stops decay from being a confounding variable in the experiment.
- Numbers which came later in the list were recalled far better, supporting the displacement theory of forgetting. If this difference was due to decay then reading the numbers faster should have improved performance, but this was found to make only a slight difference.

Evaluation

Waugh and Norman's study (1965) usefully distinguishes between decay and displacement. It suggests that both can play a role in forgetting, but that displacement makes more of a difference than decay. This suggests that when we forget things from WM on an everyday basis, it occurs mainly because of new, incoming information.

However, this research is based on an outdated concept of working memory as a passive, unitary store. It doesn't allow for the different parts of working memory that are shown in the working memory model.

Discussion point

What are the implications of decay and displacement for learning in class or for revision?

Interference

LTM seems to be susceptible to **interference** between material that is similar. This is to say, we may forget some things because we mix them up in our memories. Unlike a computer, the human mind struggles to store very similar sets of information without getting them confused. In contrast, when things are unique, or at least very distinctive, it's much easier to remember them. For example, you can probably remember the journey for a one-off school trip much better than you can remember all of your daily journeys to school.

Retroactive interference is where new information interferes with old, such as finding it hard to remember your old phone number after you have memorised a new one. **Proactive interference** is when old information interferes with new information, such as looking in a drawer where something used to be kept.

Baddeley and Hitch (1977) studied rugby players' recall of a season's fixtures. Some players had taken part in fewer games due to injury. It was found that those players had a better recall of the early season fixtures they had played – presumably because they had played fewer games to confuse. These players had not experienced as much interference in their LTM.

Evaluation

Interference appears to play an important role in LTM, and shows the importance of information being meaningfully distinctive if it is not to be forgotten. The Baddeley and Hitch rugby player study (1977) seems to show this well in a realistic context. However, as it was a natural experiment, the study lacked control of extraneous variables. We can't be certain that the players' poorer memory for fixtures was due only to interference. There could have been some other difference between the groups – perhaps the injured players spent more time thinking about the fixtures, as they were spending less time training.

The theory of interference is highly computational, fitting well with the information processing model that is popular among some cognitive psychologists (see chapter 1). However, it struggles to fit with the concept of LTM having an unlimited capacity. Experts in their field are a good example of how LTM does not appear to be limited – they learn so much about the same topic that they should suffer from a lot of interference, yet knowing a lot about a subject makes it easier to take in new information about it.

One possible explanation for this is based on schemas. When people are beginners in a subject, their schema knowledge is

Top tip

If you are asked to analyse these explanations of forgetting, a good way to pick up marks would be to compare them to each other. You could also analyse the assumptions and supporting evidence, and give real world examples.

simplistic. However, an expert makes much more subtle distinctions and will, in effect, form multiple different schemas where ordinary people only have one. For example, most people might have a schema for 'beetle', while an entomologist (insect researcher) may have formed multiple different schemas (via accommodation – see page 28) for the hundreds of different species of beetle. Two types of beetle might look the same to a beginner and be subject to interference, but will look very different to an expert and not be easily confused.

Cue-dependent forgetting

Memories may be stored accurately in LTM but not be retrievable – it is somehow difficult or impossible to bring the information to mind. The information remains in memory, but retrieval failure occurs if there is no cue to bring the information to mind. This fits with Bjork's view (1994) that information becomes inaccessible rather than being subject to decay (see above).

There are two types of **cues** that can affect memory and forgetting:

1. State cues – being in the same physical state as when information was learned, for example having consumed alcohol or not
2. Context cues – being in the same place as when information was learned, for example going back to the classroom where you studied something.

Research on state dependency showed that when learning took place after consuming a drug or alcohol, learners were able to recall the information better when they had consumed the drug or alcohol again, rather than when they had not. For example, Darley *et al.* (1973) found that people who had hidden money after smoking marijuana were only able to find it if they got high again. Of course, the same applies if something is learned sober – it is better recalled if sober at the time of retrieval.

Godden and Baddeley (1975) demonstrated the importance of context cues in an experiment on divers, conducted at Stirling University. Members of the diving club were asked to learn word lists either on land or underwater. They were then asked to recall the words either in the same physical context (for example, learn underwater/retrieve underwater) or the different one (for example, learn underwater/retrieve on land). The researchers found that retrieval was significantly better in the same context that the lists had been learned.

The tip of the tongue phenomenon has been widely studied

The **tip-of the-tongue phenomenon** is where people are sure that they know something but cannot recall it. They may be able to recall some details of the word or idea, and feel like it is almost coming back to mind; Brown and McNeill (1966, p.326) reported that a participant would *'appear to be in mild torment, something like on the brink of a sneeze, and if he found the word his relief was considerable'*.

People often suffer from the tip-of the-tongue phenomenon if they try to recall a word which is rare or that they don't use very often. This is very specific to the individual, but try to recall the following (alone, not in a group):

- The capital of Argentina.
- The name of a Jewish place of worship.
- The hero from Ancient Greece who fought the Minotaur.
- The type of triangle which has three unequal sides.
- The term for the art of stuffing animals.
- The Freudian defence mechanism where someone's behaviour is the opposite of their true feelings.

Can you remember the name of the person who fought the minotaur in the Greek legend?

For some of these (the ones you don't get immediately), you may get a feeling that you know (or should know) the answer, and can perhaps say something about the sound of the item or how long it is. Perhaps you even get a sense that you can almost recall the word. If so, it's on the tip of your tongue.

An important finding in terms of cue-dependent forgetting is that when an item is on the tip of someone's tongue, a cue such as the first letter is often enough to prompt them to recall it (Brown & McNeill, 1966). This shows that it is possible to *almost* remember something, and that in such cases of forgetting, all that is needed is a cue.

Memories may be described as being 'on the tip of your tongue'

Evaluation

Cue-dependent forgetting applies particularly to LTM, and as such it has many practical consequences. It shows that there are risks to trying to learn something in a particular biological state, and perhaps helps to explain why people forget so much after drinking alcohol (although failure to focus enough attention is also a major factor).

Using context cues and surroundings could be very beneficial to learning. However, and perhaps more importantly, learning in multiple contexts seems to be beneficial. So, for example, while it is hard to learn something in a classroom and then retrieve it in an exam hall, it would be easier to retrieve the information if it has been learned in lots of different contexts. The more variable the learning contexts, the better (Smith & Rothkopf, 1984). This could have implications for where you do your revision.

Top tip

Conduct your revision in multiple places, so that the memories are not associated with a single context.

Forgetting due to brain damage

A key assumption of the biological approach throughout psychology is that all thoughts, beliefs and memories have a physical basis in the brain. Therefore, if the brain is damaged in some way, memories can be lost. Indeed, entire areas that process particular types of memory could be destroyed through injury or illness.

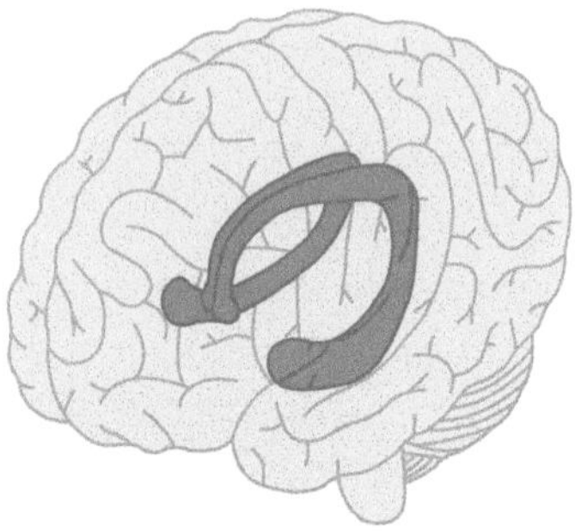
The hippocampus

One brain area in particular has been repeatedly linked to episodic LTM – the **hippocampus**. This seahorse-shaped area of the limbic system is essential for new long-term memories to be formed. While the number of neurons we have is apparently fixed in most brain areas – new neurons are 'born' in the hippocampus throughout life (Eriksson *et al.*, 1998). This structure can be larger in some people than others and it has been found to be larger in taxi drivers, perhaps because their job places an exceptionally great demand on them to learn spatial information (Maguire *et al.*, 2000). However, cells in the hippocampus can also get smaller due to the effects of stress (McEwen & Sapolsky, 1995). This suggests that stress or other lifestyle issues could potentially harm memory.

WM appears to rely on different brain areas. The frontal lobes of the neocortex seem to play a key role in tasks that require planning, keeping track of information, and making judgements. The visual areas of the neocortex also play a role in the actions of the visuospatial sketchpad.

Researchers have particularly focused on unusual cases where people have had a part of their brain removed in an operation or due to an accident. In one famous case, a patient named Henry Molaison (referred to as H.M. during his lifetime to preserve anonymity) had his entire hippocampus removed, as well as some of the nearby areas of the temporal lobes of the neocortex. This resulted from exploratory surgery, but had the unintended side-effect of destroying his ability to form any new episodic or semantic long-term memories (see key study).

Make the link

...with research ethics and the principle of anonymity.

There are also cases of people who have lost WM function due to brain damage. In one such case, a patient who had experienced a head injury through a motorbike accident had a severely reduced WM capacity, but his LTM function and learning were normal.

Evaluation

As well as telling us about the potential role of brain areas in forgetting, brain injury cases also establish further evidence that WM and LTM are largely separate, supporting the memory store model of memory. However, they don't tell us much about forgetting in everyday situations. If you forget something in your school or college exams, it is usually because it was not well learned and therefore never fully encoded to LTM, or because the information is difficult to retrieve from memory. It is not because you have experienced damage to your brain.

Make the link

...with the multi-store model of memory.

Specific memories do rely on brain function, but they depend more on the strength of connections between groups of neurons – connections that form through **long-term potentiation**. These can be strengthened via practice of the learned information.

Key study: Scoville and Milner (1957): the case of 'H.M.'

Aim: *Some of the most dramatic cases of memory loss come from individuals who have been brain damaged – accidentally or through surgery. One such case was Henry Molaison (often referred to as 'H.M.'), a young man who suffered from very severe epilepsy in the 1950s. It was not possible to improve his condition using medication, and so his doctor, William Scoville, decided to try a novel surgical procedure – removing a large area from his temporal lobe, the hippocampus. This case study aimed to find out the nature of his memory loss, and therefore deduce the role of the hippocampus in memory.*

Method: *The surgery was not part of the research. Instead, the researchers tried to investigate the effects that the surgery had on H.M. They conducted interviews with the patient and his family, and administered a range of tests including an IQ test and a memory test – the 'Wechsler Memory Scale'.*

Findings: *In the opinion of his family, Henry's personality was unchanged and his IQ was undiminished. However, he suffered from dramatic loss of memory function after the operation. He was still able to recall his early life but could no longer remember anything from around the time of the operation. More importantly still, he could not encode any new information to LTM. This left him in a permanent state of amnesia, unable to hold a sustained conversation or take in anything new. His score on the Wechsler memory test was zero in some areas and he* 'failed to improve with repeated practice' *(p.17). Curiously, however, H.M. was still able to learn new skills – Milner (1970) later reported that he was still able to learn a mirror-drawing task, even though he had no recollection of his repeated attempts at the task. This suggested that his procedural LTM might have been unharmed by the damage to his hippocampus.*

Evaluation: *It is important to realise that this research is a case study, not an experiment, and the study of H.M. should not be considered unethical – his memory loss was an accidental side effect of earlier surgery while this research focused on tests and interviews. The precise nature of the damage has made him an especially useful case to science. It was a tragic case for Henry Molaison himself, but he became the most studied man in the history of psychology. This study in particular helped to establish the key role that the hippocampus plays in memory.*

Henry Molaison in 1986, aged 60, enjoying an unmemorable memory experiment at Massachusetts Institute of Technology

Key concepts

- Trace decay
- Displacement
- Interference
- Proactive interference
- Retroactive interference
- Tip-of-the-tongue phenomenon
- Hippocampus
- Brain damage
- Long-term potentiation

Questions

1. Which memory store(s) does decay relate to?
2. What did Bjork (1994) say about decay in LTM?
3. Which theory did Waugh and Norman's (1965) experiment mainly support – trace decay or displacement?
4. Which form of interference is involved if you accidentally type your old password into a website?
5. Name two types of cues that can affect forgetting.
6. Which part of the brain plays a key role in WM?
7. For what type of memory is the hippocampus important?
8. Did H.M.'s personality or IQ change as a result of his operation?
9. What is the term for the changes in brain cell structure that occur when learning?
10. On the basis of the research into context cues, should you do all of your revision in the school/college library?

GO! Activities

1. Think of further real-world examples of retroactive interference and proactive interference.
2. On the basis of what you have covered in this chapter, there are numerous principles that you can apply to your own learning, such as the limited duration of working memory, the role of attention, the role of schemas when learning new information, or the role of interference in forgetting. There are also several popular ideas about learning that are not supported by the research evidence. Make a leaflet about practical study ideas that could be given to younger pupils. Ensure that it is clear and does not use too much terminology. Use images and make the leaflet visually attractive. Give real examples of using strategies, too. The information on studying given towards the end of chapter 7 could help you with this.

End of topic project

You will conduct a case study into memory in the context of study strategies. Select a participant from your classes or outside school, ensuring that you get informed consent. The aim will be to find out how effectively the participant is studying and revising, and to make recommendations from your knowledge of memory to improve this effectiveness (see chapter 8 for general information on the case study method of research).

- Conduct a brief case history, using a semi-structured interview, to reveal the following points. Find out, up until now...
  - How often the participant typically studies outside class in general and for exams/ tests.
  - Where, when and how thoroughly the participant completes his/her homework and revision.
  - What approach their peers and family members take/have taken to their studies.
  - The participant's views on learning and revision, and any changes that have taken place in these views.
  - Memory strategies the participant has adopted, for example, mnemonics, flash cards, etc.
  - How well the participant has performed academically, by their own estimation and by objective criteria (e.g. grades versus grade average).
- Now, follow up on this case history. Try using observation to find out how effectively the participant is studying – this could involve analysing a recording.
- Prepare recommendations based on your findings and your knowledge of human memory.
- If your participant consents, you could make a poster showing your results.

End of topic specimen exam questions

1.	Explain the working memory model, referring to research evidence.	12 marks
2.	Explain the features and functions of long-term memory.	6 marks
3.	Evaluate the decay theory of forgetting.	6 marks
4.	Analyse three explanations of forgetting.	15 marks

6 Stress

For the topic of Stress, you should be able to explain:

- The physiology of stress.
- Health effects of stress.
- Sources of stress.
- Individual differences in the stress response.
- Types of coping strategies.
- Research evidence relevant to the topic.

You need to develop the following skills:

- Explaining concepts and processes relevant to stress.
- Explaining, analysing and evaluating psychological theories and research evidence relevant to stress.
- Using research evidence to back up your explanations of human behaviour.
- Applying your understanding of stress to real situations.

! Syllabus note

Stress is a topic in the Individual Behaviour unit in Higher Psychology. National 5 students should instead study the option topic Phobias (chapter 3).

Make the link

Your studies of Biology or Human Biology will help with this topic.

We use the term stress on a daily basis

What is stress, and why do we experience it? Stress can be defined as our reaction to demands which exceed our ability to cope. However, all of the words in such a definition need further explanation. How do people react to stress? What demands cause stress? What is coping, and why are some people better able to cope than others? These issues will be explored in this chapter.

The physiology of stress

The fight-or-flight response

A short period of intense stress is known as **acute stress**. This could happen if you are in a fight, argue with your family or even if you have to give a speech. The way your body responds to acute stress is known as the **fight-or-flight response** (also called the 'acute stress response'; Cannon, 1927).

When faced by an immediate severe threat, an animal or person reacts by releasing energy and preparing for action – either self-defence ('fight') or running away ('flight'). The outcome is a group of changes in our bodies which are the same no matter whether we fight or run – either way, the body is prepared for expending energy and using its muscles. Note that psychologists tend to use the term 'stressor' to mean the stimulus that causes stress, such as an argument or a threat.

The following chart summarises several major changes during fight-or-flight:

Raised heart rate	Increases blood pressure to pump glucose and oxygen to the muscles
Sweating	Helps cool the body in a fight or when running away
Tense muscles	A side effect of increased blood flow to the muscles in preparation for action
Increased blood clotting	Reduces bleeding in a fight situation
Glucose released into bloodstream	Stored energy is used to deal with the emergency
Slowed digestion	Side effect of reduced blood flow; causes nausea and loss of appetite
Heightened vision and awareness	All focus is on immediate threat and other things are ignored

Explanations of fight-or-flight

When explaining the evolutionary approach to psychology, the first chapter of this book described the 'EEA', where humans lived a hunter-gatherer existence. It is difficult to make sense of fight-or-flight without understanding this evolutionary past. In the modern world, the fight-or-flight response is often unhelpful – for example, nobody really wants to sweat and tremble when giving a speech or just before a job interview. Nobody wants to have clammy hands or feel sick at the start of an exam. Why, then, would our bodies make things so difficult for us?

The answer can be partly explained in that many of today's stressors didn't exist for the bulk of human evolution. There were no job interviews, exams, money worries or traffic jams for the vast majority of our species' history and these things have not been around for long enough to make a significant difference to the human gene pool.

According to this approach, therefore, the fight-or-flight response evolved to aid survival. It helped our ancestors' bodies to prepare rapidly in the face of a threat, making them more likely to win fights or successfully evade predators. Any individual who had a weaker fight-or-flight response would have been more vulnerable to being killed and, therefore, less likely to pass their genes on to future generations. This helps us to understand why our heart rate rises and we release energy when stressed – even when it is no longer useful in the modern world.

You may feel acute stress if you have to give a speech

Top tip

If you are trying to describe fight-or-flight in the exam, think of a situation that you have experienced that made you very tense and when you experienced your heart beating faster. Use this as an example in your answer.

? Discussion point

What kind of things make you feel stressed?

Analysis of fight-or-flight

Acute stress is important but it is only part of the problem we face from stress. In practice, it is often the long-term effects of stress that cause more worry. In addition, fight-or-flight is not shown in every species. Some animals such as snakes use a 'play dead' strategy in response to a threat; sometimes humans also 'freeze' in a threatening situation. It is over-simplistic to view all acute stress in terms of fight-or-flight.

Your body will prepare itself if you need to run away from a threat

Some groups still live hunter-gatherer existences where the fight-or-flight response is more useful

? Discussion point

What would be the stressors in a hunter-gatherer society?

The general adaptation syndrome

Fight-or-flight focuses on the response to immediate threats, but it is now recognised that this is just part of a much larger process. Not all threats are dealt with immediately – some occur repeatedly, while other stimuli might not be threatening at all in the short term but can add to our stress over longer timescales. Psychologists refer to prolonged or repeated stressful situations as **chronic stress**. (See the next section for more on this topic.)

Hungarian-Canadian researcher Hans Selye (1956) believed that the acute stress response was the first part of a more complex syndrome.

While previous researchers had talked about fight-or-flight, Selye realised that the stress response had long-term effects and that a similar response could be triggered by a huge range of stimuli. He also suggested that the stress response to positive events could be the same as that for threats and that while stress could cause illness, some stress could be a positive thing.

Selye came up with one of the key biological theories of stress – the **general adaptation syndrome** theory. It states that stress is cumulative, just as physical stressors impact on a bridge or road. As such, it can be described as an 'engineering model' of stress. Selye also helped to popularise the modern-day concept of stress, a term that had previously been used inconsistently and in a number of different contexts (Jones & Bright, 2001).

A medical doctor by training, Selye believed that the changes his experimental rats experienced were an example of the way all animals, including humans, react to stressors such as illness. The exact nature of the stimulus wasn't important – all stressors impact on us in the same way, according to the theory, and it was therefore a 'general' response. The reaction to stress is called 'adaptation'; Selye believed that this is an important part of how the body adapts to environmental challenges. The response was called a 'syndrome' because it involves a set of biological symptoms that occur together (see key study).

Key study: Selye's (1936) study of stress in rats

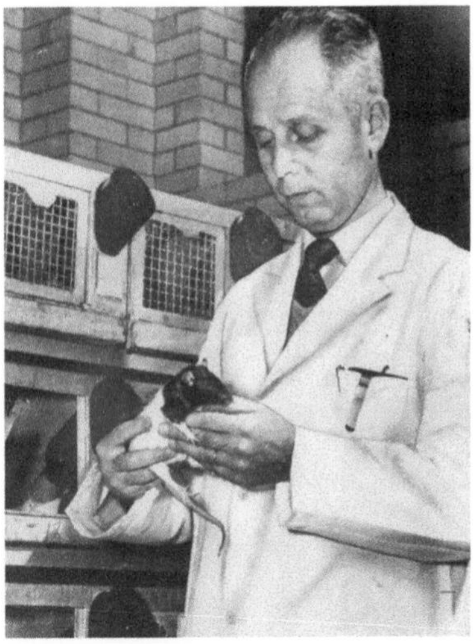

Hans Seyle carrying out the study

Aim: *Selye was trying to discover a new hormone that appeared to have an effect on the adrenal glands. He realised that his experimental rats were reacting to the stress of injections, not to the substance itself. He decided to test this out by subjecting rats to a range of different stressors and comparing the effects.*

Method: *He subjected rats to a number of different stressors, including surgical injury, extremes of temperature and injections of toxic substances such as formaldehyde. These stressors were repeated over many weeks so that the animals could not recover.*

Findings: *The animals showed a physiological triad: enlargement of adrenal glands, bleeding from ulcers in the digestive system and shrinking of lymph tissue (the body areas that produce white blood cells). After 6 to 48 hours of treatment, these systems returned to normal. However, after a further one to three months, symptoms returned, and the animal became vulnerable to disease. Because* *the response to all of the stressors was the same, Selye concluded that this was the body's general stress response to all threats.*

Evaluation: *Selye's study showed a systematic change over time, and being a lab experiment, it kept other variables constant. However, it is hard to reliably generalise the findings from rats to humans. The experiment was also highly cruel to the rats, and therefore, unethical. In addition to this, Bell (2014) has reported that Selye was sponsored by tobacco companies who were keen to blame health problems such as heart disease on stress rather than on smoking.*

Stages of the syndrome

Because the syndrome occurred in three distinct stages, Selye included three main stages of stress in his theory:

In a race, a runner's body adapts to the stress

1. **General alarm reaction**. The body's reactions are heightened and a 'fight or flight' reaction is experienced. Internally, the adrenal glands enlarge and stomach ulcers may be present. The immune system is damaged, with a shrinking of the lymph (white blood cell) system. This stage can last for several hours as the body reacts to a new stressor.
2. **Resistance**. If the stressor persists, the body starts to adapt to it. The body obtains energy by burning fats. Even though the stressor is still present, symptoms from the alarm stage disappear, as the body adapts. Selye (1956) compared this to a runner midway through a race – they are running at their peak and not yet significantly tired but they are using up energy fast.
3. **Exhaustion**. If the stress is prolonged for weeks without being overcome, the body may become exhausted. After a month or more, symptoms from the first stage reappear. Ultimately, this can result in **diseases of adaptation**, such as heart problems, and psychological disorders such as depression.

Evaluation

The general adaptation syndrome is a detailed theory of stress, based on a large body of experimental evidence. The theory is based on sound knowledge of biological systems and detailed experiments looking at changes in the body. It links mainly to the biological approach to psychology.

However, a lot of the supporting research has been done on animals (especially rats and birds), making it harder to apply to humans, as well as the obvious ethical issues of harm to the participants. In addition, the use of extreme physical stressors such as injuries and injection of toxic substances in Selye's 1936 study makes it hard to generalise the findings to everyday life. It can't be assumed that the same physical reactions would occur due to ordinary human stressors such as having an argument or being late for class.

In recent years, the idea that all stressors produce the same physiological response has been challenged. Instead, it may be the case that it is only when the stressors are at an unusually high level that the body responds to them all similarly (Goldstein & Kopin, 2007).

Key concepts

- Stress
- Acute stress
- Fight-or-flight response
- Adrenaline
- Chronic stress
- Stressor
- General adaptation syndrome
- Alarm
- Resistance
- Exhaustion
- Disease of adaptation

Questions

1. Which term means the effects of a stimulus on the body and mind, 'stress' or 'stressor'?
2. What is meant by 'acute stress'?
3. The fight-or-flight response involves an animal or person preparing for self-defence or what other action?
4. The heart rate rises during fight-or-flight. What else happens in the body? Name two things.
5. What is 'chronic stress'?
6. Give an example of a situation that could cause fight-or-flight.
7. When did the symptoms of the alarm stage disappear in Selye's rats?
8. What are diseases of adaptation?
9. What over-simplistic assumption is made by 'engineering' models of stress?
10. Were there any ethical issues with Selye's research?

GO! Activities

1. Draw a diagram of a person and label it with the changes that happen during fight-or-flight.
2. Draw three boxes in your notes, filling a whole page. Then try to explain the three stages of the general adaptation syndrome model, one in each box, without reading from the textbook or your notes. Write as much as you can and include information from Selye's 1936 experiment. If you get stuck, check back and read the section again, then go back to the task. Do this until you have written a full explanation of each stage. This 'retrieval practice' will help the details to stick in your memory (see chapter 7).
3. Read this short article by Selye which appeared in *Nature* in 1936. (It can be accessed online at http://bit.ly/1FziKxA). Prepare a short evaluation of the study to share with classmates. Consider ethical points and also issues such as external validity (see chapter 8).

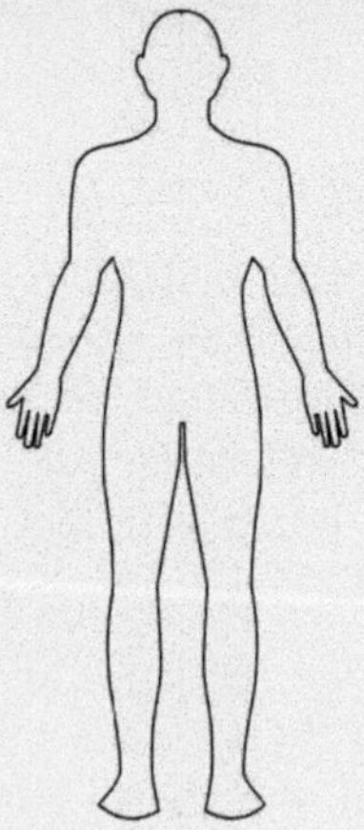

Stress and health

The role of hormones

The changes that occur during both acute and chronic stress are governed by the release of hormones in the body. Two hormones in particular are associated with stress. The release of **adrenaline** triggers the processes of acute stress. This helps the body to prepare for an immediate threat by releasing energy and raising the heart rate so that energy can be pumped to muscles via the bloodstream. Adrenaline is released from our adrenal glands.

In longer-term stressful situations, lasting hours or days, a different process occurs. A key hormone here is **cortisol**. Cortisol is released during the resistance stage of the general adaptation syndrome. While cortisol also releases energy, it does so in a different way – by using up stored energy from fats and muscles. A side effect of cortisol is that it suppresses digestion, making the individual lack their usual appetite when they are suffering from prolonged stress. This can start to have a harmful effect on the body. Cortisol is also released from our adrenal glands, but from a different part – the adrenal cortex (the outer part of the gland).

The release of adrenaline and cortisol is governed by two different systems in the body, one of which is associated with acute stress, and one of which is associated with chronic stress:

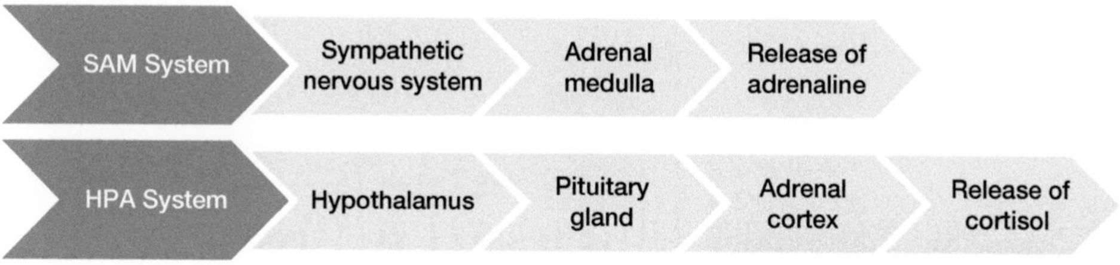

Biological processes that control our stress response

The sympatho-adrenal medullary system

The acute stress response is triggered by the nervous system – a network of neurons which includes the brain, the spinal cord and all of the nerves around the body, including those which control organs. The autonomic nervous system (ANS) is a branch of the nervous system. It consists mainly of neurons that control glands and organs (see chapter 1 for a diagram of the nervous system).

When the body is aroused by a threat, the sympathetic branch of the ANS is active. The nerves stimulate the centre of the adrenal glands (the adrenal medulla) to release adrenaline. This is called the **sympatho-adrenal medullary (SAM) system** ('SAM' for short). When a threat has passed, the parasympathetic branch of the ANS becomes active, and triggers the body to go into a more relaxed state, sometimes referred to as 'rest and digest'.

The hypothalamic-pituitary-adrenal system

The second system which contributes to stress response begins with an area of the midbrain called the hypothalamus. When we are stressed, the hypothalamus instructs the pituitary gland to release a messenger hormone called ACTH, which in turn stimulates the release of cortisol from the adrenal cortex. Overall, this set of processes is called the **hypothalamic-pituitary-adrenal (HPA) system**. It is a slower response than the SAM system, because it relies on hormones travelling around the bloodstream rather than on the fast direct connections of the nervous system.

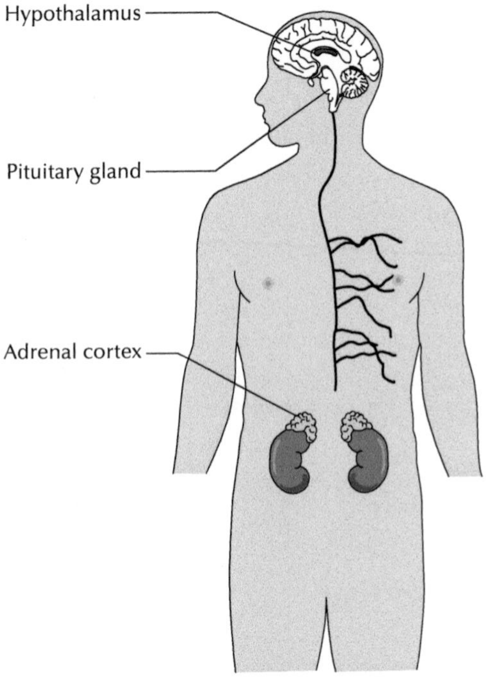

The hypothalamic-pituitary-adrenal system

Health effects

Have you ever noticed that you are more prone to getting ill at exam time? Or that when you are busy and tired, you suddenly come down with a cold to compound the problem, or develop a mouth ulcer? Some of these things can be explained in terms of the effects of stress on physical health.

Before explaining how and why stress affects health, let's first consider some of the major stress-related health problems that can occur.

Short-term health effects

Fight-or-flight can briefly boost our immune response but stress soon makes the body more susceptible to a range of infections. Cohen *et al.* (1991) found that high-stress individuals were more susceptible to the common cold. This may be because the general adaptation syndrome leads to shrinkage of the lymph system, the part of the body that produces white blood cells. The study of Kiecolt-Glaser *et al.* (1984) showing fewer white blood cells in students at exam time (see following page) demonstrates in humans what Selye had shown in his rats – the body's immune system is compromised by stress.

Acute stress will also affect **mental health** – the person may anger easily, as well as being moody and irritable. This will be seen in behaviour such as emotional outbursts. They may dwell on the stressor, have difficulty concentrating on other tasks and find it hard to sleep (Cox, 1978).

Long-term health effects

As stress lasts longer, health effects tend to become more serious and it can cause permanent damage, with an increased risk of diseases of adaptation such as **coronary heart disease (CHD)**. Appearance can be affected, with skin conditions such as psoriasis likely to worsen when a person is stressed. A person is also more liable to adopt unhealthy behaviours such as overeating, smoking or drinking, all of which can have knock-on effects on health. They may experience a long-term increase to their blood pressure (hypertension), increasing the risk of a stroke.

Psychologically, a person becomes more prone to mental health problems such as anxiety and depression. Stress can be a triggering factor in a number of psychological disorders, including eating disorders. Mumford *et al.* (1991) found that among Asian girls in the UK, those who were most traditional in their dress and outlook were more susceptible to eating disorders, perhaps because of a greater 'culture clash' making life more stressful.

Stress can result in health effects even in the short-term

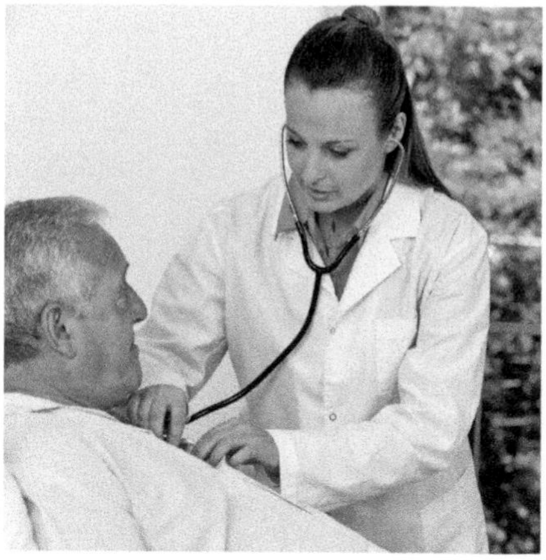

Long-term stress can result in diseases of adaptation such as CHD

The causes of health effects

What causes the health effects of stress? Some are essentially side effects of processes which occur for other reasons. Both adrenaline and cortisol function to increase the glucose (blood sugar) level in the bloodstream. This is useful for an animal that is trying escape from a predator, but in humans this extra energy is often not necessary to deal with modern stressors. Instead, the raised glucose in the bloodstream can cause damage to arteries and to the heart.

Immunosuppression

High levels of cortisol in the bloodstream can harm the immune system. This affects many parts of the body, giving an insight into why stress makes people more vulnerable to illness. This process is known as **immunosuppression**. The immune system consists of cells throughout the body, each of which plays a role in attacking infection. It is essential for healing infected areas of the body and for fighting off viruses.

A key part of the immune system is the lymph (or lymphatic) system, a set of body areas which produce white blood cells (also called 'leucocytes'). There are different types of **leucocytes**. Some produce antibodies which attack invading bacteria and viruses, helping to destroy them. The body can cope with brief periods of stress but if stress is prolonged, the production of key virus-fighting white blood cells reduces. This makes the body more vulnerable to infection.

To find out more about these processes, Kiecolt-Glaser *et al.* (1984) investigated stress among students around their exam time. In particular, they wanted to find out about virus-fighting 'killer-T' leucocytes, which play a key role in the body's response to colds and other infections. This natural experiment involved 75 first-year medical students. The researchers collected blood samples from the participants on two occasions – a month before their exams and again at exam time. They also gave out a stress questionnaire. The study found that during exam time, students showed a significantly lower level of virus fighting ('killer T') cells compared to one month previously, meaning that they had become more vulnerable to illness. The questionnaire confirmed that this was a time of higher stress for the participants, particularly those who lacked a strong social support network.

Top tip

A natural experiment is one where the researchers don't or can't manipulate the independent variable (IV). In the Kiecolt-Glaser *et al.* (1984) study, they did not directly control when the students had exams. The IV (exam time versus not exam time) was therefore naturally occurring. This type of experiment is more prone to confounding variables than true experiments, because there may be other variables besides the IV which also change (see chapter 8). For example, the students may have eaten a less healthy diet at exam time.

Long-term stress can also harm the body's ability to heal wounds and injuries. In another study, Kiecolt-Glaser *et al.* (1995) inflicted a small wound on two groups of women – one group had stressful caring responsibilities and the other was a control group. The researchers found that the wound healed faster among the control group.

As was noted earlier in this chapter, one possible factor in the harm caused by stress is that, unlike other species, modern humans do not engage in physical activity (such as fighting or running away) when faced with threats – a situation that differs from our evolutionary past. It's possible that this causes or worsens the health effects seen in chronic stress. To support this idea, Fleshner (2000) conducted a study in rats. She found that moderate regular **exercise** could prevent the negative physical health effects of stress by reducing the suppression of leucocytes.

Questions

1. What is meant by chronic stress?
2. Which has the more serious effect on health, acute or chronic stress?
3. Name the hormone that is released when stress is prolonged.
4. Name a short-term mental health effect of stress.
5. What does CHD stand for?
6. Name two psychological disorders where stress can play a role.
7. What term means that the function of the immune system is reduced?
8. What specific type of white blood cell is essential for fighting viruses?
9. According to Kiecolt-Glaser *et al.* (1984), at what point in the year were medical students most vulnerable to infection?
10. Which research study found that exercise reduced the harm of stress on the immune system?

Key concepts

- Cortisol
- The sympatho-adrenal medullary system (SAM)
- The hypothalamic-pituitary-adrenal system (HPA)
- Immunosuppression
- Coronary heart disease (CHD)
- Mental health
- Leucocytes
- Exercise

Activities

1. Draw a mind map based on the health effects of stress.
   In the centre, write 'stress and health'. Then add branches to indicate issues such as short- and long-term health problems, physical and mental health, the immune system, lifestyle factors and so on.
2. Find out more about the workings of the immune system. You could do this by questioning a friend or family member with expertise in biology or medicine, or by watching a video online.

Hearing someone walking behind you at night may make you tense

Sources of stress

Types of stressor

As previously mentioned, a source of stress is usually called a 'stressor' (a term first used by Hans Selye). Some stressors are intense but only occur for a brief period of time, leading to acute stress and the fight-or-flight response. The minutes before a job interview or walking home on a dark night and hearing someone walking behind us – these are immediate situations that make people feel tense and the heart start to race.

However, as mentioned above, it is often the longer-term stressful situations, such as exams, that have the bigger impact in terms of our general health and wellbeing. There is no strict definition of how long the stressor has to occur for it to be termed 'chronic stress', but generally, it refers to situations that last for days, weeks or even months, whereas acute stress is a situation in the here-and-now.

Engineering models such as the general adaptation syndrome suggest that the source of stress doesn't matter physiologically, because the body responds in the same way to all stressors. However, it is important to identify where we are likely to experience stress if it is to be reduced or avoided.

Stressors can be categorised into three main types:

Type of stressor	Examples
Environmental stressors	Noise, overcrowding
Occupational stressors	Workload, exams
Social stressors	Arguments, divorce

It is useful to know these terms as they often appear in books and research studies but they are not well-defined categories and they often overlap. For example, being bullied at work is both an occupational and a social stressor. Arguments with noisy neighbours would involve both a social and an environmental stressor.

Research into sources of stress

Environmental

Our surrounding environment can very stressful in many ways, with perhaps the most obvious stressor being noise. Every day, people are exposed to traffic noise, noise from machinery in the home and workplace, other people's music and dozens of other noises, much of it outwith our control. This can impact on healthy development; children in noisier homes show more frustration at school tasks (Cohen *et al.*, 1980) and higher levels of overnight cortisol in their bloodstream (Evans *et al.*, 2001).

Overcrowding is an environmental stressor

The unpredictable nature of background noise increases its stressful effects. Glass *et al.* (1969) played noises to participants who were completing puzzles. Some heard regular, predictable noises, while others heard the same noises at random intervals. Those who heard the random noises experienced frustration and annoyance and became significantly poorer at solving puzzles, even after the noises had stopped. Those who heard regular noises did not do any worse than a control group who completed the puzzles in silence.

Another major environmental stressor is overcrowding. Anyone who has had to take a long journey on crowded public transport knows how tense this can make you feel. Calhoun (1962) conducted a longitudinal observational study into the effects of overcrowding on rats. He allowed rats to breed in a 10′×14′ enclosure until it became overcrowded with 80 rats in the space for 48. Many rats became depressed and unresponsive, females failed to build nests or look after offspring, while others cannibalised or sexually assaulted other rats, sometimes attacking them in gangs. While it is hard to generalise from rats to humans, the findings suggest that the stress of brutally overcrowded conditions can dramatically impact on mental health and lead to antisocial behaviour.

Make the link

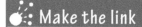

...to the topic of Aggression (chapter 14).

Occupational

One of the clearest demonstrations of workplace stress was conducted by Marmot *et al.* (1997) in the British Civil Service. These government workers are ranked in a strict hierarchy and the researchers found that those at the top – the highest ranked managers – had the lowest level of illness. What's more, the illness level increased with each rank down the hierarchy. Interestingly, Sapolsky (1995) compared humans and baboons and found very similar health changes – lower ranked individuals in the baboon troop being more stressed and less healthy compared to the alpha males and females. These findings suggest that having less power leads to stress, and consequently, to ill health.

Jobs which require focused attention for long periods can be very stressful

Some jobs require focused attention for long periods. Johansson *et al.* (1978) studied workers in a Swedish sawmill and found that one group of workers had a high level of responsibility but a monotonous task (the stage of finishing/processing the timber was monotonous but important). They also worked in social isolation. These workers were

Top tip

Control is a key concept in workplace stress. Lack of control has been linked to health problems in multiple studies.

found to have raised levels of stress hormones and to take more days off sick than a control group.

Workload also plays a role. Engineering views of stress such as the GAS model (see previous section) suggest that more work will lead to more stress, because stress is cumulative. People with a heavy workload, especially when combined with a lack of control and working in social isolation, tend to take more time off sick.

Social

Humans are highly social animals. We suffer stress from being isolated (Cacioppo & Hawkley, 2009), yet a number of our stressors come from social interactions (Sapolsky, 1995).

A number of our stressors come from social interactions

Top tip

Try out the SRRS scale, using the items listed on the following page. Compare your results with those of others in your class or school. Remember that items can be counted more than once if they happen repeatedly. Are there any that don't seem to apply to you?

Rahe *et al.* (1970) studied a range of major social stressors; they believed that the main factor in social stress was how much change or 'readjustment' a stressor causes us to make in life. Their analysis included both negative items, such as being put in prison, and positive ones, such as a new job. Using a questionnaire called the social readjustment rating scale (SRRS), they showed a positive correlation between two variables – the number of stressors a person experienced (as measured by the SRRS) and their level of ill health. The correlation was weak, perhaps because there are so many other factors that affect health, but it was significant (see table opposite on the following page).

The work of Rahe and colleagues generated a huge amount of research and helped psychologists assess the impact of life events more accurately (Jones & Bright, 2001). However, it does not account for the differences in severity of the items on the list and makes no distinction between positive and negative life events. Also, later researchers have found that day-to-day minor hassles, while smaller in scale, have a larger cumulative effect on health (DeLongis *et al.*, 1982). Kanner et al (1981) found that hassles impacted on psychological health, but positive events - termed 'uplifts' - only boosted psychological health among women. Falconier et al (2015) found that hassles put more strain on a couple's relationship, even if the hassles were not caused by either partner.

Life event	Mean value
Death of spouse (significant other)	100
Divorce	73
Marital separation	65
Jail term	63
Death of close family member	63
Personal injury or illness	53
Marriage	50
Fired at work	47
Marital reconciliation	45
Retirement	45
Change in the health of family member	44
Pregnancy	40
Sex difficulties	39
Gain new family member	39
Business readjustment	39
Change in financial state	38
Death of close friend	37
Change to different line of work	36
Change in number of arguments with spouse	35
Mortgage or loan for major purchase (home, etc.)	31
Foreclosure of mortgage loan	30
Change in responsibilities at work	29
Son or daughter leaving home	29
Trouble with in-laws	29
Outstanding personal achievement	28
Spouse begins or stops work	26
Begin or end school	26
Change in living conditions	25
Revision of personal habits	24
Trouble with boss	23
Change in work hours or conditions	20
Change in residence	20
Change in schools	20
Change in recreation	19
Change in church activities	19
Change in social activities	18
Mortgage or loan for lesser purchase (car, tv, etc.)	17
Change in sleeping habits	16
Change in number of family get-togethers	15
Change in eating habits	15
Vacation	13
Christmas	12
Minor violations of the law	11

The social readjustment rating scale (SRRS)

Individual differences in stress

Hardiness

Does everyone respond to stressors in the same way? The short answer is 'no' – there are **individual differences**, because some people are better able to cope than others, depending on individual traits, in particular the way they think about themselves and about a stressor.

Rotter (1966) studied **locus of control**. This means where the control appears to lie – that is, how much we feel in control of the things that happen to us. It is based on our beliefs about ourselves and the world. His research suggested that having a high internal locus of control – feeling that we are in control of what happens to us – led to lower levels of stress. This fits with the occupational stress research of Marmot (1997) (see p. 153), but suggests that it is what we think about control (rather than the reality) that matters.

Folkman *et al.* (1986) interviewed married couples on a weekly basis about their main stressors for the previous week. They found that those who had a high internal locus of control had better health outcomes than those who did not.

Researcher Suzanne Kobasa wanted to know why some managers and executives seem to cope better with stress than others. She believed that some exhibit a characteristic that she termed '**hardiness**', which had three key elements, sometimes termed the **three Cs**:

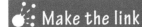

> **Top tip**
>
> Make a note of Kobasa's three Cs of hardiness on an index card.

- **Commitment**. They were highly committed to their work, their projects, and getting tasks completed.
- **Control**. As with Rotter's (1966) research, hardy people saw themselves as being in control, that is they had an internal locus of control.
- **Challenge**. They enjoyed a challenge, and saw new tasks or changes in the workplace as being a challenge rather than a threat.

> **Make the link**
>
> Hardiness is very similar to the concept of resilience. Both concern how well you are able to cope with difficulties.

Following this idea, Kobasa (1979) gave the SRRS questionnaire to 800 executives. She found that those who showed the same level of stress through their questionnaire responses had experienced different levels of illness – it appeared that the executives who scored highly on assessments of commitment, control and challenge were less likely to get ill as a result of stressful life changes.

Personality

Another individual difference that can affect stress is personality. As you will see in other topics in this book, personality can play a role in many areas of psychology, from obedience to relationships. Personality is thought to be relatively stable across the lifespan, and although there are various theories of personality types, a popular modern idea is that an individual's personality can be summarised in terms of their level (from low to high) of five key traits:

- openness (to new experiences)
- conscientiousness
- extraversion (versus introversion)

- agreeableness
- neuroticism.

In particular, the trait of neuroticism is relevant to stress. People who show a high level of neuroticism are anxious and self-critical, and therefore tend to get stressed about things that other people might not worry about.

Related to this is the idea that people's behaviour can be divided into different types. Researchers Friedman and Rosenman (1974) described several types of behaviour, but focused on two in particular:

- **Type A behaviour.** These people are highly competitive, have a strong desire for recognition, are very ambitious, tend to rush things, are very mentally alert, and tend to do several things at once.
- **Type B behaviour.** These people show a lack of ambition or drive, are relaxed about both achievements and deadlines, and tend not to rush or get involved in competitive behaviour.

Type A behaviour was associated with a higher level of stress and a higher level of heart problems such as CHD (see key study). However, neither type A nor type B behaviour was considered a personality type as such. (The researchers focused on behaviour that they could observe, rather than underlying traits.) This may mean that, unlike personality, these patterns of behaviour are open to change (Banyard & Grayson, 2000).

? Discussion point

Do you understand your own personality? Take a personality test at http://personality-testing.info/tests/BIG5.php.

Top tip

In the exam, it's fine to refer to Types A & B as either 'behaviour' or 'personality'. The important thing is to describe them accurately.

Key study: Friedman and Rosenman's (1974) study of type A and type B behaviour

Aim: *Researchers Friedman and Rosenman were cardiologists who noticed that the patients with more severe heart problems were also more impatient and aggressive when they had to wait before an appointment. A previous study (Friedman & Rosenman, 1959) had established two key types of behaviour: 'type A' individuals were rushed and hostile, while 'type B' individuals were relaxed and cooperative. The researchers hypothesised a connection between these behaviour patterns and the health effects of chronic stress, and ran a longitudinal study to test this.*

Method: *The researchers used interviews and questionnaires to put people into one of two categories. Among other things, the interviewers would speak very slowly and make deliberate mistakes in order to aggravate the participants and determine whether they were impatient! Over 3,000 participants were categorised into types, all of whom were males aged 39 to 59.*

Findings: *Eight-and-a-half years later, the researchers studied the health outcomes of these men. Even allowing for other risk factors such as diet, 70% of those who had contracted coronary heart disease (CHD) were type A, and the type A men were twice as likely to have suffered a heart attack. This seemed to establish that*

The type A behaviour pattern often involves being in a hurry and trying to do several things at once.

a rushed and hostile pattern of behaviour can be a significant risk factor in health.

Evaluation: *The study focused on men, in part because CHD is more common among men, but it is limited in that the findings can't easily be generalised to women. There may be sex differences in both the behaviour patterns and their physiological effects. The study also didn't take into account environmental factors. The behaviour (for example, rushed or competitive) may not have been a characteristic of the men, but could have resulted from an interaction between the individual and their work or family circumstances. Nevertheless, it was a large-scale study which shed light on a very serious health problem. By focusing on behaviour rather than personality, the findings leave open the possibility that changing behaviour could lead to improvements in health.*

Other individual differences

There are certain biological differences in how our bodies react to stress. For example, women release less adrenaline than men do during fight-or-flight, and it remains in the bloodstream for a shorter length of time (Frankenhauser *et al.*, 1976). There are also sex differences in the way the hormone oxytocin mediates stress. Oxytocin – sometimes called the love hormone – is associated with love, bonding, parenting and friendship. Large amounts are released when we fall in love, and it is also released when we bond with other people. Taylor *et al.* (2000) explained that oxytocin can result in lowered levels of the stress hormone cortisol when we get social support during stress. However, oxytocin is affected by sex hormones: it is boosted by oestrogen, whereas testosterone makes it less effective. This means that women benefit more from social support during stressful times than men (see also chapter 1).

There is also some evidence that age plays a role in stress. Colton and Gore (1991) studied the effects of stress on teenagers, and found that they were more likely to openly show the symptoms of stress than older adults. However, this could be due partly to experience – as people go through life, they become more experienced at coping with stress, and this may have an effect on how they react to a stressor. Also, people of different ages often experience different stressors. As a teenager, typical stressors involve social interaction at school, conflicts with parents and exam stress. A young adult is more likely to be stressed by having young children to care for, while older adults may have to cope with issues such as retirement or age-related health issues.

Make the link

...with the individual differences that affect conformity.

Questions

1. Name three types of stressor.
2. According to the study by Glass *et al.* (1969), what type of noise was more stressful?
3. Which study looked at the effects of overcrowding on rats?
4. What similarity was found between civil servants and baboons?
5. Give an example of an occupational stressor.
6. What type of locus of control is associated with lower stress?
7. What are the three Cs of hardiness?
8. Name two characteristics of type A behaviour.
9. Give an example of an age difference in stress.
10. Name one sex difference in stress.

Key concepts

- Occupational stress
- Social stress
- Environmental stress
- Hardiness
- Three Cs
- Locus of control
- Personality
- Type A behaviour
- Type B behaviour
- Individual differences
- Workload

Activities

1. Find out more about one of the animal studies mentioned in this section or in the previous section, such as Calhoun (1962) or Sapolsky (1995). Write a blog post or make a poster explaining the findings. Don't forget to evaluate the study.
   Can the findings be generalised to humans?
2. Find out about other behaviour types relating to Friedman and Rosenman's work – type C and type D. Also, try to find out about other psychology issues to which these behaviour types have been linked.

Coping strategies

There are several ways of tackling stress. Some focus on the body's physical response by trying to reduce the symptoms of fight-or-flight, while others try to change the thoughts or emotions. The strategies that a person can use, with or without the help of an expert, are known as **coping strategies**.

Drugs

One way to tackle the body's stress response is by giving a drug that directly tackles this response in the body. Such drugs are frequently prescribed by GPs both for stress and for stress-related problems such as insomnia or anxiety disorders.

Top tip

Provide context to your answer on coping strategies by explaining why stress is a threat to health (see the earlier section of this chapter). However, the majority of your answer should focus on the techniques themselves.

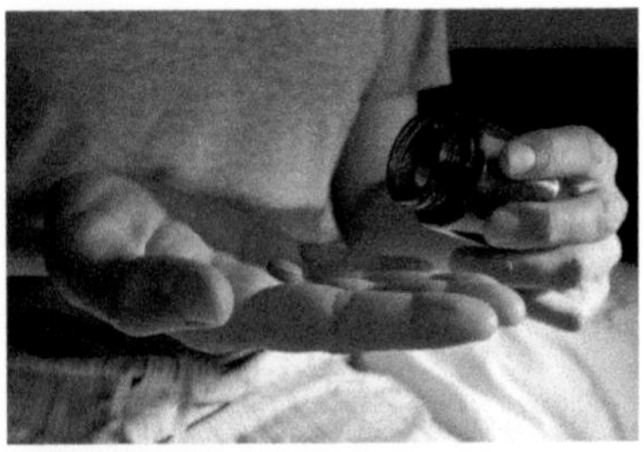

Drugs may be prescribed for stress-related problems

Make the link

Benzodiazepines are also used as sleeping pills (see chapter 2), and can be prescribed to people who are suffering from anxiety disorders (see chapter 3).

One group of drugs is the **benzodiazepines**, including Valium, Restoril and Librium. These boost a neurotransmitter called GABA, making the person feel more relaxed and sleepy. The faster-acting drugs make people fall asleep and they are used as sleeping pills; however, the slower-acting versions relax the body and this makes people feel psychologically more relaxed.

Another commonly prescribed group of drugs are called **beta-blockers**. These act directly on the nervous system, reducing the effect of sympathetic activation by blocking the 'beta' receptors that respond to adrenaline. This leads to lower heart rate and reduced blood pressure.

A possible criticism of this strategy is that it provides short-term relief without helping to solve a person's underlying problems. In addition, all drugs can have side effects. Benzodiazepines can make you sleepy, which is potentially risky for driving and other activities. In some cases, they have more severe side effects, such as confusion, seizures or hallucinations. They are also addictive. They are only recommended for short-term use (Royal College of Psychiatrists, 2018).

Beta blockers are generally considered safe for longer term use, but can have some side effects such as dizziness and tiredness (NHS, 2016).

Stress inoculation

Sometimes people who are under a lot of stress may be referred to a therapist, especially if the stress is causing, or worsening, mental health problems or making the person unable to work. A specialised form of CBT designed for stress is Donald Meichenbaum's **stress inoculation** training. This teaches people to resist stressors (just as a disease can be resisted), using techniques such as role-playing, visualisation and practice. There are three phases:

- **Conceptualisation phase**. Clients are taught to break stressors down into smaller units, in order to tackle them.
- **Skills acquisition phase**. Coping skills are taught and practised with the therapist.
- **Application phase**. Newly acquired skills are used in real-life stressful situations.

People who are under a lot of stress may be referred to a therapist

Essentially, the idea is that people learn to identify the component parts of stress and the situations that cause stress. They are then taught techniques for dealing with stress, and then they apply these to the real world outside of therapy, for example, in work, study or relationship situations.

There is good evidence that stress inoculation can be effective. A meta-analysis for the United States Army conducted by Saunders *et al.* (1996) found that it reduced performance anxiety and enhanced performance under stressful conditions. It can tackle both chronic and acute stressors and a complex mixture of both (Meichenbaum, 2007).

A positive aspect of stress inoculation is that it tries to deal with the causes of stress by making people less vulnerable and teaches strategies that can be applied in day-to-day situations. However, the therapy sessions themselves can be time-consuming and expensive; typically, a client would attend sessions once or twice per week for six to twelve weeks.

Social support

There is widespread agreement that social support can help to reduce or manage stress. As you have seen in earlier sections, people who have better social support tend to have fewer problems resulting from stress, while those who are isolated, and therefore have less social support, suffer more from the health effects of stress (as was found in the Kiecolt-Glaser *et al.* (1984) study on medical students).

Social support can play two key roles. One is to provide practical, **instrumental support** – help with practical problems. This kind of social support could include getting lifts from a friend or family member that has a car, or help with a job application or a UCAS personal statement. **Emotional support** focuses on making people feel better, rather than providing practical help. This kind of social support may be forthcoming from peers. Indeed, just talking and having someone to listen can make people feel better.

Psychological counselling and therapy tend to offer emotional support rather than instrumental support – they may focus more on making a person feel better and able to cope with stress, rather than trying to solve their problems for them or reduce their levels of stressors (although some types of therapy try to do both). For example, stress inoculation therapy (see above) teaches people coping skills.

There is a range of evidence suggesting that social support is important in reducing stress. In a natural experiment, Nuckolls *et al.* (1972) found that pregnant women under high stress had a much lower rate of pregnancy and birth complications if they had good social support compared to those who did not.

Social support can also be combined with sport and exercise. Exercise helps people to metabolise the excess glucose that is released into the bloodstream due to stress hormones such as adrenaline. It therefore has biological benefits to the person who is suffering from stress. However, sport and exercise can also be a social activity, whether via a team sport such as football or basketball, or by joining a group or club to engage in exercise such as running or swimming.

A limitation of social support as a coping strategy is that it is reliant on having other people around and willing to help. People who are isolated or very introverted would have great difficulty benefiting from this strategy. It would also be hard for people who suffer from social anxiety or agoraphobia to make use of this strategy.

Top tip

If you are asked to analyse these types of coping, a good way to pick up marks would be to compare them to each other. You could also analyse the assumptions and supporting evidence, and give real world examples.

Top tip

Social support can be either instrumental or emotional.

Make the link

...with the concepts of social anxiety and agoraphobia as discussed in the National 5 topic Phobias (chapter 3).

Key concepts

- Drug therapy
- Benzodiazepines
- Beta-blockers
- Social support
- Stress inoculation
- Instrumental support
- Emotional support

Questions

1. Which method of tackling stress tries to tackle the body's stress response directly?
2. Which group of drugs has the more severe side effects, benzodiazepines or beta-blockers?
3. What are the possible side effects of drugs used to treat stress?
4. Which drugs are suitable for long-term use with stress, and do they solve the person's problems?
5. What is the first phase of stress inoculation?
6. What does the application phase involve?
7. Give an example of something that might happen in a stress inoculation session.
8. Which type of social support involves tackling a person's problems?
9. Name the research study which found a positive effect of social support on pregnant women.
10. Which health-related coping strategy can combine well with social support?

Activities

1. Investigate a coping/stress management technique by researching sources and presenting your findings. You could focus on one of the techniques discussed above, or something different, such as meditation or exercise. You should:
   - Read more about the technique and write a short summary of it.
   - Use Google Scholar or another research website to find recent research studies (from the last 10 years or so). Choose one short article, and summarise it in your own words.
   - Briefly summarise how effective you think the technique is compared to other coping strategies and how practical it is in everyday stressful situations.
   - Present your findings from the previous three activities, for example in a presentation or blog post.
   - Share your findings with other students, for example by giving your presentation to the class or sharing a link to your blog post for others to comment.
2. Write a one-page summary of what students could do to minimise the health effects of stress. Refer back to the issues covered in the section on stress and health, as well as this section, and mention more than one coping strategy. This work could form the basis of a practice essay answer for the exam.

End of topic project

You will conduct a case study into stress at exam/prelim time. The aim will be to find out about a classmate's stressors related to studying and revising and to make recommendations based on your knowledge of coping strategies to help them relieve their stress at exam time (see chapter 8 for general information on the case study method).

- Draw up a plan showing how you will conduct the case study.
- Conduct a brief case history, using a semi-structured interview, to reveal the following points. Find out, up until now...
  - Where and when the participant studies for exams.
  - What environmental and social stressors have affected him/her.
  - What social support he/she has if any.
  - The participant's views on learning and revision.
  - Anything the participant does to relieve stress at present.
- Now, show how you would follow up on this case history. Try using observation to find out more about the participant's study techniques and what coping strategy works best for him or her – this could include video recordings.
- Prepare recommendations based on your findings and your knowledge of stress.
- If your participant consents, you could make a poster showing your results.

End of topic specimen exam questions

1. Evaluate a research study into the physiology of stress. 8 marks
2. Explain the role of stress in immunosuppression. 5 marks
3. Analyse the effects of sources of stress, referring to research evidence. 15 marks
4. Explain social support and one other coping strategy in stress. 10 marks

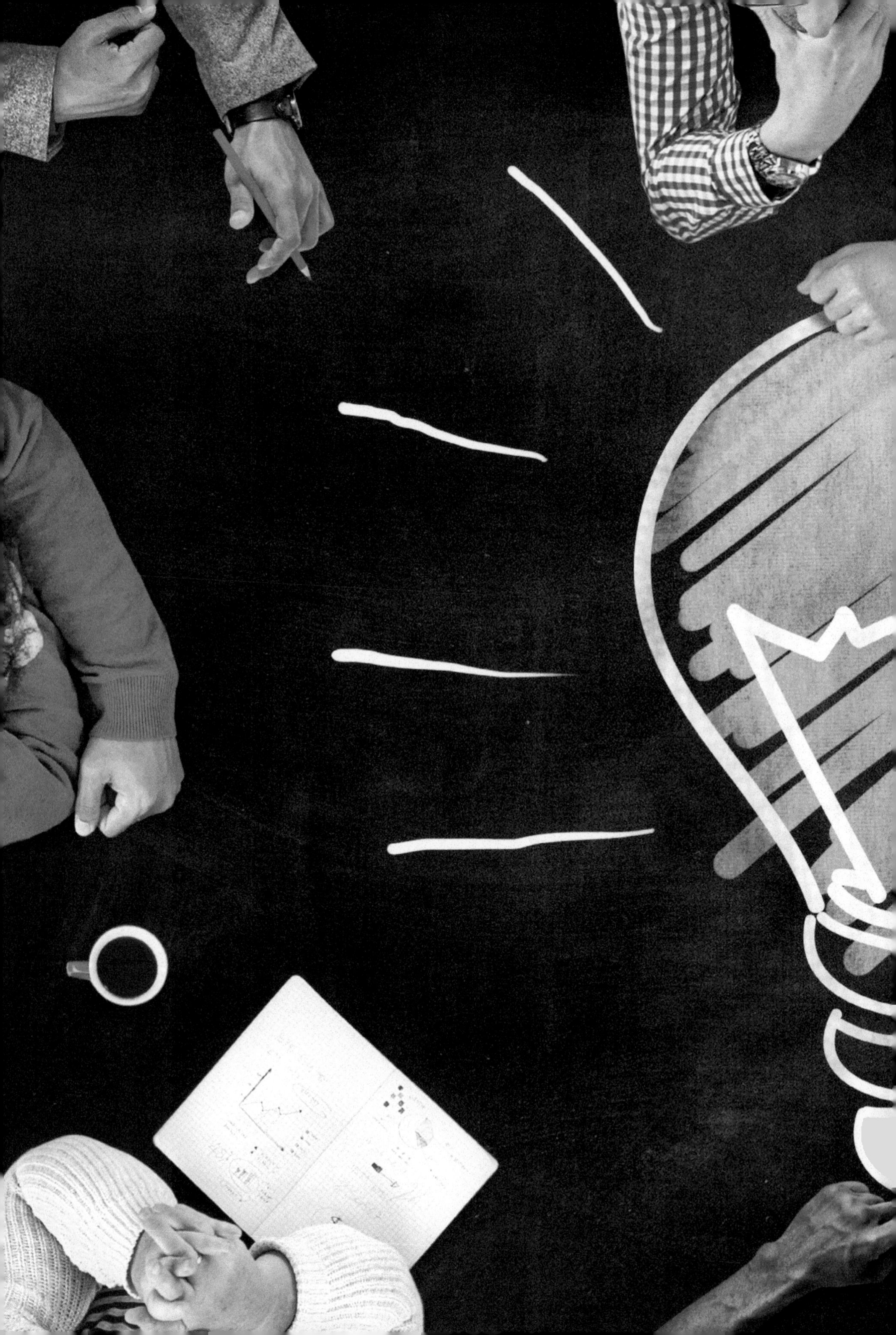

Research and Skills

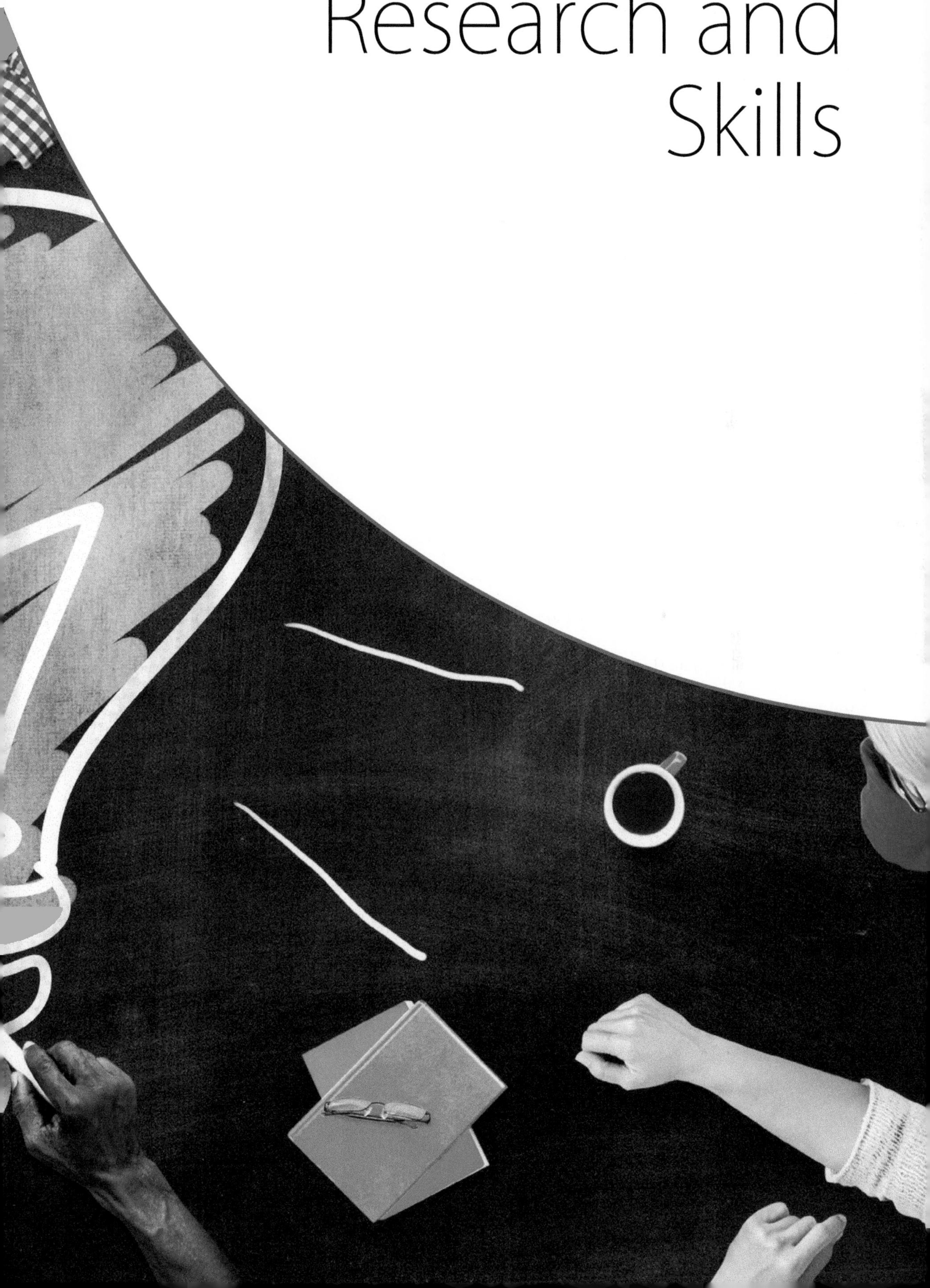

7 Key skills

Skills such as literacy, analysis, evaluation and applying knowledge are particularly essential for the exam

There are several skills that are developed during this course including literacy, writing, numeracy, information handling and personal learning. These will be developed throughout the year including on the Assignment project.

Skills such as literacy, analysis, evaluation and applying knowledge are particularly essential for the exam.

Top tip

It will be useful to read this chapter during the course, but you should also come back to it and read it again once you have finished studying all the topics.

Top tip

There are differences between N5 and Higher Psychology in terms of the skills required. Check the requirements with your teacher/lecturer, or look at the latest SQA course documents.

Main skills developed in the course: overview	
Numeracy	Numeracy skills are important in handling the data for your Assignment. You will learn how to calculate statistical concepts discussed in chapter 8, such as the mean, and be able to explain and evaluate these statistics. You may need to comment on data in a table or chart in the exam. Ensure that you practise if you are not confident with number work.
Literacy	The literacy skills developed throughout this course and in your other subjects will be important in writing a successful Assignment and in tackling extended answers in the exam. Many students with good knowledge are let down by their literacy skills. You can develop your literacy by reading more, by writing essays and getting feedback. In the exam, you will not be penalised for spelling and grammar, but it is important to be able to write extended/essay answers, especially at Higher. A common problem is writing answers that are too short. The next section will explain how to structure and plan longer exam answers.
Describing and explaining	Many class activities and exam questions will require you to describe new concepts and theories, or to explain theories and research. If you are asked to 'describe' something in the exam, this means give information and factual detail, such as the name or parts of a theory, or the methodology of a research study. 'Explain' means you need to focus more on how something works, such as how the different parts of a theory work, or how a particular type of therapy is carried out, or the steps involved in a research study.

Analysing and evaluating	Analysing concepts and theories involves identifying and commenting on features of theories and research or on the way these features relate to each other. Evaluating involves identifying what is good or bad about theories, research, etc. Both are important skills in psychology and gain a lot of credit in exam answers. Do not make the mistake of thinking that the psychology exam is just about writing down as many facts as possible! Analysis and evaluation are considered higher-level skills, that is, they are more difficult and important than memorising facts. Analysis of research studies is especially important in this course and a later section in this chapter discusses this in detail.
Applying	Another key skill is being able to apply knowledge to a situation. In other words, it means identifying links between theories and real life. Psychology research tends to have some practical use, such as the application of memory to legal situations or of psychopathology to therapy. This skill is discussed in more detail under 'Added value', later in this chapter.

Applying knowledge is a key skill

Tackling exam questions in psychology

You want to gain a good pass in the exam and have the best chance of an A grade overall in your course, but developing your knowledge of the topics is only part of the process – you also need good exam technique. This section looks at how to tackle common questions, what skills are required and how to summarise, analyse and evaluate research studies.

You will need good exam technique to get your A!

Short answer questions

Short answer questions are generally very specific about what is required and it is usually clear what the available marks are for. For example:

> **Describe one strength and one weakness of the psychoanalytic explanation of dreams.**
>
> **2 marks**
>
> **Explain two calculations that the researcher has carried out to summarise the raw data.**
>
> **4 marks**

In the first question above, it is apparent that there is one mark for each evaluation point. The points you make do not need to have an extended explanation, but you should try to answer them fully, in a sentence or two, rather than giving one-word answers. Compare these two possible points that could be used as a weakness in the first question:

Better: *Freud's idea of wish fulfilment does not really explain nightmares, because if dreams are about what we wish for, then why would we dream about something bad?*

Weaker: *It can't explain nightmares.*

Therefore, it is fine to keep these answers short but make sure that the question has been fully answered.

The second question also asks for two points to be made but this time they are worth two marks each. A similar approach is required but slightly more information should be given. If there are two marks available for such questions, try to make two separate points, as in the following example:

The mean was used – this is calculated by adding up the total of the scores and dividing the total by the number of scores. The mean allows a researcher to get an idea of a typical mid-point of the data that takes every score into account.

The range was also used – this is calculated by subtracting the lowest score from the highest score. The result gives an overall idea of how spread out the data are.

Top tip

It is very easy for a marker to give just one mark out of two if an explanation is incomplete, so it's better to say too much than too little.

Both of the above answers do two things – state how the statistic is calculated and state why it is used – and these responses are therefore worth two marks each.

Extended answers

It is very important to structure your answer

It can be harder to tackle questions that require extended answers and it starts to become very important to structure your answer. For most 'explain' exam questions an answer can be structured as follows:

- Identify the concept.
- Explain the concept (two to three sentences).
- Give a real-life example.
- Back up with research evidence.
- Evaluate the evidence.

This will work well for fairly simple concepts or as part of a longer answer. For example, a description of a factor that affects conformity:

Explain one factor in conformity. **6 marks**

Identify the concept: One factor in conformity is the size of the majority group.

Explain the concept: People feel more pressure to change what they do when faced with a large majority group with different views or actions. They are much more likely to conform to the majority when they are in a large group of peers – three or more – than when they are with just one or two other people. Asch called this 'the magic number 3'.

Give a real-life example: An example of this is when you are with friends and everyone wants to do something but you do not, such as watch a TV show that you do not enjoy. With one or two other people, you might argue but if with three or more you would just go along with it.

Back up with research evidence: Asch (1951) demonstrated this in his 'length of lines' experiment, where people had to judge which of three lines was the same length as another line. In one version of his study, participants were put in groups of six, where the other five participants were confederates who had been told to give the wrong answer several times. There was a 32% conformity rate. However, when Asch repeated this with only two confederates, the conformity rate dropped to 13%.

Evaluate the evidence: Asch's study clearly shows that a smaller group exerts less social pressure on our behaviour. It was a lab experiment so all other variables were kept constant, allowing a clear conclusion. However, it was an artificial situation and it is hard to say how well the conclusions can be applied to real life settings such as the workplace.

Top tip

Write this structure onto an index card.

Top tip

This answer does not give very much detail on Asch's study and it is not perfectly accurate, but it is sufficient for the question.

If the question is just on a theory, then the same structure can be used, but it will be necessary to spend more than two to three sentences explaining. Most theories include several components and it will be necessary to go through each component in turn, explaining what it does, as well as making relevant points about the theory as a whole:

- Explain key points about the theory as a whole.
- Name and explain each component of the theory.

The rest of the answer can use the same structure as above – give examples, support with research evidence and evaluate.

Another important variation comes when explaining a key **research study**. These are covered in the next section of this chapter.

Essay answers

It is vitally important to be able to answer an exam essay well, as they are worth such a large number of marks. Three things in particular often let people down:

- lack of detailed knowledge
- essay is too short
- not enough focus on evaluation or analysis.

This is especially true for essays that ask you to 'analyse' a theory or study. The answers given here are often too descriptive. If you are asked for analysis, simple description will not gain marks.

If the essay involves explaining several components – for example, factors that affect sleep – you can use the same structure as described above and simply repeat it for each paragraph.

However, many essays require you to explain one thing in detail rather than presenting you with several concepts. The following examples show how this can be tackled.

Exam essays are worth a large number of marks, so it's important to know how to answer an essay question well

National 5: Explain the two-process model of phobias, including a relevant research study.

10 marks

Higher: Explain the multi-store model of memory.

12 marks

Higher: Explain the role of immunosuppression on physical health.

12 marks

Each of these questions requires you to give an extended answer to explain a concept. Each is essentially a short essay, accounting for most of the marks in the particular topic.

Remember that for questions that ask you to 'explain' you need to give information about processes and how things fit together. It is not enough to list facts (which might be acceptable for a 'describe' essay).

You need to think in advance how you will use your knowledge to answer certain common essay questions

For all of these questions, you need to consider:

- what research evidence to include
- which real-world examples to give
- how to structure the essay into paragraphs.

If you have prepared well, some of these choices should be almost automatic: you should have revised a certain number of key studies (the ones from this textbook or other studies covered in class), and prepared real-world examples in advance.

The following essay plan includes an introduction paragraph (which may or may not get marks, but it is worth showing that you can define the topic accurately), followed by four key paragraphs and a conclusion. The number of paragraphs can vary.

Paragraph 1

Here you state what the essay is about, defining the overall topic or subtopic. Give a detailed definition, or a brief summary of one or more major relevant concepts. For the stress essay above, a brief bit of context regarding stress and health could be given.

Paragraph 2

Start to explain the key concept covered in the essay. For example, what is meant by immunosuppression? Give an explanation, linking it to chronic stress and giving examples of situations that might cause it. In the memory question, a diagram of the model could be included at this point, highlighting how stores link together.

Paragraph 3

Explain the first main aspect of the model or process. Ensure that you are giving explanations, not just naming things and stating facts. In the phobias essay, you should describe classical conditioning but more importantly you should explain how it can cause a phobia. In the memory essay, it is important to explain how stores link together and how they process information. In the stress essay, you might explain how the immune system works.

Paragraph 4

This should be similar to the third paragraph but move on to a different aspect or concept, for example how operant conditioning can maintain a phobia. For the stress essay, this is where you could explain how chronic stress harms the immune response, and give evidence from research.

Paragraph 5

Here you could either explain a third aspect of the essay, building on the previous two, or go into more detail with supporting research. In the memory question, this would be a good point to explain the model in terms of evidence such as the serial position effect or the case of H.M.

Paragraph 6

This is your conclusion. It is considered good style to give one but you should keep it short. You have already made your points and hopefully picked up all the available marks, so do not waste time repeating yourself.

One further issue that may arise is that questions, especially extended or essay questions, may ask you to use your knowledge to explain a scenario. For example:

- Use your knowledge of factors in conformity to explain how peer pressure can be more of a problem for some teenagers than for others.
- Use your knowledge of sleep to explain why people who travel internationally and drink a lot of caffeine may have sleep problems.

A scenario may describe a real-world example of behaviour. Below is an example essay for a question that provides this kind of scenario.

Discussion point

Can you think of other essay questions that this plan could be used for?

Top tip

Try this plan out and compare your responses with classmates.

Top tip

Consider how much time you would have to answer an essay answer by working out the number of minutes per mark in the exam (allowing for extra time if you get any), and then multiplying this by the number of marks in the question. For example, if there are two minutes per mark, then you have 24 minutes for a 12-mark question. Remember that this includes planning and thinking time.

Example essay

David is a medical student who is finding it hard to get to sleep. Explain some possible reasons for this problem and some of the ways that psychologists might attempt to treat this problem.

14 marks

David appears to have insomnia, a problem with sleep that can have several possible causes. Sleep is a state of reduced awareness, when the body is less active and less responsive to the outside world. We spend a quarter or more of our lives asleep, but some people like David find it hard to get to sleep.

Sleep can be affected by environmental factors such as drugs, zeitgebers or shift work. Zeitgebers are the things that prompt the brain to know whether it is night or day, such as light. As a medical student, David may have to work at night a lot. Then when he tries to sleep during the day, it is light outside and his body is not producing the sleep hormone melatonin so he won't feel drowsy. Another factor is drugs such as caffeine. Night shift workers may take stimulants to

A question may ask you to use your knowledge to explain a scenario

keep them awake. Then they will find it hard to sleep – caffeine can stay in the bloodstream for many hours after drinking a strong coffee! So after a long shift he may find it hard to drop off.

There are different approaches to understanding sleep and sleep disorders, and one of the most important explanations is the biological approach. This explains that sleep is controlled by certain parts of the brain and body. An area of the brain called the suprachiasmatic nucleus controls the sleep-wake cycle. It gets information from the eyes about when it's dark, and triggers the body to release the sleep hormone melatonin. We therefore find it harder to fall asleep if it's light outside or the lights are on. The approach also explains that stimulants such as caffeine block adenosine receptors in the brain, stopping our body from realising that it needs sleep.

Sleeplessness can affect our mood and make it unsafe to drive, so it could be risky for David to drive home after work. Many accidents are caused that way. Sleep can also lead to health problems (Czeisler et al., *1990). In extreme cases, like 'wakeathon' participant Peter Tripp or people who are tortured with sleep deprivation, a lack of sleep can lead to hallucinations and affect a person's mental health. It is important that David addresses his insomnia, though fortunately as a student doctor he will probably recognise the symptoms – generally, insomnia means an inability to get to sleep or that the person cannot stay asleep.*

Sometimes sleep problems are not due to zeitgebers or lifestyle, but there is a deeper problem. It could be that there is a medical problem with circadian rhythms – David could have a genetic or medical issue affecting his body clock, meaning that he doesn't follow a strict 24-hour cycle. This could lead to going to bed later and later every day. This can cause major difficulties with work, so even if he has a regular 9 to 5 job, David would have problems as sometimes his body would want to be asleep during the day.

An effective way to improve the sleep of shift workers is light therapy. This is where strong light is used to trick the brain into thinking it is daytime during a night shift. Czeisler et al. *(1990) conducted a lab experiment and found that being exposed to really bright light during a shift helped to change the body clock so that a participant felt sleepy during the day and awake at night. This would be helpful for doctors such as David. Another possibility is CBT. It is possible that David's insomnia is caused by worries and anxiety. For example, he could be disturbed by some of the medical cases he has to treat in his job, or simply worrying about the future. If so, a few sessions with a CBT therapist would be helpful. CBT is a short intervention, so six to 10 sessions may be enough. As he is a student doctor, he might be able to arrange it through work, as CBT is available on the NHS.*

Hopefully, with the correct treatment David will get over his sleep difficulties. It may be that he will need to find a more regular job though, that does not mess with his circadian rhythms by having him stay up all night on shifts.

Top tip

Note how paragraph three moves from general to specific information. There are general points about the approach, followed by specific links to the topic. This will require practice and feedback from your teacher.

Top tip

Everything is clearly linked to the scenario. Scenarios like this will be chosen to be easily recognisable – you are not being tested on your knowledge of what being a medical student is like, but you should try to use the example to bring in knowledge from the course.

? Discussion point

In a group or with your teacher/lecturer, try to think of other scenario-type questions.

Top tip

Note how the overall structure is the same as the one presented earlier, with a short introduction and four further main paragraphs, each making around three key points, followed by a brief conclusion.

Understanding research

Understanding research is essential in the study of psychology. Without evidence, we cannot say very much at all about human behaviour. Therefore, you should work on developing detailed knowledge of the research. As well as having knowledge about the evidence, though, you also need to be aware of its strengths and weaknesses and how it fits in with the topic as a whole. This section will discuss the skills of analysing and evaluating evidence.

Understanding research is essential in the study of psychology

Creating a research file

The topics in this textbook each contain three to four summaries of key research studies. Some are mandatory (e.g. Dement and Kleitman, 1957), while others have been selected because they are theoretically important, well known to teachers and examiners and easy to understand. However, if you come across other interesting studies, feel free to add those to your notes. It can be interesting to use some very up-to-date studies, for example.

It is strongly suggested that you make your own notes on studies. Reading or highlighting the examples in this book is not a good way to encode the information to your memory or to develop evaluative skills. Instead, follow this process:

- Read about the study.
- Close the book and write a draft summary including analysis points in your own words.
- Refer back to the book to check any details that you couldn't remember (e.g. number of participants) and add these to your summary.
- Write a shorter summary into a separate notebook/index cards.

Index cards are an excellent way to revise studies, as they make it easy to change the order of the studies, and therefore test yourself without it becoming repetitive. A jotter (perhaps the back pages of your main jotter), a ring binder with loose leaf A4 paper or even notes on your phone could also work well.

Top tip

For each new study you read about, try to think of how it links to theories or approaches. You can check these ideas with your teacher/lecturer.

You can make revision notes in different ways

When considering how to summarise research, remember the two main ways you might use a research study in an exam answer:

1. As evidence to back up a point that you make. Here, a short one-to-two sentence summary of the research alongside a brief strength/weakness of the study will usually be enough (as in the example essays earlier). Any more, and you may be taking up too much time on the study, and not actually answering the question!

> Example of using a research study to back up a point:
>
> *The behaviourist approach explains a lot of our behaviour in terms of simple associations formed between two stimuli. This is known as classical conditioning. An example is when Watson and Rayner (1920) taught little Albert to associate fear and a small animal. Albert learned to fear something that he had previously liked, due to learning an association.*

2. As a main answer. Sometimes you will be asked a question such as '*Evaluate a research study into sleep.*' You will need to know the key research in enough detail to tackle this sort of question. Key information should always include:

- aim
- methodology, including participants
- findings/conclusions
- evaluation.

To help you, these points are highlighted in all of the key studies in this book. Any aspect of the study can be evaluated, including the aim, methodology and conclusions.

Evaluating research

It is best to develop evaluation **as a skill**. It is much more efficient in the long run to learn *how to evaluate* than simply to memorise strengths/weaknesses for each study. For one thing, this skill will help you to evaluate other studies that you come across in the future, including newly published ones. It will also help you to evaluate your own research for the Assignment.

There are four aspects of any study that you can tackle in your evaluation:

Criticise the ethics of the study

Consider any ethical problems such as deception and stress. It is less common to *praise* the ethics of the study ('it wasn't cruel or deceptive') but it could be a valid point if this is unusual in the research area. For example, as many studies of conformity involve deception, a study that avoids using deception could be praised for good ethical practice.

Top tip

See the end of this section for an example of a study on conformity described and evaluated as a main answer.

Example: *Selye's research on rats caused rats to be in extreme pain and some of them died. This is unethical, as there was considerable harm to the participants.*

Praise or criticise the methodology

Consider the internal validity of the study – did it demonstrate cause and effect? Were there extraneous/confounding variables? Identifying the method used will be useful here. Laboratory experiments are controlled and they demonstrate clear cause and effect, while other studies, such as natural experiments and correlation studies, generally do not. You could also comment on a task for being quick and efficient or for being slow or hard to replicate.

Example: *As a natural experiment, Raine* et al.*'s (1997) study of brain abnormalities in murderers cannot demonstrate cause and effect. It is not possible to know that these people committed murders because of the differences shown in the scans – there could be some other variable affecting their behaviour.*

Discuss whether findings can be generalised from the sample to the population (external validity)

Consider the sample used – large or small, human or non-human. What age were they, what culture did they come from and was the study conducted a long time ago? All of these issues affect whether findings can be generalised to the broader population in today's society. In addition, the setting of the study, for example, a lab, can make it hard to generalise to real life (i.e. low ecological validity), as can the use of artificial tasks (i.e. a lack of mundane realism).

Example: *A strength of Friedman and Rosenman's (1974) study was that it used a huge sample of more than 3,000 participants, leading to reliable results. However, the sample were all middle-aged men and it is difficult to be sure whether the findings apply to other groups such as young women.*

Compare results to other studies/theories

Many studies are done in order to support a theory. Did the study, for example, usefully distinguish between two theories, showing that one theory was better than the other was? If so, the study helped to make progress in its field and this is a strength. In contrast, perhaps a weakness is that the study is outdated and its findings have since been disputed.

Example: *The word length effect study by Baddeley* et al. *(1975) was one of the first to show that the idea of short-term memory holding seven items was over-simplistic. The study showed that it depends on the length of the item, so previous theories of memory were flawed.*

These four points should provide a powerful guide that will help you to evaluate any research study in psychology. Write them on your jotter or notebook, perhaps inside the front cover, and practise applying them to new studies that you read about in the news or online.

Analysis of research

Factual knowledge of studies is not enough – you need to be able to think about the research more deeply, understanding why it was carried out and what it showed. In general terms, **analysis** means

There are four aspects of any study you can tackle in your evaluation

Top tip

Go forward to chapter 8 for an explanation of internal and external validity.

It is important to develop the skill of evaluation

Analysis means identifying component parts and explaining how they work together

identifying component parts and explaining how they work together. When discussing a research study, analysis could include:

- Identifying the theory that the research was based on and explaining why it supports this theory.
- Identifying aspects of method/procedure used and explaining why they were used.
- Comparing aspects of the study to other studies.
- Identifying details of the results and explaining what these mean.

Often an analytical point will start by stating a fact, but the key thing is to say something interesting about that fact. For example:

- Asch's study was different from previous research studies into conformity, as it used a task where the answer was clear and unambiguous. This allowed Asch to know whether people would be influenced even if they knew the correct answer, and therefore demonstrated normative social influence.
- Dement and Kleitman's study used only nine participants. This is fairly typical for sleep studies, as they are very time-consuming and require complex apparatus.
- Mori and Arai (2010) used two different types of glasses that caused participants to see the same lines as if they were of different lengths. This contrasts with earlier studies that relied on actors, and meant that nobody was lying or acting unnaturally.
- Czeisler *et al.* (1990) found that people's body clock, on average, had shifted forwards by around nine hours. What this means is that the light therapy had successfully shifted each participant's circadian rhythm, so that rather than just staying awake all night, their body responded as if it was actually daytime.

This skill differs slightly from evaluation, which is more about saying whether the research is good or bad for various reasons. As an analogy, if you were taking apart an appliance such as a computer, you might *analyse* what the different parts do and why they were designed that way. *Evaluation* would involve saying how well the computer works – is it fast, does it break down easily, was it cheap to buy, etc.

Top tip

The same type of analysis points should be made in the Discussion section of your own Assignment.

Top tip

There is some overlap between evaluation and analysis but it is important to stick to the correct skill as far as possible. Exam marking schemes can be strict about the difference between the two skills.

Sample answer

Analyse one research study into obedience.
20 marks

Top tip

State the aim of a study. This can gain analysis marks. This answer usefully states the background, therefore analysing the purpose of the study.

The following sample essay analyses a research study on obedience – the Milgram study, which is mandatory at Higher level. Analysis points are made both by analysing the methodology and by elaborating on evaluation with statements such as 'this was a problem because…' or 'this was a strength of the study because…'

A relevant research study into obedience was Milgram's (1963) behavioural study of obedience. Milgram wanted to test whether people would obey an instruction which came from an authority figure even if it went against their personal values. His study was inspired by the horrific events of the Second World War, and in particular the way that ordinary people participated in the Holocaust – following immoral orders and contributing to mass murder.

Milgram's study was set up as a lab experiment, with three people in the lab. One was the experimenter, and although the other two were both portrayed as participants who were given roles of 'teacher' and 'learner', one of the two was actually a confederate of the researcher. This individual was always in the 'learner' role. The 'teacher' was instructed to deliver electric shocks to the learner every time they got an answer wrong in a simple test. The electric shocks began at 15 V and increased up to a maximum of 450 V. The maximum voltage was labelled 'XXX', one higher than 'Danger, severe shock', on the apparatus.

Milgram had prepared the responses in such a way that the learner gave many wrong answers. This was done so that the true participant was under pressure to give increasingly high electric shocks fairly quickly. The true aim of the experiment was not to test learning but to see how long the participant would continue, with obedience levels measured in terms of the percentage of people who reached the maximum 450 V level.

As the experiment proceeded, participants expressed concern at the 'learner's' suffering. However, the experimenter (also an actor) used verbal prods such as 'You have no choice – you must continue.' Again, these were designed to put the participant under realistic pressure. Allowances were made for the right to withdraw – if all four prods were used and the participant still refused to continue, the experiment was halted. Despite this rule, many would argue that Milgram did not respect participants' rights.

The main finding of the experiment was that people were highly obedient, with 65% continuing to the maximum shock level. This was a surprise to Milgram's colleagues, who had predicted that only a small percentage would risk potentially electrocuting a complete stranger. Milgram concluded that the situation caused people to make an 'agentic shift', where they handed over control of their actions to the authority figure. He believed that this happened because participants were in an unfamiliar situation, and because the researcher appeared to have legitimate authority. This idea is supported by one of Milgram's later variations of the experiment where the authority figure left the room and the obedience rate fell from 65% to 20.5%. It appeared to answer one of the main questions behind the research – will people do terrible acts just because they are told to do so by an authority figure?

Milgram's study was highly influential, apparently showing that ordinary people can take part in war crimes and acts of cruelty. It stimulated many other research studies of obedience, forming an experimental paradigm that has been used worldwide. However, the experiment was criticised by other psychologists, such as Diane

Top tip

A short description of the methodology is given at the start. This is not analysis, but sets out the context clearly without taking too much time. Practise writing a 2–3 sentence summary of key studies from the course.

Top tip

In the third paragraph, note that the essay quickly moves on from facts about methodology to analysing why the experiment was set up that way.

Top tip

In the fourth paragraph, a major ethical flaw is not just stated/explained but discussed. This could gain analysis marks.

Top tip

The fifth paragraph initially states the findings as a fact. This is not analysis. However, the answer quickly moves on to discuss possible explanations for the findings, and compares the original result to Milgram's later theories and experiments. Comparisons and links to theory are excellent ways of gaining analysis marks.

Top tip

The later part of the essay contains some evaluation, but the evaluation is also discussed and argued over, not just stated as a fact. This raises the level of the answer. Again, comparisons are made.

Baumrind, from an ethical point of view because participants were put under intense stress.

Does the study generalise to everyday life? There are arguments on both sides. On the one hand, a field experiment by Hofling et al. (1966) tested whether nurses would follow an order to give a drug overdose. This study found an even higher level of obedience, suggesting that Milgram's results were not due to the artificiality of his setting. However, Milgram's use of volunteers and a university setting may have increased the level of obedience, as participants may have believed that a scientific study would do no real harm.

Mnemonics

This section looks at why we forget things and how to use your memory effectively. It should be of use in helping you to learn material effectively from both this and other courses. If you are studying the Memory topic, you could also use it as an example of how an understanding of memory has been applied in the real world.

As you may have learned, information that we learn is encoded into a memory trace, stored, and then retrieved when needed. **Forgetting** is the flip side of memory – it is what happens when things cannot be retrieved from memory or when memory is inaccurate. **Working memory** (WM) is the immediate memory for a few items, such as when you are taking down notes in class. **Long-term memory** (LTM) means permanent storage. What this means is:

- WM is important for taking in and processing new information but it is not used for recall after more than a few minutes.
- LTM involves permanent storage and it is required for all of the information and skills you need for the exam.

Your mind going blank could be a sign of stress – you could learn some relaxation techniques to help with this

Memory failures

Think of a time when you went to another room and then thought *'what did I come here for…?'* It appears that things can disappear from WM really quickly. WM also has a limited capacity (Miller, 1956); new information will take up all of the space and old information will be pushed out. An analogy is trying to squeeze items into a full suitcase – and other things popping out!

Long-term memory can last for decades, but things can be forgotten if they were not learned effectively. Similar items might be confused ('interference') or may have been forgotten due to insufficient or ineffective revision. LTM can also fail in times of stress.

The following table summarises some of these issues:

Problem	Explanation/solution
I revised for two hours but I was really tired and I couldn't focus.	Attention is essential for encoding new information to memory. If your attention level drops – or if you are distracted by other things – you will not take anything in, so it will be a waste of time. Dividing your time into several short revision sessions can make it easier to focus and make links with other knowledge rather than just going over things repeatedly (see 'Elaboration' on page 180).
I took notes in class but I didn't really understand.	LTM is based on meaning. Anything that is meaningless or poorly understood can be held in WM but will not be encoded to LTM. Therefore, it is vital to ask questions and get a good grasp of new topics.
There was so much information; I didn't know where to start.	If you try to tackle an entire topic in one day, you are trying to take in too much information at once. WM capacity is limited, and it is better to break things down into smaller chunks. In addition, learning relies on sleep in order to consolidate changes in the brain – so you cannot remember everything in one day!
I got things mixed up in my test.	LTM is susceptible to interference between very similar items. Unlike a computer, the human mind struggles to store similar sets of information without getting them confused. The more similar things are, the harder it is to distinguish them in our memories. You can make information more distinct by setting it out in different ways on the pages of your notes. Page after page of highlighted writing is easily mixed up. Make sure to emphasise the differences between concepts and check with your teacher/lecturer if unsure.
I thought I knew it but it turned out I was wrong.	Bartlett (1932) found that anything unfamiliar tended to be simplified, omitted or made more familiar. People's minds distort information based on schemas. This may happen in Psychology – perhaps you will stick with your common sense assumptions about human behaviour, and ignore the factual information from your teacher/lecturer!
I thought I knew it but I couldn't remember it later.	Problems with retrieval: it may happen that long-term memories have been stored accurately but cannot be retrieved when needed. Retrieval is more likely to fail when there is a lack of a **cue**, that is, a reminder of something that triggers off retrieval. It could be the first letter of an answer, for example. Quizzing yourself regularly is a great way of consolidating knowledge, and boosts your later ability to remember things. The use of **mnemonics**, where you create a phrase that helps you to remember the first letters, for example of parts of a theory, can help to provide cues in an exam situation.
My mind just went blank!	Stress. Have you ever been flustered and unable to remember someone's name that you are sure you should know? This shows that stress can interfere with retrieval of factual information. From a biological perspective, the release of cortisol during the stress response negatively affects the hippocampus, a structure that plays a key role in LTM. Some relaxation techniques – such as deep breathing and meditation – can be used during an exam, while others (e.g. exercise) are ideal to break up your revision time (see chapter 6 for more on stress management).

> **Top tip**
>
> In your revision, use keywords as cues to help avert forgetting under exam stress.

> **Top tip**
>
> Pin up research summaries on note-cards or post-its, with the researcher name and year as a heading, followed by the key points of aim, method, findings and evaluation. Put these around your study space, or – better still – all around your home, so that you can visualise them by taking a mental journey from room to room.

Pinning notes on your wall can really help with revision

> **Discussion point**
>
> Can you think of acrostics for the other research methods and for the theories or terms that you have studied? Share the best ones with classmates.

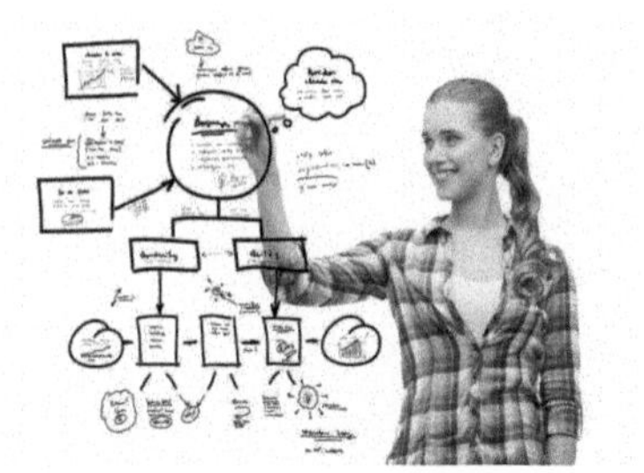

Using visual notes can help you to remember information

Types of mnemonic

A mnemonic just means a memory strategy. There are several different types; two of the most useful ones for your studies are as follows:

Acrostics

Some terminology in this course will be hard to remember, such as the names of the stages of a theory, researchers of the key studies in one topic or features of a research method.

Using acrostics means making phrases with the first letter or letters of the items you are trying to remember. For example, the features of the case study method could be remembered as:

Q-U-I-L-T

Qualitative – **U**nusual/unique cases – **I**nterviews/in-depth – **L**ongitudinal – **T**ests

Several key ethical considerations could be remembered as:

B-I-T-C-H

Briefing – **I**nformed consent – **T**reatment of children – **C**onfidentiality – **H**arm

Visualisation

Visual memory is very powerful, but unfortunately, much of what we have to learn in school and college involves verbal information. You can improve recall by combining visual and verbal encoding (Paivio, 1969). Therefore, it is a good idea to try to make visual images for the material in the course. You could make visual notes. If you make your notes very visually distinctive, you may find it easier to remember items in your mind's eye when you are sitting in an exam hall! Use cartoons, different styles and layouts, different types of paper, etc. Try associating key concepts with the images in this book or in your handouts. Mind maps and spidergrams are useful ways of making your notes visual and distinctive.

Other memory tips

What else can you do to improve your memory for information ahead of the exam? Psychology research has suggested three things that are particularly important. Again, these can apply to all of your school/college courses:

Elaboration

As mentioned above, LTM is based on meaning, and information is linked together into meaningful schemas. The result of this is that simply reading over things is an ineffective study strategy – even though you understand them at the time, you have not linked the information to anything that you already know.

Elaboration involves making meaningful connections between new information and things you already know. Craik and Watkins (1973) found that this made a much bigger difference to LTM compared to just spending more time trying to remember the item.

Elaborative links could include real life examples of psychological concepts, such as thinking of how the factors in conformity have happened in your life, or considering real-world implications of topics – what would happen if we stopped using psychiatric drugs and everyone was treated using CBT? Linking topics together and making links with other subjects such as Biology and Modern Studies is also great elaborative learning.

The **Cornell note-taking** system involves dividing your page into three sections, using a large margin at the side to write the key questions and essential terms, with your more detailed class notes alongside. A section is left blank at the foot of the page to write an overview later and make links to other topics (see image). This is a good way of making connections.

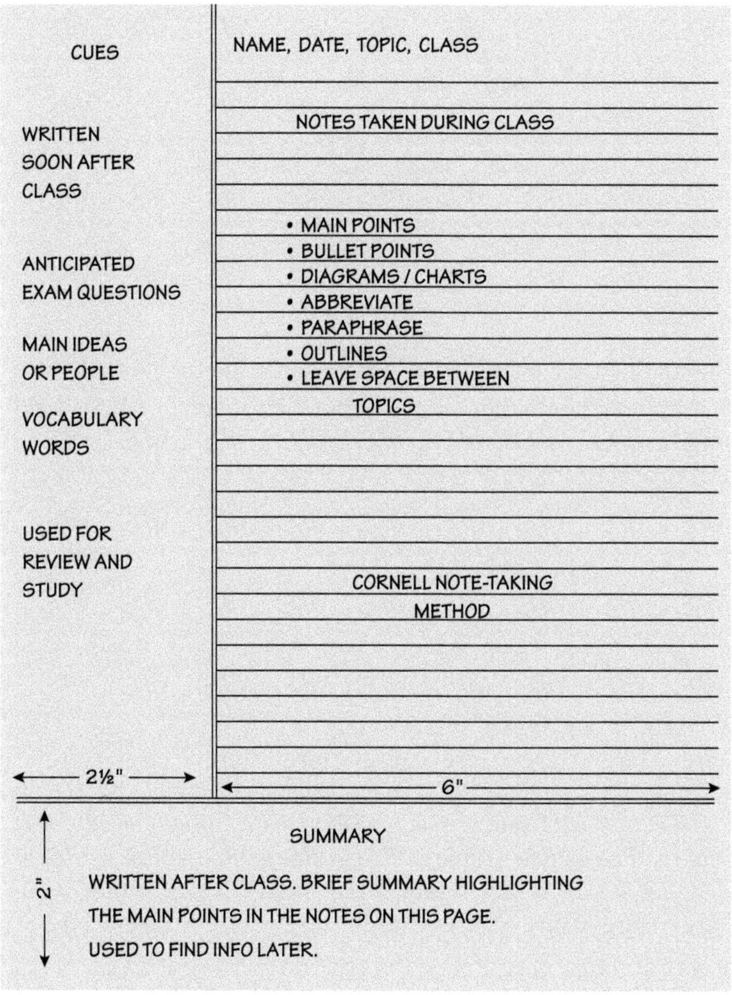

The Cornell note-taking system

Elaboration will also help to practise the skill of applying information to real-world situations – a key part of the course.

Spacing

Many studies of memory have shown that a pattern of spacing out learning over time can make a big difference to retention (e.g. Cepeda *et al.*, 2008). This **spacing effect** could include:

- Revising something soon after studying it (e.g. later the same day).
- Looking at the material again a week or two later (e.g. one weekend later in the month).
- Revising it again a couple of months later (e.g. at prelim time).

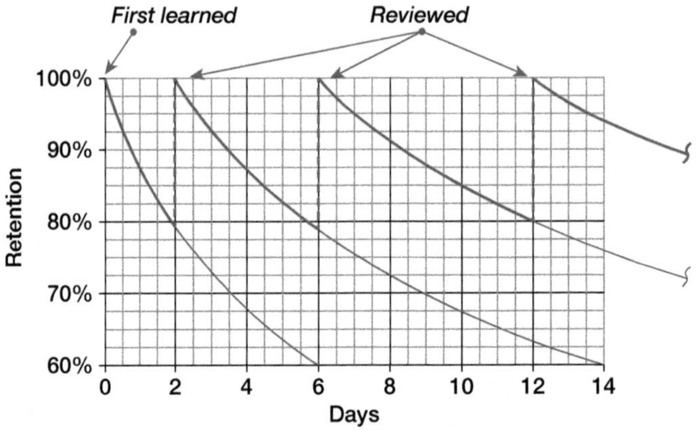

Typical forgetting curve for newly-learned information

This gradually increasing schedule is thought to be the most effective way of encoding information. For example, Kapler *et al.*, (2015) found that with lecture-type material, an eight-day gap before revision resulted in better long-term recall than a gap of just one day before revision. In both cases, students were tested five weeks later.

If you have used index cards as suggested, then by the end of the course you should have established a stack of cards summarising different theories, studies and applications. Study them, then set them aside, and come back to them again after a few days. The key is to leave a gap of time before reviewing the information.

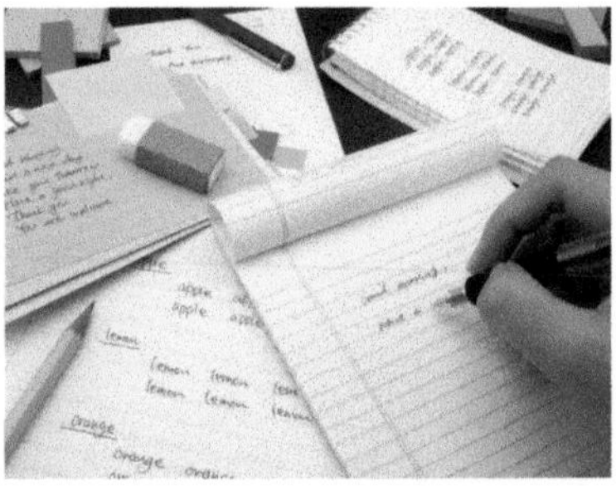

Testing yourself is highly effective in improving recall

Top tip

The testing effect is also known as 'retrieval practice' because it involves practising the process of recalling information from memory.

Top tip

Promote retrieval practice by trying to remember items or discussing them rather than just looking over them. Just highlighting your notes is not an effective study strategy!

Testing

Perhaps most importantly of all, testing yourself is highly effective in improving recall (McDaniel *et al.*, 2007). This is known as **retrieval practice**. One reason for this is that by making the revision harder, it has a larger effect on LTM. Unfortunately, it may have to be difficult in order to be effective!

Again, index cards make it easy to test yourself – just look at one side and try to remember what's on the other side. For example if you have facts about a theory on one side, you could test yourself on the evaluation points written on the other.

Added value

Added value means the extent to which you have gone beyond simply learning facts and skills. The main things that it refers to are:

- Breadth of learning – knowing more theories/explanations for a particular concept or a broader range of relevant research.
- Depth of learning – learning about a single concept in more detail.
- Ability to apply your learning to real situations

Added value is assessed in the exam by your ability to demonstrate these three aspects and it is important if you want to get an A grade. The best preparation is to develop good study habits and find opportunities throughout the course to broaden and deepen your learning. It is a good learning habit to always look for ways in which new information is relevant to real life. As mentioned earlier, application is a skill, and it can be developed by using elaborative memory strategies rather than simply reading over notes.

It is not necessary to achieve the same level of breadth and depth in your learning in every area of the course. Ideally, it will derive from having an interest in particular areas. The main message is that finding out more about a particular theory or area is always beneficial and you should not try to do just the bare minimum to pass!

Activities such as project work and additional reading on a topic help to promote breadth and depth of learning. Relevant activities are suggested in each section of the topics after the review questions.

Exam questions on Research

The current format of the National 5 and Higher exams does not include a separate section on research (although you may see this on some past papers). Research is certainly assessed in the exam but this is done in the context of the various topics. So, for example, you may be asked about lab experiments as part of a question on Sleep, or you may be asked about the interview method within a question on Stress. You may also be asked about research design, data or ethics when explaining a key study from any topic. The sample questions at the end of chapter 8 provide some practice of this format.

Added value means the extent to which you have gone beyond simply learning facts and skills

Top tip

Improve your ability to quickly take in and analyse research summaries by regularly reading research blogs such as the BPS's 'Research Digest' – **digest.bps.org.uk**.

Key concepts

- Index cards
- Analysis
- Forgetting
- Short-term memory (STM)
- Long-term memory (LTM)
- Cue
- Mnemonic
- Acrostic
- Visualisation
- Elaboration
- Cornell note-taking
- Spacing effect
- Testing effect

8 Research

For the topic of research, you should be able to explain:

- The main stages of the research process.
- The key features of different research methods, experimental and non-experimental.
- The key features of different types of sampling.
- Variables and how these affect research.
- Ethical codes of conduct in research.
- Data analysis including mean, mode, median and range.

You need to develop the following skills:

- Evaluating experimental and non-experimental research methods.
- Selecting appropriate research/sampling methods for different scenarios with an awareness of their strengths/weaknesses.
- Explaining and applying ethical standards.
- Analysing research examples.
- Calculating descriptive statistics.

! Syllabus note

Psychology is a scientific subject and an understanding of research is essential. It is required both for conducting your own research and to answer certain questions in the exam.

In this chapter you will learn about sampling and about experimental and non-experimental research methods. This will prepare you to make key decisions when planning your Assignment. You will also learn about the key ethical principles that underlie psychological research. Your understanding of all of these things will have an impact on your course grade via the Assignment. The details of planning and writing up the Assignment are covered in chapter 9.

You will also need to show an understanding of research during the exam, as you may be asked to explain research methods, sampling and ethical principles, or to analyse data or identify variables in any section of the exam.

The scientific method and the research process

The scientific method

The vast majority of academic psychology is based on the **scientific method**. This is the idea that theories must be backed up with valid, reliable evidence that has been gathered from practical research. This will be a theme throughout every topic in National 5 and Higher Psychology. Contrary to what you might hear from people outside the subject, psychology is not 'all common sense'! Even ideas that *seem* obvious need to be put to the test and confirmed with objective evidence.

The scientific method involves a cyclical **research process** of generating ideas, conducting practical research, analysing the findings of the research and then generating new ideas. This is the process by which we attempt to find out more about psychology and other subjects. We often take it for granted, but the scientific method is an incredibly powerful tool – Dartnell (2014) describes its *'knowledge-generating machinery'* as humanity's greatest invention. It has certainly contributed to our understanding of the world in all of the scientific subjects.

The scientific method involves practical research, such as experiments

Scientific standards

Although research in psychology is conducted on humans or animals, the same logical processes are followed as in the other sciences. This includes gaining empirical data and using statistics to analyse it. In addition, it must be possible to **replicate** studies (i.e. repeat them using the same methodology by other researchers, to test the findings).

Precise wording is important for researchers because we need to be clear about what we mean, and communicate ideas in such a way that others in the field will understand them. Even if you are new to the subject, you should try to use terminology accurately and consistently. It is worth bearing this in mind when people talk about scientific 'facts'. A fact in science is a piece of evidence that has been repeatedly confirmed. A theory is not the same as a fact. A **theory** is an idea that is supported by the current evidence – alternative ideas may have been rejected due to this evidence. Essentially, a theory is an explanation of how and why processes occur (Schmidt, 1992).

It is generally agreed that a theory should be stated in a way that can be tested. This means it must be possible to prove the theory wrong – it can't be so vague that no evidence could ever disprove it. If new evidence is found that the theory cannot explain, then one of two things can happen:

- The theory is changed to accommodate the new finding.
- The theory is abandoned in favour of a better theory.

Scientists also tend to avoid saying that theories have been 'proved', as it can only ever represent an explanation of the available facts. In the scientific method, a theory cannot be proved – although it can be disproved!

The research process

This leads to a research process of gathering data and developing/changing theories. The process goes through the following stages:

- **Generating a theory**. A statement is made about how a process in psychology (e.g. memory or prejudice) works.
- **Forming a research hypothesis**. From the theory, researchers make a prediction about what they will find in a particular situation.
- **Gathering data**. Researchers conduct experiments and gather data based on their prediction.
- **Analysing data**. The findings are analysed and compared to the hypothesis.
- **Publishing findings**. The data and analysis are published so that other scientists can comment on them.
- **Debating and amending theories**. If the evidence does not support the theory, it may need to be changed. However, usually findings must be replicated before anyone will accept the need to change a theory.

New hypotheses can be then generated from the (amended) theory, and so it goes on, in a cyclical process.

The process mentions the use of the experiment. This is in many ways the most useful research method, as it is highly controlled. However, there are four other major research methods described in this chapter that all contribute to our understanding of human behaviour – the observation, interview, case study and survey methods. These all have their limitations, but in combination can provide a range of evidence that contributes to the research process.

A key idea in research is that knowledge is **cumulative** – it builds up over time. No one research study is going to provide all of the answers but many individual studies each provide a piece of evidence that adds to our understanding.

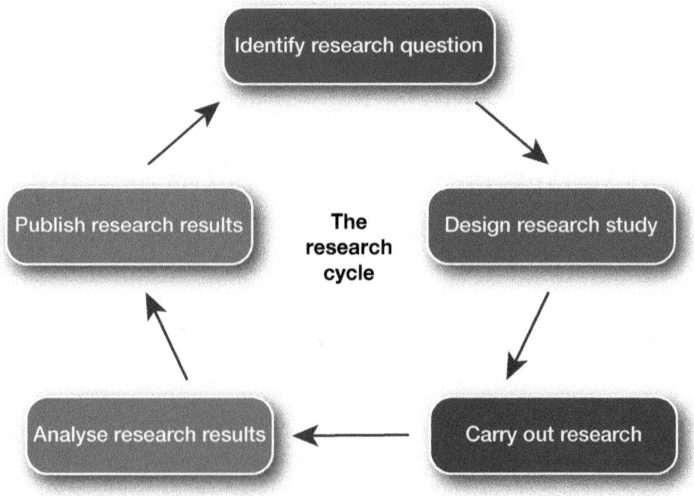

Revision of theories

Where does this research process end? Ideally, it ends with a full understanding of the particular issue – after major questions have been answered, researchers can move on to new questions and deal with those.

In practice, according to philosopher Karl Popper, the scientific method only leads to a progressively better understanding of an issue. This is in part because experiments cannot prove a theory to be true. They can only lead us to reject incorrect ideas. Therefore, the scientific community as a whole can move towards a better understanding of psychology (and other subjects) but never reach a perfect understanding of them.

Contemporary theories are, by definition, the best explanations that we have at present. We should just remember that every idea in science is open to being reconsidered, if new evidence becomes available.

Summary: the research process

In summary, psychology is based on the scientific method and research in the subject goes through a series of stages. These stages form a cycle, with theories being gradually improved over time. A theory represents the best available explanation of a psychological process, but there is always room for improvement, and any idea in science is open to evidence-based criticism.

Questions

1. Can research studies prove a theory right or wrong?

2. Define a theory.

3. Why is psychology not confined to applying 'common sense'?

4. Which philosopher said that scientific understanding of an issue could never be perfect?

5. Is it ok to criticise theories?

6. What are the main research methods used in psychology?

7. What process comes after generating a hypothesis?

8. What is meant by knowledge being 'cumulative'?

9. Does it matter if research findings can be replicated or not?

10. What is the final stage of the research process?

Key concepts

- Scientific method
- Research process
- Replication
- Theory
- Cumulative

Activities

1. Using a psychology topic of your choice, find an example of how research has followed (or could follow) a cyclical course. You may focus on a particular aspect of the topic if you wish. Draw a diagram of the process in your notes.

! Syllabus note

In both Higher and National 5, your understanding of research will be assessed indirectly, through the exam and the Assignment. However, be aware that you could be asked about research concepts directly, and that in your exam answers and Assignment it is important to use terminology accurately. Take time when you are revising to make sure you understand key concepts, and test yourself on terminology.

Populations and samples

What is a sample?

The people that a psychology researcher studies are collectively known as a **sample.** They are drawn from a larger group known as a **population**.

A 'population' does not have to mean the entire population of the country (or the world) – the term can refer to any specific group such as workers, students, pensioners, the unemployed, etc. The population that a particular study is interested in is called the **target population**.

Sampling means selecting people to take part in your research. There are two logical steps:

- Define the target population that you want to study. Perhaps you live in Dundee and you want to do a survey on elderly people in your city.
- Unless the target population is very small, you can't study all of them. Therefore, you pick a smaller group from this population – the 'sample' – and conduct the research on them. A good sample will have three key features:
  - it should be **unbiased**
  - it should be **representative** of the population as a whole
  - it should be **large**.

The people that a psychology researcher studies are collectively known as a sample

Being representative means that the sample should contain the same variety of people and behaviours as found in the target population.

This is less likely to happen if the sample is biased, that is, distorted by having too many/too few people from certain groups within the target population. For example, if your target population is people in their 20s, and you obtain your sample in a university library, the sample will be biased by including lots of students and very few people from other occupations.

A large sample is always better – it helps to even out random error and stop results being distorted by individual differences among participants. There is no perfect size for a sample but the larger the better.

? Discussion point

Think of how the term 'sample' is used in other areas such as geography, medicine, or just in everyday life. Does it have a similar meaning?

Generalising from a sample

If you have studied geography/geology and collected rock samples, the concept of sampling is logically similar. Rather than taking the whole rock/mountain, you collected a small piece and studied that. The problems are also similar. What if the area of the mountain that you collected the rock sample from just happened to have a different type of rock from 99% of the mountain? The problem is that the sample is not representative of the whole, and so the results of the study on that rock sample can't be **generalised** to the whole mountain.

It is very similar in psychology. Imagine you want to conduct research into elderly people in the UK. If you selected a sample of elderly people by asking your grandmother's friends, they might not be representative of the whole population. Perhaps they are in better health or better educated than the average. Perhaps they are not as ethnically diverse as the whole population. If your sample is not representative of the population, then what you find out about the sample might not be true of the target population – making the research less valid (see 'external validity', page 215).

Top tip

People commonly mistake the words 'bias' and 'biased', perhaps because they sound very similar when spoken. Remember – bias is a noun and biased is an adjective. As discussed in the previous section, it is important for researchers to use language accurately!

How to select a sample

There are several sampling methods to choose from, each with strengths and weaknesses:

Opportunity sampling

An **opportunity sample** means a sample that is chosen based on convenience. This could be done by asking members of your class to take part in an experiment, or asking friends, or approaching strangers who walk past in the street and asking them to complete a survey. The sample may not be representative at all, because the researcher just uses whoever is easily available. This tends to lead to a biased sample but it is often used because it is quick and easy to do.

- Strength(s): usually the quickest and easiest sampling method – it is based on convenience.
- Weakness(es): suffers from bias – some members of the population will be under-represented. Researchers may be unconsciously biased when they choose people to ask.

Opportunity sampling could involve recruiting strangers in the street

? Discussion point

If you gather your sample by approaching people who walk past your classroom/lecture theatre, what kind of biases might there be in the sample?

Top tip

Most assignments use opportunity or volunteer sampling. If you are considering random sampling, discuss this with your teacher or lecturer. Unless the target population is very small, it is likely to be an impractical choice.

Random sampling

A **random sample** means that everyone in the population studied has *an equal chance of being chosen*. This is a lot more difficult than it sounds! How do you ensure that everyone has exactly the same chance? Putting all the names into a hat might work, but it is not practical if there are thousands or even millions of names. Psychologists typically use **random number** software, together with a numbered list of every member of the population.

It may be that a random sample is not perfectly representative of the target population just by chance, but this method avoids any systematic bias and so it is generally considered the ideal method of sampling to use in most situations. However, the people who have been randomly selected may not want to take part in the study, leading to a high refusal/drop-out rate. In short, this is a very good method of sampling but it has many practical problems.

- Strengths: the best way of ensuring a representative sample.
- Weaknesses: time-consuming to carry out and people chosen may not be willing to take part.

Self-selecting sampling

A **self-selecting sample** (or 'volunteer sample') means that participants come forward of their own choice, responding to an advert or email request for participants. The key defining feature is that they come to you, rather than you selecting them. If you put up a sign asking for people to contact you/come to a lab at a particular time to be tested, then you are obtaining a self-selecting sample. Milgram's (1963) study of obedience (see chapter 10) used people who responded to a newspaper advert – a self-selecting sample.

Advertising for participants would result in a self-selecting sample

This type of sampling is simple to arrange but the sample may be biased because participants may differ from other members of the population in various ways, for example, by being more interested in helping scientific research, being more generally helpful ('pro-social') than others or just having more free time. They may also be more in need of the money paid to participants, resulting in a bias in the occupation/income level of the sample. Another cause of bias is that the sign/advert/email may not be seen by everyone – for example, the sample might contain an unrepresentative number of people who read newspapers.

- Strengths: a simple way to get a large number of participants. People want to take part, making it ethically sound.
- Weaknesses: people who come forward may not be representative of the population, for example by being more pro-social. In addition, the placement of the sign/advert asking for volunteers may lead to bias.

Systematic sampling

A **systematic sample** involves picking people at fixed intervals from a list of the whole population. For example, if you have a list of 1,000 students in your year and you pick every 20th name, you will obtain a systematic sample of 50 participants in total. Going through the telephone directory and picking the top person from each page would also be systematic. Another means of conducting systematic sampling would be to do it over a particular time and place, for example, asking every 10th person who walks past you in the street. The main reason for sampling this way is that it removes any choice from the experimenter, eliminating **researcher bias** – the tendency for researchers, often unintentionally, to distort research results through their actions.

- Strengths: it is generally a representative sample. Avoids researcher bias and avoids the biases of self-selecting samples.
- Weaknesses: The list chosen (e.g. phone book) may be incomplete, therefore, excluding some members of the population. If done in the real world (e.g. asking every 10th person) then it suffers from some of the drawbacks of opportunity sampling.

Picking the person at the top of each page of the phone book would be systematic sampling

Make the link

Do you carry out research on people in your other subjects? If so, how are your samples obtained?

Stratified sampling

With a **stratified sample**, the researcher makes sure that key groups within the population are represented fairly within the sample, such as by selecting a 50:50 mix of males and females. The exact details of this may depend on what is important to the research. If religious belief is an important aspect of a study then researchers might ensure that their sample has the same proportions of religions as the population as a whole.

However, stratified sampling is not a complete sampling method and it must be combined with another method. For example, if you decided to pick 12 males and 12 females, you must then apply some other sampling method, for example opportunity sampling, to actually obtain these participants. It ensures a representative sample but only in the identified areas; in other areas, for example personality, they may not be representative.

Picking an equal number of men and women to take part in a study would be stratified sampling

- Strengths: helps to make a sample more representative in key variables, for example sex, religion, ethnic background.
- Weaknesses: the sample might be representative in terms of sex or religion but still unrepresentative in other ways, for example in occupation. It is not a complete sampling method – it must be combined with another method, and therefore, suffers from the drawbacks of whatever other method is used.

Quota sample

A **quota sample** is similar to stratified sampling, but here, the researchers specify numbers of participants from the key groups/categories and then fill these 'quotas'. This helps to ensure representation of minority groups. Unlike stratified sampling, the researchers do not try to keep the proportions of each group the same as those in the population. For example, a quota sample may require a minimum of five people from every major religion; this would avoid missing out groups that have a very tiny population, and therefore,

Quota sampling might be used to ensure a numer of categories are represented by the sample

Top tip

For the Assignment, students often combine quota sampling with opportunity sampling. For example, if you aim to find 20 male participants and 20 female participants, then you could pick people leaving the school/college library until you have reached those numbers.

might not be included in a stratified sample at all because they make up less than 1% of the target population.

Again, quota sampling is not a complete sampling method – once the quotas have been set, some other method (e.g. opportunity sampling) must be used in order to fill the quotas.

- Strengths: helps to ensure small minority groups are represented within a sample.
- Weaknesses: does not always result in a representative sample as proportions of small groups are distorted. It is not a complete sampling method – it must be combined with another method, and therefore suffers from the drawbacks of whatever other method is used.

Key concepts

- Sample
- Population
- Target population
- Sampling
- Bias
- Researcher bias
- Representative
- Generalising
- Opportunity sample
- Random sample
- Random numbers
- Self-selecting sample
- Systematic sample
- Stratified sample
- Quota sample

Questions

1. What is meant by a 'sample' in psychology research?
2. Which is bigger – the target population or the sample?
3. How large should a sample be?
4. Why is it important for a sample to be representative?
5. Which methods of sampling are least likely to produce a biased sample?
6. Is a random sample always representative of the target population?
7. State three features of a good sample.
8. Why is random sampling often considered the best sampling method?
9. Why is quota sampling not a 'complete' method of sampling?
10. Which method of sampling is better at ensuring that the size of groups within the sample are proportionate to the size of groups within the target population – stratified or systematic?

Activities

1. Which, if any, of the following methods would guarantee you a random sample? Discuss them with your classmates:
    - Picking every 100th name out of the phone book.
    - Putting all target population names into a box and pulling 10 out.
    - Writing a list of names on a sheet of paper and putting a pin in with your eyes shut.
    - Picking people 'at random' from the street or corridor.
2. Find out about the sampling methods used in at least two research studies in different topics in psychology. What effect might the sampling method have had on their results? Are particular types of sampling more common and/or more suitable in particular topics? Write a short explanation.
3. Try out sampling in the classroom by picking coloured sweets from a bag. What can you do to ensure a representative sample in terms of different colours? Try experimenting with different proportions of sweets in your 'population', for example 5% red, 20% blue, 75% yellow sweets.

Experimental methods

What is an experiment?

Experiments are the main tool of the scientific method. Every experiment involves making a comparison between two or more things, in order to find out something about them and to uncover an objective piece of evidence.

The logic of an experiment is that if you change one thing and keep everything else the same, then any difference must have occurred because of the thing that you changed. In other words, you change one **variable**, and try to measure its effect on another variable, while keeping everything else constant. Therefore, experiments aim to study **cause and effect**.

A variable can be any aspect of behaviour, for example heart rate or any stimulus that affects behaviour (e.g. noise). The two key variables in any experiment are:

- The IV: **independent** variable (the variable that the experimenter changes).
- The DV: **dependent** variable (the variable that the experimenter measures).

Sometimes primary school children run a simple experiment where they put one plant in a dark place and another on a windowsill. The result? If everything else is kept the same, the one on the windowsill grows more and is greener. This result may seem obvious to us nowadays, but such experiments throughout history have allowed researchers to uncover previously unknown facts in science, such as the presence of chlorophyll in plant leaves.

Discussion point

In the example experiment with the plants, what variables need to be kept constant? (Hint: things to do with the plant and environmental conditions...)

Conditions of the IV

Every experiment involves a comparison. In order to make a comparison, there must be two or more experimental **conditions** – parts of the experiment that are different. For example, if you want to study the effect of background noise on revision, you would have a low noise condition and a high noise condition, and compare the effect on people's exam scores. The IV in this example would be noise and the DV would be how well they perform in the test/exam.

Conditions are determined by the IV. Sometimes there is only one **experimental condition**, so the researchers use a **control condition** too. It establishes a baseline by measuring how things are under relatively normal circumstances.

The independent variable is the noise level

Other variables

As you have seen, an experiment manipulates an IV to see what effect it has on the DV. In order to be sure that the IV is actually affecting the DV, everything else needs to be kept constant.

A well-designed study will keep the effect of other variables to a minimum or ideally eliminate them altogether. Outside variables that may cause random errors in results are called **extraneous variables**. These include environmental variables, such as background noise, and participant variables – differences between participants such as intelligence.

Example experiment 1

A student research team are testing the effect of caffeine on short-term memory. In one condition, participants will be given a fairly high level of caffeine and in another condition they will be given no caffeine. To control for extraneous variables and demand characteristics, they decide to give the caffeine in the form of a mug of coffee and to give the control condition a mug of decaffeinated coffee without telling participants which one they are getting. An opportunity sample – students from a nearby class – are tested over two days. One day they get the normal coffee and then five minutes later do a memory test. The following day they are given the decaffeinated coffee and then five minutes later do a different memory test.

Does caffeine affect short-term memory?

Some variables cannot be eliminated. For example, a researcher cannot avoid the fact that participants have different personalities and life experiences or that they may be tired or in a bad mood. A researcher will try to keep the effects of such variables to a minimum by designing the experiment well but there will always be some **random error**.

However, if an extraneous variable influences one condition more than the other, it becomes a **confounding variable**. It then becomes difficult or impossible to know what causes a change in the results – the IV or the confounding variable.

In example experiment 1 (see p.194), participants may respond differently to caffeine. This is an extraneous variable but it is not a confounding variable, because the same participants are used in both conditions.

In example experiment 2 (see p.198), if the experimental group who used the memory strategy were also given more time to study the material, then *study time* would be a confounding variable. If the experimental group did better, it would be impossible to know whether this was due to the memory strategy or just because they had more time to learn the material.

Top tip

Identifying extraneous or confounding variables can be an excellent source of evaluation and analysis marks. The topics of Sleep, Depression and Stress all make use of natural experiments which often feature possible confounding variables.

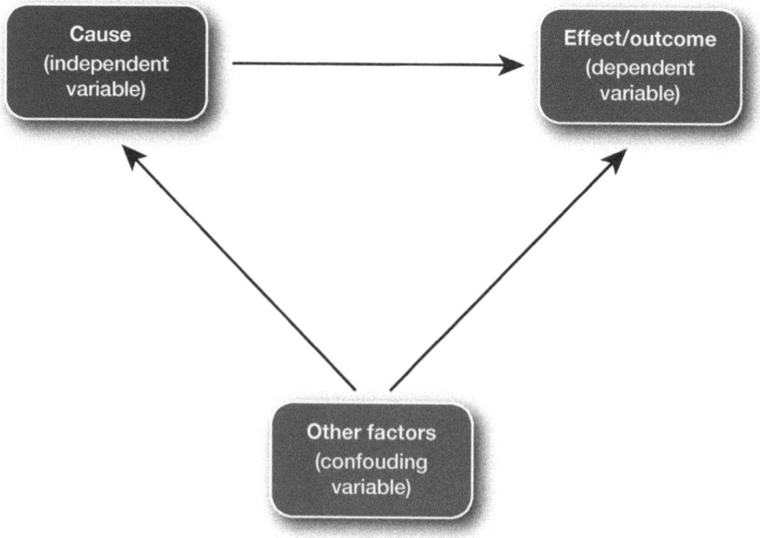

If there is a confounding variable, it is impossible to know which variable caused a change in results

Design

Design has a very specific meaning in the experimental method – it means the way in which participants are allocated to the different experimental conditions. There are two main options: either participants take part in every condition – a **repeated measures** design – or they are divided up into groups and each group completes one condition – an **independent groups** design.

Discussion point

Example experiment 1 used a repeated measures design. Do you think that was a good choice? Are there any other extraneous or confounding variables that the researchers did not control in example experiment 1?

Repeated measures

In a repeated measures design, every participant completes every condition. However, it is important to **counterbalance** the order in which participants complete the conditions. If there are two conditions, half will do condition 1 first and then condition 2, while the other half will do condition 2 first and then complete condition 1. Failure to counterbalance would lead to **order effects** – people will do better (or worse) in later conditions than they did in the first condition, due to practice or fatigue/boredom. Counterbalancing helps to balance out order effects between conditions but does not eliminate them.

The main advantage of this design is that participants' scores in one condition are being compared with the same participants' scores in another condition, rather than comparing two separate groups of people. This reduces the effect of a particular type of extraneous variable – **participant variables**. These are things that vary from one participant to the next, such as personality and ability levels.

In repeated measures studies, order effects can be a problem, and **demand characteristics** are likely. This means that participants will alter their behaviour according to perceived requirements of the situation, in particular, to a researcher's wishes. According to Orne (1962), participants who do two or more conditions will find it easy to guess the study's aims and will modify their behaviour to fit expectations.

In a repeated measures design, every participant completes every condition

Independent groups

An independent groups design, as mentioned above, uses two entirely separate groups of participants. It is not ideal to compare two separate groups of individuals – the main reason for doing so is when a repeated measures study is not possible, for example, if there is an element of deception that would make the aims of the study obvious if participants did both conditions. This is the case in some conformity and obedience experiments – the same participants could not have been used in more than one condition of Milgram's experiment, as they would have realised the second time around that the electric shocks were fake (see chapter 10).

For an independent groups design, there needs to be one group for every condition, and therefore, the total number of participants in each condition is smaller with this design, especially if there are many conditions. For example, if you have selected a sample of 28 students and there are four conditions, then only seven would take part in each condition. In a repeated measures design on the other hand, all 28 complete every condition, resulting in more data overall.

An independent groups design uses two entirely separate groups of participants

Another limitation of the independent groups design is that with completely different individuals in each condition, the results can be strongly influenced by participant variables. It is possible that participants in one condition do better compared to those in the other, not because of the IV, but because they are different individuals and they just happen to be better at the task.

Matched participants

To minimise participant variables when a repeated measures design is not an option, a third experimental design is sometimes used – **matched participants**. This is essentially very similar to independent groups, except that each participant is matched up with one or more others and these matched (similar) participants are then allocated to separate conditions. For example, participants could be paired up with someone who is very close to them in age, and then from each pair, one person will be put into the first condition, and the other into the second condition.

There are many variables on which participants could be matched, for example age, sex, IQ and personality type. The choice of what to match will depend on what is being studied, and therefore, what extraneous variables especially need to be controlled. In a memory experiment it may be a good idea to match participants on their memory ability before they take part to ensure that participants in the different conditions have similar ability levels. However, to do so makes a study more time consuming and it might not be practical if participants are recruited gradually over a long period of time.

Top tip

'Design' and 'condition' are both cases where you need to use terminology accurately. They mean different things in the context of a research study than they do in everyday life.

In a matched participants design, each participant is matched with the participant from the sample that is most similar to themselves. In the following simplified example, six participants are given a memory test, with a maximum score of 50. They are then matched up – Lauren and Leah form one pair, Courtney and Adil the second pair, and Roisin and Duncan the third pair:

Courtney: 28

Adil: 34

Lauren: 18

Roisin: 41

Leah: 10

Duncan: 43

Pair 1: Lauren and Leah

Pair 2: Courtney and Adil

Pair 3: Roisin and Duncan

In a matched participant design participants are grouped with others who are similar to them in a specific way

Types of experimental design

Type	Description	Advantage	Disadvantage
Repeated measures design	The same participants do all conditions of an experiment	Participant variables kept to a minimum	Order effects and demand characteristics
Independent groups design	A separate group of participants in each condition	No order effects – participant only does one condition	Participant variables
Matched participants	Matching pairs/groups of participants, then dividing them between conditions	Avoids order effects and controls some participant variables	Time consuming and not always practical to conduct

Example experiment 2

Lorna is a researcher who wants to know whether a memory technique will improve students' grades. She recruits 40 volunteer 16-year-old school pupils during the summer holidays. She randomly picks 20 to be the experimental group and 20 to be the control group. Those in the experimental group are taught the memory strategy and then given 10 pages of information about satellites and space travel to learn. The control group are given the same material to learn but are not taught the memory strategy. Both groups are told that they will be tested on their memory for the information after two weeks.

Those in the experimental group are taught the memory strategy

Random allocation

In example experiment 2, the researcher randomly chose half of the participants to do condition one and the other half to do condition two. Any true experiment must **randomly allocate** participants to conditions. In an independent groups study, the researcher allocates every participant to one of the experimental conditions randomly, for example, by tossing a coin to see whether they go in condition one or condition two. In a matched design, each matched participant is randomly allocated to one of the available conditions (if there are just two conditions, then one member of the pair is randomly selected for condition one and the second is then assigned to condition two).

A repeated measures study is slightly different because everyone does all of the conditions. However, randomisation is still necessary. Here the researcher must decide randomly which condition each participant does *first*.

In example experiment 2, the researcher starts with 40 volunteers and then randomly puts 20 into each of the two groups. This could be done by putting the names into a hat and drawing them out or by tossing a coin. In practice, though, most researchers would prefer to use a computerised random number generator. The participants could be numbered 1 to 40, and then a computer programme could generate a list of the numbers 1 to 40 in a random order. The first 20 are put in one condition and the next 20 into the other.

Note that random allocation to conditions is not the same thing as random sampling. Experiments using other types of sample, such as opportunity, should still randomly allocate participants to conditions.

? Discussion point

Why is random allocation necessary in a true experiment? (See p.382 for feedback.)

Top tip

Try the website http://www.random.org/sequences to set a maximum number and then generate all of the numbers in a random order.

It might occur to you that random allocation does not guarantee that the participants in the two conditions are the same as each other, and you would be right – as mentioned previously, there could be participant variables that affect the findings. It might happen just by random chance that the participants in an experimental condition are superior in some way to those in the control condition. In example experiment 2, the experimental group might have done better on the test anyway, regardless of whether they had used the memory technique or not. However, this chance is small (especially with a large group of participants) and a small amount of random error is accounted for in statistical tests. The important thing is that random allocation avoids systematic bias.

Lab or field?

Every experiment is conducted either in a controlled environment (laboratory) or in a natural environment (the 'field'). These are called **laboratory experiments** and **field experiments**:

- Laboratory ('lab') experiment: conducted in any controlled, artificial environment.
- Field experiment: conducted in the participants' natural environment, for example, home or the workplace.

There is no universally agreed standard for what a lab should look like; typically, it will be a plain room with no distractions – it is best if it does not have a window, as the researcher cannot control what might happen outside. A typical lab experiment would be conducted in a small room with a computer on a simple desk. Of course, some lab experiments might need more elaborate apparatus.

An advantage of lab experiments is that environmental variables are controlled. With no distractions, random error is reduced, allowing the researcher to conclude that any changes in their DV are due to the manipulation of the IV.

The disadvantage of any lab-based study (not just lab experiments) is that being in an artificial environment, they lack **ecological validity** – participants may not behave in the same way in the lab as they would in their everyday life.

Most research that you will conduct in your school, college or at home will involve field experiments. The field experiment has the opposite strengths and weaknesses of a lab experiment: ecological validity is higher, as participants behave more naturally in their usual surroundings, but environmental variables are not controlled. It is possible that noise or other distractions could affect the findings, reducing their reliability.

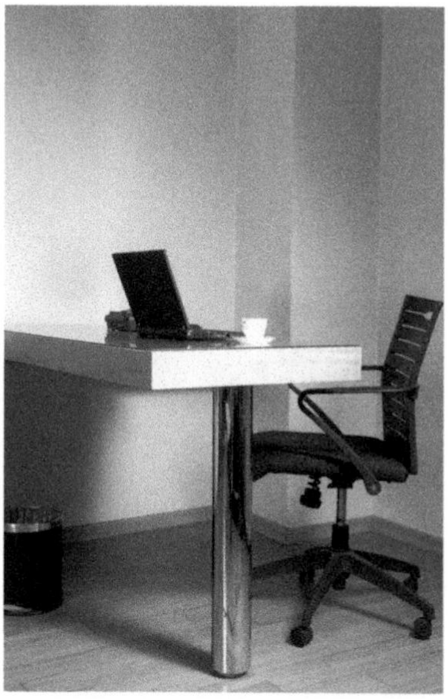
A lab where a psychology experiment could be carried out

? Discussion point

Should example experiment 2 be conducted as a lab or a field experiment?

Top tip

All true experiments are artificial because the situation is set up by the researchers. However, they are more artificial if they use a controlled setting (lab) and/or an unrealistic task. Compare the observation method described in the following sections and consider why it might be preferred to an experiment in some circumstances.

Other types of experiment

A **quasi-experiment** (meaning 'partial experiment') is in most respects the same as a true experiment. It could take place either in a lab or in the field. However, there is something fundamental about the design that means that it lacks the control of a true experiment. The most common reason is that the IV is something that is fixed in a participant or otherwise cannot be controlled, and it is therefore impossible to randomly allocate participants to experimental or control conditions. Examples include:

- comparisons of males versus females
- comparison of extraverts versus introverts (or any other personality difference)
- comparison of vegetarians versus meat eaters.

Because there is not full control over the IV, participants are in pre-existing groups rather than being randomly allocated. This means that there is no randomisation of extraneous participant variables either. There could be a confounding variable.

A **natural experiment** is not controlled by a researcher at all but the structure resembles an experiment – one variable changes and another is measured. However, the IV and DV occur naturally and all the researcher does is measure and analyse the DV. This might happen for ethical or practical reasons. For example, Nuckolls *et al.* (1972) studied the effect of high or low levels of social support on the health of women who were stressed during pregnancy (see chapter 6). They studied women who naturally experienced either a high or a low level of stress, because it would have been unethical to deliberately cause stress to pregnant women. The researchers also did not provide social support. These variables were naturally occurring.

In the Nuckolls study, it is possible to treat social support like an IV and health outcomes like a DV, but important to remember that with no control and no random allocation, this is not a true experiment – confounding variables cannot be ruled out and we cannot be certain that one variable caused a change in the other.

? Discussion point

Can you see why a quasi-experiment is considered to be less controlled?

Top tip

Many popular Assignment topics involve quasi-experiments. For example, a study where the independent variable is males versus females is a quasi-experiment. An Assignment that compares personality types is also a quasi-experiment. State this in the design sub-section of your Method section.

It would be unethical to deliberately cause stress to pregnant women

Top tip

Most students find quasi- and natural experiments difficult to understand at first. Take notes on both and refer back to them regularly. Look for examples of types of experiments as you work through other topics in the course.

Questions

1. What type of experiment uses controlled conditions?

2. Name the two variables that an experimenter manipulates and measures.

3. Which experimental design uses the same participants in every condition?

4. Which of the following is a key feature of all true experiments – being in a lab or control over variables?

5. Complete the following sentence: 'The most important feature of the experimental method is that it allows a researcher to establish…'.

6. Give a weakness of the experimental method.

7. What is the difference between a field experiment and a natural experiment?

8. What is the difference between a natural experiment and a quasi-experiment?

9. A researcher testing the effect of music on memory uses four different types of music. They also want to have a control group which does a memory test in silence. How many experimental conditions will they use in total?

10. Name three common examples of extraneous variables.

Key concepts

- Variable
- Cause and effect
- Independent variable (IV)
- Dependent variable (DV)
- Conditions
- Experimental condition
- Control condition
- Extraneous variables
- Confounding variables
- Random error
- Experimental design
- Repeated measures
- Independent groups
- Counterbalance
- Participant variables
- Order effects
- Demand characteristics
- Matched participants
- Random allocation
- Laboratory experiment
- Field experiment
- Ecological validity
- Artificiality
- Quasi-experiment
- Natural experiment

Activities

1. How should you identify extraneous variables in your Assignment or a research example? Try to do so with the simple example below. Then try to do the same with your own Assignment or plan.

   Amina, Jamie and Calum are 18-year-old students who are conducting a quasi-experiment investigating gender differences in IQ estimates. Each of them selects two participants. Amina chooses her brother and sister, while Jamie selects his mother and father, as does Calum. Each asks these participants to estimate their own IQ, telling them that the population average IQ is 100. Calum asks this question at home; the others ask the question when out shopping. The group thus obtains six sets of data; three from male participants and three from female participants.
2. Briefly explain in your own words the difference between an extraneous variable and a confounding variable. Give examples.
3. Look at example experiment 2 in the box on page 198. Identify the method (type of experiment) used, the design, the IV and DV. Are there any extraneous or confounding variables that the researcher has to consider?
4. Imagine you are going to conduct an experiment to see whether sleep affects memory for a skill. You will compare two groups of participants – one will train on the skill once before sleep and once after a night's sleep. The other will train on the same task twice in the same day, without sleeping in-between. Everyone will be tested after the second training session to see how well they have learned the skill.
   - What skill would you use and why?
   - What issues are there in terms of selecting a sample? Are there any people you would avoid using?
   - What extraneous variables would you have to control for? That is, what things would have to be kept constant for both groups? Think of as many as possible.
5. Look for examples of the four main types of experiments and the three experimental designs in other chapters of this book. Can you find at least one example of each? Take a note of your examples and compare them with a classmate's notes.

Non-experimental methods

Experiments are arguably the best method to use in most situations, as they allow the researcher control over variables. However, sometimes behaviour in an experiment may differ from real everyday behaviour because of the artificiality of experiments. In other cases, it is impractical or unethical to run an experiment. For example, it would be unethical to run an experiment into the effect of pollution on a person's behaviour by deliberately exposing an experimental group to high levels of pollution. Therefore, it is helpful to have the option of using other, **non-experimental methods** on occasion.

The main non-experimental methods you should be aware of include:

- survey
- interview
- case study
- observation.

Surveys and interviews

A **survey** involves handing out a list of questions – a **questionnaire** – to participants, usually a very large sample of participants. An **interview** is conducted face-to-face, but otherwise has certain key similarities – in particular, both gather data by asking questions to participants.

You may have already come across versions of these methods outside of Psychology, for example in job interviews and marketing surveys. In scientific studies such as psychological research, however, the design of interviews and questionnaires needs to be especially careful to avoid misleading participants or introducing bias.

A questionnaire is a non-experimental method

Top tip

Often students use the terms 'experiment' and 'case study' to refer to any type of research study. Try to use terminology precisely – don't call something an experiment if it actually uses a non-experimental method and vice versa.

Writing the questions

For both surveys and interviews, questions will be carefully considered and written out in advance. Good question wording is essential in gathering valid and reliable data. There are various pitfalls that a researcher must avoid, as shown in the following table:

Issue	Explanation	Bad example question	Improved example question
Leading questions	This kind of question 'leads' participants to pick a particular response, often by using strongly emotional language.	'Do you think that buying a new car from a car dealer is a complete waste of money?'	'Do you think that buying a new car from a car dealer represents value for money?'
Loaded questions	A 'loaded' question includes an unwarranted assumption, perhaps reflecting bias on the part of the researcher. The following example includes an assumption that *some* immigrants should be prevented from accessing benefits and it is therefore not neutral.	'Do you think that all immigrants should be prevented from claiming housing benefit?'	'Do you think that any immigrants should be prevented from claiming housing benefit?'
Jargon	A question should use everyday language, avoiding technical terms that a participant might not understand.	'Do you struggle to focus your attention on brief cognitive tasks?'	'Do you sometimes lose concentration after revising for 10 to 15 minutes?'
Avoid vague/ ambiguous language	The question should be as clear and specific as possible, avoiding statements that could be interpreted in different ways by different participants.	'Are some age laws of this country problematic?'	'Should the legal age for driving be raised from 17 to 18?'

Types of questions

Questions fall into two main categories: **open questions** (also called 'open-ended questions') and **closed questions**. Open questions allow the respondent to use their own words in response, whereas closed questions provide a selection of answers – yes/no, or a set of options. Some interviews/surveys use a mixture of both.

Generally closed questions are easier to analyse but don't allow people to express themselves as fully – this is a trade-off between detail and ease of analysis (see the following section, page 220, for a discussion of qualitative and quantitative data).

One of the most common types of closed question is the **Likert scale**. This is where a question is followed by a numerical scale, for example, 1–5 or 1–7, often labelled from 'strongly agree' to 'strongly disagree'.

Strongly disagree	Disagree	Undecided	Agree	Strongly agree
(1)	(2)	(3)	(4)	(5)

The Likert scale

Bias

Even if questions are carefully worded, there is the possibility that data gathered will be biased in some way. Two of the main reasons for this are as follows:

- **Acquiescence bias**: some participants tend to agree more than disagree, regardless of the question. For example, if asked 'do you have a good memory' a participant may say 'yes', but the same participant may also agree if asked, 'are you always forgetting things?' It is therefore important to have a balance of both positive and negative questions on the same issue.
- **Social desirability bias**: participants may distort the truth in order to look good. For example, if asked whether they are prejudiced, most participants will say 'no', even though their opinions and behaviour may indicate otherwise.

Top tip

A Likert scale is a good way to gather numerical data for your Assignment if you are using a survey.

Make the link

...between research bias and bias in a sample.

Distributing a survey

With a survey, the questionnaire is designed in advanced and then sent to participants. All potential problems must be thought of beforehand, as the researcher will not be there to guide participants when they fill in the questionnaire. It is important for questions to be clear and it helps if the questionnaire is fairly short – if it takes too long to complete, participants may give up and stop filling it in.

The questionnaire must then be distributed to participants. In the past, this would typically have been done by post, but it is now very common to use Internet-based questionnaires.

Top tip

A popular tool for creating online surveys can be found at www.surveymonkey.com. There is a free version that is ideal for students.

A questionnaire

Types of interview

The key characteristic of the interview is that questions are asked face-to-face, making research more time consuming, but allowing misunderstandings to be clarified. Interviews can be divided into three main types:

- A **structured interview** uses a fixed list of questions that will have been carefully planned as described above. It is similar to a survey, except that it is conducted face-to-face; the interviewer will not to go beyond the questions on the list, except to make clarifications. They mainly use closed questions. Structured interviews are useful when interviewing a large number of participants.
- A **semi-structured interview** also uses a set list of questions but allows the interviewer some freedom to expand on these. The interviewer may ask the respondent to elaborate on some answers, prompting them with simple follow up questions, such as 'Can you tell me more about…?'
- An **unstructured interview** does not stick to a fixed list of questions, allowing the interviewer to vary the questioning depending on how a participant responds. It is more like a natural

conversation. Many open questions will be used, providing rich, detailed data. However, responses are difficult to analyse and there is a danger of researcher bias.

As well as being used as the main method of research, interviews are also used in combination with other methods. For example, a participant may do a short interview at the beginning or end of an experiment.

In an interview questions are asked face-to-face

Observation

Observation is another major research method that can be used either on its own or in combination with other methods. Most experiments involve an element of observation but a typical observation study is less controlled than an experiment and it gathers data from watching behaviour as it happens. For example, you could observe a classmate as they are revising, and take notes on body language and how much time they spend looking at books/writing/looking at their phone, etc.

There are certain key design considerations when conducting an observational study:

Observation is another major research method

Naturalistic versus structured

A **naturalistic observation** involves simply watching and recording whatever unfolds in a natural, everyday situation. Naturalistic observation is the only method in psychology that gathers data on spontaneous behaviour as it happens. However, it lacks control over the many variables that could influence a person's behaviour. It is also impossible to replicate because the situation is natural and not set up by the researcher.

An alternative is to put participants into a lab and observe them doing a task – a **structured observation**. Here there is more control, and the situation could be replicated. One fairly common example is to set up a lab with particular toys/games and observe a child playing. A structured observation is more controlled but it may lack ecological validity – participants may not behave the same way in a lab as they would in an everyday situation.

Disclosed versus undisclosed observation

Any observation can be either **disclosed** – participants know they are being observed – or **undisclosed** – kept secret. Disclosing the observation has the problem that if people know they are being watched, the presence of the observer may affect the results (would you behave the same way when revising if a classmate was observing you?) This is known as the **observer effect**.

Undisclosed observation provides more natural results. However, undisclosed observation may be unethical, as participants haven't consented to take part in the research. It is never ethically acceptable to make secret observations of people in private, although some ethical codes accept observation in public places, where people would expect to be observed by strangers (British Psychological Society, 2009). For example, a researcher might conduct an observation into the behaviour of sportspeople during a match/competition without disclosing the research beforehand (it would still be best to ask for consent retrospectively).

One way of reducing the observer effect while still disclosing the observation to participants is to use discreetly placed video cameras. As cameras are less intrusive, behaviour may be more natural. Another way is to spend some time allowing participants to get used to the observer before starting to gather data.

> **Top tip**
>
> Ethics are highly important in research. Do **not** make undisclosed observations or recordings of other people for your Assignment. Discuss all research procedures with your teacher/lecturer before starting to gather data.

Participant versus non-participant

In the example described at the start of this section, the researcher is on the outside and does not influence the situation, rather like watching birds or animals through a pair of binoculars. This is called **non-participant observation**. By staying out of the situation, the researcher tries to avoid directly influencing participants' behaviour. However, as described above, they may still affect results because of the observer effect, if the observation is disclosed.

In **participant observation**, however, researchers take part in the social situation and interact with the people that they are observing, resulting in a more natural situation. In a classic example of a participant observation, a researcher and his colleagues pretended to be hearing voices in their heads and were admitted to a psychiatric hospital as if they were real patients (Rosenhan, 1973). They then took part in ordinary hospital activities, observing how psychiatric patients are treated by hospital staff.

> **Top tip**
>
> Unless otherwise stated, descriptions of the observation method usually refer to naturalistic, non-participant observations.

Participant observation gives the observer a unique insight into a social situation and participants can more easily get used to their presence. However, it can lead to subjectivity, as the researcher becomes personally involved in the situation.

Participant observation can be either disclosed or undisclosed.

Observation schedules

Some observation studies use a list of key behaviours called an **observation schedule**. This may require the observer to tick key behaviours each time they occur or take note of what happens during a particular time period. By focusing the observer's attention on particular things, they help in gathering the data that the researchers are looking for and avoiding distractions. They may provide an objective timescale as well.

> **? Discussion point**
>
> What could be included in an observation schedule to use on fellow students to find out what behaviours take place while eating? What about for observing behaviours in the corridor?

By providing an objective standard, observation schedules can also improve the reliability of recordings taken by more than one observer. Reliability means that results are consistent across different occasions and **inter-observer reliability** means the extent to which two observers produce the same results when looking at the same data. This is never perfect, but well-trained observers using observation schedules usually display high inter-observer reliability.

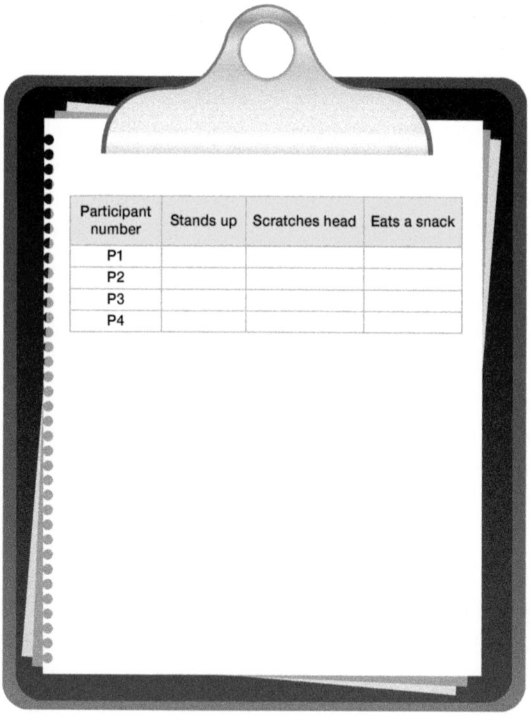

Participant number	Stands up	Scratches head	Eats a snack
P1			
P2			
P3			
P4			

An observation schedule

Case studies

A case study is another example of a non-experimental research method. It is an **in-depth** study, which is usually based on one individual but could also be conducted on a small group such as a family or team. Case studies were famously used by Freud to build up his psychoanalytic theories (see chapter 2).

A case study is generally **longitudinal**, that is, it follows the individual or group over an extended period of time. Rich, detailed information is built up, including a range of historical information such as family details, education, relationships and employment. In this way, the researcher builds up a full picture of the participant(s). This would include any brain injury or psychological trauma, if relevant to the case. This background information in a case study is called a **case history**.

Case studies typically use a range of techniques to gather data. They may use interviews and observations as well as ability tests (e.g. IQ, personality and memory tests) and brain scans.

Research examples

Case studies are done for various reasons. Some of the most well-known case studies in psychology are of individuals with unique psychological problems. Other important examples include:

- In cognitive psychology, several case studies have been conducted into the effects of brain damage on memory.

Top tip

The study of little Hans (see chapter 2) and the study of HM (see chapter 5) are both examples of case studies.

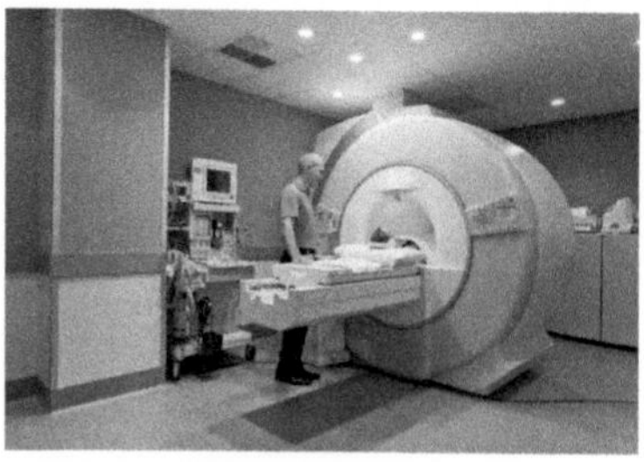

Brain scans may be used in case studies to gather data

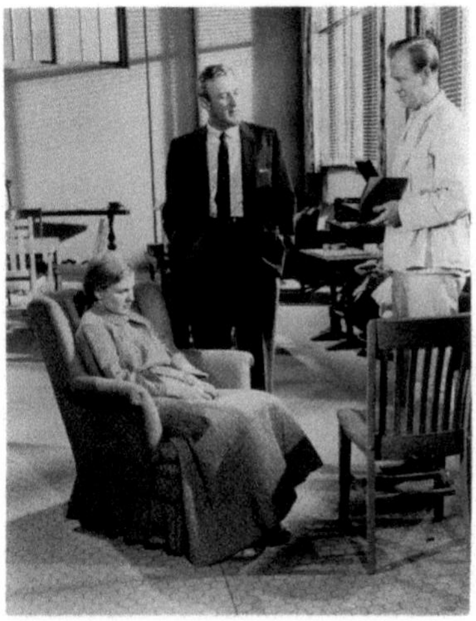

A still from the film The Three Faces of Eve

Top tip

Look for footage of Eve's case (Thigpen and Cleckley, 1954) on YouTube.

- In developmental psychology, case studies of deprived children have been useful in understanding the psychological effect of neglect or abandonment.

In all of such studies, the case study method is particularly suitable because the individual involved was unique. Thigpen and Cleckley (1954) presented a famous case of dissociative identity disorder (also called 'multiple personality disorder'). In their interviews with a female patient, it became apparent that she had more than one personality. One, calling herself 'Eve White' was uptight and law abiding, while another who introduced herself as 'Eve Black' was flirtatious and shallow. Personality tests and IQ tests confirmed the differences between the two personalities, which could be brought out through hypnosis. A third, more reasonable personality emerged through therapy, and the case was made into a film, *The Three Faces of Eve*.

Evaluation of case studies

Case studies are an extremely useful, sometimes essential tool for studying unique cases, including rare brain damage that would be unethical to cause deliberately. However, as a researcher builds up a personal acquaintance with a participant and their case, (s)he may start to show researcher bias due to developing a relationship with the patient/client. It is also hard to generalise the results of a case study to the wider population. Because of these problems, case studies are limited and no area of psychology relies on them entirely.

Overlap between methods

When considering what method is being used in a study, consider first whether it is an experiment or not. Many experiments use observations or surveys, but they should still be described as experiments rather than surveys/observation studies.

In particular, many experiments use observations as part of their procedure. However, these are not observation studies, as they manipulate an IV and record one or more numerical DVs, instead of passively gathering observational data. It is useful to remember that there is a degree of overlap between research methods in psychology.

Some studies draw on several methods. A case study is not in itself a single method of gathering data; it typically involves one or more of the other methods described in this book. Typically, the participant will be interviewed and they may fill in some questionnaires as well. The researcher may decide to observe the participant, either in their own environment (naturalistic observation) or doing a structured task in a controlled environment.

Summary of strengths and weaknesses of non-experimental methods

Non-experimental methods	Strengths	Weaknesses
Survey	• Well-designed questionnaires with closed questions are relatively quick and easy to answer and can gather a lot of data. • Answers can be analysed easily, forming totals and percentages.	• As the answers to structured questionnaires are a fixed choice, they do not allow respondents to express opinions that are different from those offered. There may also be researcher bias in the selection of options. • Participants cannot usually ask for further explanation – risk of misunderstanding. • There is a low response rate for postal and Internet questionnaires.
Interview	• Face-to-face format allows questions to be explained if necessary. • Unstructured interviews can be personalised to each participant and provide rich data.	• Suffer more from social desirability bias than surveys do, due to being face to face. • Unstructured interviews are costly and time-consuming to run, and questions may be biased or leading. The data from open questions is harder to analyse.
Observation	• Detailed record of real-life behaviour as it happens. • Captures behaviour in its true social context.	• Lacks the control of an experiment, so cannot infer cause and effect relationships. • Hard to replicate the results of an observational study as social situation is unique.
Case study	• Allows the researcher to focus on a specific instance and identify processes and variables. • A source of very rich and meaningful data (qualitative). • Insights from participant(s) may reveal an unusual and highly relevant perspective.	• Results are specific to the individual – often impossible to replicate. • Time consuming and expensive to carry out. • Close relationship between researcher and participant(s) potentially interferes with objectivity.

Activities

1. What problems might there be with the data from an unstructured interview? Consider each of the following, and rank them in order of importance from 1 to 4 (in your opinion):
   - biased results
   - unreliability of answers
   - difficulty to analyse
   - too much/too little data.
2. Draw a table showing the strengths and weaknesses of the different types of observation.
3. Design a survey to investigate an area of your choice relating to attitudes. Decide what type of questions to use, then design three or four questions. Get feedback and then complete a questionnaire with a total of 8–10 questions. Give copies of the questionnaire to other students for them to fill in and comment on.
4. In pairs, make an observation of a classmate volunteer for two minutes. Then compare your results with your co-observer to assess your 'inter-observer reliability'.

Classroom Observation Schedule
Duration: 2 minutes

Observer name: Participant name: Date and time:

Mark one tally mark for each time a behaviour is exhibited.
Ignore the first 20 seconds of observation.

Looks up at observer
Turns the page
Rubs/picks nose or sniffs
Licks lips/dribbles
Laughs or chuckles
Yawns
Scratches head or chin
Folds/crosses hands or arms or legs
Looks at other person in the room
Picks up pen or other nearby object

Questions

1. What is a closed question?
2. Give an example of an issue that needs to be avoided when writing survey questions.
3. Which type of interview mainly sticks to a list of questions but can include follow-up questions?
4. Why might you choose to use a structured interview instead of a survey?
5. Which type of observation involves watching participants in their everyday environment?
6. Being observed causes behaviour to change. What is this effect called?
7. Give a strength that is always true of observation.
8. Give three characteristics of the case-study method.
9. What techniques are used to gather data in a case study?
10. True or false: every study uses just one of the research methods?

Key concepts

- Non-experimental methods
- Survey (research method)
- Questionnaire
- Interview (research method)
- Open questions
- Closed questions
- Likert scale
- Acquiescence bias
- Social desirability bias
- Structured interview
- Semi-structured interview
- Unstructured interview
- Observation (research method)
- Naturalistic observation
- Structured observation
- Disclosed (observation)
- Undisclosed (observation)
- Observer effect
- Participant observation
- Non-participant observation
- Observation schedule
- Inter-observer reliability
- In-depth
- Longitudinal
- Case history

General research issues

There are certain issues that apply to every research method. All of these should be considered when planning and running your own research including the Assignment. Understanding them will also provide you with the tools to evaluate other studies. These issues include:

- hypotheses
- internal and external validity
- ethics
- data analysis.

Hypotheses

Every study will include one or more hypotheses. A **hypothesis** is a statement of what a study expects to find. Regardless of the type of

Top tip

Your two hypotheses should be located at the very end of the introduction section of your Assignment. Ask a classmate to check them and give you feedback.

experiment, the researcher will have a prediction that they are looking to test. This should be stated clearly towards the start of a research write-up.

Experimental and null hypothesis

In an experiment, the **experimental hypothesis** is based on the prediction that the treatment applied to an experimental group will cause them to be different from the population – manipulating the IV will have an effect on the DV. For example:

People who take a vitamin pill once a day will do better in their exams than those who do not.

OR

The group who are taught a memory strategy will recall more foreign language words than the control group.

Note that the variables in hypotheses should be **operationalised**. This means that they are put into a specific, testable form. Rather than *'memory'*, for example, you could say *'number of items recalled from a list of words'*.

Another hypothesis is usually stated – the **null hypothesis**. This makes a baseline prediction, essentially stating that the experimental group will be no different from the rest of the population.

A good way to phrase the null hypothesis is to state that the IV will **not** affect the DV and any difference between conditions is due to chance (e.g. participant variables or background distractions). For example:

The null hypothesis is that there will be no difference between group 1 and group 2 other than random error as a result of chance factors.

Sometimes you may see these hypotheses termed H_1 (experimental) and H_0 (null).

Directional hypotheses

Compare these two hypotheses:

Stress will have an effect on scores in a memory test for celebrity names.

Stress will reduce scores on a memory test for celebrity names.

Here the IV is stress and the DV is memory for celebrity names. The researcher wants to find out whether stress will affect memory. There is good reason to think that stress will harm memory, rather than improve it. Therefore, it would be more logical to predict the direction of the effect, and use the second of these example hypotheses. This is called a **directional** or **one-tailed** hypothesis.

Discussion point

Why do you think the terms 'one-tailed' and 'two-tailed' are sometimes used to describe hypotheses?

A hypothesis that just says the IV will have an effect and does not say whether it will increase or reduce DV scores is called a **non-directional** or **two-tailed** hypothesis. If the experimental hypothesis is directional, it would be logical to have a directional null hypothesis as well, for example:

Stress will ***not*** *reduce scores on a memory test for celebrity names and any changes found will be due to chance.*

Alternative hypotheses

Of course, not all studies are experiments, and as you might expect, the term 'experimental hypothesis' is only used in experiments. With a non-experimental study (e.g. a survey), the prediction is termed an **alternative hypothesis**. A null hypothesis is also used. For example, in a playground observation:

The alternative hypothesis is that younger children will play in larger groups than older children.

Internal and external validity

Whether or not a study is valid relates to whether it is possible to draw a logical conclusion from its findings.

Internal validity

If an experiment has high **internal validity**, it means that it is well designed and research can draw a sound conclusion about whether the IV had an effect on the DV or not. Many of the design issues discussed so far in this chapter relate to internal validity – in particular, control of extraneous and confounding variables so that cause and effect can be determined.

External validity

Even if a study is high in internal validity, the results could be worthless if it tells us nothing about real life. Some studies are highly artificial. If it can be hard to generalise from the results in the study to a real life situation, then the study is said to lack **ecological validity**.

A study that takes place in a participant's natural environment is often considered to be more realistic. As discussed earlier in this chapter, lab experiments are seen as more controlled but less realistic, while field experiments are the opposite. Therefore, lab experiments usually have higher internal validity and lower external validity, while for field experiments the situation is reversed.

However, the level of artificiality depends a lot on the task that is done. Even in a field experiment, participants might be asked to do something quite unnatural. Experimental tasks that are not typical of everyday life are said to lack **mundane realism**.

These two issues both relate to a more general concept – can we generalise the results from a study to other situations? If not, the results are next to useless. The ability to generalise from a study is known as its **external validity** – whether the findings hold true outside of the experimental situation. A third type of external validity has also been raised earlier in this chapter – can results from a sample be generalised to the population as a whole? This is called **population validity**.

These three main types of external validity will be helpful when you evaluate research studies, as they are three of the most common criticisms made of experiments throughout psychology. In every study that you have to evaluate, consider whether these might be a problem.

Even if they are not a problem, for example, if mundane realism is high, you should be aware of this as a strength of the study!

Top tip

Look at chapter 7 of this book for more guidance on evaluating research – note how important internal and external validity are to making strong evaluation points.

Types of external validity

Ecological validity: can the results be generalised to another environment, for example from the lab to the workplace or the home?

Mundane realism: how closely does the experimental task resemble something that people do in the real world?

Population validity: can the results be generalised from the sample to the population as a whole?

Discussion point

Do example experiments 1 and 2 (see p.194 and 198) at the start of this chapter have external validity? If not, why not?

Top tip

Write the three types of external validity on a post-it note and stick it up in your study area. Consider them every time you have to evaluate a study.

Research ethics

Psychologists want to find out answers to their questions and that means carrying out research on people. However, people are very different from the objects of study in other scientific subjects – they have rights that must be respected and feelings that must be taken into account. Psychology researchers therefore must follow a set of moral principles known as a **code of ethics** that states what is and is not acceptable in research. Such codes are published by professional organisations such as the British Psychological Society (BPS). Some of the key ethical principles are as follows, based on the BPS code of ethics (British Psychological Society, 2014).

As well as following these guidelines in your own research, you should raise ethical issues when discussing research in the other topics of this course. In particular, ensure that you are aware of the ethical flaws of classic research studies. These issues don't necessarily invalidate the results of the studies, but in some cases they might make it impossible to replicate the research.

It is important that participants give informed consent

Consent and deception

At the outset of a study, participants should give their consent to take part, meaning that they agree to be part of the research. However, people should be in full knowledge of what they are agreeing to do, including how long it will take. This is called **informed consent**.

Deception is where participants have been deliberately misled about the nature of a research task. An example is Asch (1951) – a study of conformity, but participants were told it was a study of perception. Deception is unethical, and cases where it has been used in the past are controversial.

Getting informed consent does not mean that participants need to be told the aims or hypothesis of the study but they do need to be told what they will have to do. There are some areas of research where it is impossible to get fully informed consent because telling the participants about the experiment's procedure will distort the results and researchers must therefore use an element of deception. An example is the Mori and Arai (2010) study of conformity. BPS guidelines recognise this and state it is acceptable only when there is no other alternative and that consideration must be given to how participants will react when they are given the full information (British Psychological Society, 2014). Also, participants must be given as much information as possible at the earliest opportunity.

Briefing and debriefing

A **briefing** should be given, explaining what the study will entail. Usually this takes place after consent has been given. The researcher gives a summary of what the experiment involves and what to expect. The briefing is a general overview of the study in more detail than was given during the consent process. The researcher will also provide specific task **instructions**, telling them what they have to do.

Participants must also be **debriefed**, meaning that after the study has taken place, all relevant aspects are explained to them. In particular, the aims of the study should be explained. If participants took part in only one condition of the IV, researchers may choose to tell them what the other condition involved. Participants are typically provided with the researchers' contact details, in case they want to withdraw their consent later. They may also be interested to find out the conclusions of the study once all of the data have been analysed.

Note that in relation to the previous section, the BPS code of conduct states that debriefing people afterwards does not excuse or justify unethical research (British Psychological Society, 2014).

> **Top tip**
>
> When debriefing participants in a classroom experiment or as part of the Assignment, it is helpful to have a short written statement to read out. This ensures that you won't forget anything important. Don't forget to thank participants for taking part!

Avoiding harm

Arguably, the most important and universal rule of research ethics is to avoid **harm** (or the risk of harm) during the research procedures or as a result of them. Of course, harm can happen accidentally (e.g. a participant falls off a chair and hurts themselves) but the principle set out by BPS and other research organisations is that the risk of physical or psychological harm should be no greater than in everyday life.

Psychological harm was shown in the Milgram (1963) study of obedience (see chapter 10). Participants later reported that they found it traumatic – but most reported that they were happy to have taken part (Milgram, 1974). Modern research guidelines ensure that such experiences could not happen nowadays.

Closely related to the risk of harm is that participants should not be exposed to any degrading or humiliating treatment.

Research on children

Some theoretical advances have been made through ethically dubious research on children, such as Watson and Rayner's (1920) study of 'little Albert' (see chapter 1). However, rules are much stricter nowadays: student researchers must not carry out experiments on children at all, and professional researchers take particular care to avoid any distress to child participants.

Children must be willing to take part and in addition to the child showing willingness, their parents must give written informed consent.

Parents must give written consent for a child to participate in a study

Top tip

If a research study that you are evaluating involves child participants, you should raise the issue of parental consent.

Top tip

Give careful consideration to the ages of participants for your own Assignment – you must identify a way of obtaining enough research participants who are aged 16 or above.

Discussion point

When conducting the Assignment, you must keep data confidential yet be able to identify which findings relate to which participant so that you can delete them at a later date if they withdraw consent retrospectively. How in practice are you going to achieve this? What steps should you take to ensure that all materials and results are kept secure and confidential?

This is because under-16s are vulnerable and may be too young to fully understand what they are consenting to.

Confidentiality

Confidentiality must be maintained. This means that data should be kept secure, and when results are published, no names or identifying information should be included. This ensures that participants are not embarrassed by their participation. In some cases, initials are used (e.g. 'the case of H.M.' in the famous case study of memory; Scoville & Milner, 1957). As well as being fair and respectful, this avoids unwelcome attention for the participants and also avoids putting people off from participating in the first place.

Right to withdraw

Participants also have the **right to withdraw** from any study at any time if they feel unhappy or uncomfortable or simply change their mind. They may also retrospectively withdraw consent when the study is over, in which case their data must be deleted/destroyed.

Example study: Piliavin's 'Good Samaritan' study

Irving Piliavin and colleagues were interested in diffusion of responsibility – the tendency for bystanders not to help a person in need if there are other people who could help. In a study that generated a considerable ethical debate, they conducted an observational study in a public place, where an actor faked a collapse on a subway train in New York. Researchers hid among the bystanders taking notes of who helped and how quickly they helped (Piliavin *et al.*, 1969).

Irving Piliavin conducted his 'Good Samaritan' study on the New York subway

Ironically, for a study into the unethical behaviour of strangers, there were several ethical problems in this methodology, including deception, a failure to gain informed consent from participants and psychological harm (stress).

For this study, it is vital to appreciate the historical context of ethical guidelines gradually tightening up. Such studies have helped to advance the ongoing process of deciding what is, and what is not, ethical in research.

Questions

1. What is an experimental hypothesis and when is it used?
2. Is it necessary to operationalise the IV and DV for an experimental hypothesis?
3. Which type of validity means that the experiment is well designed/set up and controls extraneous variables?
4. What does ecological validity mean?
5. A researcher asks participants to count backwards in threes while clicking coloured squares on a screen. Does this task have mundane realism?
6. Which type of validity relates to the issue of whether results from a sample can be generalised to the wider population or not?
7. Do laboratory experiments always lack mundane realism?
8. What is meant by a 'code of ethics' for research?
9. What is the term for the ethical principle whereby research findings have to be kept secure and names of participants should not be disclosed or published?
10. Can children give consent to take part in a study?

Key concepts

- Hypothesis
- Experimental hypothesis
- Null hypothesis
- Operationalisation
- One-tailed/directional hypothesis
- Two-tailed/non-directional hypothesis
- Alternative hypothesis
- Internal validity
- External validity
- Ecological validity
- Mundane realism
- Population validity
- Code of ethics
- Informed consent
- Deception
- Briefing
- Instructions
- Debriefing
- Harm
- Parental consent
- Confidentiality
- Right to withdraw

Activities

1. To operationalise means to put variables in a testable/measurable form. How could you operationalise the following variables?
   - Noise level
   - Concentration
   - Popularity
   - Stress level
   - Success at school
   - Amount of caffeine
   - Long-term memory
   - Ability at sports
2. Write out possible experimental and null hypotheses for studies based on these three research questions:
   - Does smoking cannabis harm your short-term memory?
   - Does what a researcher is wearing affect participants' performance on a task?
   - Are men better than women at parking cars?
3. Summarise the three main types of external validity into a chart in your notes. Ask a classmate to test you on them. Now identify an example research study that lacks each of the three types.
4. Briefly describe the procedure of a famous study where unethical research has been conducted, and give your views on whether such research should be conducted in the future or not.

Data and graphs

Research aims to produce good quality, valid data. But what do researchers do with their data? Data analysis is a key part of any research process and a useful transferrable skill to learn. This builds on basic concepts that you will have come across in other subjects on the curriculum.

Qualitative versus quantitative data

Some types of studies, for example, unstructured interviews, produce **qualitative data**. These are non-numerical data, especially verbal data such as descriptions. Images and videos (e.g. made during an observation) are also qualitative.

Other studies, in particular experiments, produce **quantitative data** – data based on numbers. The data can be analysed, or displayed in graphs.

In some cases, such as with observation methods, it may be matter of choices – verbal descriptions could be written during an observation, or quantitative data could be recorded (e.g. a record of the number of times that a behaviour is observed), or the study could use a mixture of both.

Sometimes qualitative data is converted into quantitative data to make it easier to analyse. For example, a researcher could ask interviewees an open question about prejudice and then score their responses out of 10 based on how much prejudice they showed. This is quite subjective. A more objective way to convert the data is to use a software package to search for the frequency of key terms or phrases in people's answers.

Descriptive statistics

Descriptive statistics are ways of calculating numbers that describe the data in some way – that is, summarise a set of data in a single number. The most obvious example is to calculate an average.

Averages

People use the term **average** in everyday speech but there are three main ways of showing the average or most typical value of a set of data:

The mean	The **mean** is calculated by adding together all of the values and dividing by the number of scores. It is the most useful score statistically as it includes all of the scores in the calculation and is the basis of other calculations such as the standard deviation. However, it can be distorted by extreme high or low scores.
The mode	The **mode** is the most common score. This can be useful to avoid extreme values of the mean, and although less useful statistically, it may be of interest to know which score was actually the most common. However, some sets of data do not have a mode. Sometimes there are two modes ('bi-modal') or several (multi-modal), that is, two or more scores that are equally the most common.
The median	The **median** is the midpoint of the data, obtained by putting scores in order, low to high, and finding the one in the centre. If there is an even number of scores, the mean of the middle two scores is calculated.

Dispersion

The mean, mode and median are useful statistics but having the average alone gives us no indication of whether scores are generally close to or far away from this midpoint. **Dispersion** means how widely data are spread out and it is calculated using a different set of descriptive statistics:

Top tip

At National 5 and Higher, *descriptive statistics* are required but you do not have to calculate the *inferential statistics* that more experienced psychology researchers use. Inferential statistics are useful because they tell us whether the difference between two groups is likely to have occurred by chance or not. They are essential for published research. Although time-consuming, they are not especially difficult to calculate. Ask your teacher or lecturer for more information.

Make the link

When journalists talk about averages such as 'average income', ask yourself – and try to find out – which statistic they are using. Sometimes it can make a huge difference!

The range	The **range** is a very simple summary of the spread of data, based on the difference between the lowest and highest scores. It is easily calculated by subtracting the lowest score from the highest. However, it is limited in that it does not reflect the distribution of the other data. Worse still, the lowest and/or the highest score are extreme values, which may be abnormal in some way. For example, if the data were based on time to do a task, you may find that the highest values are very much out of line with the bulk of scores due to one or two people giving up or misunderstanding the instructions. This affects the value of the range as a summary of the data.
The interquartile range	An easy way to avoid the extreme scores used by the range and still get a simple-to-calculate figure is to use the **interquartile range**. This involves listing numerical data in order from lowest to highest and then finding the difference between the scores at the 25% and 75% points, that is, the difference between the score one quarter from the bottom of the distribution and the score one-quarter from the top.
The standard deviation	For a more reliable calculation of the spread of scores, the **standard deviation** (**SD**) shows the typical amount by which the scores in the distribution differ from the mean. The calculation is based on finding the difference between each score and the mean and then calculating the average of these differences. A large range could be the result of just two people failing to conform; however, the SD takes everyone's response into account.

? Discussion point

Note that Jenness (1932, see chapter 10) used the range rather than the SD. However, his groups only had three members. Why would this make a difference to his choice of statistic?

! Syllabus note

Correlation is not mandatory in this course but a basic understanding of the concept will help you understand research evidence that uses correlation.

Correlation

A typical correlation study in psychology uses a non-experimental source such as a survey to obtain numerical values on two variables (e.g. IQ and extraversion). The researcher then uses a statistical technique to find the relationship between these variables, typically called the 'co-variables'. This technique gives the research a number which tells them if the relationship between the two variables is:

- strong (closely connected) or weak
- positive (rise and fall together) or negative (move in opposite directions).

The strength of a correlation is shown via a number between 1 and 0, with the closer it is to 1, the stronger the correlation between the two variables. Negative correlations show strength in the same way, but they are shown using a negative number (i.e. between 0 and –1).

A scattergram is used to display the relationship: for each participant, a point or cross is marked at the point on the graph where their scores on the co-variables meet.

A correlational hypothesis should state that a relationship will be found, instead of saying that one variable will affect the other. For example: *'The correlational hypothesis is that there will be a strongly positive relationship between the number of hours of sleep a student gets and their grade average.'*

> **Top tip**
>
> A positive or negative correlation means that the variables do have a relationship but cause and effect cannot be assumed – just because two things seem linked, it doesn't mean that one is causing the other to change. A classic example is that the time your alarm clock goes off is correlated with the time the sun comes up but this doesn't mean that the sun is making your alarm clock go off or that your alarm clock is making the sun rise!

Graphs

Graphs are used to present results and to perform a basic visual analysis. You may have to interpret a graph in the exam or suggest a suitable graph for a set of data. It is also an essential skill for your Assignment. Some of the most common types include:

A **bar graph** shows scores as heights on two or more separated 'bars', which often represent the different conditions of an experiment. It allows for an easy comparison of means.

Note that the IV is shown along the x-axis, at the bottom of the graph.

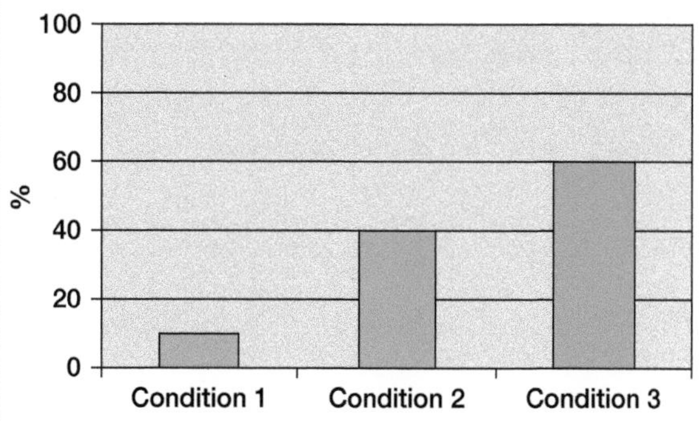

A **histogram** looks similar to a bar graph, except for the lack of gaps between the columns. This is because a histogram shows a range of values from the same category, e.g. scores on a test. The height of the columns shows frequency.

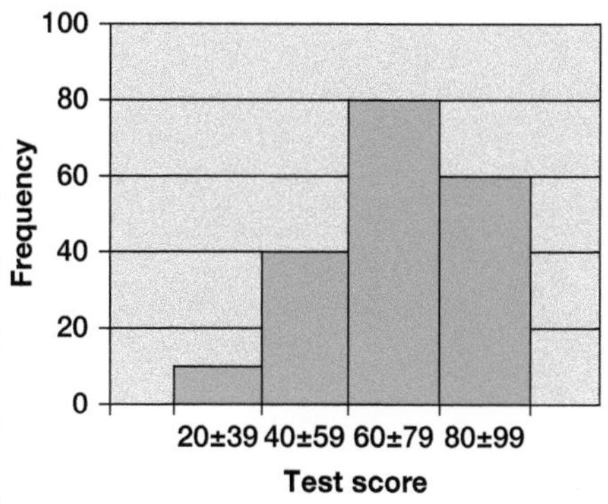

A **pie chart** is not commonly used in psychology but it can be helpful for showing the percentages of a population which engage in a behaviour. The size of each slice represents its proportion and the total should add up to 100%. Scores on a DV, such as memory test scores, should not be presented on a pie chart.

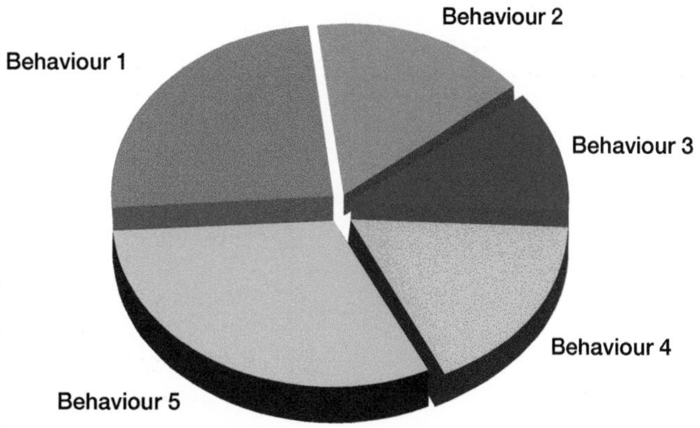

Top tip

Draw a scattergram using data on two variables for your class, for example, scores on a test and number of hours spent revising.

As mentioned above, scattergrams are widely used in psychology, but only for correlational studies. They should not be used to present experimental data.

Percentages

Finally, you should be aware of the use of **percentages**. As you will be aware from your studies of maths, percentages are easily calculated by dividing the score by the maximum and multiplying by 100.

(score/maximum) × 100

Percentages help to standardise scores, making them easier to compare. For example, if participants have done two tests, one out of a maximum of 80 and one with a maximum of 65, it can be hard to compare the results. Is 49/80 better than 38/65? A percentage makes it immediately clear – the first result converts to 61.2% and the second is 58.5%. Therefore, the first score is superior.

Key concepts

- Qualitative data
- Quantitative data
- Descriptive statistics
- Average
- Mean
- Mode
- Median
- Dispersion
- Range
- Inter-quartile range
- Standard deviation
- Bar graph
- Histogram
- Pie chart
- Scattergram
- Percentages

Questions

1. Name three ways of calculating the average.
2. Name three graphs.
3. Which descriptive statistic shows the midpoint of the data?
4. When is a mean not the best way of calculating the average of a set of data?
5. Name the statistic that is calculated by subtracting the lowest score from the highest.
6. Summarise verbally what the SD is.
7. What major disadvantage does the mode have?
8. Why is the SD considered the most 'powerful' way of calculating dispersion?
9. What is the difference in appearance between a bar graph and a histogram?
10. Why is it often useful to use percentages to summarise scores?

Activities

1. Calculate the mean, mode, median and range of ages in your classroom, <u>or</u> of members of your family. Does this task highlight weaknesses of any of the statistics?
2. Calculate descriptive statistics for the following scenario:

> The following data were obtained from an independent groups study in which two sets of participants (total n=26) studied a section of a psychology textbook and were then given a 20-question multiple-choice test. In condition 2 only, a memory strategy was used.
>
> Scores on condition 1:
>
> 3 7 10 8 14 2 9 8 7 13 7 5 11
>
> Scores on condition 2:
>
> 19 10 11 8 9 9 11 14 3 6 3 10 17

3. Fill in the following table.

Type of graph/chart	Appearance/key features	Example(s) of when to use
Bar graph		
Histogram		
Pie chart		

4. Draw examples of the three types of graph from the previous task. Find out about other kinds of graphs, and add them to your notes too.

9 The Assignment

For the Assignment, you should know and understand:

- The importance of planning practical research.
- The purpose of and correct way to express an aim and hypothesis.
- The correct way to express methodology in a research write-up.
- Using background information to inform a research plan.
- How to apply ethical evaluation in a practical context.

! Syllabus note

For National 5, the Assignment is based around a research plan, and gathering data is not compulsory. There is an open choice of topic for the plan.

At Higher, you must conduct a practical study and gather data. The write-up will be based on the data that you gather.

Planning, conducting research, and scientific writing are valuable skills to learn

Understanding the Assignment

Place in the course

The **Assignment** is a mandatory part of both the Higher and National 5 courses in Psychology. It is a research project that forms part of the Research section of your course and it is externally marked by the SQA. It forms around a third of your overall marks for the course – enough to bring a poor exam mark up to a pass, or turn a C into an A, so it is essential to complete it as well as possible. Chapter 8 has equipped you with the skills and knowledge needed to conduct research. In this part of the course, you will develop those skills and put them to use. You will complete a piece of scientific writing based on a practical research project. This will then be submitted to the SQA for marking.

Planning, conducting research, and scientific writing are valuable skills to learn, which will be of great use to your future studies, not just in psychology but in business, medicine or any scientific subject, and to careers such as working for local or national government, the police, management or a range of other areas. In this topic, you will learn how to write a report in a formal style, including in-line citations, references and appendices. You will also learn how to evaluate your own research activities.

Evidence and spot checks

Your school or college will put measures into place to ensure that your Assignment is your own work. This could include short interviews with you to ensure that you understand what is included. It is vitally important that you write it all yourself. Copying from any source (including this textbook!) is out of the question and could lead to you failing the whole course. Likewise, getting anyone else to help you write your Assignment is unethical as well as highly risky, while cheating is generally easy for teachers/lecturers and markers to spot.

Working as a group

You can (where relevant) conduct the data gathering element of your Assignment in a small group, provided your teacher/lecturer agrees. There are some research situations where it is helpful to have more than one person available, for example to hand out materials or debrief participants. However, the analysis of data and all report writing should be your own work. Also, do not show the work you have done on your Assignment to a classmate, as to do so puts you at risk of being copied.

Deadlines and drafts

It is a good idea to get started with the Assignment early – perhaps after you have studied the first topic or two of your course. You will then work on it over a period of months, completing by the SQA deadline, which is usually in the spring. It is important to be organised and much easier to produce an excellent piece of work if you work at it regularly. Keep detailed notes and make sure you back up all saved files.

Your teacher will support you through the process and will look at drafts that you write, but ultimately, this is your work. You should not expect detailed corrections of your drafts, but more general feedback.

! Syllabus note

At Higher, the Assignment is worth 40 marks in combination with 80 marks for the exam. At National 5, the Assignment is worth 30 marks, which is combined with 70 marks for the exam.

At Higher, the guideline word count is 2,000 to 2,500 words, excluding references and appendices; for National 5, the Assignment should be 800 to 1,200 words in length.

You can plan and conduct the data gathering element in a small group

Skills for the Assignment

Background reading

In order to fully understand the topic area of your Assignment, you should conduct some independent background reading as you work on the Assignment. The background will feed into the introduction section of your plan/write-up.

It is important that you keep track of your sources. If you come across a useful website or book, make sure that you take a note of it (or bookmark the site or take a photo) to help you find it again later. This is good research practice and will save you wasting time later when you come to write your references section.

Copy-and-pasting text from the Internet, even if you plan to re-word it, is strongly discouraged. In any case, you will get a much better end result if you read the material and then try to explain it in your own words without looking at the source.

Speak to your school/college library, as they will be able to direct you towards suitable books. Every textbook has different background research studies so look around. Most also have a section on writing research reports.

! Syllabus note

Background reading is required at both levels. At National 5, your teacher/lecturer will direct you to suitable sources. At Higher, you are expected to be more independent.

Top tip

Published research usually includes a short summary at the start, called an 'Abstract'. You are **not** required to write an abstract for the Assignment in Higher/National 5 Psychology.

As well as books, there are several useful online sources for you to look at:

Name	Source	Comments
The SQA Assignment research guidelines	www.sqa.org.uk or via search engine	Your school/college may provide some additional background information or a scenario.
This textbook and other suitable books	Library	Any psychology textbook can be useful for background – it doesn't need to be a book aimed at your course.
BPS research digest	digest.bps.org.uk	Summarises the best current research studies each week. Began in 2005, so it now contains a great database of studies from over 12 years of psychology.
Psyblog	spring.org.uk	A more populist blog, but it contains very interesting articles on a huge range of topics and has links to all research studies mentioned.
Google Scholar	scholar.google.co.uk	Don't forget to look for a link to a pdf version of the study – these links are sometimes out of date, but often you can read the full original article.

You should conduct some independent background reading as you work on the Assignment

Avoid using an ordinary Google search for your background reading. Wikipedia and other encyclopaedias are best used just as a starting point for your reading, if at all. The introduction section of your write-up will include a review of background research, in which you will outline the topic area and summarise the most relevant previous studies.

References

You will have noticed in your studies of psychology so far that there are many references to previous research, which often look like this:

Smith and Bond (1993)

or

Cohen *et al.* (1981)

You will include **references** in a standard format in your Assignment. In the main body of the text, put the author's name and year in brackets, each time you are referring to an idea or a research finding that came from their work. This is called an **in-line citation**. Then, at the end of the document, there should be a reference section, which will give full publication details of the sources that you refer to – what book, website or journal the findings were published in. This allows a reader to find and check these sources.

There is no single correct way of formatting the reference section, but it is important that it is well presented and consistent. The key is to pick an appropriate standard format and then stick to it. The following is suggested as it is based on British Psychological Society guidelines:

Books like this:

Baddeley, A.D. (1999). *Essentials of human memory*. East Sussex: Psychology Press.

Journal articles like this:

Craik, F.I.M. and R.S. Lockhart (1972). Levels of processing: A framework for memory research. *Journal of Verbal Learning and Verbal Behaviour, 11*, 671–684.

Websites like this:

Harkness, T. (2014). Does brain structure determine your political views? Retrieved 21 May 2014 from *http://www.bbc.co.uk/news/uk-politics-27437799*.

Writing style

It is important to present the Assignment clearly and to make it look like a professional piece of work. It would be a good idea if possible to word-process the Assignment, as it makes it much easier to edit and improve it as you go along. Present it with 1.5 or 2.0 line spacing, in a standard-looking font such as Times, Arial, Optima or Tahoma, and in 11 or 12 point text size.

It is also standard in scientific writing to use the **passive voice**, for example: '*questionnaires were handed out*' (instead of: '*I handed questionnaires out*'). There are many exceptions, but at this early stage it would be best to stick to the passive voice as it sounds more formal.

Scientific writing is generally done in the **past tense**, and in the Higher, most of the write-up will be in the past tense as you are reporting on an experiment done in the past (remember this if you start writing before gathering your data). However, for National 5, the Assignment is based around a plan, so in some elements it will be more suitable to talk about what you are *going to* do in the future. See the sample Assignments in the following two sections for examples of this.

Key concepts

- Assignment
- References
- In-line citation
- Passive voice
- Past tense

National 5: planning and writing the Assignment

Skills for the National 5 Assignment:

- Developing a research idea into a workable research plan.
- Identifying ethical issues that will affect your study.
- Writing up the plan in a standard scientific format and formal language.

! Syllabus note

The details of planning and writing-up the Assignment are very different for Higher and National 5. The following sections focus on National 5 planning; for Higher, skip to page 237.

At National 5, you have an open choice of topic. However, it will be easier to do something linked to one of the topics that you have studied so far, or will study soon, because material from the topic will help you to develop research ideas and conducting the Assignment will consolidate what you have learned so far.

Note that you have to consider ethical issues as part of the assessment. Do **not** plan a highly unethical study on the basis that it will give you more to talk about! Even if you don't actually run the study that you describe in the plan, it must be something that you could practically and ethically carry out. Showing ethical awareness is part of the task.

The suggestions in the following section might help you to decide on a topic. However, it is possible that your teacher/lecturer will want everyone in the class to do the same topic, so take advice on acceptable choices before you begin.

SQA's general assessment requirements for N5

A. Describe behaviour associated with a chosen psychological topic

B. Explain features of the topic with reference to psychological research evidence

C. Describe an aim for research on this topic

D. Give an experimental/alternative hypothesis for the proposed research study

E. Describe a suitable research plan, including method, sampling, variables and procedure

F. Describe ethical issues and ways of addressing these in the research plan

G. Use appropriate terminology and provide basic references

Source: www.sqa.org.uk

Top tip

Note that any conformity study that involves social pressure from a group discussion (whether or not actors are used) could be considered unethical due to the stress it might cause participants, and should therefore be avoided.

National 5: suggested studies

The following suggestions draw on popular psychology topics, including those described elsewhere in this textbook.

Conformity. A replication of Jenness's classic study of conformity (see chapter 10) could be planned. This would involve a stimulus of some kind, such as a jar of sweets. Measurements of estimates could be taken individually, and then further estimates taken after allowing participants to view what other people have estimated. The range and mean of estimates could be compared.

For a variation of the study a sheet of faked high or low answers could be prepared and shown to half of the participants. A control group are asked to estimate the number of sweets without being influenced, while others are shown the (fake) guesses of previous participants and then asked to give estimates. Variations of this idea could include using illusions, to see whether people conform to previous answers when stating what they see.

Sleep. A questionnaire study could be conducted to look at the relationship between hours of sleep and cognitive function. Questions could be asked about how late people go to bed and how many hours of sleep they get, as well as about ability to concentrate. Grades at school/college could also be studied or an IQ or memory test given to students.

Memory. A study could be conducted to look at the 'primacy/recency effect'. This is where items at the beginning and end of a list are better remembered compared to those in the middle. Typically, a list of words are read out or shown on screen, or a set of items/pictures shown. Items must be shown one at a time, not all together. Recall is then immediately tested by asking participants to name or write down the items. Usually people remember items at the beginning and end of the list, but not the ones in the middle.

Phobias. As described in chapter 3, some researchers have suggested that people are more fearful of animals that appear ugly due to being alien-looking. You could conduct a study where you show images of animals to participants, and ask them to rate the animals on the basis of how attractive they are, and on how scary they find each animal.

NVC: there are individual differences including cultural differences in how body language and facial expressions are interpreted. Plan a study that looks at these differences. It could be a quasi-experiment comparing males and females. For example, each participant could be shown pictures with examples of body language, and asked what the different gestures/postures/expressions mean.

Top tip

For more research ideas, have a look at the suggested studies for Higher in the following section – although these may involve more work in terms of background reading.

Top tip

The word counts for sections are not mandatory but they should help you to write a suitable amount in order to pick up all of the available marks.

It is fine to choose a different idea to those mentioned above, but give some thought to practicalities and to research ethics – as mentioned previously, you should not plan a study that is impossible or highly unethical. If any deception is involved, consider how participants will feel after the deception is revealed to them during debriefing – if it is likely that they will be upset or annoyed then it is best to rethink the procedure.

National 5: sections of the write-up

The following describes a standardised structure for your write-up based on section headings used at other levels of psychology, including Higher, HN and degree level. Although the SQA does not provide a mandatory structure, it is suggested that you follow this guide as the section headings fit the task well, and will be recognisable to your marker.

Each section is allocated a particular number of marks on the marking scheme. The table below explains what should be included.

Section	Must include
Introduction/ background (350–550 words)	Define topic with relevant behaviour described. Explain relevant previous research. Aim and hypothesis.
Research plan (350–450 words)	Should cover: **Method:** state proposed method (e.g. lab experiment) and state its strengths and weaknesses. **Sampling:** proposed sampling method must be described and reasons given for the choice. **Variables:** key research variables (usually IV and DV). **Procedure (including materials):** description of procedure – steps to be followed and materials that will be used.
Ethics (100–200 words)	Must be specific to plan. Four or more ethical points must be made, including both the ethical principles and how they will be considered in the plan.
References and terminology	Accurate terminology should be used throughout. References to previous research should be listed at the end (should be clear enough that a reader can identify the sources).

Bear in mind that marking guidelines can change and you should consult the most recent SQA documents.

The overall Assignment will be 800 to 1,200 words in length.

For National 5 your Assignment should be 800 to 1,200 words in length

Title

You don't get marks for your title but you should include one – it is part of good presentation to do so. Something simple, such as 'the effect of ___ on ___' usually works best. Include this on a separate title page along with your name, school and Scottish Candidate number.

Contents

It is good style to include a **contents page** with page numbers matching the page number of each section.

Introduction

In the first main section, usually called the **introduction** section in published research, you describe the behaviour that your research aims to study. The section starts by stating the topic of study and general area of psychology (e.g. social psychology). It should then progress from general background (the topic/area, e.g. conformity) to more specific similar previous research studies (e.g. a study that you are replicating).

- Define the topic.
- Discuss two to three real world examples of behaviour relevant to this topic, using relevant terminology.
- Describe one relevant theory/model.
- Briefly explain how one of the approaches has been used to study the topic.
- Explain the methodology and findings of the study that your Assignment is based on.
- Explain one other relevant study.

> **Top tip**
>
> The introduction should simply describe the research area *without mentioning your own study*. In many ways, it is like a short essay on the topic.

State the aim and hypothesis

Next, state your aim in general terms. This is what you say about what the study is trying to do. Perhaps it could say that the aim is to replicate a previous study, or to find out the effect of something, or to test/find support for a theory. Example:

The aim of this project is to test the effect of cultural differences on how facial expressions are interpreted.

Key concepts

- Contents page
- Introduction
- State aim
- State hypothesis
- Research plan / methodology
- Ethics
- References

Now, give the **hypothesis** – the predicted finding of the study. If it is an experiment, put this under the heading 'experimental hypothesis', otherwise it should be titled 'alternative hypothesis'. If it is a correlational study, use the heading 'correlational hypothesis' and remember that is should be described in terms of the relationship between two variables (see page 222 for more about correlation).

Explain the research plan

The **research plan** is where you explain what the proposed practical research will involve. Use the heading 'Methodology'. Include:

- Method to be used, for example field experiment.
- Sampling method, for example opportunity sampling, volunteer sampling.
- Variables: the IV and DV to be studied (or the two co-variables for a correlation).
- Materials or apparatus to be used, for example, questionnaires, experimental apparatus.
- A description of the procedure.

Where appropriate, explain why a choice was made, such as why you plan to use a field experiment instead of a laboratory experiment.

Sub-sections can be used here if it seems clearer, such as method/sample/variables/procedure. If the materials are especially complex (e.g. a long questionnaire) then it might be best to have a separate section under the subheading 'Materials', as well.

Ethical procedures

The **ethics** of your study must be carefully considered. Under a suitable heading such as 'Ethics', describe any ethical problems that will arise and procedures that should be used to avoid or minimise these. For example:

> *It is anticipated that participants may feel stressed and want to stop doing the experiment. To deal with this problem, they will be told at the start that they can withdraw at any time. A classmate will be available to debrief anyone who leaves early.*

Think of things about this study in particular that could upset, stress or harm participants. Also consider general ethical principles such as briefing/debriefing, consent (participants under the age of 16 are generally considered too young to consent on their own behalf) and confidentiality of results. If there is any deception involved, this should be considered and discussed.

Top tip

A top quality plan will include several ethical points, carefully analysed. Strengths of your research procedure can be mentioned, as well as problems.

References

It is essential that you provide basic references. These are the sources that you mentioned in your introduction/background section. Simply including the name, year and title of sources is acceptable (with a url if it is a website), although you are encouraged to start using a standard reference in the British Psychological Society or APA format. See the previous section of this chapter for more information or just use the same format as the references at the back of this book.

National 5: example plan

The following is an example plan in the popular topic of non-verbal communication. The same structure could be used for any topic. This example follows the structure suggested in the previous section and covers all of the essential points, although it is relatively short and there would be room to give more detail in places.

Top tip

In a real Assignment, a contents page would be included as well.

The effect of attractiveness on pupil dilation

By Nadia Bachmann

Dundee Academy
SCN: 0900011991

Background

The term non-verbal communication (NVC) refers to processes by which people communicate with others without using words, such as gestures and postures.

Some aspects of NVC are relatively automatic — we don't even realise we are doing it. In some cases these behaviours are innate, and universally the same for everyone regardless of culture. Facial expression is thought to be a cultural universal in NVC; people from all cultures show the same basic facial expressions (Ekman & Friesen, 1971).

Eye contact can be a form of non-verbal communication. The way we move our eyes to look at another person can show interest (Argyle & Cook, 1976). We prefer people who catch our gaze as long as this is not brief or shifty (Kuzmanovic et al, 2009).

Related to this, the pupils of our eyes may engage in subtle and automatic NVC. It is well known that a person's pupils are wider when it's dark. However, dilated (i.e. wider) pupils also make a person appear more attractive. In an experiment by Tombs and Silverman (2004), graduation photos were edited using Photoshop to make the pupils appear larger or smaller. Images with larger pupils were rated as better looking.

What's more, a person's own pupils appear to dilate more when they are speaking to someone that they find attractive. This could be an innate reaction, a way of communicating mutual interest by automatically showing that they find someone attractive. This would fit with the evolutionary approach to psychology.

However, it's also that case that a person's pupils get wider if they are doing a difficult task (Granholm & Steinhauer, 2004). It's therefore possible that in some of the past research, participants' pupils didn't dilate as a form of communication because they find another person attractive, but instead because the person was concentrating hard on the situation when they saw someone attractive. Perhaps they were imagining what it would be like to be such a stunning person, or else mentally composing a chat-up line.

Aim

Is pupil dilation upon seeing beautiful faces purely an automatic form of NVC? Or could it be due to the processing demands that come from concentration? This study aims to investigate this issue. It will keep the cognitive demands of the task constant by giving every participant the same complex processing task to do while they look at images of faces. This will ensure that any change in pupil dilation is linked to attraction and not due to cognitive effort.

Experimental Hypothesis

Participants doing a counting task will show more pupil dilation when viewing highly attractive faces than when viewing average/unattractive faces.

Methodology

A laboratory experiment will be used, with a quiet tutorial room as a lab, helping to keep all distractions to a minimum and avoid errors creeping in.

Opportunity sampling will be used – this will involve taking conveniently available participants i.e. friends from other courses. Pupil dilation is thought to be a universal reaction, so random sampling is not really necessary.

The IV of the proposed study is whether faces are attractive or not, and the DV is the size of participants' pupils. The IV will be operationalised by getting a group of classmates to all name five attractive celebrities and five that they find unattractive. The 10 most commonly named individuals from each group will then be chosen.

The DV will be operationalising by taking photos of participants' eyes at a fixed distance, and then measuring their pupils using a ruler.

A key variable to be kept constant is the amount of mental effort. This will be done by asking every participant to count backwards in 3s from 500 throughout the task. The time they view the faces will be kept constant by showing the images on a timed slideshow. A final consideration is participants' sexuality, as this is likely to influence results. To keep things simple, the research will show an even mix of both male and female faces in both conditions.

Procedure

The procedure will be as follows: participants will be brought into the laboratory by the researcher. They will be asked to sign a consent form, and told that the experiment is on non-verbal communication and will take a few minutes.

They will then watch a slide show which will show them the images of 20 celebrities (10 attractive, 10 unattractive). In each case the main image from the website IMDB will be used. There will also be an instruction slide at the start, at which point they will begin counting. The slideshow will be set up so that each face displays for two seconds, and after each one a blank slide will show for two seconds. A photo will be taken of the participants' eyes after each celebrity is shown.

At the end they will be debriefed, given information about the study's background, and thanked.

Ethics

People may find the counting task very hard. If they are showing signs of stress, the researchers will stop the test early and discard their data.

Researchers will not tell participants whether they are expected to find t he c elebrities attractive or not. To avoid psychological harm from this mild deception, the researchers will debrief them and explain why this was necessary.

Participants should not be children. To avoid choosing any participants who are under 16, friends from college classes will be used. In addition, the consent form will ask them to declare their age.

An ethical strength is that this kind of research is controlled, and does not expose participants to real-world harm or embarrassment.

WORD COUNT: 915 words.

Higher: planning and writing the Assignment

> **! Syllabus note**
>
> The following section applies to Higher – for National 5, refer to the previous section.

Skills for the Higher Assignment:

- Developing a research idea into a workable research plan.
- Identifying ethical issues which will affect your study.
- Identifying variables which will affect your study and controlling these where possible.
- Creating clear materials relevant to your topic, for example, questionnaires.
- Identifying a sample of participants and gathering data.
- Writing up the study in a standard scientific format using formal language.

The topic for your Higher Assignment must stick to the guidelines provided by SQA. Make sure you have the documents for the current year's course. You might also be given specific instructions by your school or college about what topics are acceptable. It's best to follow this advice, as it means you will benefit from guidance given by your teacher/lecturer to your whole class.

SQA's general assessment requirements for Higher

1. Review the topics and related research you have studied.
2. From these, choose a topic for your own primary research.
3. Plan primary research based on this topic and following BPS ethical guidelines
4. Carry out primary research according to the research plan and following BPS ethical guidelines
5. Produce a report that conforms to the style and format of a psychology research report

Source: www.sqa.org.uk

Higher: suggested topics

The following will give you some ideas of how to develop your chosen Assignment research topic or scenario.

Line drawing task apparatus

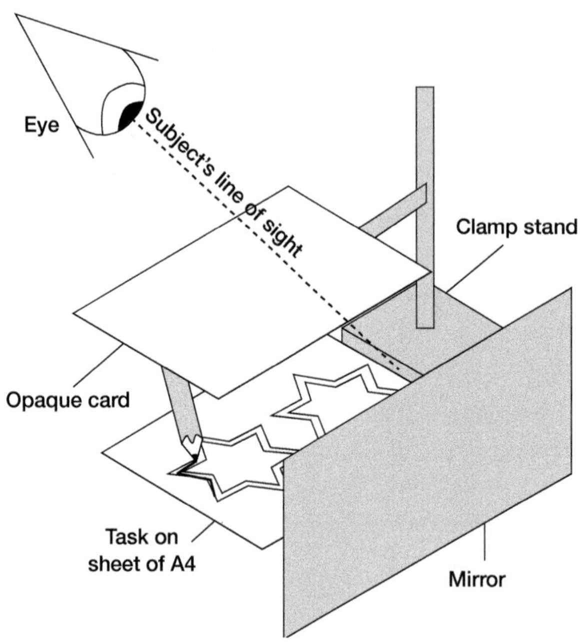

Mirror drawing is a classic way of testing improvement on a procedural (skill-based) memory, and was used with the memory patient H.M. (see page 139). It could be used for a number of studies, such as testing age differences, comparing skill/improvements on mirror drawing with other memory tasks or with IQ, or even looking for the effects of sleep on procedural memory – do people improve more after a night's sleep rather than in the same day, keeping the amount of practice the same?

Link to research topic or scenario: this task could be connected to the topics of Memory, Stress or Sleep, or to a scenario that asks you to investigate individual differences in learning and memory.

Multi-tasking – give participants two things to do at once, such as completing a simple video game while answering questions. The wire game pictured is a good visuospatial task for such experiments and it could be used for other studies including stress and reaction times. Card sorting tasks or following a moving spot with a pointer could also work well. Stoet *et al.* (2013) found evidence that women are better than men at multi-tasking, but there are still many unanswered questions – does the gender difference depend on the type of task participants are trying to do?

Link to research topic or scenario: this task could be connected to a scenario that asks you to investigate learning or education, individual differences or anything to do with the workplace.

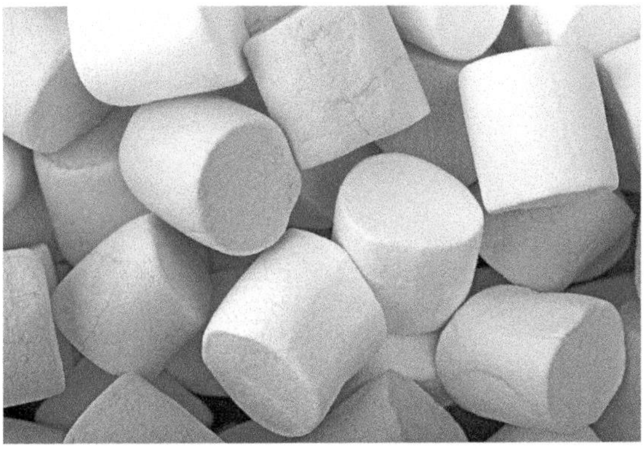

The 'marshmallow test' is a classic test of willpower. Typically, a sweet is put in front of a child and they are told that if they can resist eating it for 10 minutes, they can have a second sweet and eat both. Those who could resist were later found to score better on school tests and be less likely to commit crimes (Mischel *et al.*, 1972). Perhaps you could compare classmates' ability to resist this temptation with their school exam results? Mischel *et al.* also noted that people could successfully use strategies for resisting temptation (e.g. thinking of something else rather than looking at/sniffing the sweet). Perhaps you could try teaching these strategies to classmates (see http://bit.ly/1tZ08zi for a simple summary).

Link to research topic or scenario: this task could be connected to topics that involve individual differences, anything to do with children, or cultural differences. It could also be linked to some scenarios in political or environmental psychology.

Illusions are fun and interesting and they can be used in various studies. Visit www.michaelbach.de/ot for an excellent selection of illusions, most of which can be modified in various ways. Illusions can be used to investigate the nature-nurture debate, as things such as culture and experience can affect how we see them.

Link to research topic or scenario: this task could be connected to topics involving individual differences, especially cultural differences. Although you probably won't be conducting brain scans, the role of visual areas of the brain could in principle be investigated using illusions as a stimulus. It could also be used as part of a memory experiment.

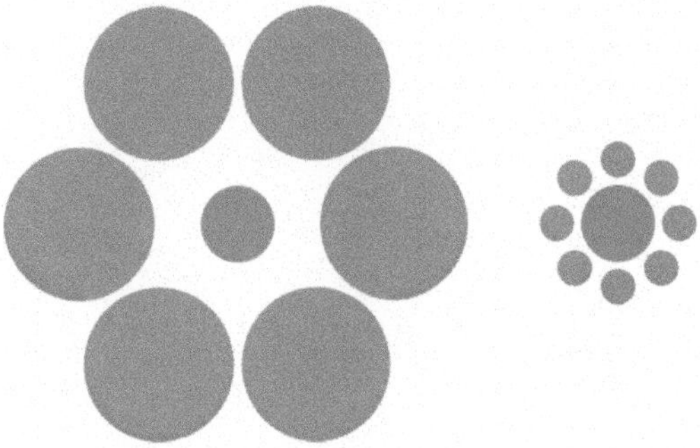

The orange circles are the same size

Adorno's (1950) F Scale, or the more modern version, Altemeyer's RWA scale, is a great way to conduct a practical study of prejudice. Versions are available online – see for example http://www.panojohnson.com/automatons/rwa-scale.xhtml. Another option would be to give people information to remember that either fits or goes against prejudiced schemas, and see how well these are remembered, similar to the study by Cohen (1981; see page 303).

Link to research topic or scenario: this task could be connected to most psychology topics involving social psychology or culture, and to scenarios where prejudice could play a role. It could also be linked to memory, upbringing, personality or individual differences.

There are a number of quick and simple ways of studying the body's response to stress, such as 'stress dots' that measure skin temperature, a heart-rate monitor or even just taking the participants' pulse rate by hand. Note that any study of stress **must** be ethical and it is not acceptable to stress people more than they would experience in everyday life, for example, during a typical class. Consult with your teacher/lecturer on the research ethics of this area.

Link to research topic or scenario: this task would most obviously connect to a health-related scenario but it could be linked to any aspect of the Stress topic, or other topics where stress is involved.

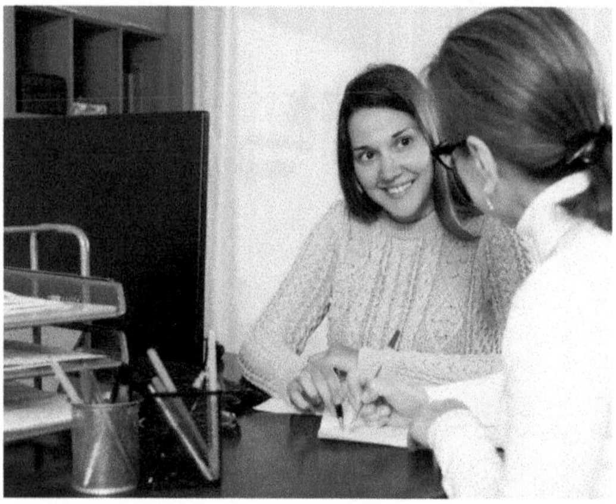

'Happiness' is a concept that has gained increasing attention in psychology, as researchers have realised that economic prosperity is not enough to make people feel happy. The 'Oxford Happiness Inventory' is a widely used survey to investigate happiness. This could be used on its own, for example to compare gender, age differences or some other naturally occurring variable such as quantity of sleep per night. Alternatively, it could be compared with the results of another survey such as the F-Scale (see previous page) or a personality test. It can easily be accessed online, http://happiness-survey.com/survey/.

Link to research topic or scenario: this task would link to any scenario relating to personal wellbeing or improving society as a whole. If you are focusing on the mandatory topic of Sleep, this could fit well. It could also be linked to cultural differences in stress.

Bower (1972) looked at how linking two items (e.g. a cat and wall) into a single mental image led to better recall of both items. A version of this could be done in various ways, such as using objects, cards with words on them or a PowerPoint. Ensure extraneous variables, such as timings and familiarity of the objects, are controlled.

Link to research topic or scenario: this task will link well to any scenario relating to education or memory. It could also be linked to topics that involve skills or the workplace.

PURPLE YELLOW RED
BLACK RED GREEN
RED YELLOW ORANGE
BLUE PURPLE BLACK
RED GREEN ORANGE

Stroop (1935) tested people's ability to state the colours of words, when the word said a different colour to the ink it was printed in, for example, 'green' or 'yellow'. Reading is so automatic for most people that we cannot 'switch off' the process. Even when asked to name the ink colour, we automatically read the word at the same time, resulting in two conflicting pieces of information, therefore slowing down the correct response. This is an easy experiment to run on classmates – ask others to read random coloured words as a comparison and time how long each list takes. There are good computerised versions available such as http://www.psytoolkit.org/experiment-library/stroop.html.

Link to research topic or scenario: this task could be connected to a scenario that involves learning or education, or to the role of attention in the multi-store model of memory.

Note that the above are just examples of tasks that could potentially fit with some of the Higher topics. A good research study will usually make some kind of comparison, between two different types of tasks (e.g. long words versus short words) or groups (e.g. ages, sexes, personality types).

You can get many other ideas from looking at the research studies described elsewhere in this book – although note that some of the 'classic' studies would nowadays be considered unethical.

Once you have selected a general area to work in and the aim of your study, you can work on planning your experiment at the same time as reading more background research.

Higher: preparing materials

Once you have selected a topic and planned all aspects of your study carefully, you will need to prepare all of the materials required for data gathering. These will depend on the study, but as general guidelines, ensure that you have:

✓ Consent forms (see p.255 – example consent form).

✓ Instructions. Should be standardised, that is, written/typed in advance to ensure that they are the same for all participants. Could appear on a PowerPoint slide or at the start of a questionnaire.

✓ Task materials. Any questionnaires or apparatus as described in the previous section. If you need to borrow apparatus, ensure that you do so in plenty of time.

✓ Clipboards/paper/spare pens. For example, you may need blank paper for responses in a memory test.

✓ Debriefing. Again, this should be standardised. Make sure that all aspects of the study are explained and that participants are thanked.

Higher: data gathering

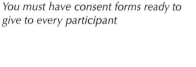

You must have consent forms ready to give to every participant

Once all materials are ready, it is time to gather the data. As with all aspects of the Assignment, it is important to be organised and to communicate well. If you have arranged with a participant to test them at a particular time and place, ensure you are punctual and have everything you need. The experiment should be run smoothly and professionally.

If things don't seem to be going to plan, it is very important that you don't change the procedure mid-way through the experiment. To do so would invalidate all of your findings. Don't worry if the findings do not seem to be turning out the way you expect. In many ways, it can be more interesting to interpret and discuss unexpected findings. There are classics of psychology such as Milgram's (1963) obedience experiment that obtained unexpected findings.

Remember – you must not carry out your research on children.

Sample

You need participants to complete your task. For practical reasons, this will probably be an opportunity sample rather than a random sample. For ethical reasons, participants must be at least 16 years of age. If you are based in a school, then only fifth or sixth year pupils can be used (and make sure they actually are 16 or over, as some may not be). You may also use your friends and family.

Pilot study

It is advisable to test out the procedure/materials before you actually collect data. How this is done can range from running a full **pilot study**, which is similar to the actual experiment but with fewer participants, to researchers simply trying the tasks themselves. For things such as memory tests, you need to ensure that it is not too hard or too easy. For questionnaires, it will allow you to ensure that all of the questions are understandable. As well as checking for problems, a pilot study allows you to estimate how long data gathering will take.

Gathering data

When everything has been prepared and checked, you can begin to collect your data. In experiments, each participant in the study should be randomly allocated to an experimental condition – tossing a coin is an acceptable way to do it.

Take care to follow the same standardised procedure with all participants and to follow ethical guidelines, including obtaining written consent, and giving a debrief.

Higher: data analysis

If you have run an experimental study (or a quasi-experiment or natural experiment) for your Assignment, it should be a fairly simple matter to analyse the data. For each condition, you have a set of scores. Calculate the mean, mode and median (as described on page 221) to get an idea of the average/typical score on each condition. Calculate the range and (optionally) the inter-quartile range and standard deviation to get an idea of the spread of data. These findings will go into the results section of your write up.

With a survey or observation, it depends largely on the type of data that you have. Some observation studies will result in numerical data such as time taken to do a task.

Higher: how to structure a write-up

The write-up should use headings and sub-headings. There is a very standard structure in psychology research and it is best to stick to it as far as possible. If you go on to HNC or degree level, you will see that these courses use much the same format for write-ups, as do published research studies. Perhaps you will be publishing your own psychology research articles one day.

Each section is allocated a particular number of marks on the SQA marking scheme. The following table explains what should be included.

Section	Must include
Introduction (600–800 words)	Background research and theories Aim Hypothesis
Method (500–700 words)	Four subsections: **Design**: states method (e.g. lab experiment), design (e.g. repeated measures), variables (e.g. IV and DV plus controlled variables). **Participants**: sampling method and group/participants must be described. **Materials**: should be described. **Procedure**: description of procedure; ethical procedure.

(*continued*)

Section	Must include
Results (200–300 words)	Usually does not have subsections but should include: A description of how data were analysed (e.g. use of mean, standard deviation etc.) A table of statistical results. One or more appropriate graphs. A summary of the main findings and whether they support the hypothesis or not.
Discussion (700–900 words)	Structuring this section into subsections is optional – doing so may make it easier for you to organise your ideas. It is best not to think too much about the marking scheme here but to attempt a full and detailed explanation of your results, linking them to previous theories/studies, and critically evaluating your own study.
Supporting information/ overall style and presentation	Must include references – cite sources in text and include a reference list at the end that allows a reader to locate these sources. Should include supporting materials such as questionnaires used as **appendices.** Should be well presented in an appropriate format with page numbers, contents page and correct headings. Overall should be in an appropriate style for a scientific write-up.

Top tip

Bear in mind that marking guidelines can change and you should consult the most recent SQA documents.

Top tip

The introduction should simply describe the research area *without mentioning your own study*. In many ways, it is like a short essay on the topic.

The overall Assignment will be 2,000 to 2,500 words in length.

Title

You don't get marks for your title but you should include one – it is part of good presentation to do so. Something simple, like 'the effect of ___ on ___' usually works best. Include this on a separate title page along with your name, school and Scottish Candidate Number.

Contents

It is good style to include a **contents page** with page numbers matching the page number of each section.

Introduction

In the first main section, 'Introduction', you describe the behaviour that your research aims to study. The section starts by stating the topic of study and general area of psychology (e.g. social psychology). It should then progress from general background (the topic/area, e.g. conformity) to more specific similar previous research studies (e.g. a study that you are replicating).

- Define and explain the topic (in more detail than would be required at National 5 level).
- Discuss how this behaviour can relate to everyday life.
- Describe one or more relevant theories/models/approaches and explain how they link to the aims of the investigation.
- Explain the methodology and findings of a range of relevant previous studies (a small number in detail or a larger number in less detail).
- Use accurate terminology throughout.

The introduction sets the scene for your own study, describing the background in a 'funnel' shape – starting general and narrowing in focus until you state the aim and hypothesis.

Top tip

It is essential that the background you present in the introduction is relevant to the aim and hypothesis. Irrelevant previous studies will not gain any credit.

State the aim and hypothesis

First state the aim in general terms. This is where you say what the study is trying to do. Perhaps it could say that the aim is to replicate a previous study, or to find out the effect of something, or to test/find support for a theory. Example:

The aim of this project is to test the primacy and recency effect in order to evaluate the multi-store model of memory.

Next, give the **hypothesis** – the predicted finding of the study. If it is an experiment, put this under the heading 'experimental hypothesis', otherwise it should be titled 'alternative hypothesis'. If it is a correlational study, use the heading 'correlational hypothesis' and remember that it should be described in terms of the relationship between two variables (see page 222 for more about correlation).

Overall, a good introduction is around 600 to 800 words long – any longer and you may be using up too much space within the overall word limit.

Top tip

Although the introduction should start with a general definition of the topic under investigation, you should move rapidly from the general to the specific, so that the majority of the introduction is highly relevant to your aim.

Method

The method section is divided into four sub-sections as follows: design, participants, materials and procedure. Use **subheadings**.

- **Design**. This sub-section explains the design of your experiment – RMs or IGs or matched – and states IV, DV and controlled variables (things you kept constant).
- **Participants**. This subsection says who your participants were – how many there were, what sex and age, etc. The sampling method should be stated.
- **Materials**. Here you describe materials used such as sheets and apparatus – give precise details.

> **Top tip**
> Rather than being included within the Procedure section, ethics could be formatted as a separate (5th) subsection of Method. Ensure that you devote specific attention to it, as markers consider it very important.

> **Top tip**
> Remember to label columns and axes, and give the overall table or graph a title. Failing to do so can lose you marks.

> **Top tip**
> Ensure that your analysis of results is detailed. Cut words from other sections if you need to, in order to stick to the overall word count.

- **Procedure**. This subsection states what the participants actually did. Do not include things the researchers did, for example, analyse data. You should also explain the research ethics in detail here. Identify at least four relevant ethical concerns, stating specifically why they were a potential problem and how you addressed them.

Results

Start with a statement of how the data were analysed (e.g. mean, range) and justify this choice of statistics. After that, this section will largely include tables of results/graphs, but it should also include description and a final summary of the main findings in terms of the experimental hypothesis.

Discussion

This section includes two main elements:

- Analysis of your findings.
- Evaluation of your methodology.

To start with, summarise the main findings, making appropriate points about whether these supported the research hypothesis and how/how not. It is important to make links to theories and previous research here. This is one of the biggest sections in terms of marks and it is important to go into detail.

One good way to approach the analysis is to brainstorm all of the things that occur to you about your results, good or bad. Are they reliable? Do they fit with other studies or theories? Were any results unexpected in some way?

Don't forget to discuss the implications of all of your main statistics, including both the averages and the measures of dispersion. For example, if you found a very high standard deviation, this can suggest that the effect of your IV was not consistent – it had a much bigger effect on some participants than others. Conversely, a low standard deviation suggests that the IV had a similar effect on everybody.

This section should also evaluate your methodology. Ensure that you include at least four to five well-explained points. Ethical flaws must be covered and you could include extraneous variables that should have been controlled, ecological validity, any possible sources of bias (for example, in the sample used), differences from previous studies mentioned in the introduction or any weaknesses of the data collected. You should also suggest improvements for future studies.You should then discuss the relevance of the findings, for example, applications and future research. The findings could have some potential benefit to people's wellbeing and this could be explained – studies of memory can help people to study effectively, for example. In terms of future research, think about what you would do next if you were a professional researcher (suggestions should be more imaginative than just 'do the same study again'!).

Finally give a brief conclusion – this could come under a separate subheading. Keep the conclusion down to a couple of sentences – don't ramble.

> **Top tip**
>
> Many students spend far too long on the introduction and then write a rather short discussion section. Discussion should be the longer of the two sections, as it is worth more marks and is where you demonstrate your analytical skills.

References

Include references to all sources named in your text in a standard format. Make sure they are in alphabetical order by the first author's surname. At this level you should be producing accurate references, so make sure you check them carefully.

Appendices

Many studies will include one or more appendices at the end. These are not awarded marks but must be included for completeness and will contribute to your marks for presentation. Examples include calculations, task sheets, instructions, debrief, consent forms and apparatus.

> **Top tip**
>
> Ensure that all sections are completed in your first draft – don't miss chunks out. It is much easier to improve a section than to add it from scratch.

Higher: example Assignment

The following example shows how an Assignment report can be structured, following the sections and subsections described above. This example is short – at the lower end of the recommended word count – but of reasonable quality. As a Higher Assignment, it deserves a B grade. An A grade write-up would be very similar but more detailed, especially in the discussion section, the introduction would be more closely linked to the aim rather than talking about the topic in general and there would be more on ethics.

> **Top tip**
>
> In a real Assignment, a contents page would be included as well.

Title:

The Effect of Noise on Concentration

by Salwa Bugaighis

SCN: 90101202

Word count: 2,003 words.

INTRODUCTION

Stress can be defined as the body's response when the perceived demands of a situation exceeds a person's perceived ability to cope. Researchers into stress study how things in our environment affect our thoughts, our mood and our health. Things which cause stress are

(continued)

called 'stressors'. Stressors can come from our job (occupational), our social life, or from the environment around us. People get stressed from a huge range of situations, such as noisy classrooms, overcrowded trains and arguments with parents.

The study of stress draws heavily on both the biological and cognitive approaches to psychology. Biological psychologists see stress as a bodily response and study the hormones such as adrenaline and cortisol. They view stress as they body's response to things which are detected by the nervous system, and lead to a response by the PNS and endocrine system. Biological psychologists are more interested in how the body reacts to stress than in the cognitive processes – what we think about stress. A lot of research in this area has been conducted on animals, on the basis that they have a similar nervous system and endocrine system to us and therefore the stress response is roughly the same. For example, Selye (1936) studied rats and exposed them to various stressors, e.g. spinal shock, surgical injury, and injections of formaldehyde. He found a predictable pattern of biological responses including enlarged adrenal glands, shrunken lymph (white blood cell) system and stomach ulcers (the 'physiological triad'). This study and others like it paved the way for an understanding of how stress affects the body. It suggested that all stressors – from background noise to injuries – can have the same effect on the body. However the studies were unethical due to animal cruelty, and Selye was later questioned over research bias when it emerged that he had been funded by tobacco companies, keen to blame health problems on stress rather than on smoking (Bell, 2014).

Noise is an environmental stressor. People might be exposed to noise due to neighbours having a party all night, and this would cause stress. They might be trying to work in the school library when other pupils were annoyingly talking. They might experience stress from the noise of traffic or machinery.

A classic study into the effects of noise on stress was conducted by Glass *et al*. (1969). This study compared reaction to impossible puzzles with unpredictable random background noise. Participants felt frustrated and their ability to solve the puzzles was reduced. This was not found among a control group who heard predictable, regular noises.

The cognitive approach has increased in importance in the study of stress over the past three decades. Cognitive psychologists feel that perceptions and beliefs are of the utmost importance in our behaviour and feelings. A theory called the transactional model of stress by Lazarus & Folkman states that people appraise a stressor (primary appraisal) and they also appraise themselves (secondary appraisal), then decide how they will attempt to cope with the stressor. The model can be applied to how we react to noise – the perception of whether or not it is a threat (e.g. panicking that you won't be able to concentrate on homework) affects how stressed a person actually gets.

A more recent study into stress was conducted by Evans and Johnson (2000). They conducted a lab experiment which simulated the effects of a noisy office. The participants they tested showed higher levels of adrenaline after 3 hours, and had poorer posture, and were less likely to attempt difficult puzzles, compared to a control group of participants who had been in quiet conditions. This study has high ecological validity and demonstrates the risks of stress in the real world.

Aim: Due to this previous research it can be seen that noise, especially unpredictable noise, can lead to stress, causing it to be hard to concentrate. The aim of this study is therefore to test the effect of unpredictable noise on concentration, using a recording of unpredictable random bleeps or regular bleeps as people try to solve puzzles, some of which were impossible. This study will find out about the ability of people to concentrate when they are exposed to unpredictable noise, and therefore has relevance to education.

Hypothesis: The experimental hypothesis was that the participants who listened to unpredictable noises would spend less time on the impossible puzzles than those who heard regular noises.

Null hypothesis: The null hypothesis was that participants who heard unpredictable noises would not spend less time on the puzzles. Any differences found would just be due to chance variations.

METHOD

Design:

This was a lab experiment. A classroom was adapted to take the form of a lab. The design of the study was independent groups – participants were either in the unpredictable noise condition or the predictable noise condition. This allowed the same puzzles to be used for both conditions, without practise effects distorting the results. Allocation to conditions was done randomly.

The independent variable of the study was the presence or absence of unpredictable background noise. The dependent variable was the length of time in seconds spent on the puzzles.

Several things needed to be kept constant. Every participant was given the same instructions and the same tasks. The experiment lasted for the same amount of time for every individual participant. In order to control extraneous variables like temperature and distractions, the study was conducted in a small quiet classroom that had been set up as a lab, and each participant was tested separately. Both conditions were conducted at the same time of day (lunchtime).

Participants:

An opportunity sample of 20 participants was used. All of the participants were pupils of a secondary school in Dundee. They were selected by asking people in the cafeteria. Most were known to the researchers, but were not psychology students. The age range was 16–19. The mean age was 18.1 and out of the 20, 12 were male and 8 were female. They were naive to the research, as none had ever studied Psychology.

After they agreed to take part, participants were randomly put into one of the two conditions by tossing a coin, and a time to test them was arranged within the same week.

Materials:

The researchers prepared two short tracks of beeping noises using a computer application. The tracks each lasted for 10 minutes. One had a bleep every 10 seconds, and therefore 60 bleeps overall. The other also had 60 bleeps, but these were spaced at uneven intervals. These were put into an iPod.

A sheet of puzzles was used. It had eight puzzles on it. Puzzles number 1–6 were straightforward (a pilot study of classmates found that most people could solve each of these within one minute) while puzzles 7 and 8 were impossible to solve. This sheet can be seen at the end of this assignment (see Appendix 2).

(*continued*)

Procedure:

Participants were tested at school lunchtimes as far as possible, though some were tested during free periods. At prearranged times they were brought to the student laboratory (empty psychology classroom) and seated at a desk, where they were asked to read and sign a short ethical statement and consent form. This informed them of their right to withdraw from the study at any time.

Standardised instructions were then read to each participant. This told them that they would be given puzzles of varying difficulty to do, they had a maximum of 10 minutes to do the puzzles, but they could stop at any time when they were finished or if they decided to give up.

Participants were then handed a sheet of puzzles, face down. They were asked not to turn the paper over until they heard the first 'bleep'. The track was then started, and was played using an iPod with small plug-in speakers. The iPod was around 2 meters away from the participant as they did the puzzles, and the volume was set to a medium level so that it could clearly be heard but was not unpleasantly loud.

A researcher began a timer after the participant had turned over the paper, and stopped the timer when the participant said that they were finished/gave up; if the participant continued to the maximum 10 minutes then they were stopped and '10.00' was recorded as their time.

At the end the participants were debriefed and thanked. The aims of the study were explained to them, and they were reminded of their right to withdraw.

RESULTS:

The results were gathered together and a mean and range were calculated. The mean showed the overall average score, while the range indicated the spread of the scores. This statistic was chosen because it takes all of the raw scores into account. A median was also calculated. This calculation is not distorted by extreme outliers, and can therefore be a more typical midpoint. To measure dispersion in the scores, a simple range was calculated, and again to avoid the problem of outliers and to take every score into account, a standard deviation was calculated too.

These scores can be seen in table 1, below:

	Mean	Median	Range	SD
Predictable noise	473	450	350	95.6
Unpredictable noise	359.5	298	427	159.2

Table 1: Results of study (seconds)

The main findings are shown on the following graph, which provides a useful visual summary. As can be seen, there was a difference between the mean scores for the two conditions of over 110 seconds. Clearly participants persevered longer in the condition where there was predictable background noise during the task. The range and SD were both larger in the unpredictable condition.

The large difference in mean and median scores supports the experimental hypothesis, and the null hypothesis can be rejected.

(*continued*)

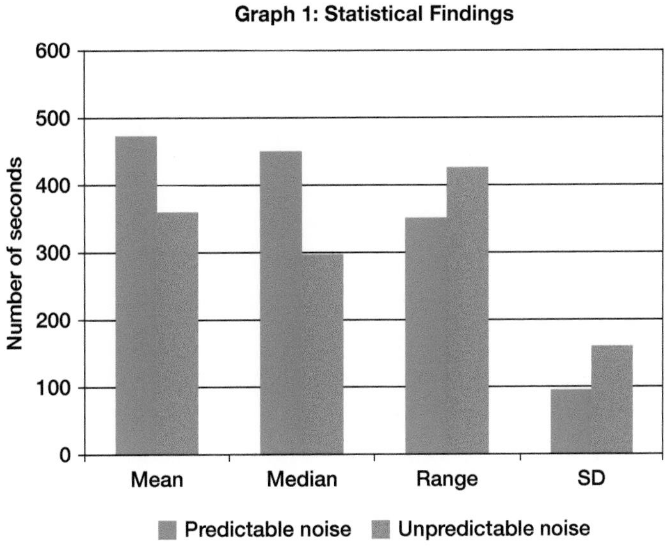

DISCUSSION

The results show a clear difference between the two conditions of over 110 seconds (mean). Participants in Condition 2 (unpredictable noise) spent less time on the impossible puzzles than the participants in condition 1. This supports the work of Glass *et al.* (1969). It appears that an inconsistent noise is more stressful than a regular one, resulting in a poorer ability to concentrate on difficult puzzles. The findings support the experimental hypothesis.

The statistics also showed a wider dispersion of results in the noise condition. Both the mean and range were higher. This suggests that there were individual differences in how long people were willing to concentrate despite the background noise.

Together, what these findings suggest is that people will spend more time trying to solve a difficult or impossible puzzle if background noise is regular. People find random noise distracting, and will give up quicker. However, as shown by the range, some people will persevere for longer than others, while some will give up very quickly.

These findings link noise and stress, supporting previous research studies. The stress of background noise apparently reduces people's ability to focus. These findings have practical uses. They may link to the real world because workplaces and classrooms are often very noisy. Factories might have predictable noises due to the regular action of machinery. Classrooms and offices might have unpredictable noises. Noisy neighbours and annoying people on public transport make unpredictable noise that can stress someone out. This study shows that such unpredictable noises are especially likely to harm a person's mental health and concentration.

To evaluate, this study had several weaknesses. The researchers did not check the hearing abilities of participants. If any of them had had poor hearing due to listening to excessively loud music then they would have been less sensitive to noise. There were also some extraneous variables that were not controlled, for example, time of day. People might have been more or less stressed depending on the time of day, and that could have affected their results. Some participants may have had undiagnosed learning disabilities which affected their concentration.

In future studies, participants should all be tested at the same time of day, and a questionnaire should be used to ask about hearing or learning disabilities.

(*continued*)

The predictable noise group spent a mean time of 7.9 minutes working on the tasks, compared to just under 6 minutes by the unpredictable noise group. This suggests that unpredictable background noise makes it more likely that people will get frustrated and give up.

REFERENCES:

Bell, V. (2014). The concept of stress, sponsored by Big Tobacco. Retrieved 01 December 2014 from *http://mindhacks.com/2014/07/14/the-concept-of-stress-sponsored-by-big-tobacco/*

Evans, G. and Johnson, D. (2000). Stress and open-office noise. *Journal of Applied Psychology, 85*(5), 779–783.

Glass, D.C., Singer, J.E. and Friedman, L.N. (1969). Psychic cost of adaptation to an environmental stressor. *Journal of Personality and Social Psychology, 12*(3), 200–210.

Selye, H. (1936). A syndrome produced by diverse nocuous agents. *Nature, 138*, 32.

APPENDICES:

Appendix 1: The following table shows the raw data gathered, alongside statistical calculations.

			Unpredictable noise						Predictable noise		
	Scores	mean	x–mean	Squared			Scores	mean	x–mean	Squared	
	190	359.5	–169.5	28730.25			302	473	–171	**29241**	
	186	359.5	–173.5	30102.25			391	473	–82	6724	
	210	359.5	–149.5	22350.25			406	473	–67	4489	
	233	359.5	–126.5	16002.25			421	473	–52	2704	
	270	359.5	–89.5	8010.25			430	473	–43	1849	
	288	359.5	–71.5	5112.25			435	473	–38	1444	
Median:	**298**	359.5	–61.5	3782.25		Median:	**450**	473	–23	529	
	340	359.5	–19.5	380.25			486	473	13	169	
	371	359.5	11.5	132.25			488	473	15	225	
	501	359.5	141.5	20022.25			501	473	28	784	
	559	359.5	199.5	39800.25			578	473	105	11025	
	611	359.5	251.5	63252.25			609	473	136	18496	
	617	359.5	257.5	66306.25			652	473	179	32041	
			SUM:	**303983.25**					**SUM:**	**109720**	
TOTAL:	4674		/n–1	25331.94		**TOTAL:**	6149		/n–1	9143.33	
MEAN:	**359.5385**		**SQ Root:**	**159.2**	**SD**	**MEAN:**	**473**		**SQ Root:**	**95.6**	**SD**
Range:	**427**					Range:	**350**				

Appendix 2: Copy of task used

You have up to 10 minutes to complete these puzzles. You can stop (give up) at any time.

1. Three frogs catch three flies in three minutes. How many frogs are needed to catch 30 flies in 30 minutes?
2. A toad is at the bottom of the well which is 20 meters deep. Every day the toad climbs 5 meters upwards and then fall back by 4 meters. How many days it will take for the toad to reach the top?
3. If x is 3 and y is 4 and $x^2 - 3y + 4 = z$, what is z?
4. Use only the numbers 1, 9, 7 and 5 in that exact order to calculate the numbers 33 and 79. You can use any mathematical symbol (for example, you could make 59 by calculating 1 + 9 x 7 – 5).
5. Tom wants to measure out 4 litres of water into a soup pan. He doesn't have a measuring jug, but he does have a 3 litre and a 5 litre bottle. How can he do it?
6. What is the missing number in this sequence: 0, 1, 4, 15, __, 325
7. You have two types of square tile – one type has sides of length 1cm and the other has sides of length 2cm. Find a square with sides of under 10cm that can be covered by an equal number of each type of tile.
8. This diagram shows the walls of five rooms. Cross every line in the diagram once (and only once) using a continuous line. You must cross both internal and external walls.

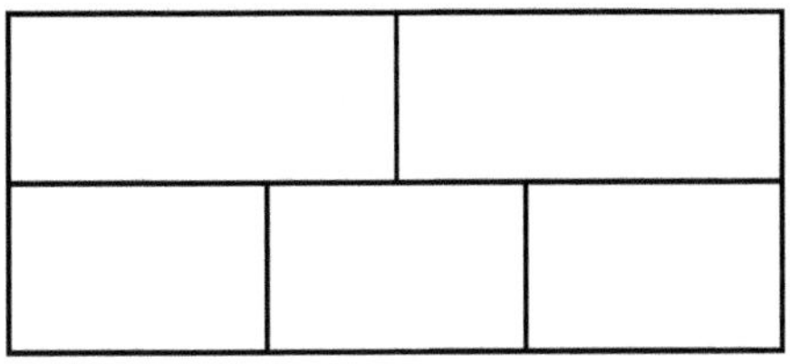

Finalising the write-up

Final checks

You should allow enough time to check through your Assignment document before you submit it. Remember that it is worth a large percentage of your course marks, so you want it to be excellent.

Backup

This project forms a huge part of your mark for the National 5/Higher course, and it would be disastrous to lose it though a computer problem. Ensure that you keep a backup version (or versions) using a pen drive, cloud storage, emailing drafts to yourself and occasionally printing a hard copy. Save a new version each time you make significant revisions. Don't forget to back it up when it is complete, too, in the unlikely event that it gets lost by your school/college or by the SQA.

! Syllabus note

This section applies to both National 5 and Higher.

It is a good idea to regularly save your Assignment on a pen drive!

Checklist

This checklist will help you to look out for common problems.

- [ ] You have a front cover with your name on it, and the title of the study
- [ ] You have given a definition of the topic of study (e.g. Sleep)
- [ ] You have cited at least two relevant studies in your introduction and included in-line citations
- [ ] Terminology is used accurately and consistently
- [ ] You have stated an aim for research on this topic
- [ ] You have linked the aim to previous research
- [ ] Check the hypotheses. Are they phrased like the examples on pages 213–215?
- [ ] Variables are explained in detail (depending on the study, for example, co-variables, or IV and DV plus any variables kept constant)
- [ ] You have explained why the sampling method is suitable for this study
- [ ] The method used (e.g. questionnaire/survey/lab experiment) is explained including main strengths and weaknesses of the method
- [ ] Apparatus/materials required have been explained
- [ ] Procedure has been explained, with steps to follow
- [ ] Type of data to be gathered has been explained, as well as how to analyse it
- [ ] Potential ethical issues have been identified
- [ ] Strategies to avoid/minimise ethical issues have been explained
- [ ] Presentation: a title page and contents are included
- [ ] References: the studies cited have a reference at the end
- [ ] Word count: check this using your word processor and state it at the end or on your front cover

Higher only

- [ ] Write-up includes labelled table(s) and graph(s) which are referred to in the text.
- [ ] The discussion includes evaluation of the study
- [ ] Analysis section compares research to other studies and links it to theories
- [ ] Suggestions for future research studies are included

Key concepts

- Pilot study
- Introduction
- Method
- Results
- Discussion
- Appendices
- Subheadings

Top tip

Markers can stop marking if you exceed the word limit by 10%.

Top tip

You do not need to include the title page, contents page, references or appendices in your word count. Count your words from the start of the Introduction to the end of the Discussion.

Top tip

Note that the Discussion section includes both analysis and evaluation. Some of your evaluation points should reflect on the ethical points identified in the Method – did your ethical procedures work as planned, or could they be improved upon? It's absolutely fine to criticise your own procedures!

Appendix: Research materials for Assignment

Example Consent Form

I consent to take part as a participant in this psychology research study. I have received information about the nature of the research and I understand that I have the right to withdraw at any time. I understand that the researcher(s) are working under a code of ethics, which prohibits them from putting me in harmful situations and any data obtained from my participation will be treated confidentially.

Name ______________________________ Date ____________________

Top tip

The consent form should be accompanied by information about the study, so that consent is informed. This often involves handing out a participant information sheet.

Social behaviour

10 Conformity

For the topic of Conformity, you should be able to describe:

- Types of conformity.
- Factors affecting conformity.
- Factors affecting obedience **(Higher only)**.
- Research evidence.

You need to develop the following skills:

- Distinguishing between types of conformity.
- Using research evidence to support statements about the topic.
- Identifying the process of conformity/obedience in a real-world context.
- Explaining the links between concepts and real-world situations.
- Analysing and evaluating research relevant to the topic.

Conformity usually results from 'peer pressure'

! Syllabus note

Conformity is a mandatory topic in both Higher and National 5 Psychology. This chapter will provide the key information for both courses. Your teacher or lecturer will be able to guide you to the sections most relevant to the exam that you are sitting.

The nature of conformity

Conformity can be defined as changing behaviour or beliefs in order to come into line with others in a group, in response to social pressure. Conformity usually results from 'peer pressure', meaning pressure from your **peers** (people similar to yourself), but we can also feel pressured to go along with groups of strangers, as several studies demonstrate. We are also influenced by **media pressure** – people that we identify with via the media can have a strong influence on behaviour.

Conformity is typically unspoken, that is, we respond to what we observe others doing and change our behaviour to fit in. However others can sometimes ask us to do the same as they are doing, such as to have another drink or wear different clothes.

Types of conformity

Conformity can be responded to by simply going along with the group situation – or it can affect us more deeply. The term **compliance** refers to the first type – when a person pretends to agree with the group, while maintaining their own beliefs.

If the group has a deeper effect on the person, and they come to agree with the group and adopt the same behaviours even when alone, then the person has shown **identification** with the group, but this may well be temporary – meaning that if the individual leaves the group, the behaviour will stop.

Sometimes a group has such an influence on a person that they permanently adopt the behaviour and carry it out even if they are no longer a group member. This is known as **internalisation** (Kelman, 1958).

Internalisation is when a person permanently adopts a behaviour

Examples

Compliance	Tom notices that everyone else has taken their food off their tray in the cafeteria, so he decides to do the same.
Identification	Dave supports his school hockey team, but then he moves school and starts to support the team of his new school instead.
Internalisation	Ava spends a lot of time with a group of friends who love rock climbing and comes to take up the sport. Long after she no longer sees those friends, she still goes rock climbing.

Top tip

The term 'comply' is also used more generally to mean going along with any kind of social pressure, including obedience. 'Dissent' means refusing to conform or obey.

Motivation to conform

Why do people feel the need or desire to conform? There are times when we feel an urge to do the same as others that is very hard to resist. Where does that motivation come from? According to Deutsch and Gerrard (1955) there are two separate reasons motivating conformity, which might occur separately or both at once:

Informational influence: when uncertainty leads to a person adopting the behaviour of others – they conform because they don't know what to do and they want to be correct.

Normative influence: when a person is not in doubt but is influenced by social norms. The pressure comes from the group, based on a need to be liked and accepted by it.

? Discussion point

Distinguish between compliance, identification and internalisation by asking if a person would exhibit a behaviour in private or just in group situations and whether they would continue the behaviour if the social group ceased to exist or they were no longer a member.

Classic research into informational influence

Jenness (1932) conducted a study where individuals were shown beans in a bottle and asked to guess their number. There were over 800 beans and it was impossible to count them, so nobody could be entirely sure of their estimate. Participants were then put in groups of three and asked to discuss the number and give a group estimate. When later given the option of changing their first guess, most participants wanted to change to a number closer to the group estimate. They were motivated to be correct because Jenness offered the reward of an A grade for the most accurate guess in their class. It appeared that when unsure of the correct answer, people will tend to be influenced by a peer group – even though there is no reason to believe that the group are any more accurate.

Jenness's study was supported by Sherif (1935), who obtained similar results using an illusion called the auto-kinetic effect where a point of

? Discussion point

What types of groups and situations lead to identification?

Top tip

Normative influence is often called 'normative social influence' or NSI. Informational influence is often called 'information social influence' or ISI.

? Discussion point

Do you consider informational influence to be true conformity? What about internalisation? Or do you think the term 'conformity' should only apply when people are acting against their own wishes and beliefs?

How many beans are in the bottle?

The auto-kinetic effect was first noticed in stars

light appears to move in a darkened room. There was no true answer, but when estimates were called out aloud in a group of three, people's estimates conformed to those of group members.

Classic research into normative influence: the Asch experiment

Early studies such as the Jenness (1932) 'bottle of beans' study put people into ambiguous social situations, to see whether people follow the crowd when they don't know what to do or say.

However, a study by Asch (1951) tested whether social pressure would result in people denying something they could see quite clearly with their own eyes. He tested people's judgement of the length of lines. In a simple task, participants were asked to state which one out of three 'comparison' lines was the same as the 'standard' line – 'C' in the example in the Key study below. Asch found that 75% of people conformed on a least one occasion – demonstrating that most people are willing to say something that they know is wrong due to social pressure (see key study).

Key study: Asch's (1951) experiment into length of lines

A photograph of the study

Aim: *In contrast to previous studies of conformity, Asch wanted to see whether people would conform to others' incorrect estimates if the task was easy and the correct answer was obvious.*

Method: *Fifty male American participants were used and they were told that this was an experiment into visual perception. They were placed in a group with seven other individuals. Unknown to the true participant, everyone else in the group was an actor whose responses had been prepared in advance.*

The group were shown a series of 18 cards and asked to match the line to a choice of three comparison lines each time. The confederates (actors) had all been briefed to give the same wrong answer on 12 out of the 18 examples – these are described as the 'critical trials'. The true participant was always last or second last to answer. This put them in a position of having to choose between giving the clearly correct answer or conforming to the majority and giving the wrong answer.

Top tip

Many sources focus on a later replication of this 'length of lines' study. You can gain credit for these instead of the original study, as long as they are accurately explained. In the replication, Asch (1955) calculated an overall conformity rate of 36.8%, based on 123 participants.

Findings: *Two main issues arose. First, the majority group generally had a large influence on the true participant. Over all of the critical trials, 32% were incorrect – despite the fact that participants could see the correct answer very clearly. There was a mean of 3.84 errors out of the 12 trials; in contrast, a control group made a mean of 0.08 errors. Asch believed that the main reason for these findings was that people do not wish to be ridiculed and excluded by a majority. Some participants reported that they started to doubt their own perceptions.*

Second, there were considerable individual differences in how people responded; 25% of participants did not conform at all (by the same token, 75% of participants gave a wrong answer at least once). Asch noted that even when participants gave correct answers, the way they expressed their answers was influenced by the presence of the majority, with participants often appearing withdrawn or embarrassed. The largest number of incorrect responses was 11 out of 12; Asch noted that this participant 'appeared nervous and somewhat confused... The primary factor in his case was a loss of confidence' (p.228).

Evaluation: *The Asch study was a powerful demonstration of how a group can influence our behaviour – even a group of strangers can make people respond very differently to how they would when alone. The study was hugely influential and many other studies have used a similar task. However, it lacked ecological validity, as it was an artificial lab experiment. The task itself lacked mundane realism, as real-life situations where we are pressured to conform tend not to be so clear-cut.*

It may also be the case that the culture of 1950s America encouraged conformity and the findings can't necessarily be generalised to social behaviour in other places and eras. Perrin and Spencer (1981) replicated the Asch study using British engineering students and found a much lower level of conformity than the original study. They suggested that the findings depended on how people interpret the social situation and on their cultural norms.

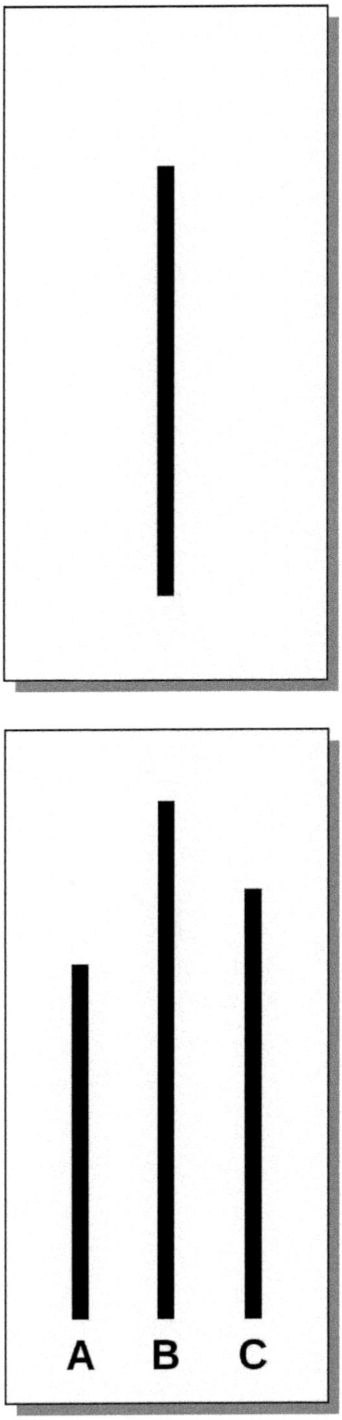

Asch used clear images of lines

Minority influence

Most studies of conformity investigate the effect of a majority on an individual or a small group. But what about the reverse? Moscovici (1981) believed that in the real world, compliance with a majority viewpoint rarely has any long-term impact on a person's behaviour. Instead, it is often minorities that cause a real long-term change by exerting consistent pressure on the majority. Examples could include feminism or the environmental movement.

Minority influence is when an individual or a minority within the group changes the behaviour of the larger group. In a classic study of the phenomenon, Moscovici *et al.* (1969) planted two confederates in a group of six that had the task of naming the colours of a set of slides. The confederates had been told to call certain blue slides 'green'. True participants showed signs of being influenced – 8.42% of their responses followed the minority, considerably more than the control

Top tip

Fake participants in studies such as Asch (1951) are called confederates or 'stooges'.

Discussion point

Can you think of any examples of minority influence among school or college students?

Discussion point

Why might pressure from a minority have a greater long-term effect on behaviour and opinions compared to a majority?

group. Interestingly, the effect disappeared if the two confederates were not consistent with each other – influenced responses from the true participants dropped to just over 1%. Therefore, it appears that if a minority is to exert an effect on the majority, it has to present its viewpoint consistently.

The women's suffrage movement is an example of minority influence

Key concepts

- Conformity
- Peer pressure
- Media pressure
- Compliance
- Identification
- Internalisation
- Normative influence
- Informational influence
- Minority influence

Questions

1. Which type of influence means that we conform in order to be liked and accepted – informational or normative?
2. What type of conformity occurs if you feel part of a group but stops if you leave the group?
3. What term means that someone refuses to conform?
4. What type of objects did participants have to estimate in Jenness's study?
5. How many of Asch's participants conformed at least once?
6. If you laugh at a joke that you don't find funny, just because everyone else is laughing, which type of conformity is occurring?
7. If a person becomes a socialist because their school friends are, and then maintains these political beliefs throughout life, which type of conformity is occurring?
8. Which type of influence has a long-term effect on behaviour, according to Moscovici?

9. Was Asch's study a lab or a field experiment?

10. Who were the participants in Perrin and Spencer's replication of the Asch study when no conformity was found?

GO! **Activities**

1. Over the following week, take notes of situations where you observe informational or normative influence. Do you sometimes see both together? Be prepared to discuss this with fellow students.
2. Find out more about Jenness's study. Could you replicate it with students today? Do you think the results would be the same?
3. How does conformity affect other areas of Psychology? For example, does it affect sleep habits, attitudes to psychopathology, or other areas of social psychology such as prejudice? Write a short summary or blog post on this issue.

Factors that affect conformity

What makes some people conform when others don't, or conform on some occasions and not others? In other words, what **factors** affect levels of conformity?

The factors that affect conformity can be divided into two types: **situational factors** and **individual differences**. Situational factors are things that vary from one situation to another, while individual differences refers to the fact that some people are more likely to conform than others due to things such as their personality.

How does group size affect conformity?

Key situational factors

Asch's study helps to illustrate some of the key factors that make conformity levels rise or fall depending on the situation.

Group size

The most obvious situational factor is group size – it might be assumed that a large majority will have a much bigger influence than one or two people. Asch (1951) put this to the test by varying the number of participants in his 'length of lines' experiment. He found that with fewer than three confederates, the level of compliance diminished greatly. However, increasing group size only made a difference up to a certain point:

- With only one confederate, there was almost no conformity.
- With two confederates, the conformity rate was 12.8%.
- With three confederates, the rate rose to 33.3%.
- The addition of further confederates made only a slight difference to results.

! Syllabus note

Informational and normative (social) influence can also be given in exam answers as factors that affect conformity, because the presence or absence of these will increase or decrease conformity rates.

Top tip

Three was the 'magic number' in Asch's (1955) study – with a majority of three-to-one, conformity rose above 30% and further increases in the majority group size beyond this did not make a significant difference.

Discussion point

How might conformity affect a car driver if the passengers outnumber the driver three (or four) to one?

How would conformity affect this driver?

Conformity tends to fall when participants are able to write their answers down secretly

Top tip

Use the 'S' initials of these factors to help remember them – situational: size, support, secrecy. Write these on an index card or a page of your notebook.

In his replication of the study, Asch (1955) varied the number of participants from 1 to 15 and found very similar results (see graph).

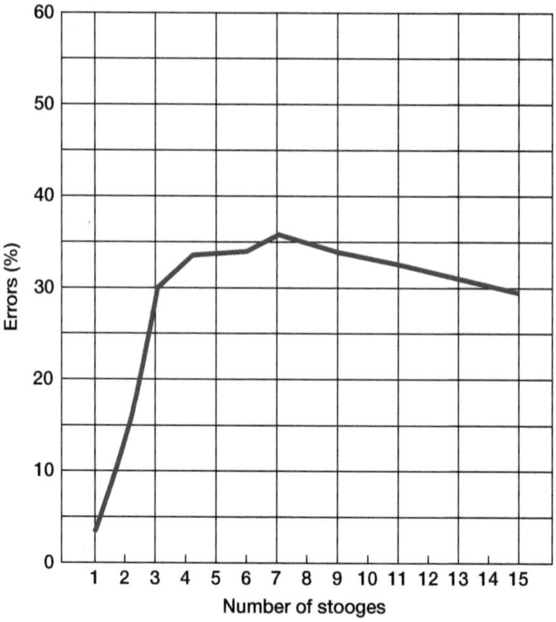

Results of Asch's 1955 study

In summary, the rise in group size from three to four is critical. After that, adding an additional person (e.g. increasing group size from five to six) only made a slight difference. It could be that beyond this point, the others are perceived as 'a group' rather than as a particular number of individuals. It is also possible that true participants may suspect a trick if a large number of the other participants all give the same wrong answer; in the real world, a larger group may have more of an influence (Baron & Byrne, 1997).

Social support and unanimity

In another variation of Asch's basic procedure, he instructed one confederate to act as an ally to the true participant by disagreeing with the others so that the majority were no longer unanimous. The ally was seated fourth, and therefore answered before the true participant. This produced a sharp decrease in total conformity, which fell to 5.5% (Asch, 1951). Interestingly, the participants reported greater feelings of warmth and liking towards the ally, but did not believe they had been influenced by him (Asch, 1955).

Secrecy of response

Asch's classic study mainly tested public compliance. In another variation of the study, a participant was told that they had arrived late and they had to write their answers down privately, while everyone else spoke theirs aloud. The experiment was otherwise identical to the original study, with confederates giving incorrect answers. The conformity level fell to 5%. This suggests that in real situations where we can hide our response or avoid responding in front of other people, compliance is much less likely to occur.

Task difficulty

Asch's task was easy – everyone could see which line was longer. But what would happen if the lines were more similar to each other in length? Asch (1956) varied this and found that conformity increased. It may be that the stimuli being more similar made it less embarrassing for the participants to conform, allowing them to save face. Interestingly, Mori and Arai's (2010) experiment (see page 267) was apparently more difficult, with more errors than the Asch study. Real life situations are often more ambiguous than the lines task, and may therefore lead to more conformity.

Perceiving that other people in a situation are in-group members is another factor that could also increase the rate of conformity

Individual differences in conformity level

Looking at the classic research on conformity described above, it is hard to escape the idea that some people are more susceptible than others to social pressure; 75% conformed at least once in the Asch study but how were the remaining 25% able to maintain their independence on every trial?

This question links to an important concept in psychology more generally – that people's behaviour is strongly affected by **individual differences**. Some of the main individual differences to consider here (as in other topics) are age, sex, cognition, personality and culture. These are the things that make us fundamentally different from one another and all of these things could potentially cause people to conform.

Age

Some age differences have been found in conformity. A review of studies reported that conformity levels remain static between the ages of 10 and 14, after which, the ability to dissent rises steadily up to age 18. Thereafter it remains steady through early adulthood (Steinberg & Monahan, 2007).

How likely are you to conform to a younger sibling?

When considering age, it is important to consider the age of the group. We conform more to people like ourselves in a Jenness-type experiment. For example, would you conform to a group of young children? What about a group of people a year or two older than yourself? In this sense, age is also a *situational* factor in conformity, affecting the context of the situation.

Personality

Certain personality characteristics link to conformity levels. Santee and Maslach (1982) found that people who have higher self-esteem were less likely to conform. Burger (1992) showed that people who value control are less likely to conform: participants rated as high in their personal desire for control conformed less in an Asch-type experiment where they had to rate the funniness of cartoons.

Women tend to conform more to promote group harmony

However, in the Stanford prison experiment (see p.274), Zimbardo *et al.* (1973) did not support the idea that social behaviour comes from personality. They concluded that behaviour is mainly influenced by social context.

A rally in support of same-sex marriage in Sydney, Australia, May 2015

Sex

Some researchers have found sex differences in conformity, with women tending to conform more compared to men (Mori & Arai, 2010; see key study). Eagly (1987) suggested that this happens because women tend to take a communal role and promote harmony in the group, while men are more comfortable maintaining independence. However, the behaviour of males and females varies greatly over time and depends on culture. Some older studies of gender differences in conformity may be culturally biased and outdated, while even more recent ones, such as Mori and Arai (2010), cannot be generalised to all cultures.

Top tip

Ensure that you can explain both situational factors and individual differences. Cultural factors must be included, as this is a mandatory part of the course content.

Thought processes

There are differences in cognitive processes from one individual to another in a conformity situation – everyone interprets the situation differently. This was noted by Asch (1955) who stated that some participants genuinely doubted their own judgement, while others knew that they were right but followed the crowd in an attempt to avoid disapproval.

Hornsey *et al*. (2003) found that if someone had a strongly held conviction about an issue, they are less likely to conform. They studied 205 Australian university students who had reported being in favour of same-sex marriage and showed them faked graphs supposedly of other students' views that seemed to show that the majority disagreed with them. In terms of how they would act privately, those with weak beliefs conformed, while those with stronger beliefs did not. In terms of public behaviour the difference was even greater – those with strong beliefs in favour of the topic showed **counter-conformity**, meaning they became even more strongly in favour of same-sex marriage than before, in defiance of the supposed majority who were against them.

? Discussion point

What subcultures exist where you live? Consider groups related to age, occupation, fashions and hobbies. Are you a member of a subculture? Do people from subcultures appear to conform more or less than the majority? Do some of them display counter-conformity?

Culture

One problem with interpreting the classic research by Jenness and Asch is that they studied young Americans in the mid-20th century and findings can't necessarily be generalised beyond that cultural context – a culture that has been described as highly conformist (Perrin & Spencer, 1981). Follow up studies have not always replicated the findings, perhaps because of varying cultural attitudes about the value or necessity of maintaining group harmony.

Collectivist cultures tend to show higher levels of conformity than individualist cultures

One consistent cultural difference is that **collectivist cultures** tend to show higher levels of conformity than **individualist cultures**. Collectivist cultures – including most Central American and South East Asian countries – value the family and society over the needs of the individual while individualist cultures – including most Western countries – have the opposite emphasis. Smith and Bond (1993) reviewed conformity research from around the world and found Belgians to have the lowest level of conformity and Fijian Indians the highest. Some subcultures are strongly associated with counter-conformity – punks are a good example of this. It may be the case, though, that members of the subculture conform to each other (see chapter 1 for more information about culture).

Key study: Mori and Arai (2010): length of lines study

Aim: *This study aimed to replicate Asch's experiment without the need for actors, to ensure that nobody was acting unnaturally. It also included both males and females, thus contributing to our understanding of individual differences in conformity.*

Method: *The researchers replicated an Asch-type situation with length of lines but with an important twist – there were no actors. Instead, everyone wore a pair of specially designed filter glasses that allowed them to look at the same image but see different things. This meant that everyone was a true participant – but one had been given a different type of filter glasses that meant that they perceived a different correct answer. 104 Japanese student participants were used in groups of four. Participants stated their answers aloud, with the minority participant going third.*

Findings: *For female participants results were similar to those of Asch (1955), with conformity to the majority shown on 4.41 out of 12 critical trials (versus 3.84 in the original). However, it was found that the male participants did not conform to the majority view. Another difference from the Asch findings was that it made very little difference whether the majority were unanimous or not. In other words, having an 'ally' did not make the radical difference shown in Asch (1951) and led to a small reduction in conformity rate.*

Evaluation: *The researchers explained the gender difference in terms of the different expectations and social roles of males and females. They concluded that the reduced conformity in males compared to the Asch study may reflect generational changes since the 1950s. Culture could also be a factor, as gender roles can be different from one culture to another.*

In this study, the participants knew each other (compared to the strangers used in the Asch study), which could have affected results. Mori and Arai believe this was a strength of the study because how we conform to our friends and acquaintances is more relevant to real world problems than conformity to strangers.

Specially designed glasses were used in the experiment

Top tip

A later study by the same research team found that males and females showed similar levels of conformity in early primary school, after which males became gradually more independent.

Discussion point

What effect do you think culture or social role could have on the gender differences found in conformity? Would similar differences be found among your groups?

Summary and analysis

The Asch experiment has certain limitations mentioned in the previous section and its findings cannot necessarily be generalised to all situations. Nevertheless, the way that the study varied several aspects of the procedure provides useful objective evidence to help you analyse situational factors. For example, it can be used to support a claim that group size affects behaviour or that having social support can make us less likely to conform.

It is useful to consider the categories of individual difference such as age, personality and culture. In real situations, these factors may all play a role and may interact with each other, making it hard to be sure which is the most important.

Key concepts

- Factors in conformity
- Situational factor (conformity)
- Individual differences
- Counter-conformity
- Collectivist culture
- Individualist culture

Top tip

Can you think of examples of countries which have primarily collectivist and individualist cultures? Think of three examples of each, ready to use in an exam answer.

Top tip

In order to tackle exam evaluation questions, ensure that you can give at least two strengths and two weakness of key studies such as Mori and Arai (2010) and Asch (1951). See chapter 7 for advice on how to evaluate studies.

Questions

1. At what point in Asch's study did rising majority group size make the biggest difference to conformity?

2. True or false: writing answers in secret made no difference to conformity level in Asch's study?

3. True or false: having the support of an ally dramatically reduced conformity?

4. Name three types of individual differences that can affect conformity.

5. Which study showed that low self-esteem affected conformity level?

6. What is meant by 'counter-conformity', as shown in the Hornsey *et al.* study?

7. Which group of cultures tend to show higher levels of conformity?

8. How did Mori and Arai (2010) avoid the need for confederates in their study?

9. What two major differences were there in the findings in Mori and Arai compared to the original study by Asch?

10. Who were the participants of Mori and Arai's study?

Activities

1. Draw up an A3-sized poster on either the Jenness, Asch or Mori and Arai study. Ensure that you include the aim of the study and the background. Choose a suitable image and describe the procedure. This could be used to decorate your study area and will help you to remember the details of the study.
2. Make a mind-map in your notes of the main individual differences that can affect behaviour – personality, age, sex, thinking style, culture. As well as individual differences in conformity, you could link these to other topics such as stress or sleep on your mind map.

Obedience

Obedience can be defined as changing behaviour or beliefs in response to a direct command or instruction. While pressure to conform comes from peers, obedience is the result of an **authority figure** – someone in a position of power – telling you what to do. In addition, the person giving the order is typically not doing the same thing themselves. It is a case of 'follow my instructions' rather than 'follow my example'.

Obedience to rules and to authority figures is a key part of everyday life, and is arguably a useful thing that allows society to function effectively. For example, rules about behaviour in school allow everyone to learn without disruptions, while rules about paying tax allow the government to collect money that can then be spent on socially useful things such as health care. However, if an authority gives a harmful instruction and people obey it, then obedience becomes problematic. One of the biggest questions for social psychologists since the mid-20th century has been why people followed instructions to commit atrocities such as the Nazi Holocaust (the mass murder of Jews, disabled people, gypsies, communists and homosexuals under Hitler's regime in the Third Reich).

Perceived legitimate authority

Many parts of society, such as schools and workplaces, are structured as **hierarchies**, meaning that people with lower ranks or status are expected to obey those in higher positions. For example, employees usually obey their manager and school pupils usually obey their teachers and headteacher. These figures are considered in society to be **legitimate authority** figures.

Sometimes, however, the legitimacy of an authority figure is not clear – someone may give an order but people are not sure whether to obey or not, asking themselves, 'does this person have the right to tell me what to do?' This problem is familiar to student teachers or babysitters, as children may not recognise them as authority figures, and therefore, behave more disobediently than usual!

Someone who receives an order tends to look for clues in the situation and a major one is the way someone is dressed. Bickman (1974) conducted a study where actors gave orders to passers-by, such as '*pick up that litter*' or '*give that person a dime*'. There were three conditions – actor dressed as security guard, in a milkman's uniform or in casual clothes. The security guard outfit led to the greatest level of obedience. Even though a security guard is not a legitimate authority – they don't have the right to tell members of the public to pick up litter – their uniform conveyed a sense of power and legitimacy.

! Syllabus note

This part of this topic is only required at Higher, not National 5.

Obedience is the result of an authority figure telling you what to do

Top tip

Although it forms part of the same topic, obedience is **not** a type of conformity. Both conformity and obedience are types of **social pressure**.

The commandant of the concentration camp in Landsberg, Germany, stands among dead prisoners

Employees usually obey their manager

Sociologist Max Weber said that legitimate authority and the right to give orders comes from three main sources (cited in Howitt *et al.*, 1989):

- Tradition: in each society, some groups are considered to have the right to give instructions, for example parents.
- Legal: some people have a legal authority, and it is rational for others to obey them because failing to do so would have negative consequences such as punishments.
- Charisma: some people have great personal charm and manage to persuade others that they should be listened to instead of the traditional authorities, sometimes claiming religious inspiration or moral superiority. Political rebels and religious dissidents fall into this group.

Children may not recognise a babysitter as a legitimate authority figure

However, there are some limitations to this view. It is a descriptive summary, which doesn't really explain *why* people obey instructions from these sources. Also, as is clear from the Milgram study (see below), the power of the authority figure plays less of a role than variations in the social situation and factors such as experience.

The Milgram study of obedience

According to social psychologist Stanley Milgram, orders can result in a clash between a person's morals and the social situation. He wanted to know if there was something uniquely obedient about German soldiers and concentration camp guards who had followed immoral orders during the Second World War.

Milgram devised an experiment where people would be asked to deliver increasing levels of electric shocks on the demands of an experimenter – although the shocks would be faked, the participants would think that they were real. He asked his colleagues, researchers and PhD students, whether people would obey and most said that only a tiny minority of people would obey, and those would be psychopaths. Essentially, the experts had predicted that the American participants would not obey immoral instructions and that German people during the war were somehow different. In fact, his volunteers proved highly obedient to authority (see key study).

Top tip

In your exam answer, wearing of a uniform – or other symbols of power – can be explained as a factor that affects obedience level.

? Discussion point

School pupils typically wear a uniform and teachers do not. Who has the power in that social situation? And why?

In Bickman's study the security guard's uniform conveyed a sense of legitimate authority

? Discussion point

Who are the legitimate authority figures in your life?

Key study: Milgram's (1963) study of obedience

Aim: *Milgram wanted to know how obedient ordinary people would be to an authority figure. This would allow him to have a baseline level of obedience in a normal population, for comparison in later studies.*

Method: *Milgram recruited 40 volunteers by advertising for a 'memory and learning experiment'. An experimenter introduced each participant to 'Mr Wallace', who they were told was another participant – but was actually a confederate working for Milgram. The pair was then told that one of them would take the role of a 'teacher' and one would be a 'learner' in the memory experiment. The teacher, they were told, would have to give an electric shock to the learner each time they got an answer wrong. The participant was given a mild 15-volt electric shock as an example. The pair drew lots – but this was fixed; Mr Wallace was always placed in the role of learner and the true participant placed in the role of teacher.*

The electric shock apparatus had a series of switches, the first of which was labelled 15V, and participants were asked to increase the shock level with each wrong answer. There were labels below the switches, for example, 375V – 'Danger, severe shock'. The last switch was labelled 450V. The confederate deliberately got many answers wrong and the participants found themselves under pressure to give stronger and stronger shocks.

The confederate participant grunted with pain at first, and as the faked shocks continued, began to shout in protest, including saying that he had a heart condition and refusing to take any further part. After 315V, he was silent. If the true participant hesitated, the experimenter could use a verbal prod such as 'the experiment requires that you continue', or 'you have no choice, teacher – you must go on'.

Findings: *Twenty-six out of 40 (65%) continued up to the maximum shock level of 450 volts. Many showed signs of becoming highly stressed but nobody stopped before 300V. Milgram concluded that most people can be highly obedient in certain social situations. Here, they were obedient because they were in a novel situation and therefore unsure of how to act. They perceived the experimenter as a legitimate authority and they believed he would take responsibility for any harm done.*

Evaluation: *This was a groundbreaking and highly influential study that was well controlled in a lab. However, it can be criticised on ethical grounds, as participants were both stressed and deceived. In his defence, Milgram stated that in a subsequent survey, 84% of participants said that they were 'glad to have been in the experiment' and that participants showed no signs of long-term harm in psychiatric assessments (Colman, 1987).*

A photograph from the study

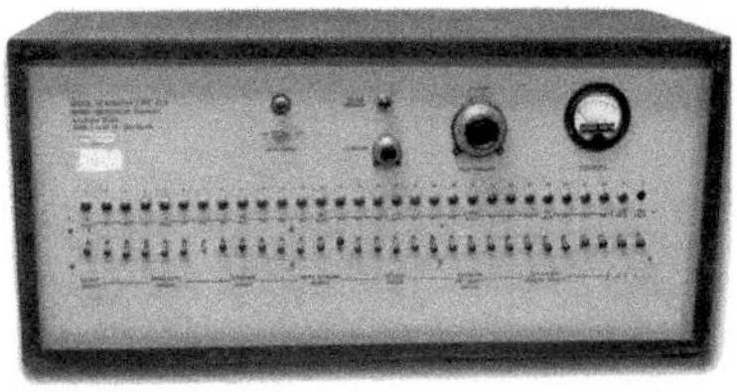

The electric shock apparatus used

Top tip

When analysing this study, ensure that you link it to concepts such as agency theory (see p. 273) and to its historical background. You can also compare it to other studies of obedience, and analyse the methodology.

? Discussion point

Would you pick up a piece of litter if told to do so by a fellow student? What about by a teacher/lecturer? The headteacher or college principal? If it was a fellow student, would it matter what year they were in – if they were older or younger than you?

? Discussion point

Besides clothing, what aspects of an individual's appearance and behaviour can convey a sense of authority?

The dose requested by the doctor was twice the maximum shown on the label

The obedience rate was higher in the prestigious setting of Yale University

Was the Milgram study realistic?

Milgram's study was a fascinating demonstration of obedience in a lab but it is not clear if it can be directly compared to everyday life – it lacked ecological validity. Orne (1962) doubted whether Milgram's participants really believed in the electric shocks and suggested that such a high level of obedience in the face of harmful consequences would not be found in the real world.

However, another research study in the 1960s demonstrated a very high level of obedience in the real world. Hofling *et al.* (1966) conducted a field experiment on nurses. A fake drug labelled 'Astroten' was left in the ward and each nurse received a phone call from an unknown doctor, calling himself 'Dr Smith'. The doctor told the nurse to prepare a dose of the drug (which was double the maximum dosage indicated on the label) and give it to a patient, 'Mr Jones'. Despite having the opportunity to refuse, 21 out of 22 nurses prepared the medication and they were going to administer it until stopped by the experimenter.

Why people obey: effects of the situation

We like to feel that we have a choice over our actions and that whether we obey an immoral command or not is due to our own moral values. Some participants in Milgram's study did refuse to obey. One participant, Jan Rensaleer, was an electrical engineer, and refused to continue, stating '*I know what shocks do to you*' (Milgram, 1974, p. 52).

However, the overall findings of his work led Milgram to believe that individual factors have a very limited role in obedience behaviour. People don't obey because of their personality, he thought, but because of the social situation they find themselves in. His results went against the idea that Nazi soldiers were somehow different from other people and suggested that in particular circumstances, nearly everyone will obey authority.

According to Milgram, there were several variables that could have affected the results and in order to test the role of each variable he repeated his experiment 20 times with a slightly different procedure each time. Every time he used a different 40 participants, and obedience level was always based on *the percentage who went up to the maximum shock level*.

Legitimate authority

Milgram (1974) thought that one reason for the high level of obedience in his original study was that its setting was prestigious – Yale University. What would happen if it was conducted in a more everyday setting? He replicated the experiment in an office in the city centre, with the experimenter wearing casual clothes. Obedience rate dropped to 52% – a fairly small difference that suggests that the appearance and social power of the experimenter was not the main cause of obedience.

Proximity

Milgram felt that having a wall between the participant and Mr Wallace acts as a **buffer**, making it easier to deliver the shock, as the suffering is not immediately visible. One variation of the experiment – the 'proximity' variation – involved the teacher sitting in the same room as Mr Wallace, so they could see as well as hear him. However, obedience rate only fell to 40%, and even when the teacher had to hold Mr Wallace's arms down, believing that shocks were delivered through metal plates on the chair arms ('touch proximity'), obedience rate stood at 30% (Milgram, 1974). It appears that the lack of a buffer has an effect but that there is still a lot of obedience.

Children tend to be less obedient if their teacher or parent leaves the room

Presence of authority

In the classic version of the study, the authority figure, that is, the experimenter was in the room (note that the 'experimenter' was an actor as well and not Milgram himself). Life experience suggests that if the authority figure is removed, obedience tends to fall, just as when children stop working if their teacher or parent leaves the room. In the 'remote authority' variation, the experimenter gave initial instructions and then left the room, delivering further instructions by phone. The obedience rate fell to 20.5% (Milgram, 1974).

Top tip

If asked about proximity, you could include the proximity of the authority figure, or their presence/absence. Use real world examples.

Peers

Milgram wanted to see how peer pressure would interact with obedience. To do this, he added two confederate teachers who were instructed to dissent at specific points (150V and 210V). The obedience rate fell to 10%. However, in another variation, a confederate teacher pressed the electric shock switches, so that the true participant just had to read the questions, thereby playing along with the suffering of the 'learner' but not directly causing it; 92.5% continued to the maximum level in this variation (Milgram, 1974).

Top tip

Proximity is a key factor and easy to explain, but statistically it made less of a difference to obedience rate than the presence of peers.

Why people obey: effects of society

Agency theory

According to Milgram, people's decision to obey or dissent from an authority figure can depend on the mental state in which they find themselves. Most of the time, we act based on our own wishes and desires. Milgram called this the **autonomous state**. However, at times of stress and conflict, there is a tendency to look for the person in charge – the authority figure in the situation – and follow their orders. This happens because we are used to hierarchical systems throughout society where there are both leaders and followers. Therefore, when people are under moral strain such as in the Milgram experiment, they relinquish their own moral responsibility and act on the basis of this authority figure's commands. This is known as entering the **agentic state**:

- Autonomous state: seeing yourself as being in power; acting on your own wishes and morals.
- Agentic state: seeing another person as having power; acting on behalf of their principles/commands.

? Discussion point

Considering both Milgram's research and the Hofling *et al.* (1966) study, what can be concluded about the role of location on obedience level?

At times of stress and conflict, there is a tendency to look for the person in charge

Parenting style will have an affect on a child's level of obedience

Socialisation

One of the reasons we enter the agentic state is that society has taught us to respect and obey authority figures. Childhood is the time when we learn society's rules, including learning who is considered to be an authority figure and who is not – parents, teachers and so on. The effect of childhood experiences on making us behave according to social norms is known as **socialisation**. It is the result of collective social pressures from family, teachers, peers and other significant people encountered as a child grows up. As Andersen and Zimbardo (1984, p. 200) state:

'The 'good child' learns his place in all social settings, stays put in her seat, is polite, speaks only when spoken to, is cooperative, does not make trouble, and never makes a scene. As children we are rewarded for going along with the group and for not insisting on getting our way. It is the wiser course of action, we are taught, to go with (or around) power, not to challenge it.'

Parenting

One of the biggest influences on a child's socialisation is its parents. However, not all children are raised in the same way by their parents. Some are encouraged by their parents to think for themselves and make rational choices. This is called **democratic parenting**. In this parenting style, rules are not absolute; instead, children are encouraged to negotiate reasonable boundaries.

Other parents teach their children that obedience to, and respect for, authority figures is the top priority and that rules should be obeyed and not discussed. This is known as **authoritarian parenting**.

However, it is hard to put parents into a particular category. In addition, as we grow older, peers begin to become more influential. Nevertheless, the beliefs about the world that we learn in early childhood tend to stay with us.

Top tip

Find out more about the Stanford prison experiment and its follow-up, the BBC Prison Experiment. As well as being relevant to obedience, they are also useful evidence for the Prejudice topic – the two groups quickly became hostile towards each other, rather like in Sherif's 'summer camp' experiment (see p.310).

Summary and analysis

The variations of Milgram's basic study provide powerful evidence of the role of situational factors in obedience. They are supported by the hospital study of Hoffling *et al.* (1966), which demonstrated that obedience plays a role in real life settings.

Another study that showed the importance of the situation was the Stanford prison experiment by Zimbardo and colleagues (Zimbardo *et al.*, 1973). Student volunteers were randomly divided into two groups – prisoners and guards – and put into a mock prison, which was actually set in the basement of Stanford University Psychology Department. The researchers observed the students changing their behaviour to suit their new roles, with prisoners becoming demoralised and depressed while many guards became aggressive and demeaning, and used their power to humiliate the prisoners.

However, despite the importance of the social situation, individual factors can play a role in obedience too. You have already seen how the personal experience level of some of Milgram's participants made them more likely to dissent. Sex differences have been found too, with Kilham and Mann (1974) reporting significantly lower levels of obedience among women in a Milgram-type experiment.

Make the link

...with the concept of authoritarian personality (see chapter 11).

Kohlberg (1969) described the importance of an individual's level of moral development in whether they obey authority or not (see box below). He stated that only some people reach the highest level of moral development – **post-conventional reasoning** – and that these people are better able to disobey an immoral command.

- Pre-conventional reasoning: the individual's view of right or wrong depends on the standards of adults around them, and on the outcome of their actions. At this stage, typical in children under the age of nine, anything that results in punishment is 'bad', and anything that results in a reward is 'good'.
- Conventional reasoning: the individual's view of right or wrong has come to be based on the standards of their society as a whole – they see law breaking as always wrong, for example, while obeying the rules is seen as good behaviour.
- Post-conventional reasoning: at this stage, the individual goes beyond the norms of their society and comes to realise that rules/laws themselves are not always morally right. Such individuals may consider it morally correct to break a law if it results in a greater good.

Questions

1. True or false: obedience usually results from unspoken social pressure?
2. Two sources of authority according to Weber are traditional and legal – what is the third?
3. What is the name of a social structure where people with lower ranks or status are expected to obey those in higher positions?
4. How many participants took part in Milgram's original (1963) study?
5. How many of the participants obeyed up to the maximum level?
6. What were the main ethical issues with the Milgram study?
7. In what setting did the Hofling *et al.* (1966) study take place?
8. Which variation of Milgram's basic procedure produced the highest level of obedience?
9. What are the two states that form Milgram's agency theory?
10. True or false: democratic parenting encourages children to blindly obey authority?

Key concepts

- Obedience
- Authority figure
- Social pressure
- Hierarchy
- Legitimate authority
- Buffer
- Autonomous state
- Agentic state
- Socialisation
- Democratic parenting
- Authoritarian parenting
- Power
- Uniform

Activities

1. Think of three examples of when obedience is a positive/useful thing in society and three examples of when it can be negative/harmful. For example: 'obedience is a bad thing if someone obeys their partner in an abusive relationship.' Compare your answers with a classmate. Do you agree about when obedience is good or bad?
2. Draw up a table summarising the main variations (including the original) of Milgram's study ('proximity', 'peer gives shock', etc.) and the obedience level that was found with each one.
3. Give a real example of how the following factors can affect whether people obey or not:
   - power of the authority figure
   - presence/absence of the authority figure
   - proximity to victim
   - personality/personal experience
   - peers
   - parenting style.

If possible, draw the examples from your own experience.

End of topic project

In your class or another suitable group of fellow psychology students, conduct a simple experimental study, as follows:

- First, identify a suitable stimulus, such as that used in the Jenness or Hornsey *et al.* studies.
- Now identify a way of applying group pressure – for example, a faked list of prior responses.
- Using opportunity sampling, find participants to look at, and respond to, the stimulus.
- Make a distinction between two groups, for example, with versus without social influence (fake guesses or no fake guesses).
- Analyse results and draw conclusions.
- Write a summary of the study and your findings. Find at least one relevant background research study that is not from your notes or textbook.

End of topic specimen exam questions

National 5

1. Give one example of a situation where people might conform. 2 marks
2. Explain two types of conformity. 4 marks
3. Describe one research study into conformity. 5 marks
4. Explain the difference between minority and majority influence. 4 marks
5. Look at the following scenario:

   Rebecca is a school pupil aged 14. When on a school trip, she finds herself sitting with a group of four pupils from a different year group. When they start talking about how much they like shopping at Tesco, Rebecca agrees, even though she never goes there.

   Referring to the scenario, explain two factors that affect conformity. 6 marks

Higher

1. Some people are more vulnerable to peer pressure than others. Explain two or more factors involved in conformity that could account for this difference. 8 marks
2. Analyse one research study relevant to conformity. 8 marks
3. Explain the concept of obedience, referring to research evidence and factors that affect obedience. 20 marks
4. Look at the following scenario:

   Pooja is trying to study Psychology in the school dining hall during a free period but two other sixth year pupils on the other side of the hall are distracting her by chatting. She glares at them but they ignore her. After a few minutes, a depute headteacher walks past and tells the pair that they must work quietly. They immediately stop talking.

   Analyse the scenario in terms of the roles of perceived legitimate authority and proximity in obedience. 6 marks

11 Non-verbal communication

For the topic of Non-verbal communication, you should be able to explain:

- Types of non-verbal communication.
- The functions of non-verbal communication.
- The role of nature and nurture in non-verbal communication.
- The methodology and findings of relevant research.

You need to develop the following skills:

- Explaining concepts and processes relevant to non-verbal communication.
- Explaining and evaluating theories and research relevant to non-verbal communication.
- Using research evidence to back up your explanations of human behaviour.
- Applying your understanding of non-verbal communication to real situations.

! Syllabus note

Non-verbal communication is a topic in the Social Behaviour unit in National 5 Psychology. Higher students should instead study one of the following option topics: Prejudice (chapter 12) OR Social Relationships (chapter 13) OR Aggression (chapter 14).

Non-verbal communication includes facial expressions and body language

Non-verbal communication (NVC) means communicating without words. There are several aspects to NVC, such as body language, eye contact and facial expression. Just as with verbal communication, non-verbal cues such as your expression or posture can communicate information to others. They can reveal your mood and how friendly you feel towards the person. This chapter will look at the functions of key forms of NVC, as well as exploring an aspect of the nature – nurture debate: is NVC innate, or do we learn it from people around us?

Types of non-verbal communication

Body language

One of the most obvious and important aspects of NVC is a person's **body language** – the way they communicate using their bodies rather than (or as well as) words. Gestures, a person's posture and how close they stand to another person are all examples of body language. The following section explains three major types of body language that are apparent in everybody when communicating.

Proximity. This is how close we are to another person. Generally, people stand closer to those that they like better – and proximity can therefore communicate liking – or dislike – to the other person. On the other hand, standing too close is rated unfavourably – there are social norms regarding how close people can stand without making the other person feel stressed, unless the person is already a close friend (Freedman, 1975). If **personal space** is invaded, people tend to back away (Felipe & Sommer, 1966). People also keep a greater 'social distance' from members of groups that they have prejudiced feelings against (Norman *et al.*, 2010).

Proximity can depend on liking

'Thumbs up' is a gesture

Gesture means the things that we do, primarily with our hands and arms, to communicate non-verbally or in addition to words. Examples include pointing, clapping, 'thumbs up', waving arms around, and, of course, sticking fingers up! A gesture may support the content of speech, such as a rising hand motion when talking about climbing (McNeill, 1992). There are certain ritual hand gestures in religion, politics or the military (e.g. saluting) and they can form part of games (e.g. 'rock, scissors, paper'). Gestures are typically done using the hands, but shrugging shoulders, nodding, shaking the head, etc. are also usually considered to be examples of gestures.

Posture is another aspect of body language. Broadly, this can include things such as sitting, standing or lying down, but on a more precise level, things such as the angle of a person's shoulders, neck and back can signal their mood – a straight back and relaxed shoulders indicating confidence, for example, while slouching does not (Krauss Whitbourne, 2012). Furley and Schweizer (2014) showed participants images of athletes, without giving away the score or showing any clear examples of celebration or disappointment. They found that child participants could guess the score from the body language of the athlete – in other words, they could reliably tell who was winning or losing just by looking at them.

Posture can communicate mood

? Discussion point

What body language indicates that someone is bored? What about when they are interested/excited?

Top tip

Use visualisation to help you remember major elements of body language. You could imagine someone you know keeping their distance, slouching and making a rude gesture!

Ambady and Rosenthal (1992) believe that these cues lead people to make unconscious but yet very accurate judgements of others. In their research, they discovered a reliable correlation between people's own reports of their personality and short clips of their body language observed by others. They used the term **thin slicing** to mean immediate judgements that are made about a person or situation and observed that taking more time or paying more deliberate attention to an observation did not make people's judgements more accurate – a 30-second observation was just as effective as five minutes.

Therefore, it appears that these aspects of NVC affect us on a very basic psychological level – we make fast, accurate judgements of others based on their body language and we are generally unaware of doing it. And of course, other people are doing the same to us all of the time.

Eye contact

Eye contact means whether we look at another person's eyes/face or look away. This can indicate interest in them or what they are saying, or other emotions such as embarrassment. Another term for eye contact is **gaze**. If both people look at each other at the same time, this is known as **mutual gaze**.

Making eye contact signals that you wish to communicate

Failure to pay attention to some's gaze is usually interpreted as a sign of not being interested, or not listening to what they are saying (Argyle & Cook, 1976). In particular, gazing at another person's face and making eye contact indicates that you wish to communicate (DeSteno *et al.*, 2012).

Kendon and Cook (1967) found that there are individual differences in length of gaze, with some people tending to look at faces for longer than others regardless of who they are speaking to. However, people find long interpersonal gaze, particularly from strangers, uncomfortable, due to the sense that someone is staring at them. In a research study, people preferred the eye contact to last for three seconds or less – but were comfortable with longer gazes as long as the person who was looking at them seemed trustworthy (Moyer, 2016).

Other points to note about gaze include:

- It can make it easier to process information about a person, such as what they are saying.
- It makes a person more memorable by engaging your attention.
- A gaze can have multiple uses during a social interaction, such as indicating boredom (with an 'eye-rolling' gaze) or surprise.
- We like people more when they look at us, particularly when their gaze is not too brief (Kuzmanovic *et al.*, 2009).
- However, having someone looking at you makes it harder to focus on other events and tasks, even if you are not looking back at them (Conty *et al.*, 2010).

Top tip

Note down some of the points about gaze on an index card. They can form the outline of an exam answer on eye contact.

Top tip

Some researchers use the term 'eye contact' to refer to mutual gaze only.

Some researchers have expressed concern about how technology may affect eye contact as a part of NVC. As noted above, failing to pay attention to someone's gaze suggests that you are not interested, and so if young children find that adults are not looking at them (for example, because they are looking at a screen instead), this could affect the development of communication skills. Indeed, paying attention to gaze and eye contact appears to be at least partly **innate** – newborn babies have been shown to spend more time looking at an image of a face that is looking at them than one that is looking away (Farroni *et al.*, 2002; see next section of this chapter). Learners appear to remember more if a teacher makes eye contact with them, while eye contact can also lead to an increase in helpful behaviour. Reduced child–parent eye contact during a child's upbringing could therefore have negative effects.

Facial expressions

Facial expressions play a huge role in understanding what another person is feeling. The most obvious one is the smile. It was recognised in the 19th century that there are two key types of smile – one that involves the mouth muscles and the muscles around the eyes – a so-called **Duchenne smile** – and one that just involves the mouth. Subsequent research shows that a smile involving only the mouth is more likely to be false, while a smile involving both the mouth and the eyes is universally associated with positive emotions (Messinger *et al.*, 2001).

Researcher Paul Ekman has done extensive work on facial expression, stating in the 1960s that there are certain basic facial expressions that are the same for everyone – they are **culturally universal**. Ekman (1999) believes that these indicate universal basic emotions.

A smile involving both the mouth and the eyes is universally associated with positive emotions

Ekman (2009a) also noted that faces display brief **microexpressions** – momentary appearances of emotion on the face, sometimes too fast to see without a slow-motion video, which the person then deliberately hides. For example, if someone's boss gives them extra work to do, there may be a momentary sign of anger on their face, which they then hide by deliberately smiling and nodding. Their initial brief micro-expression may be a truer indication of what they are feeling. Polikovsky *et al.* (2009) supported the idea of microexpressions and suggested that they can be a clue to violent and criminal intentions. However, Ekman (2009a) noted that microexpressions are hard to spot and that NVC in general is easy to misinterpret.

Ekman states that there are seven emotions that have universal signals in people's facial expressions, often revealed in their microexpressions:

- anger
- fear
- sadness
- disgust
- contempt
- surprise
- happiness.

Can you tell how this girl is feeling from her expression?

The idea of microexpressions suggests that our facial reactions are, to some extent, controlled by automatic emotional responses and that these are quickly suppressed as our awareness of the social situation

People may try to hide their feelings by changing their facial expression

takes control. Therefore, there are at least two processes controlling facial expressions: one more immediate that leads to automatic reactions, and a slower, more deliberate, cognitive reaction that allows us to modify our own expressions.

There is some evidence that facial expressions are universal – the same across all cultures. Ekman and Friesen (1971) conducted a study of the **Fore people** in Papau New Guinea, a group that had been isolated from the rest of the world for thousands of years (see key study). This study found that despite the people's isolation, the labels they gave to facial expressions (such as happy or angry) were very similar to those used by outside observers. However, it is possible that people learn to modify their facial expressions, depending on the norms of the culture in which they live, and they may therefore be only partly innate. The relative roles of nature and nurture in NVC are discussed in the next two sections.

Key study: Ekman and Friesen (1971): the universal nature of facial expressions

Aim: *Ekman and Friesen aimed to find out whether facial expressions are universal to all humans.*

Method: *The researchers studied the Fore people in Papua New Guinea, a group that had been isolated for thousands of years, living in a Stone Age culture. The tribe had very little contact with outsiders before the 1950s, and although some had since met and interacted with many outsiders, the researchers picked participants who had experienced very little of such contact. They had never learned a Western language, seen a movie or worked for an outsider. The sample included 189 adults and 130 children – around 3% of the total Fore population. For comparison, researchers also studied 23 adults who had extensive contact with Westerners. A difficulty was that none of the participants could read. Therefore, a task was chosen that involved looking at two to three pictures of facial expressions while the researcher read out a short scenario that indicated an emotion, for example, 'her mother has died and she feels very sad' (p.126). The participant then had to point to the face picture that indicated the emotion. The scenarios were read by Fore translators who were instructed not to prompt.*

Findings: *Responses were very similar to those previously found by Western subjects, with a very high percentage – in some cases 100% – applying the same label. Importantly, there were no significant differences between the Westernised and isolated groups, suggesting that exposure to Western colonists had not affected Fore perceptions of facial expressions. The one 'error' that was commonly found was in distinguishing fear from surprise. No sex differences were found, except that Fore women were less enthusiastic about taking part in the study. There were also no age differences found, with six- to seven-year-old children responding the same as older Fore individuals and with as much accuracy. The researchers concluded that certain facial expressions are* *universally associated with particular emotions in all human cultures. They accepted that fear had not been well distinguished from surprise and noted that it was unclear whether this is because culture does play some role in modifying innate facial expressions, or because among the Fore people, fearful events (such as an attack by another tribe) are generally also surprising.*

Evaluation: *A strength of the study was the relatively large sample who had very little contact with the outside world. It was also supported by a number of other findings; for example, work with blind children who show the same facial expressions as sighted children. The research supports the views of researchers such as Darwin, Wundt and Asch that facial expressions are universal. However, Smith and Bond (1993) argued that relatively few emotions are truly universal, while Matsumoto (1989) found that Japanese people were poorer at identifying images of negative emotions – perhaps because it is less culturally acceptable to express these emotions in Japan than elsewhere.*

Photographs of one of the Fore men studied – can you match the expressions to the following emotions: happy, sad, disgusted and angry?

Questions

1. Three major types of body language were described at the start of this chapter. One is proximity, what are the other two?
2. Which of the three types is this an example of: pointing?
3. Which of the three types is this an example of: backing away?
4. How do people usually interpret mutual gaze?
5. How easy is it to see a microexpression?
6. How easy is it to interpret a microexpression?
7. There are two key types of smile. Which parts of the face do they involve?
8. Who were the Fore people and what made them unique?
9. How many participants were there in Ekman and Friesen's study?
10. Give three examples of what Ekman considers basic facial expressions.

Key concepts

- Non-verbal communication (NVC)
- Proximity
- Personal space
- Gesture
- Posture
- Gaze
- Mutual gaze
- Eye contact
- Thin slicing
- Duchenne smile
- Facial expression
- Microexpression
- Fore people
- Innate

Activities

1. Use your phone to take pictures of yourself (or a classmate) making the seven basic facial expressions described by Ekman. If possible, add these photos to your study notes. Can you think of a situation when you would make each of those faces? Note those down as well.
2. What do the following gestures mean to you?

Arguments for nature in NVC

As is apparent from other topics in psychology, there is an ongoing debate between approaches and theories that emphasise the role of nature – our biology and genetics – in behaviour, and explanations that say that culture and/or experience have greater roles. This is known as the **nature–nurture debate**.

In terms of theories of NVC, the nature side of the debate suggests that NVC is innate and due to our genetics, and is therefore **universal** – the same in all societies. The nurture side of the debate suggests that the major part of NVC is learned from society around us, and therefore varies from culture to culture.

Biological factors

A major issue in the nature/nurture debate in NVC is the extent to which body language and other NVC functions are controlled by universal biological systems. Evidence here that mainly supports the 'nature' side of the debate is the study of the biology of NVC, closely linked to the biological approach to psychology (see chapter 1).

This view says that a brain area called the **amygdala** plays a central role in regulating our response to other people's NVC. The amygdala is part of the limbic system, a set of brain areas associated with emotion (see chapter 1). It plays an important role in regulating emotions, especially fear and aggression, in all animals, and in humans it seems to be very important in responding to faces – people who have had their amygdala damaged tend to trust unappealing, unfamiliar faces that other people react negatively to (Adolphs *et al.*, 1998).

When viewing faces, the amygdala is probably involved in the rapid 'thin slicing' reactions described in the previous section. In other words, this part of the brain produces our 'gut feelings' about a person or situation. The amygdala is also involved in recognising body language, as are several other brain areas; motor cortex – the area of neocortex that controls movement – is vital for mentally representing the actions that we see (De Gelder, 2006).

Although these processes could be affected by culture, on the whole biological evidence suggests that the way we respond to other people's NVC, such as facial expressions or threatening body language, is rapid and largely innate.

NVC in babies

Researchers have discovered that our reaction to NVC and the appearance of other people arrives early. Most babies start to smile at around six to eight weeks old, suggesting that this is biologically programmed in humans. As mentioned earlier, babies appear to recognise faces and prefer them to non-faces – in experiments, they respond more to face-like pictures than pictures with the same features jumbled up (Fagan, 1976). They also imitate the facial expression of adults long before they learn to imitate other actions (Meltzoff & Moore, 1977, see key study). Together, these findings suggest that the way we respond to people's faces and body language occurs at a very basic (unconscious) level, which is under biological control.

Key study: Meltzoff and Moore (1977): babies' imitate facial expressions and gestures

Aim: *The researchers noted that earlier experts on infant development such as Jean Piaget had assumed that imitation does not develop until eight months of age or older. Their aim was to show that it could occur in babies who are less than three weeks old.*

Method: *The researchers studied six babies aged 12 to 19 days. In a laboratory experiment, the researchers initially displayed a*

Top tip

The nature side of the argument states that NVC is universal, while the nurture side states that NVC is learned from our culture.

The amygdala is important in responding to faces

Most babies start to smile at around six to eight weeks old

? Discussion point

What other things that occur during a baby's early development might be innate? Think about how they feed, move and communicate.

neutral face. They then showed one of four stimulus faces/gestures in a random order:

- *tongue out*
- *pouting face*
- *wiggling fingers*
- *wide open mouth.*

Each stimulus was displayed four times over 15 seconds, and for the following 20 seconds, the experimenter made a neutral face again and the baby's reaction was recorded. In order to allow for the possibility that the baby might not be paying attention, this process was repeated up to three times in total if required.

Findings: *Undergraduate observers were then shown the video recordings in a random order and they were asked to estimate which of the four gestures they thought the baby was copying. They were significantly more likely to guess the correct gesture than the other options. The researchers concluded that the ability to imitate NVC is largely innate, developing before a child is able to consciously control its own actions.*

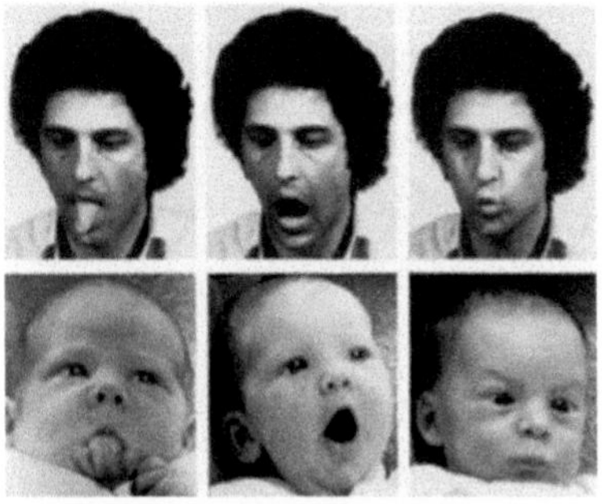

Photographs from the study

Top tip

The Ekman and Friesen (1971) study on facial expressions among the Fore people also supports the nature side of the nature–nurture debate.

Evaluation: *A strength of the study was its careful control of possible confounding variables that had to be avoided, for example:*

- *The effects of two similar facial expressions were compared, for example, tongue sticking out versus wide mouth.*
- *Distance between the baby and the adult was kept constant.*
- *Observers were shown the baby's face only on a video recording and they were not told what gesture the infant had been shown.*

The study was highly influential in showing that some NVC occurs very early and it is apparently linked to others' NVC at a very young age. It led to the development of a model of infant imitation that has been used by researchers Breazeal and Scassellati (2002) in teaching robots to imitate. However, Jones (2009) disputes the findings. She points out that imitation of finger wiggling and the pouting face have not been reliably replicated, while sticking the tongue out is a very typical response in babies to anything that interests them – it does not necessarily mean that they were imitating.

Universals in NVC

The **evolutionary theory of NVC** favours the nature side of the debate and states that NVC is the product of evolution by natural selection. Drawing on Darwin's theory it suggests that functions such as facial expressions and body language have evolved because they gave our ancestors a survival advantage. As humans are all genetically very similar, we can be expected to have very similar body language, too.

Darwin considered human behaviour to consist of evolved traits that, as in animals, have given an advantage to our ancestors and have been passed on through the generations. In terms of NVC, Darwin made four key claims that have been supported by subsequent research (Ekman, 2009b):

- There are several basic emotions that are fundamentally separate from each other.
- Facial expressions are the main way of conveying these emotions through NVC.
- Facial expressions are culturally universal.
- Gestures are cultural conventions, learned within a social group.

Emotion in primates can only be studied through observation

Darwin believed that all human emotions were linked to our origins as apes and he saw parallels with expressions of emotion that he observed in other primates. It is difficult to study emotion in primates as it can only be done through observation, however Ekman (1999, p.54) states there is '*no convincing evidence*' that humans have any emotions that are not also present in our near relatives such as chimpanzees.

Chimps make a 'begging posture' with outstretched hands

As well as facial expressions, body language in grief among other apes is strikingly similar to that in humans. Chimpanzees have been observed stroking the hands of ill relatives, hugging bereaved individuals and sitting in a nightly 'vigil' after a death (Anderson *et al.*, 2010). Their posture and proximity to the dying and deceased also changes, with a tendency to avoid places associated with death. Chimps also make a 'begging posture' with outstretched hands (Premack & Premack, 1983). These similarities suggest that such gestures are based in our ancient evolutionary past.

Evaluation of the nature side of the debate

There is good evidence that brain systems play a role in NVC, and that there are some aspects of NVC that are similar in all children, including those who are blind. However, the idea that the development of our reactions to NVC may be linked to basic biological systems does not rule out the possibility that these functions come under conscious control as we get older, and therefore become influenced by culture.

Although the principle of natural selection is generally accepted, researchers do not always agree on why NVC functions evolved – what use these behaviours had for human ancestors. Ekman (2009b) states that emotional facial expressions are largely universal because it was essential during human evolution that individuals gave clear signals to the social group of what they were feeling and what they might be just about to do. Zajonc (1985) disputes this view, arguing that it would not have been an evolutionary advantage to let enemies know one's intentions.

Key concepts

- Nature–nurture debate
- Amygdala
- Natural selection
- Universal
- Evolutionary theory of NVC

Questions

1. On the whole, which side of the nature–nurture debate is supported by the role of brain areas in NVC?
2. Which area of the brain is particularly important for regulating our emotional response to NVC?
3. At what age do human babies start to smile?
4. Do babies learn to imitate facial expressions before or after learning to imitate other actions?
5. What is most likely to happen if you showed a baby two cartoon faces, one with normal features and one with jumbled up features?
6. What four forms of NVC did Meltzoff and Moore (1977) use in their study?
7. For how long were the forms of NVC shown to the babies in the Meltzoff and Moore (1977) study?
8. What problem could there be with interpreting a baby's 'imitation' of the tongue sticking out?
9. Name one of Darwin's four claims about the universality of NVC.
10. Give one example of how body language in chimpanzees is similar to that in humans.

Activities

1. Make a list of at least four arguments in favour of the nature side of the debate. On the left side of a piece of paper, summarise each argument in one or two sentences. On the right side of the paper, make a note of research evidence or real-world examples for each argument. This sheet could form the basis of an essay answer on the nature side of the debate – each argument would become a paragraph.
2. Find out more about gestures used by other primates. Perhaps you could watch a documentary or YouTube clip and report back to the rest of the class. Try to find more examples of NVC which resemble that found in humans. If you find examples of gestures and body language that are different in humans compared to other primates, try to find out if there is an evolutionary explanation for the difference.

Arguments for nurture in NVC

As noted in the previous section, some aspects of NVC are thought to be culturally universal, that is, the same in everyone regardless of their upbringing and culture. However, other aspects appear to be strongly influenced by what are called **nurture influences** – culture, parental upbringing and life experience. The key evidence tends to be the extent to which NVC differs in different parts of the world. Learned individual differences also support the nurture side of the debate.

This section considers aspects of NVC which seem to be most highly variable depending on culture and life experience. It also looks at smaller differences in things like facial expressions, proximity and posture. Even areas of NVC which are largely innate may have subtle but important variations that depend on upbringing and culture.

Personal space

As noted earlier, there are social norms regarding how close people can stand without making another person feel stressed, and people don't like to have their **personal space** invaded by others coming too close. Hall (1966) described four 'zones' of personal space.

Name of zone	Distance	Purpose	Features
Intimate distance	Up to 50 cm	Interaction with very close personal friend or lover	Close enough for smell, or to hear breathing
Personal distance	50 cm to 1 m	Regular interactions with friends	Touching is still possible
Social distance	1 m to 4 m	Interactions with acquaintances, colleagues	Some cues are lost but facial expression and body language is easily seen Distance may convey a lack of warmth
Public distance	4 m or more	Public behaviour, such as listening to a speech	Harder to make out details of facial expression Distance shows that closeness is not wanted

Although management of one's personal space is a general trait seen in all cultures, the details seems to be learned across childhood like any social skill (Hall, 1966). There are also differences on the basis of life experience, with people who have a history of violence preferring a larger space. These aspects suggest that personal space is highly influenced by nurture.

Holland *et al.* (2004) found that activating people's beliefs or prejudices led to variations in how close to strangers people chose to get, suggesting that proximity is at least partly affected by social processes and can even vary from situation to situation.

There are **cultural differences** in how the personal space of the home is interpreted. In Western cultures, the home is usually considered to be a private space, which people outside of the family wouldn't enter without knocking. However, Altman (1975) reports that in traditional Javan cultures, the home is no more private than a street or public square, and people walk through freely.

Norms of personal space vary across cultures

There appear to be some cultural differences in terms of how much personal space people prefer. For example, southern Europeans appear to prefer a closer personal space for interactions than do northern Europeans (Hogg & Vaughan, 1998). However, evidence on this is mixed, changes over time and appears to depend on the social situation as much as the culture. That is to say, it's not clear that some cultures prefer more personal space – it would depend on whether it was a friendly or formal interaction, and whether the person they were speaking to was from the same or a different culture, among other factors.

Cultural differences in gestures

Culture can make a huge difference to gesture – gestures can have very different meanings in different cultures and some are unique to particular cultures. Darwin accepted this fact, despite supporting the nature side of the argument! Even things that seem fairly simple, such as sticking your tongue out, can range widely in how they are interpreted.

How would you interpret this gesture?

Meanings of sticking tongue out:

- Western cultures: seen as cheeky and provocative.
- Tibet: seen as friendly.
- Māori: seen as angry/defiant and used as part of war dances.

This can of course cause problems to a traveller – as you may know if you have been abroad, attitudes to things such as public hugging, kissing and holding hands can vary between cultures, for example the norm of kissing-to-greet in some Mediterranean countries. These behaviours can also vary within cultures; in some situations within your own culture it may be more socially acceptable than others to hold hands or make rude gestures – among a group of teenage friends rather than a work meeting, for example.

Kissing-to-greet is very common in some Mediterranean countries

How do people learn differences in gesture? As you may remember, Alfred Bandura developed the work of the behaviourist approach (see chapter 1) to explain how people learn from those around them, not just from stimuli in the environment. One key concept from this research is known as **observational learning**. This means that just as an action can be rewarded directly, we can observe others doing an action and are more likely to do it ourselves. This helps to explain how we can learn a gesture rapidly from those around us, particularly if we see it being used in a way that leads to some kind of social or practical reward.

The chameleon effect describes the way that people tend to unconsciously mimic the body language and gestures of others, in much the same way that a chameleon mimics the colour of its surroundings. Chartrand and Bargh (1999) carried out a lab experiment where a confederate was instructed to make gestures such as tapping their feet or rubbing their face. They found that participants who observed this were much more likely to copy the gestures compared to participants in the control group, despite having no awareness of doing so. They also found that a confederate who mimicked a participant was better liked than one who did not. This suggests that we may adapt to NVC in our cultural surroundings, and that there is a social benefit from doing so.

Participants were much more likely to rub their face if the confederate was doing so

Cultural differences in facial expressions

Despite the strong evidence that facial expressions are highly similar across cultures (see previous section), there may also be slight but significant cultural differences. A useful analogy to this is in spoken languages and accents – it is innate to learn to speak, yet spoken language varies from place to place. Could there also be local languages or accents in facial expressions or posture? Yuki *et al.* (2007) found evidence that this could be the case. They argued that people modify their facial expressions according to local norms and expectations (see key study).

? Discussion point

Have you ever noticed people mimicking each other's body language?

Key study: Yuki *et al.* (2007) study of culture and facial expressions

Aim: *As noted earlier, Ekman and other researchers had provided evidence that some aspects of facial expression are innate. However, this doesn't completely solve the question of how these expressions develop and how people use them to communicate, as there appear to be differences between cultures in terms of how expressions are recognised and interpreted. For example, Matsumoto (1989) found that Japanese people were poorer at identifying images of negative emotions than were Americans. There is also evidence that the more familiar you are with a culture, the better you are at judging emotions in people from that culture, suggesting a role for nurture as well as nature. Could it be that there are different local 'accents' in facial expressions? This is what the researchers aimed to find out.*

Research by Friesen (1972) had found that when watching a stressful film, Japanese participants tended to mask their emotions more than American participants did. However, it is harder to control the movements of your eyes than the movements of your mouth. Yuki et al. *therefore predicted that Japanese individuals would focus more on the eyes than the mouth when viewing and interpreting facial expressions.*

Method: *The researchers had noticed that people from the two cultures under investigation tended to use different keyboard characters to indicate emotion, for example :-) to denote a happy face in the USA, compared to ^_^ in Japan. They therefore decided to use emoticons with various combinations of the eyes and mouth to test their participants. There were 118 American and 95 Japanese participants in the study, all university students and all volunteers. Each filled in a questionnaire that showed them emoticons one at a time and asked them to rate each one on a scale ranging from 1 (extremely sad) to 9 (extremely happy).*

Findings: *the results were consistent with the hypothesis; Japanese participants gave higher happiness ratings to faces that had happier eyes (such as, happy eyes and a neutral mouth), while American participants gave higher happiness ratings when the mouth was happier than the eyes (such as, neutral eyes and a happy mouth). There were no gender differences in either culture. From this, the researchers concluded that there are genuine cultural differences in terms of how people perceive facial emotions, thus supporting the nurture side of the nature–nurture debate.*

Evaluation: *A limitation of the study was that the emoticons used were not real faces, and it could be argued that familiarity with particular types of emoticons would bias the study. To tackle this issue, the researchers ran a follow-up study using six real faces that had been manipulated with Adobe Photoshop to change the eyes or mouth. This subsequent work supported the original finding – American participants focused more on the happiness of the mouth, while Japanese participants focused more on the happiness of the eyes.*

The original study was further limited by the use of only students, and the sample was biased towards younger ages. The study did not allow for differences in how people of different ages perceive the emotion of faces. It may be the case that changes in status as people get older affects how they show and interpret NVC. Despite these limitations, the large sample was an advantage to the study.

Overall, the study supports the idea that despite some aspects of non-verbal communication being innate, how we use and interpret them can be influenced by local cultural differences.

Gender and status differences

Aspects of NVC that depend on culture and upbringing could also be affected by gender and status. After all, gender roles and status can vary from culture to culture. What is the evidence that males and females differ in terms of their NVC?

As described above, the study of facial expressions and emoticons by Yuki *et al.* (2007) found no **gender differences** between the two cultures studied. However, gender differences have been found in other areas, such as:

- Men appear to prefer more personal space than woman, both in seating and face-to-face conversation.
- Women engage in eye contact more than men do.
- Women tend to speak in higher pitched tones than men, though this depends a lot on the social context.

Gaze can be used to assert dominance and control, a sign of **status differences**. You may have noticed that teachers sometimes use a gaze to control behaviour, without using any words. When two people are speaking, it is usual for the listener to gaze more than the speaker, but it is common for people in positions of power to gaze as much, or more, when they are speaking. It is also common for leaders to gaze in a fixed way towards a speaker of lower status. This characteristic is known as **visual dominance behaviour**.

? Discussion point

In your experience, do males show more of a desire for personal space in terms of where they sit around a classroom?

Personal space is another indicator of status: a manager may have a larger desk or office than their subordinates, while a headteacher may stand on a podium to speak to a group of pupils or be seated in the centre of a row of teachers. People usually interact with those from other social groups at a greater distance, and this can include giving more distance to those with disabilities and psychological disorders.

Top tip

Look for examples of visual dominance behaviour among the villains in popular movies and cartoons!

Evaluation

In general, it is useful to remember that some aspects of NVC may be due to nature and others due to nurture. For example, facial expression seems to be largely universal, while gesture is culturally specific. However, as we have seen, it's not always quite that simple. Even within a particular aspect of NVC, such as posture or facial expression, there may be a combination of influences from both nature and nurture.

It may seem surprising nowadays, but some historical writers considered cultural differences in NVC to be based on racial groups – an idea that was also popular in Nazi Germany. Writing at a time when the Nazis were in power, Efron (1941) dismissed this idea, noting that cultural differences in NVC among Jewish and Italian communities in New York largely disappeared as they assimilated into the broader American community. The fact that people can change and adapt and that cultures change their NVC over time supports the idea that these are learned from society, and not innate. The research of Bandura on observational learning, as well as the study of the chameleon effect, gives useful insights into the mechanisms by which NVC can be learned from one's society.

Italian immigrants arriving in America

Key concepts

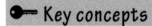

- Nurture influences
- Personal space
- Cultural differences
- Observational learning
- Gender differences
- Status differences
- Visual dominance behaviour

Questions

1. What is the name of the debate about how much of our behaviour is innate and how much is learned?
2. Give three examples of nurture influences.
3. According to Hall's (1966) four zones of personal space, how large is intimate distance?
4. According to Hall's (1966) four zones of personal space, what may be conveyed by maintaining a social distance (1 m to 4 m) when speaking to someone?
5. Give one cultural interpretation of sticking out your tongue.
6. What concept, linked with the behaviourist approach to psychology, suggests how we may learn gestures from people around us?
7. Which two gestures were used in Chartrand and Bargh's (1999) chameleon effect research?
8. In the Yuki *et al.* (2007) study, which culture focused more on the eyes than the mouth when viewing smiles?
9. Name one gender difference in NVC.
10. What status differences are shown by gaze when two people are conversing?

Activities

1. Find out more about cultural differences in gestures. Write a list of examples in your notes of where gestures can mean different things in two or more cultures with which you are familiar. You could conduct interview research with other people in your school or college to find out more.
2. If someone you knew was going for a job interview in another country, what would you tell them about the following:
   - posture
   - gesture
   - gaze and mutual gaze
   - the chameleon effect?

End of topic project

In your class or another suitable group, conduct a simple observation study into NVC, as follows:

- First, identify a suitable piece of video footage. For ethical reasons, do not use footage of anyone you know. It is best to avoid any acted/scripted behaviour such as dramas/soap operas/music videos. Some better options include:
  - an interview, for example of a politician
  - a piece of sports footage
  - a conversation during a reality TV show.
- Now prepare an observation schedule (see chapter 8). Brainstorm likely NVC cues that you may see – posture, gaze and so on. For this type of observation, a good choice would be to make a tally mark each time a behaviour occurs. Alternatively, you could write verbal descriptions at 30-second intervals.
- Compare your results between the two observers, checking for inter-observer reliability. If necessary, watch the clip again.
- If you can, play the video in slow motion and watch for microexpressions!
- Draw conclusions.
- Prepare and deliver a short talk to your class on what you found and concluded from this observation. Refer to at least one relevant background research study.

End of topic specimen exam questions

1. Explain how eye contact can be used to communicate. 3 marks

2. Besides eye contact, describe two types of non-verbal communication. 4 marks

3. Look at the following scenario and explain two aspects of NVC which may have been influenced by nurture. 6 marks

Alan is a guitarist who is giving his first solo concert. He comes out on to the stage in his local village hall and gives a thumbs up sign to the small crowd who are several metres away. As he starts to play the first song, someone at the front of the crowd starts to wave their arms in the air, and then others in the crowd do so as well.

4. Explain the role of nature in NVC, referring to one research study. 8 marks

12 Prejudice

For the topic of Prejudice, you should be able to explain:

- Different types of discrimination.
- Explanations of prejudice.
- The methodology and findings of relevant research.
- Techniques for reducing prejudice.

You need to develop the following skills:

- Explaining concepts relevant to prejudice.
- Explaining and evaluating theories relevant to prejudice.
- Using research evidence to back up factual statements and evaluation.
- Analysing research evidence relevant to prejudice.

! Syllabus note

Prejudice is a topic in the Social Behaviour unit in Higher Psychology. National 5 students should instead study the option topic Non-verbal communication (chapter 11).

Prejudice is an attitude, usually negative, towards another person based on their perceived membership of a group

Prejudice and discrimination

Prejudice is an attitude, usually negative, towards another person based on their perceived membership of a group. The word prejudice literally means to 'pre-judge', that is, to judge another person on the basis of their appearance or social group before learning the facts. For example, if you assume that someone who is older than you must be boring and decide not to talk to them, then you have pre-judged the person, and are showing prejudice.

Note that in social psychology, the term **in-group** is used to refer to any group that a person is part of, while **out-group** means a group that they are not part of. These terms are widely used in this topic.

In his classic work on prejudice, Allport (1954) notes that an in-group is any group about which we would use the word 'we', but notes also that these are flexible – people will broaden and narrow their definition of their in-group depending on the situation. For example, on a local level, someone in a different part of town is an out-group member, but if you are focusing on your whole town/country versus other towns/ countries, the same person is seen as an in-group member.

Prejudice is an attitude, meaning that it is an emotional reaction to a type of person, object or situation, based around our likes and dislikes. Prejudice typically includes colder feelings towards the out-group (Fiske *et al.*, 2007). This tends to be associated with an increase in desired social distance – the extent to which we wish to separate ourselves from members of the out-group – for example by not sitting near them, not talking to them or avoiding places where they go.

Cognitive, affective and behavioural biases

Generally, prejudice is used to refer to biases in thinking, feelings or behaviours which mean that some people are treated differently from others for no reason other than their group membership. Note that some researchers use the term 'prejudice' to refer to both thoughts and feelings, while others refer just to the feelings, and define it as part of the broader concept of **intergroup bias**, that is, any behaviour – thought, feeling or action – that favours one's in-group over out-groups (e.g. Hewstone *et al.*, 2002). According to this point of view, intergroup bias can be divided into three main aspects:

Cognitive The cognitive aspect of intergroup bias is the thoughts or beliefs a person has about an out-group. An example would be the belief that women are more emotional than men are (or vice versa). As discussed in chapter 1, a schema is a cognitive term meaning a set of ideas, knowledge and beliefs; a schema about a particular out-group is called a **stereotype**.

Affective The term 'affect' (as a noun) means emotion. This aspect means a person's biased feelings towards the out-group, such as judging them, fearing them, hating them or viewing them as making a positive or negative contribution to society. As discussed above, this aspect is usually called prejudice.

Behavioural This aspect refers to what people actually do towards an out-group – any action that involves treating the members of that group differently. The most obvious example is **discrimination**, that is, treating the out-group unfairly or harming or oppressing them (see below). Another major behavioural aspect of intergroup bias is **aggression**, ranging from physical and verbal assaults to genocide (Hewstone *et al.*, 2002).

As you can see, there are differences in how some of the terms in this topic can be defined. It is possible for a person to display differences between these different aspects, with some more positive than others. For example, a person could think that young people are lazy but not dislike them for it (cognitive but not affective) or they could hate communists but never act on their hatred (affective but not behavioural).

Assuming an older person is boring is an example of a prejudiced attitude

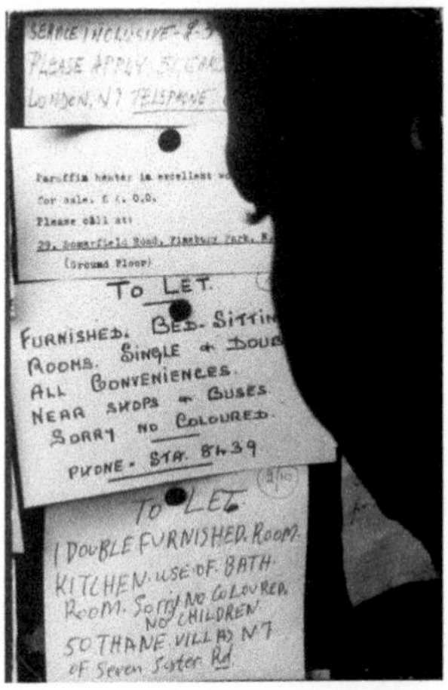

Advertisements discriminating against people who are not white, London, 1967

Top tip

There isn't universal agreement about how prejudice should be defined. Some researchers see it purely as emotional reaction, some include cognitive aspects such as beliefs, while others see it as a synonym of intergroup bias.

Discrimination

Discrimination is a behavioural aspect of intergroup bias. It means treating other people better or worse because of their membership of a social group, or some personal or physical characteristic such as a disability. Usually, it refers to unfair treatment of minorities or vulnerable people. For example, it would be discriminatory to deny someone a place on a good university course based on a stereotype about their race or social class or to deny a woman a job because she was pregnant if she would otherwise be considered the best candidate.

Prejudice could be based on any perceived group difference, but discrimination tends to be especially prominent and problematic in the context of certain social groups. Four of these groups concern sex, race, age and sexuality.

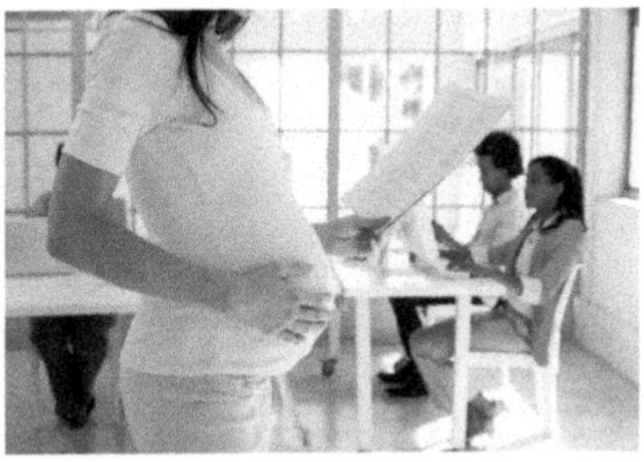

It would be discrimination not to employ a woman because she was pregnant

Supporters of the campaign for equal wages for women outside the Houses of Parliament in 2014

A rally in Baltimore, USA, in May 2015 protesting the death of Freddie Gray, a black man who died after being injured in a police van

A protest against homophobia at the Swedish embassy in Berlin, 2014, following the stabbing of members of the 'football fans against homophobia' group in Sweden

Sexism means prejudice against someone on the basis of their biological sex or their perceived gender identity. Typically, it refers to prejudice against women, although in principle the term applies equally to prejudice against men. Some sexist attitudes appear positive (for example, 'women deserve more protection than men'), but Glick and Fiske (2001) state that such views link to harmful sexism as well; in a cross-cultural study, they found that the countries with the most positive/protective sexist attitudes also showed the highest levels of harmful and violent attitudes towards women.

Racism means prejudice and discrimination against a target based on their assumed race. In fact, this term is often used loosely, for example, to describe conflict between neighbouring countries that have relatively few, if any, racial differences (such as Scots versus English) when the word **xenophobia** – a fear/dislike of foreigners – might be more appropriate. Sometimes, racism is directed at a specific religious group, for example Muslims ('Islamophobia') or Jews ('antisemitism').

Ageism means prejudice based on age. In workplace and community settings, this often refers to the elderly but there is also considerable ageism against younger people. For example, teenagers may be banned from accessing certain services or benefits, or they may be prevented from gathering in particular places. Ageism is an unusual form of prejudice in that everybody could in the future become a member of the target group as they get older (or has been in the past, in the case of ageism against the young). As with sexism, there is a positive, protective form of ageism towards the elderly that is often seen as patronising.

Heterosexism means discriminating against people based on their sexuality – the heterosexual majority showing prejudice against other sexual orientations. It is sometimes taken to include prejudice against transgender groups or people who identify as queer. Some people find this a problematic term, as it does not apply in both directions (i.e. homosexual people cannot be 'heterosexist'), and because sexuality itself is complex and people cannot be easily categorised.

Abrams and Houston (2006) found that British people surveyed were more likely to admit to prejudiced attitudes against some groups than others. In particular, they were happier to admit to prejudiced attitudes against homosexual people, Muslims and women than against disabled people or the elderly. Therefore, it appears that prejudice depends on the social context and social norms and it is not just a characteristic of the individual or how different they are from the out-group.

Direct discrimination

Most of the examples of discrimination so far are **direct discrimination** – doing something directly and knowingly harmful towards a target group, such as denying them a job or excluding them from membership of a club.

Discrimination is usually illegal; under UK legislation – the **Equality Act of 2010** – it is against the law to discriminate against people with certain 'protected characteristics'. These include the four classifications mentioned earlier in this chapter – sex, age, race and sexual orientation – as well as five others: religion/beliefs, disability, gender reassignment, marital status and pregnancy. It is illegal to deny somebody a service or refuse them equal opportunities based on any of these things. Examples could include:

- Refusing to serve someone in a shop because of their race.
- Denying an employee a promotion because he/she is an atheist.
- Paying a woman less than a man for the same work.
- Not allowing someone to book a hotel room because of their sexuality.

There are certain exceptions – it is legal to specify the race and sex of an actor for a role, for example. More controversially, some religions are allowed to discriminate when choosing religious leaders or teachers for faith schools, even if someone from outside of the religion could do a better job.

Top tip

A social norm is a behaviour that is widely accepted in a particular group or culture, but which is not inevitable and may change over time. Social norms include fashions and attitudes to relationships. If something deviates from the social norm, it tends to be perceived as weird. A person's attitude to an out-group may be based upon a social norm.

Indirect discrimination

As mentioned earlier, the cognitive, affective and behavioural aspects of intergroup bias are separate. Someone could have a prejudiced attitude and yet not discriminate against an individual because it would be illegal to do so. Likewise, someone might discriminate even though they do not hold a prejudiced attitude themselves – perhaps because they work in an organisation that has discriminatory policies.

Some policies, laws or rules apply equally to everyone but affect some groups in a more harmful way than others. This is called **indirect discrimination**, and can be hard to spot unless you fully think through the implications of the rule. On the face of it, nobody is being unfairly treated, but the end result is similar to direct discrimination – some people are worse off than others or face a disadvantage, simply on the basis of what group they are a member of.

For example, if a law said that anyone who fasted during the working day would be fined £100, this would, in principle, apply to anyone. However, it is much more likely to be a problem for practising Muslims, who tend to fast during the month of Ramadan. Such a rule would constitute indirect discrimination.

Indirect discrimination is not always illegal, but the person responsible for the policy or rule is legally obliged to show that there is a good reason for it. For example, it is necessary to have a certain level of physical health to work in the police or army and this may indirectly discriminate against people with certain health conditions or disabilities, but it is considered necessary in order to do the job.

If there isn't a good reason for a policy or practice, and it puts a protected group at a disadvantage, then it may be against the law.

Discussion point

Can you think of ways that immigrants to a country might be discriminated against, directly or indirectly?

In 2010 civil partners Martyn Hall and Steven Preddy sued the owners of a B&B in Cornwall who would not allow them to stay in a double room together

Key concepts

- Prejudice
- In-group
- Out-group
- Attitude
- Intergroup bias
- Cognitive
- Affective
- Behavioural
- Discrimination
- Sexism
- Racism
- Ageism
- Heterosexism
- Xenophobia
- Equality Act of 2010
- Direct discrimination
- Indirect discrimination

It would be indirect discrimination to have a policy against headscarves in class

Questions

1. What does 'prejudice' literally mean?
2. What term is used to refer to a group that we are not part of?
3. How did Allport (1954) define 'in-group'?
4. Is there complete agreement about how prejudice should be defined?
5. Would aggression be considered an example of the cognitive or behavioural aspect of intergroup bias?
6. Is sexism all right if it's done in a positive way?
7. True or false: Abrams and Houston (2006) found that British people did not admit to being more prejudiced towards some groups than others.
8. Give two examples of groups who commonly experience discrimination.
9. What law makes it illegal to discriminate against people on the basis of their race, age and other 'protected characteristics'?
10. What is indirect discrimination?

Activities

1. Think about which aspects of intergroup bias link to the example situations in the table. Fill in any that apply.

Example	Cognitive	Affective	Behavioural
R decides not to invite someone in her class to a party because they are 'too old'.			
D decides to give his niece a pink doll for her birthday.			
X invites his male friends to play football but does not consider inviting his female friends.			
A children's film has four lead characters – a heroic young white male, a pretty white female who needs to be rescued a lot, a wise old man and a funny male from an ethnic minority.			
A toy manufacturer decides that a popular play set is not appealing enough to girls so they bring out a new version featuring toy horses and shopping.			

2. Think of examples of rules/restrictions in the workplace that could lead to indirect discrimination. If you are stuck, try searching for news stories about discrimination online. Share your examples with your classmates.

Explanations of prejudice

Stereotyping

One explanation for prejudice is that it is based on a person's thoughts and beliefs about the out-group. If a person holds negative, inaccurate stereotypes about a group, they are more likely to engage in discrimination, according to this view.

The belief that women are more emotional than men is a stereotype

A **stereotype** relates to the cognitive aspect of intergroup bias. A stereotype is an over-simplified, distorted or inaccurate belief about a particular group. Common examples include stereotypes of men or women, stereotypes of age groups (such as teenagers) and stereotypes of nationalities. Groundskeeper Willie from *The Simpsons* is a good example of a Scottish stereotype and it is not unusual for stereotypes to form the basis of humour – although this is often found offensive.

The term is also used to describe specific people/characters in the media and elsewhere – we might say that the characters in a bad novel

Groundskeeper Willie is an example of a stereotype

or TV programme are stereotypes, meaning that they show socially conventional examples of sex roles, social class, nationalities, etc.

The process of stereotyping involves generalising from a stereotype to an individual person. When they are aware of a social stereotype of a group, people may then apply that to members of the group, so that assumed characteristics of the group are applied to members of a group. For example, if somebody believes that men generally like eating meat, they might assume that a specific man will not want to eat a vegetarian meal. Of course, this assumption may be incorrect. This highlights two main problems with stereotyping:

- The stereotype itself may be inaccurate.
- Even if the stereotype is broadly true as a generalisation, it might not apply to a specific member of the group.

A stereotype of a French person

Stereotypes can relate to any group within society of which people are aware. There are stereotypes of both high and low status groups. Many jobs and careers have stereotypes associated with them – scientists might be assumed to be 'mad', teachers to be stressed or politicians to be dishonest. There are also stereotypes of styles, clothing, disabilities or hobbies– for example, the stereotype that people who wear glasses are intelligent.

Chartrand and Bargh (1999) describe stereotypes as *'categories gone awry'* (p.907), stating that categories are generally useful but a stereotype is a distorted and harmful version of a category.

The idea that those who wear glasses are intelligent is a stereotype

Effect of stereotypes

Stereotypes can have harmful effects. One issue in education is called **stereotype threat** – this is where awareness of a negative stereotype leads to poorer performance. Ambady *et al.* (2001) found that when girls were reminded of gender differences using a questionnaire, they did more poorly on a maths test compared to a control group (responding to a common gender stereotype that girls are worse at maths). This effect disappeared between the ages of 8 to 10 – when girls tend to have a strong sense of superiority over boys – but reappeared from age 11 onwards. Spencer *et al.* (1999) found a very similar effect with female undergraduates.

Is there anything wrong with **positive stereotypes**? Having a positive stereotype can improve performance (sometimes called 'stereotype lift'). These can cause harm, though, by disadvantaging other groups who do not receive the same benefit – a positive stereotype implicitly judges other groups as negative.

Why do stereotypes form?

Stereotypes appear to be learned from society as a whole and people are aware of them even if they do not agree with them (Karlins *et al.*, 1969). They are learned early; from the age of 2 or even before, children choose toys that are stereotypically associated with their gender (Caldera *et al.*, 1989). Children's books often portray some stereotypes, and although this situation has improved in recent years, there are still inequalities such as the presentation of females as the main caregivers for children (Anderson & Hamilton, 2005; see final section of this chapter).

? Discussion point

Are you aware of the stereotypes of different nationalities? Is it ok to make jokes about these?

Make the link

...with Modern Studies and Politics. You may be able to identify certain stereotypes when politicians talk about national groups, especially in the context of immigration, as well as benefit claimants, teenagers, the elderly, etc.

Why do people not just reject inaccurate stereotypes? Cognitive psychologists believe that some human thought processes show bias and take shortcuts in order to conserve mental resources such as attention. They believe that stereotypes are a form of shortcut, limiting the need to think about each person individually, and therefore freeing up attention for other tasks. This forms the basis of **cognitive miser theory**.

'Like it or not, we all make assumptions about other people, ourselves, and the situations we encounter ... much of the time our expectations are functional, and indeed, we would be unable to operate without them.'

Source: Fiske and Taylor (1991, p.97)

The quote above implies that stereotypes exist to simplify the world. From this point of view, attention is limited and treating everything we encounter as unique and separate would take too much processing power; therefore, stereotypes are useful because they save the mind unnecessary work. This view implies that stereotyping is largely automatic.

Bargh and Chartrand (1999) reviewed the evidence and concluded that much of our decision making happens automatically, that is, without intention or conscious awareness.

Aboud (2003) found that in-group favouritism is strongly apparent from the age of 5, supporting cognitive miser theory. This follows Allport (1954, p.29), who stated that strong in-group prejudice is apparent from age 5, and although the child does not fully understand the group differences until age 10, it *'doesn't wait for this understanding before [developing] fierce in-group loyalties'*.

However, not everyone agrees that stereotypes are based on unconscious biases or that they are simply shortcuts, making incoming information easier to process. Rutland (1999) states that stereotypes are a meaningful attempt to make sense of the world around us and that we choose to use them. He considers group categories useful and largely accurate.

Cohen (1981) conducted a study into the memory of stereotyped features of common jobs. Participants were shown a video of a young woman but in one condition they were told she was a waitress, and in the other condition they were told she was a librarian. The video contained some information that was consistent with each stereotype (e.g. the librarian had spent the day reading/the waitress has no book shelves) and other points that were inconsistent with each stereotype.

Aboud found that in-group favouritism is strongly apparent from the age of 5

? Discussion point

Think of some films that you have seen recently. How many male and female characters did they have? Were male characters shown in a more positive way than female characters, for example, more skilled/brave? What other stereotypes did you notice?

When girls were reminded of gender differences they did more poorly on a maths test

Children often choose toys that are stereotypically associated with their gender

Make the link

...with the topic of Memory.

? Discussion point

Do you agree that people's behaviour is often biased and irrational? How does the idea that humans are irrational affect theories in other subjects such as Politics and Economics?

Top tip

If asked in the exam for an "explanation of prejudice", you could choose stereotyping, or one of the theories described over the next few pages.

Participants tended to remember the information that fit the stereotype better than stereotype-inconsistent information. This finding was supported by a meta-analysis of 26 studies which showed an overall effect of the stereotype-consistency of information on how well it was remembered (Fyock & Stangor, 1994).

Therefore, it appears that stereotypes are learned early, they derive from society around us and are largely inaccurate but can be reinforced by biases in our memory.

Authoritarian personality theory

Why is one person prejudiced while another is not? The **authoritarian personality theory** states that prejudice results from the disturbed mental processes of certain individuals who desire order and are aggressive to minorities (Adorno *et al.*, 1950).

This theory follows the approaches to psychology that emphasise the effect of childhood on behaviour – in particular, the psychoanalytic approach (see chapter 1), which states that childhood and unconscious motivations play a huge role in a person's adult personality. The authoritarian personality theory sees authoritarianism as a syndrome that develops in childhood, resulting in certain key characteristics that make a person more prone to **fascist** tendencies.

The authoritarian personality theory was developed around the time of the Second World War. The researchers wanted to explain the appeal of the Nazis and other fascist parties. Hitler himself can be seen as an example of an authoritarian personality, but more importantly, it applies to people who *follow* harsh, controlling ideologies like that of the Third Reich.

Oswald Mosley, leader of the British Union of Fascists, with supporters in 1936

The researchers said that authoritarian individuals had repressed anger and a weaker than usual superego due to strict parenting – they were thought to have over-dominant fathers and strict mothers (van Ijzendoorn, 1989). Because of their fear of authority, they show an exaggerated respect for conventional values and their unconscious anger would be displaced onto weaker targets – usually minorities. The personality type was characterised by nine key traits, as follows:

- **Conventionalism**: traditional social values.
- **Authoritarian submission**: submissive attitude to power and authority.
- **Authoritarian aggression**: hatred and rejection of minorities.
- **Anti-intraception**: dislike of reflective thinking or imaginative ideas.
- **Superstition**: belief in fate; tendency to think in rigid categories.
- **Power and 'toughness'**: obsessed with the idea of strong versus weak people.
- **Destructiveness**: general hostility/anger.
- **Projectivity**: belief that wild and dangerous things go on in the world.
- **Sex**: obsession with sexual 'goings-on'.

The overall picture is of people who are angry and hostile, paranoid about anything new and different, and very willing to take orders from traditional sources of power. Such people made perfect followers for fascist politicians.

Recent research has also linked authoritarianism with support for certain politicians in the current era, including Donald Trump and members of the political far right in Europe (Pettigrew, 2017).

Research evidence

A key tool used by Adorno *et al.* (1950) was a questionnaire called the **F-scale**. 'F' stood for 'fascism', and the scale aimed to measure fascist sympathies, including aggressive racism and intolerance. Items on the scale consisted of a series of statements, which participants were asked to agree or disagree with. Each statement had been uttered by the researchers' previous research participants, for example, '*people can be divided into two distinct classes: the weak and the strong*' and '*what the youth needs most is strict discipline, rugged determination, and the will to work and fight for family and country.*'

Participants had to respond on a scale from one to six, from 'disagree strongly' to 'agree strongly'.

What is fascism?

Hitler and Mussolini

The *F-scale* is based on the idea of **fascism** – the ideology of several political parties beginning in the 1920s and 1930s, most notably in Italy – Mussolini's *National Fascist Party* – and in Germany – Adolf Hitler's *National Socialist Party* ('Nazi Party'). Both of these leaders and their parties are considered to have extremely right-wing politics with an emphasis on state control and an intolerant, rather than supportive, attitude towards minorities, as well as towards anyone who could not contribute to the industrial economies of the time, such as disabled individuals.

In general, fascist politicians support strict limitations to personal freedom, regulated morality and behaviour, and strong state control. Unlike the totalitarian communist states of North Korea or the former USSR, fascist states tended to support capitalism/business interests and favour traditional moral values.

Fascism is often contrasted with **democratic** views, held by people who, on the whole, favour personal freedom, diversity and people-power rather than strict control by the state (Meloen, 1993).

One example of this in practice is human rights policies, such as the right to freedom of expression and belief, or to freely join any groups you like. Fascist groups/governments and their supporters are highly likely to ban groups or religions that disagree with them.

Make the link

...between fascism/the F-scale and your knowledge of History or Modern Studies

Evaluation

A weakness of the F-scale is that all of the 'agree' options led to a higher F-score, making it hard to distinguish between people who agree with all the statements and people who would agree to anything (see section on acquiescence bias, p.205). Bass (1955) concluded that this had a large effect on Adorno *et al.*'s findings.

Some findings have been consistent – authoritarians are found to believe very strongly in the rights of the established authorities and they are much more likely to consider illegal government actions as acceptable (Altemeyer, 2006).

This theory is now marginal, with little research support for the view that a strict upbringing leads to prejudice. Altemeyer (1981) has found that of the nine authoritarian traits, only the first three (conventionalism, authoritarian submission and authoritarian aggression) correlate together reliably. He suggests that the term be replaced by **right-wing authoritarianism (RWA)**, which should be seen as an attitude rather than a personality type.

By viewing prejudice as an individual trait, the theory doesn't take account of cultural values and the influence of political events. It struggles to explain why the same individual can be prejudiced against some groups but not others.

The connection between prejudice and authoritarian traits remains consistent in later studies, and van Ijzendoorn (1989) suggests that rather than reject the theory entirely, researchers should try to explain this pattern in cognitive, rather than psychoanalytic, terms.

Top tip

Authoritarian personality theory views prejudice as a personality type, whereas social identity theory sees it as a social process.

Social identity theory

Social identity theory (SIT) states that people's behaviour is driven by group membership. People make decisions about which groups they are or are not part of, then show prejudice against other groups to try and put their own group on top, thereby boosting their own self-esteem.

Origins of the theory

Henri Tajfel was the son of a Polish-Jewish family and most of his relatives died in the Holocaust. He himself survived as a prisoner of war by hiding his own Jewish identity. This traumatic background may have stimulated his interest in prejudice, as he developed a theory of how personal identity links to our membership of social groups.

In experiments on schoolchildren, Tajfel (1970) tried to find the minimum requirements for discrimination to emerge (see key study). The main finding from this research was that people could be prompted to discriminate very easily and for trivial reasons. People seem to be highly motivated to boost their self-esteem by giving their group an advantage over other groups.

Key study: Tajfel's (1970) minimal groups experiment

Aim: *The study aimed to find out what the minimum conditions are for discrimination to emerge. Will people discriminate if they have no good reason to do so, if the task is trivial and both groups are very similar?*

Method: *Tajfel studied schoolboys aged 14 to 15 in Bristol. They were shown 12 images of paintings by the modern artists Paul Klee and Wassily Kandinsky. The boys were then randomly grouped but were told that their choice of artwork was the reason for the grouping.*

Tajfel then put the participants into groups of 16 and gave them a task of allocating small cash rewards to the other boys. Each had to fill out a booklet that allowed them to give small monetary rewards. Choices were designed so that they could pick from these three options:

- *Maximum joint profit: the biggest overall number*
- *Maximum in-group profit: the best reward for the in-group member*
- *Maximum difference: the amounts that caused the in-group to be as far ahead of the out-group as possible*

For example:

Choice	(a)	(b)	(c)
Boy-IN	12	16	14
Boy-OUT	19	13	6

Choice (a) would give the biggest overall reward (31) if the group was not considered. If the aim was to do as well as possible for the in-group, choice (b) would be favoured, while choice (c) would suggest that participants wanted to emphasise group differences.

Findings: *Despite the trivial nature of the groupings, the boys' responses clearly favoured in-group members, giving them higher rewards. Crucially though, the biggest factor was putting their own group ahead, even if it meant getting a lower reward overall. Choices like (c) were picked most – the boys seemed to want to create the biggest advantage of in-group over the out-group, regardless of the fact that this sometimes led to a lower reward for the in-group and a lower total reward.*

Evaluation: *One problem with this study was that the task was highly artificial and short-term, therefore making it hard to generalise to real cases of prejudice. In addition the participants were all teenage boys and therefore not representative of the population as a whole. However, Tajfel's experiment was helpful in suggesting that prejudice can't be explained in terms of conflict over limited resources – being the top group was found to be more important than getting more money. It demonstrated that we discriminate very easily and for trivial reasons. This finding played a key role in developing social identity theory.*

Henri Tajfel

Green church and steeple *by Paul Klee*

Composition VI *by Wassily Kandinsky*

Our political views are part of our social identity

In a crowd of sports fans we may follow the norms of the group

? Discussion point

Which of these two components of identity – individual or social – makes more of a difference in your everyday life? Brown and Turner (1981) note that it can depend on the situation we find ourselves in – for example, when chatting to a close friend we may behave according to our individual identity, while in a crowd of sports fans, we may follow the norms of the group.

Make the link

...between social identification and the topic of Conformity and also with the issue of social norms in defining psychopathology (see the Phobias and Depression topics).

The theory

Tajfel teamed up with a group of British psychologists, including John Turner, to develop these findings into a theory. The basic premise of SIT is that we are strongly motivated by our social identity and this can result in us trying to make our groups do better than others. It begins with an automatic process of dividing the world up into 'them and us' groups that Tajfel and Turner (1979) called **social categorisation**. Tajfel (1982) states that social categorisation is necessary and sufficient for discrimination and prejudice to occur and although it can sometimes be harmful, it is essentially a normal thing to do.

The next process is identifying the groups we belong to. Our social identity is one of two components to our self-image:

- **Personal identity:** a sense of who we are in terms of unique personal characteristics, e.g. appearance, personality, likes and dislikes.
- **Social identity:** a sense of who we are in terms of groups we belong to, e.g. male/female, nationality, political view.

In other words, people's sense of what groups they belong to is a fundamental part of who they are. The process of identifying with certain groups and building up our social identity is called **social identification.** This can have a large effect on behaviour – when people start to identify with a new group, they relate the characteristics of that group to themselves and change their behaviour accordingly (Reynolds *et al.*, 2015). For example, if a teenager moves school and makes a new set of friends, they may change their likes and dislikes to fit in.

According to the theory, social identification is followed by a third stage – people making a **social comparison** between groups they are members of and other groups. This third process plays a key role in prejudice, as it boosts self-esteem if our own groups appear to be superior (Hogg & Abrams, 1988). When people see their groups doing worse, they will attempt to boost their own group, perhaps by harming the other group. They also want to appear clearly different from members of other groups. The drive to maintain a positive social identity is called **positive distinctiveness**.

Evidence

As shown by the Tajfel's (1970) participants, people will begin to treat other people differently if they start to perceive them as out-group members. If they perceive that the in-group is not sufficiently distinct or not superior then they will try to change that via discriminatory behaviour.

Judd and Park (1988) found evidence that people think differently about out-group members. Their study showed that people we categorise as being different from ourselves are evaluated less favourably and are seen as more alike in behaviour and appearance than the in-group.

Evaluation

Although it has its origins in the early 1970s, social identity is very much a mainstream theory today, with the general principles largely unchanged. It has been successfully applied in a large number of areas such as education (e.g. Reynolds *et al.*, 2015). It has successfully argued that our group identity is a vital part of who we are.

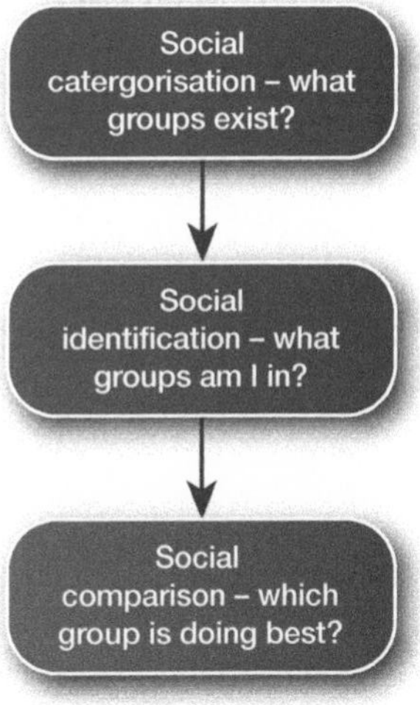

However, SIT's view of prejudice as based on a drive to boost self-esteem by promoting the in-group may be over-simplistic. There are numerous other influences on self-esteem, not least a person's position within the group, as well as their individual achievements and image. Rubin and Hewstone (1998) dismissed the idea that intergroup discrimination boosts self-esteem or that low self-esteem motivates discrimination.

In addition, the concept of SIT doesn't entirely explain why interrelations between groups change over time. For example, boys and girls aged 8 show considerable prejudice towards the opposite sex but this reduces by the mid-teens (Ambady *et al.*, 2001). This change is more easily explained in terms of sex hormones and an evolved drive to seek out potential sexual partners than in terms of social identity.

Boys and girls aged 8 show considerable prejudice towards the opposite sex

Realistic conflict theory

Like Tajfel, Muzafer Sherif believed that intergroup prejudice can't be explained purely in terms of the characteristics of the individual (their stereotypes or personality) but is instead a social process. His theory, **realistic conflict theory**, places an emphasis on situations where groups compete over resources.

Sherif realised that groups often compete over resources which are limited, meaning that both sides cannot achieve their aims, rather like attempting to win in games or sports. He believed that intergroup conflict is likely to arise in these situations. He also thought that these situations were likely to lead to high levels of **ethnocentrism** – a situation where everything is judged with reference to the in-group, and out-groups are looked on with contempt.

Sherif believed that intergroup relationships are structured by goals. A group will stay strong where people have common or compatible goals, or people may form a group where one does not already exist. However, if individuals' goals are incompatible, they will not form into a group. Where members of an existing group hold incompatible goals, the group will be put under pressure, and may fracture into factions or break up altogether (Sherif, 1966).

In most board games, winning is a limited resource over which people compete

Evidence

In order to investigate realistic conflict theory, Sherif and colleagues set up a field experiment where groups of boys were taken to summer camp in Robber's Cave, Oklahoma. In the study, the researchers attempted to generate conflict between boys who were initially quite alike – there were no pre-existing group prejudices – by making them compete over limited access to sports facilities and prizes. This research became known as the 'Robber's Cave study' (see key study).

Key study: Sherif *et al.* (1954): the Robber's Cave study

Teams are held together by having compatible goals

Aim: *Sherif believed that conflict arises due to groups having incompatible goals, such as countries disputing the same area of land. He had conducted two previous summer camp studies, during which he refined a set of techniques to cause conflict between groups. This summary is based on the third published study, which had the key difference from the earlier studies that the conflicts were resolved. The aim was to test realistic conflict theory, as well as to find ways in which conflict could be reduced.*

Method and Findings: *The participants were 22 middle-class Protestant boys from Oklahoma City. They were carefully selected to be similar to each other in background and schooling. It was also carefully established that none of them previously knew each other. The participants were divided into two groups of 11, again keeping them as closely matched as possible, and taken to the Robber's Cave National Park for their camp – a large isolated hilly area with plenty of space for outings, swimming and boating, which took its name from its past as a hideout for the outlaw Jesse James.*

In week one of the study, the boys were kept separate, for example by staggering meal times and keeping them in separate areas. The aim of this stage was to allow a strong in-group identity to form; the groups nicknamed themselves 'Eagles' and 'Rattlers' (i.e. rattlesnakes) and developed group norms including status, nicknames and favourite songs. A recognised 'leader' emerged amongst both groups of boys. Gradually, each group was allowed to 'discover' that there was another group in the area and the idea of competing against them at baseball was raised.

The two groups competed in tug-of-war contests and at other games

In week two, the aim was to cause the groups to come into conflict due to incompatible goals, in particular a tournament that only one side could win. The tournament included baseball, tug-of-war and other contests. Sherif and colleagues announced the tournament gradually, wanting it to appear to be the boys' own idea. The prizes – a trophy, medals and a penknife each – were displayed prominently. The researchers hypothesised that this would lead to negative attitudes and stereotyped views of the out-group. Early in this stage, the boys met the other group for the first time and name-calling began immediately. Some tournament events were judged by the researchers, allowing them to manipulate the scores and keep the contest even. The researchers also noticed that a sense of 'good sportsmanship' was prominent at the start but gave way quickly to name-calling and resentment. The Eagles lost the first two events and proceeded to burn the Rattlers' flag. By the end of the tournament, won by the Eagles, there was such bad feeling that fights broke out and had to be stopped to prevent injury. The Rattlers raided the Eagles hut and stole their medals and knives, though these were later returned to them by Sherif. Both groups were asked to identify friends 'from the entire camp' and in each camp, over 92% of choices were boys from the in-group.

A test of judgement was also used to follow up on stage 2, where each boy had to put beans into a bottle within a time limit and then everyone estimated how many they had managed to put in. Rattlers' in-group estimates were 3.7 higher and the Eagles estimated their own group 7.2 higher on average compared to the out-group, even though the stimuli were fixed, and everyone was shown the same number of beans (35).

In week three, Sherif and colleagues set out to replace the conflict with cooperation. To start with, seven unstructured 'contact' situations were arranged, but groups continued to jeer at each other, sit only with in-group members and some meetings resulted in food fights. Then the researchers introduced superordinate goals, most notably a vandalised water supply and a truck that had broken down on a camping excursion. These events were set up but required all of the boys to work together to solve them (for example, the whole group pulling the truck with their 'tug-of-war' rope until it started). The key finding was that after working together with superordinate goals, group hostility dropped away. The boys willingly travelled together in a single truck and laughed about the raids that had caused so much hostility the previous week. They alternated singing the songs that each group had previously adopted. At the end of the last week, they arranged and organised a group campfire, and agreed to travel back to Oklahoma City together on the same bus. In-group identities still existed, but the groups mingled readily, and name-calling had more or less disappeared.

Penknives were awarded as prizes

***Evaluation**: The study had high ecological validity – later, Sherif (1977) commented that a lack of a control in research is less of a risk than a lack of real life relevance! It made a huge impact in social psychology, and the study of prejudice in particular; there have been few, if any, other field studies with such elaborate procedures. It has great real-world relevance as a model for how to reduce prejudice.*

A limitation in terms of external validity was that the sample were all boys. However, Sherif cited Avigdor (1951), who similarly found among a group of 10-year-old girls that cooperation led to positive stereotypes and conflict led to negative stereotypes. Also, the sample were children and all of the same nationality, race and religion as each other. This makes it harder to relate to real-life conflicts.

There were considerable ethical issues. Child participants were deceived and put into situations where physical fights broke out. They were also provided with knives as prizes. One task involved depriving them of drinking water. The area contained significant natural risks as well, including poisonous snakes. The conflict was highly stressful; observers noted signs of bedwetting, homesickness and attempts to run away among some participants (Perry, 2014).

Evaluation

Realistic conflict theory usefully puts the focus on group and individual goals, and provides some compelling evidence that competition can lead to conflict and hostility. However, its view of goals is rather absolute. In reality, goals are quite fluid, and can change due to social processes such as conformity and obedience. The theory lacks the sophistication of social identity theory, which shows how group identities are constantly in flux, and how our different identities can become salient in different situations.

The Robber's Cave study is interesting in that the boys were very similar and had a lot of contact with each another, but yet prejudice easily developed. There was no particular difference in status between the two groups of boys, who were chosen to be as similar as possible to each other. The study also benefits from being a field study with a high level of ecological validity. Other research has also found examples of high levels of conflict and ethnocentrism where groups find themselves in conflict over scarce resources – for example, the Stanford prison experiment by Zimbardo and colleagues, which demonstrated high levels of intergroup hostility (Haney *et al.*, 1973). Similar effects have been shown to take place between real-world populations (e.g. Brewer & Campbell, 1976).

However, this explanation of prejudice is generally seen as too narrow, as not all conflicts involve limited resources, and as a theory it has largely been superseded by social identity theory. As you may remember, the Tajfel (1970) study showed that people prioritise group superiority, even when it means that their group gets less of a reward. This can't easily be explained in terms of conflict over resources.

Scapegoat theory

Scapegoat theory describes the process of scapegoating, an extreme form of prejudice where an in-group unfairly blames a specific out-group for a set of problems (Glick, 2005). For example, at the time of the Nazi party's rise to power in Germany in the 1930s, the party attempted to blame the Jewish community for economic problems which the country had been experiencing. More recent examples of scapegoating include:

- blaming minorities for problems such as crime, unemployment, underfunding of services, or housing shortages
- blaming a small number of team members or colleagues for an overall bad performance by the team
- blaming teenagers for all vandalism, dropped litter, etc.

As noted earlier, ethnocentrism means viewing situations from the perspective of one's in-group, while treating out-groups with contempt. Hostility towards scapegoated groups suggests high levels of ethnocentrism among those who engage in scapegoating.

Generally, a scapegoated group will be visually distinctive, such as being members of a minority race or being from a particular age group.

Evidence

Scapegoat theory links to an interesting cognitive shortcut – **confirmation bias**. This is where people tend to notice information that fits their stereotypes, while ignoring information that goes against them. In other words, what we notice and remember is biased in a way that reinforces existing stereotypes, making it harder to learn from experience and overcome those stereotypes. This fits with the evidence from the Cohen (1981) study on memory for stereotype-consistent information, as discussed earlier in this chapter.

According to this idea, simplistic, stereotyped ideas about a group (such as the idea that the group commits a lot of crimes) are then activated by one or more incidents, such as a member of an out-group committing a crime, and this being seen on the local news. The mental shortcut of confirmation bias would then lead in-group members to notice and remember further examples of people from the out-group committing crimes, while ignoring the (possibly much more frequent) examples of in-group members doing so.

Young people are sometimes the victim of scapegoating

This fits with the idea that schemas about out-group members tend to be much more simplistic. Brewer (1988) notes that people may begin with a highly abstract 'prototype' schema of an out-group member, but will gradually form a more realistic schema after having more real-life opportunities to encounter members of the group. Scapegoating is therefore more likely to occur when in-group members have little knowledge of and infrequent interaction with out-group members.

Evaluation

Scapegoat theory is a largely outdated idea of prejudice. Although it can describe a common problem, it can't fully explain why it happens, either on a social or cognitive level. For example, why are certain groups scapegoated and not others? This process could be more fully explained by some of the other theories in this section, such as realistic conflict theory or SIT.

Nevertheless, the ignorance and bias that tends to accompany scapegoating makes cognitive sense, and provides some clues as to what might be an effective way to tackle and reduce prejudice. That will be the focus in the final section of this chapter.

Key concepts

- Stereotypes
- Cognitive miser theory
- Authoritarian personality theory
- F-scale
- Fascism
- Right-wing authoritarianism
- Social identity theory
- Personal identity
- Social identity
- Social categorisation
- Social identification
- Social comparison
- Positive distinctiveness
- Realistic conflict theory
- Ethnocentrism
- Scapegoat theory
- Confirmation bias

Questions

1. Why do researchers such as Fiske and Taylor (1991) think we are 'cognitive misers'?
2. Why did Rutland not agree with the idea that a stereotype is a cognitive shortcut?
3. Which approach to psychology is the authoritarian personality theory linked to?
4. Where were the statements on the F-scale taken from?
5. Out of the nine traits of the authoritarian personality, which three reliably correlate together?
6. Name the processes of SIT theory.
7. Give a criticism of Tajfel's (1970) experiment.
8. Why do you think Sherif et al (1954) chose participants who were all very similar to each other?
9. Name an ethical issue with the Sherif et al (1954) study.
10. What cognitive process could maintain and strengthen the process of scapegoating?

Activities

1. How prevalent are fascist-type views among your group of students? Try out the F-scale online or make up your own survey. You must strictly observe ethical principles in research, such as confidentiality of results.
2. Find out more about stereotypes – find at least one recent research study or science news article that talks about stereotypes either being useful/meaningful or being a shortcut/distortion. Which view do you agree with? Report your findings and your thoughts on them back to the class.

Reducing prejudice

Psychologists want to help to reduce and, if possible, eliminate prejudice. There are many programmes and interventions that have been used to reduce prejudice and these fall into four main categories:

- **Education**: raising awareness of prejudice, its effects and why it is irrational and harmful. An example of this is Jane Elliott's blue eyes/brown eyes exercise (see next page).
- **Affirmative action**: the idea that prejudice will reduce if minority groups are given help to access more privileged positions, thus tackling discrimination and increasing intergroup contact (see page 316).

- **Superordinate goals**: creating situations where members of different groups have to work together to achieve a shared goal. An example of this is the broken truck in the Sherif study.
- **Media**: the media is able to either challenge or perpetuate stereotypes. Negative news coverage of minorities or highly stereotyped roles in movies can increase prejudice, while positive media role models may help to reduce it.

Education

Education involves tackling prejudice and discrimination, and generally occurs in schools, though it could involve any educational setting or context, including books and leaflets. The main aims of this education are:

- Raising awareness about stereotypes and discrimination.
- Teaching strategies to reduce prejudiced thought processes.

Martin Luther King addressing the crowd at the Lincoln Memorial in Washington D.C. in 1957

Evidence

Perhaps the best known example of an educational intervention to reduce prejudice was conducted by a schoolteacher, not a psychologist. Jane Elliott was working in a small town in Iowa, USA, at the time when civil rights activist Martin Luther King was assassinated. Shocked by the event and by some of the reaction to it – expressions of prejudice against black Americans in the white-dominated media – Elliott decided to tackle prejudice directly among the third grade (age 8 to 9) children she taught. She set up a scenario where children's eye colour would determine how they were treated, allowing everyone to understand what it felt like to be the victim of discrimination (Elliott, 1977). It became known as the **blue eyes/brown eyes exercise**.

A photograph from Elliott's study

On day one, blue-eyed children in Elliott's class were told that they were the social superiors, and received privileges such as extra playtime. Prejudice spontaneously emerged, with name-calling against the out-group. Those labelled inferior did worse at a card-sorting task, suggesting that stereotype threat could have an immediate impact on school performance. On the second day, the roles were reversed, with brown-eyed children being put into the superior role. The effects were repeated, with the blue-eyed children now doing more poorly on the card task.

Top tip

This section includes information on practical ways of tackling prejudice. It also provides several examples of research evidence that could be used to answer an exam question.

Elliott's technique worked well with her all-white schoolchildren but it has not always been successful with more diverse groups (Anthony, 2009). It is confrontational and caused some distress in the children – although on the positive side, the original group of children later said that they had found the process educational and it had raised their awareness of prejudice.

Overall, education is the most common intervention against prejudice – most school systems teach children about the issue. It is relatively cheap to do, as it can be conducted as part of the general social education curriculum. However, despite its prevalence in education, prejudiced attitudes are still widespread.

Diversity training can be effective in combatting prejudice

In adults, **diversity training** is a form of education aimed at reducing stereotypes, prejudice and discrimination. Some workers are offered it as part of their job (e.g. certain police forces). People are sometimes ordered to attend such courses after discriminatory or abusive behaviour, such as when Football Association referees' chairman David Elleray was sent on such a course for allegedly making racist comments to a colleague (Percy, 2014). Bezrukova *et al.* (2012) reported that such courses are more effective when integrated with other workplace activities (rather than a one-off, 'stand-alone' format), but that such a format is rarely used.

Affirmative action

Affirmative action is a political programme whereby underrepresented groups are given preferential treatment when applying for jobs or courses. The idea is to balance out the discrimination that they face and the disadvantages that they have previously experienced. It also aims to make employers or educational establishments more equal in terms of representation. It doesn't mean that people who are unqualified are given the job, but if there are several qualified applicants, then minority candidates are preferred.

For example, if the police force in a particular country employed predominantly white males, the organisation may decide to give preference to female candidates or to men from ethnic minorities in order to redress this imbalance.

Affirmative action may reduce stereotypes by promoting equal status contact between different groups. According to Allport (1954), we are more likely to form stereotypes if we are ignorant of out-groups, but if we get to know them as individuals we will become less prejudiced. This idea is known as the **contact hypothesis**. Allport thought that to be effective in reducing prejudice, contact must be equal status contact – that is, individuals must cooperate on an equal basis without either group being superior or inferior.

In addition, selecting people on the basis of their sex or race will increase the diversity of an organisation, and provide role models for others. This could have a broader social benefit, including encouraging other people to apply or train for these roles, or making young people more likely to consider such roles for their future. An organisation with a more balanced workforce may also be more approachable to customers who are themselves from minorities. For example, increasing the number of politicians who are from ethnic minorities may make parliament seem more relevant to people from these groups, and make them more willing to contact their representatives.

Evidence

Investigating the role of contact, Laar *et al.* (2005) studied Dutch students who had been randomly allocated a university roommate of a different race. After sharing a room for several months, participants became less prejudiced, according to questionnaire data. Although it was a natural experiment, this appeared to demonstrate cause-and-effect. However, it may not be possible to generalise from young students in an individual setting to other social groups. In addition, the

Make the link

...with your studies of Politics, Modern Studies or Business. Is parliament equal in terms of the sex and race of politicians? What about the executive boards of major corporations? What could or should be done to address imbalances?

Discussion point

Can you think why some people might complain about affirmative action? Are their complaints valid in your view? Are some complaints misinformed?

In Laar's study students who lived with someone of another race became less prejudiced

level of contact involved in sharing a room is much greater than is possible in most other settings.

It's possible that a person employed via affirmative action could suffer some negative psychological effects. Brown *et al.* (2000) found that when women felt that they had been selected for their gender, their performance was worse. This could be due to stereotype threat (see previous section of this chapter).

Pettigrew and Martin (1987) argue that recipients of affirmative action suffer from what they call 'triple jeopardy' – three major negative effects. These are:

- negative stereotypes within the organisation
- solo status – being the only member of the group, leading to increased stress
- token status – the sense that they are only employed because of their characteristic, leading to unduly negative judgements by other employees.

Superordinate goals and the jigsaw technique

As you have seen in previous sections, there is evidence that having shared, superordinate goals (as in the Sherif *et al.*, 1954, experiment) and having contact with people from other groups (as happens with affirmative action) can reduce prejudice. The **jigsaw technique** was developed to put these ideas into practice in a school classroom.

The key idea is that every member of a group must have an essential piece of information needed to complete a larger task – they have one piece of the 'jigsaw' (although this could be any kind of school task, not an actual jigsaw). Therefore when a group works on the task or project, each member has to contribute and must be listened to. The information they each bring to the task must be respected, because – like a jigsaw – the task is impossible to complete without having every piece.

The whole group must work together in order to complete the task. This promotes listening and a respectful exchange of information. Here, the superordinate goal is the completion of the project.

Evidence

In the USA after desegregation of schools, children from different races were finally spending time together in the same school classrooms. It was hoped that prejudice levels would reduce due to contact, but they remained high. Aronson and Bridgeman (1979) used the jigsaw technique with 10 classes of elementary (primary) school pupils over seven schools in Texas. Another three classes were used as a control group. Tasks involved working in jigsaw groups, which took 45 minutes as part of their school day. After three weeks of this intervention, the researchers found increases in three key areas:

- self-esteem increased
- students reported higher levels of liking for both in-group and out-group members
- academic performance increased

Discussion point

Do you have any experience of getting to know people from a group that you previously had no contact with? Did it change your attitude towards that group?

Top tip

As in other topics, if you are asked to analyse ways of reducing prejudice you could compare the possible techniques with each other, weighing up the supporting evidence. You could also analyse the evidence and the aims of the techniques.

The jigsaw technique was developed to reduce prejudice

Meanwhile, there was less evidence of negative stereotypes of other ethnic groups. The Sherif *et al.* (1954) study (see earlier section in this chapter) seemed to suggest that contact alone is not enough. The Robber's Cave study involved a lot of contact, as does an everyday classroom situation in a school, but prejudice and stereotypes can remain strong. These research studies suggest that while contact is necessary, it is not sufficient to reduce prejudice. In the Sherif study in particular, there was no particular difference in status between the two groups of boys, who were chosen to be as similar to each other as possible. This supports the importance of intergroup superordinate goals, and using situations where conflicting groups are motivated to work together.

The media's role in prejudice

Media is a term used to describe various methods of mass communication. It includes newspapers, books, TV, movies and the Internet. In particular, the term tends to be used to describe ways of broadcasting messages, including both factual information and stories.

The media can either challenge or perpetuate stereotypes. Highly stereotyped roles on drama programmes or in books can boost levels of prejudice. For example, if science jobs in books or TV dramas were always done by men, this could inaccurately present these roles as being unavailable to women, and cause children to develop a biased schema about such jobs that might affect their later career choices. Similarly, the language used in the media can be prejudiced – many people have highlighted the negative, stereotyped language used by some sections of the UK press.

However, if the media can contribute to prejudice, there is also the potential to reduce it. Certain studies have looked at interventions to reduce prejudice via the media (see below).

> **Make the link**
>
> ...between research methods and Paluck's (2009) study. What difficulties are there in terms of experimental control and sampling when broadcasting a radio show to your participants? Why might you conduct a study this way, rather than bringing people into a lab?

> **Make the link**
>
> ...with your studies of History and Modern Studies. The aftermath of the Rwandan genocide continues to have effects in the region, with soldiers who committed atrocities having fled to neighbouring countries.
> It's also worth noting that at the time of the genocide, national radio stations played hateful messages about the Tutsi ethnic minority, a factor that is thought to have greatly increased the hostility and violence.

Evidence

Riggle *et al.* (1996) experimented with the effects of watching a film on people's attitudes. They showed a video about the life of a homosexual politician, and questioned participants before, during and afterwards. The film had a significant and positive effect on attitudes, reducing the level of prejudice that participants expressed in questionnaires. However, such research is small scale, and doesn't investigate the real-world timescales over which prejudice develops.

Paluck (2009) conducted a large-scale field study in Rwanda, an African country which has experienced major problems with intergroup conflict, most notably the Rwandan genocide of 1994, during which one ethnic group was responsible for the mass murder of another. In Paluck's study, two versions of a radio soap opera were played for a year. The experimental group heard a version which portrayed an out-group in positive ways, while the control group heard an informative health-based radio show. After one year, attitudes were tested. It was found that attitudes towards social norms, including inter-marriage with the out-group, had changed. However, participants' personal opinions showed much less sign of change. This suggests that the media can set the agenda in terms of what is seen as normal, but is less impactful in terms of privately held prejudices.

Despite the importance of the media, its role in prejudice is still not fully understood. This is partly because it is difficult to conduct controlled experimentation. It is also because media sources are controlled by members of society, and so it is difficult to know whether prejudiced attitudes have changed because of the media, or if media have changed because of a change in attitudes.

Questions

1. What is meant by 'raising awareness'?
2. What physical feature did Elliott use as a model of prejudice?
3. What is diversity training?
4. What groups are given an advantage in affirmative action?
5. Does affirmative action mean that jobs are given to people who are not fully qualified?
6. What term is given to the idea that simply spending time together with people from other groups will reduce prejudice?
7. What is the key idea behind the jigsaw technique?
8. According to Aronson and Bridgeman, what three things increased when the jigsaw technique was used?
9. Why might it be a problem if the media shows gender-stereotyped role models to children?
10. In Paluck's study, did participants change their perception of social norms, or their personal beliefs, or both?

Key concepts

- Education
- Contact hypothesis
- Superordinate goals
- Blue eyes/brown eyes exercise
- Diversity training
- Equal status contact
- Jigsaw technique
- Affirmative action
- Media

Activities

1. The jigsaw technique is based on superordinate goals. Think of other tasks, perhaps from your own life, which involve superordinate goals. Make a list. The examples from Sherif's study may also give you useful ideas.
2. Find out about a current issue relating to prejudice. It could be one that affects you directly or from the news/your own reading. Which of the techniques described could realistically be used to reduce prejudice and promote positive interactions? Make a list of practical suggestions. If you have time, you could develop this into a presentation and/or record it as a YouTube video (an example of using the media!).

End of topic project

Conduct an observational study of prejudice. This can be done using seating distance, as follows:

- Obtain volunteers to take part in a study on health treatments, using adverts or similar.
- Obtain consent from the participants.
- Half of the participants will be briefed about the importance of treating minorities equally and fairly, while the other half will not (randomly decide which condition participants will be in).
- All participants are told that they are first to arrive for a group discussion on health treatments that will be observed. They will be told that the school/college has a visiting speaker who is a health campaigner and used to suffer from schizophrenia.
- Arrange nine seats in a circle. Put a sign on one seat marked 'visiting speaker'.
- Observe how close the participants sit to the visiting speaker's place, that is, how many chairs away from one to four in either direction. In reality, there is no speaker, and once the participants have sat down and their seats have been noted, they can be debriefed.
- Prepare and deliver a short talk to your class on what you found and concluded from this observation. Refer to at least one relevant background research study that is not from your notes or textbook.

This study is based on Norman *et al.* (2010).

End of topic specimen exam questions

1.	Describe two types of discrimination.	6 marks
2.	Explain the role of stereotyping in prejudice.	8 marks
3.	Evaluate the authoritarian personality theory of prejudice.	8 marks
4.	Analyse one research study that relates to explanations of prejudice.	10 marks
5.	Explain the use of the jigsaw technique to reduce prejudice.	5 marks

13 Social Relationships

For the topic of social relationships, you should be able to explain:

- The nature of relationships, including online relationships and parasocial relationships.
- Factors in interpersonal attraction.
- Theories of relationships.
- Relevant research evidence.

You need to develop the following skills:

- Explaining concepts relevant to relationships.
- Explaining and evaluating theories relevant to relationships.
- Using research evidence to back up factual statements and evaluation.
- Analysing research evidence relevant to relationships.

The nature of relationships

A **social relationship** can mean any social connection that we have with another person. Of course, it includes **romantic relationships**, but also the relationships that we have with friends, colleagues and even enemies.

Social relationships can be very beneficial. They provide **social support** that helps to reduce stress. Cutrona (1996) found that stress levels were lower among people who experienced a lot of social interaction. Loneliness tends to lead to feelings such as helplessness, boredom, insecurity or depression (Rubenstein *et al.*, 1979) and overall, it is a factor in ill health comparable with smoking or alcohol consumption (Holt-Lunstad *et al.*, 2010).

Relationships can also be a cause of stress and conflict. This chapter will consider relationship problems and the ways in which psychologists have tried to explain relationships.

Remember that the term 'relationship' has a broad definition in psychology. This section begins with the broadest sense of the word and then considers closer interpersonal relationships and finally romantic relationships.

Affiliation

Affiliation is a very broad term meaning the desire to form connections with other people to avoid social isolation or for strategic reasons.

! Syllabus note

Social relationships is a topic in the Social Behaviour unit in Higher Psychology. National 5 students should instead study the option topic Non-verbal communication (chapter 11).

Social support helps reduce stress

! Syllabus note

Relationships is a very current topic, with lots of interesting new research coming out all the time. Higher pupils should try to engage with new research into relationships. It is also easy to think of examples from our lives.

Shy people may be defending themselves against the unpleasantness of social rejection

Top tip

Social identity theory is discussed in more detail in chapter 12.

Make the link

...with the concept of social support in the topic of Stress (chapter 6).

Strategic affiliation may be highly significant in the workplace

Affiliation as a need

Some researchers, for example, Maslow (1943), believe that affiliating with others is a fundamental human need. Maslow states that after a human's most basic needs such as food and shelter have been met, then people are motivated to seek love and belongingness (see chapter 1: humanist approach). Baumeister and Leary (1995) agree that humans have a need for **belongingness**, which, they say, is biologically prepared, and can be compared to the social behaviour of other animals. They point out that although shyness seems to go against the idea of a need for affiliation, shy people are actually very socially-oriented, and may be defending themselves against the unpleasantness of social rejection.

Relationships can be a cause of stress and conflict

Social identity

Tajfel and Turner (1979) believed that a person's concept of who they are depends fundamentally on their membership of groups. They call this a person's **social identity**. If someone else is seen as a member of the same group, this makes us more likely to affiliate with them and more likely that we will have an influence on their behaviour (Haslam *et al.*, 2009). We are also more likely to gain social support from people who see us as members of the same group.

Strategic affiliation

Sometimes we form social relationships out of necessity. DeScioli and Kurzban (2009) state that friendships can be seen strategically, as **alliances** that can be of benefit in potential conflict. Supporting this hypothesis, they found evidence that people have a ranking of their friends' importance, which they conceal from these friends. People ranked their friends based on their perceived social ranking in the whole group, as well as perceived similarity to themselves. Similarly, Taylor *et al.* (2000) believed that the drive to affiliate with others is prompted by survival needs. They suggest that this was particularly relevant to women, while a 'fight-or-flight' response was more advantageous to males during evolution (see chapter 6). As well as among friendship groups, strategic affiliation may be highly significant in the workplace.

Attachments

We affiliate with a broad range of people – some of whom we do not actually like. However, what about our deeper, more personal social relationships? These more significant relationships feature an **attachment** or 'attachment bond'. An attachment is an emotional connection that we have with another person – typically family members, partners and close friends. The term is often used when in ordinary speech, we would say 'love', but it is preferred by researchers as a less subjective term. A person's earliest attachments are formed to the **caregiver**(s) that look after them as small children, from whom separation causes distress and sadness (Ainsworth & Bell, 1970). One feature of getting older is that we are able to tolerate separations from loved ones. However, the loss of an attachment bond through a social break-up or death can result in grief at any age.

An attachment is an emotional connection that we have with other people, such as family members

Parental attachments

The British psychologist John Bowlby developed a comprehensive theory of attachment in childhood. His **attachment theory** said that bonds must develop before the age of 2 (the 'critical period') to avoid permanent psychological damage. He also said that an infant's first attachment shows three key features (Bowlby, 1958):

- The parent acts as a secure base from which the infant can explore the environment. Infants cling to adults who can protect them against danger.
- The infants show social releasers, such as smiling and crying, to get parental attention.
- The attachment helps the child develop a schema for how relationships work.

A person's earliest attachments are formed with their caregiver

Mary Ainsworth developed Bowlby's theory by providing a theory of why some infants develop a **secure attachment** and others are insecure – she believed that this is due to how responsive mothers are to their infants' needs, in terms of noticing them, responding to them quickly and accurately interpreting these needs (Ainsworth *et al.*, 1971). She argued that insecure children fall into two categories – an **avoidant** type, who avoided contact and comforting, and an **insecure-resistant** type, who could not stand separation and were overly clingy.

? Discussion point

How do people react to fathers as caregivers for babies and how do these reactions differ from how mothers are treated?

As adults, relationships change considerably, as people form very strong bonds, sometimes life-long, with others outside their immediate family. For many people, the most significant relationship at this stage is a pair bond with another – that is, a romantic relationship.

The most significant relationship for most adults is a romantic relationship with another person

Adult attachments

Romantic love typically processes through stages, with a predictable series of changes in the brain (not the heart!):

Attraction. When someone feels sexual attraction (or 'lust'), their brain becomes aroused in a similar way to a person who wins at gambling or takes drugs. This attraction stimulates the brain's pleasure centre, the **nucleus accumbens** and their sensitivity to pain reduces (just viewing an attractive face can have a similar effect on this system to taking a painkiller!). Noradrenaline is released and the body is generally in a more excited/aroused state. Interestingly, being in a situation that causes the body to be aroused or even scared, for example, walking across a high bridge, increases the chance that we will find someone that we meet attractive – possibly because the same brain systems are already active (Dutton & Aron, 1974).

Make the link

...with the approaches to psychology. Bowlby was influenced by both the psychoanalytic and the evolutionary approaches.

Studies have found that in dangerous situations we are more likely to find anyone we meet attractive

Marriage is a long-term attachment

? Discussion point

Do you believe that people's behaviour in romantic relationships can be described in terms of Ainsworth's classification of three types – secure, avoidant and insecure-resistant?

You can study attraction bevaviourally by looking at physical closeness

Love. Once we have fixed on a particular partner, there are certain processes that change in the brain as the relationship is either established or not. Chemically and behaviourally, the individual exhibits similar features to someone with obsessive-compulsive disorder, including obsessive thoughts and repetitive behaviours; in other circumstances, the lovers might be assumed to have OCD (Marazziti & Canale, 2004). This process may be useful in establishing a successful long-term bond.

Long-term attachment. While other hormones return to normal levels, the hormone oxytocin is elevated – just as it is when parents are bonding with a new baby. This hormone is further boosted by physical closeness, including kissing. Adults who have multiple sexual partners may try to avoid a bond being formed by minimising frequency of contact and avoiding certain types of physical contact, for example, kissing (Hazan & Zeifman, 1999).

As discussed in chapter 1, Sigmund Freud thought that our early childhood could affect later behaviour. Hazan and Shaver (1987) also believed that childhood social experience can affect our relationships later and claimed that the same attachment types discovered by Ainsworth can apply to adult romantic relationships. In a questionnaire study, they found that romantic relationship behaviour has a key similarity to the attachment types in babies:

- some individuals form a secure bond
- some are 'clingy', that is, insecure-resistant
- some are avoidant – tending to keep others at a distance and avoid closeness.

Factors that affect attractiveness

As mentioned above, finding another person attractive is the beginning of a process that can lead to a romantic relationship being formed. However, what causes us to find some people more attractive than others?

Psychologists have considered several factors that could affect attraction, ranging from physical appearance to behaviour and status. Attraction can be studied either subjectively, for example, by asking people who they find attractive – or behaviourally, such as looking at people's physical closeness to another person.

Facial symmetry	Rather than being unusual, people who are viewed by others as physically attractive actually have very typical, average features, and the two sides of their faces tend to be highly symmetrical (Langlois and Roggman, 1990).
Responsiveness	We are more likely to want to form a relationship with people who are especially responsive to our needs.
Similarity	How alike people are. Contrary to the popular notion that 'opposites attract', similarity has a positive effect on social relationships and we tend to be attracted to people who are like ourselves – in personality, ethnicity, interests, etc. This can include appearance (see 'matching hypothesis' on the next page).
Familiarity	In terms of emotions, we tend to react more positively to familiar stimuli (Zajonc, 1968), so if a person's face is familiar, they will be more appealing to us.

Although this issue has mainly been researched in terms of romantic relationships, attraction is also a factor in friendships and other connections. In particular, more attractive males tend to have more friends of both sexes (Berscheid *et al.*, 1971; see below). If there is a work colleague that you choose to spend time with, it may be because you find them attractive on some level or that you are just affiliating with them to help advance your career.

We tend to be attracted to people who are like ourselves

Matching hypothesis

Closely linked to the concept of similarity, the **matching hypothesis** states that people will tend to select romantic partners of the same level of physical attractiveness as themselves. This is because the choice of a potential partner may be affected not just by that person's desirability but also by the likelihood of success in attempting to form a relationship with them (Walster *et al.*, 1966). In other words, the matching hypothesis says that people tend to make realistic choices, rather than aiming for people who are out of their league!

More attractive males tend to have more friends of both sexes

In one study, photographs of real-life engaged couples were judged based on similarity to one another in attractiveness. Judges consistently rated them as more alike than randomly paired photographs (Murstein, 1972). However, with couples that already exist, it is difficult to know what other factors may have played a role (e.g. personality, familiarity, etc.).

Walster *et al.* (1966) failed to find support for their hypothesis using an artificially set up student dance – they found that students tended to want the most attractive partner possible. However, a study by Berscheid *et al.* (1971) tried to remedy problems in the Walster study and did find support for the matching hypothesis (see key study).

Key study: Berscheid *et al.* (1971): the matching hypothesis

Aim: *The researchers wanted to test the matching hypothesis. They believed that Walster* et al. *(1966) failed to support the hypothesis because their experimental set up had not been realistic.*

Method: *In the first study, adverts were circulated for a 'computer matching dance', and from the applicants, 170 female and 177 male participants were selected, all first year university students. Some were given an element of realistic risk by telling them that the partner may not agree to go with them. In a second study, 113 mixed male and female participants were each shown six opposite sex photos and asked to choose a date. In one condition, they were told that they would automatically get their choice, and in another condition, that the date would happen only if the partner agreed. All participants were rated on a nine-point scale for physical attractiveness by four student accomplices.*

The study was based around choosing dates for a dance

Findings: *Overall, the researchers found evidence supporting the matching hypothesis – participants who had been rated as more physically attractive tended to choose more attractive dates. Surprisingly, the elements of risk/realism made no difference to the* *outcome – participants did not choose less attractive dates, even if warned that they could be rejected. The researchers concluded that previous studies didn't find support for the matching hypothesis because they had not focused enough on a partner's initial choice. The researchers also surveyed their participants and found that attractive males had more friends, while attractive females had been on more dates.*

Evaluation: *The two studies provided useful experimental support of the matching hypothesis. The first study used a large sample size and both were well controlled. However, a limitation is that they used photographs to judge attractiveness – in real life, students would tend to meet potential dates face-to-face. There are cultural differences in what people find attractive, making it hard to generalise from American students in the 1970s. The students were young and knew this was an artificial one-off date for an experiment, again making findings hard to generalise.*

Most people find symmetrical faces attractive

Top tip

In the Higher exams, any relevant research studies will be credited – they don't need to be the ones you have studied in class.

Relationship universals and variations

So far, it has been assumed that the same processes in attachment and attraction affect everybody, but there are many **cultural variations** about how relationships are conducted in different parts of the world. This section will look at what is universal – what occurs in every human society – and what varies by culture.

Relationship universals

The following are some of the aspects of relationships that can be considered the norm in every human society, and are therefore, **culturally universal**:

- Age differences in heterosexual relationships: men prefer younger females and women prefer older males (Buss, 1989).
- Facial appearance: symmetrical faces with features signalling health are found to be attractive (Perrett *et al.*, 1994).
- Most people form long-term pair bonds (Walker *et al.*, 2011).

When traits are culturally universal (or near universal), it is often assumed that these traits may have an evolutionary basis. Supporting research studies tend to treat heterosexual relationships as the norm, possibly causing bias in the selection of participants.

Cultural variations in relationships

The following are some of the aspects of relationships that vary widely between societies:

- Whether love is seen as a romance or companionship (Goodwin, 1999).
- The way that couples/marriages form, independently or via family arrangement (Walker *et al.*, 2011).
- Attitudes towards prior relationships (Buss, 1989).

Parenting also varies with culture, and attachment types in children vary in prevalence. In a review of studies, Van Ijzendoorn and Kroonenberg (1988) found the highest proportions of securely attached children in Britain and Sweden. European countries tended to have higher levels (20% plus) of avoidant children than insecure-resistant, while in Israel and Japan, the opposite pattern was found.

According to Ainsworth's theory, this could relate to cultural differences in parenting style and responsiveness in different countries. In some countries only one or two studies have been done, making it hard to draw firm conclusions.

Japan has a higher level of insecure-resistant children than European countries

Questions

1. Does having an affiliation with someone mean that you like them?
2. Which is the broader term – attraction or affiliation?
3. Name a researcher who thought that affiliation is a basic human need.
4. What are the key features of infant-parent attachments, according to Bowlby?
5. Give one feature of attachment behaviour in later childhood.
6. What brain area is particularly active in the early stages of love/romantic attachment?
7. Which of Ainsworth's types of attachment can be linked to adults in romantic relationships being 'clingy'?
8. Do opposites attract?
9. Give two examples of factors that affect attraction.
10. Explain one flaw in the methodology used by Berscheid *et al.* (1971).

Key concepts

- Relationships
- Affiliation
- Attachment
- Attachment theory
- Caregiver
- Secure attachment
- Avoidant
- Insecure-resistant
- Nucleus accumbens
- Attraction
- Familiarity
- Similarity
- Matching hypothesis
- Cross-cultural variations
- Cultural universals

Activities

1. Matching hypothesis – find out three to four examples of famous couples or couples from movies or TV shows. Do they match in terms of physical attractiveness? If not, what other factors may have affected these relationships?
2. What effect does it have if children fail to form an attachment bond in infancy? Find out about evidence regarding children brought up in orphanages or being very severely socially deprived.
3. Find out about how minority relationship types can lead to prejudice. For example, what kind of attitudes do people have towards those who are gay, single or in 'open relationships'? You could conduct a short survey into one such aspect and report back to your classmates.

! Syllabus note

You could be asked about any of these theories in the exam. You may have to explain, evaluate or analyse theories. Ask your teacher or lecturer which supporting evidence your class will study for each theory.

Theories of relationships

Social exchange theory

Social exchange theory, proposed by Thibaut and Kelley (1959), suggests that human relationships can be looked at as a series of exchanges, in which each partner tries to get a good deal. It helps to explain why relationships change over time, as the relative costs and benefits to each partner change.

Social exchange theory is an example of what are generally called 'economic theories' of human behaviour. These theories see relationships and other human behaviour as a series of rational choices based on conscious thought processes. They are influenced by the cognitive approach to psychology and view humans as essentially rational. The study of Economics looks at decision making in areas such as personal finance on the assumption that people want to maximise profit and minimise losses. Similarly, economic theories state that when people form and maintain relationships, they fundamentally want the best deal for themselves.

When we ask someone on a date we might weigh up what we will gain and what we will lose

Costs and benefits

According to Thibaut and Kelley, a relationship involves a series of social exchanges between partners. What this means is that when we ask someone on a date, form a relationship or move in together, we are essentially weighing up what we will gain and what we will lose. In these transactions, each partner can get either a good or a bad deal; every individual will try to minimise their **costs** and get as much **benefit** as possible out of the relationship. This might change as a relationship progresses – greater familiarity could cause some costs to reduce (e.g. less risk) but also some benefits to reduce (e.g. not new, so less exciting).

Top tip

Making connections with the psychological approaches from chapter 1, as well as with other topics such as Stress, can be a good source of analysis marks in an exam answer.

The table below gives some examples of typical costs and benefits, but these depend entirely on the situation. For example, in some cases, money may be a cost (having to subsidise a partner) but in other cases, it will be a benefit (being funded by a generous partner).

Rewards	Social support, childcare, companionship, fun, sex, improved reputation, money
Costs	Effort, time, money, missed opportunities with other potential partners

At first, this theory does not explain why some people have much more successful relationships than others do and why people stay in bad relationships. Thibaut and Kelley explained that a person judges the relationship they are in against a **comparison level** (**CL**), a schema for relationships that is unique to the individual. As the CL prompts people to decide whether relationships are acceptable based on their past experiences, everyone's judgement will be slightly different. For example, if their parents' relationship featured a high level of conflict and violence, then they may view a medium level of conflict and violence as being acceptable. Someone who has had a series of lazy boyfriends/girlfriends develops a lower comparison level to judge new ones by.

Explanation of attraction

Economic theories try to explain the factors that affect attraction in terms of costs and benefits. For example, similarity may have a function such as facilitating communication and making it easier to find shared activities (Rubin, 1973). The matching hypothesis is explained as follows: people want the best deal they can get but avoid costs, such as time wasting and disappointment, by aiming only as high as they can achieve.

Relationship stages

According to Thibaut and Kelley, the costs and benefits of relationships change over time. For example, the early **stages of a relationship** have high costs and a high risk of rejection, while in a longer-lasting relationship, demands are lower and costs are more predictable. This leads to a series of four stages that a relationship will progress through: sampling, bargaining, commitment and institutionalisation (see right).

Evaluation

Social exchange theory helps psychologists explain why so many people stay in bad or abusive relationships (investment is high and alternatives are unattractive). However, in reality, people do not seem to accurately retain a record of what they are 'owed' in relationships (DeScioli & Kurzban, 2009).

The theory can explain the matching hypothesis in principle but struggles to explain the findings of Berscheid *et al.* (1971), which showed that the risk of rejection made no difference to people's choices.

The theory suggests that there tend to be more romantic gestures (e.g. gift giving) at the start of a relationship because potential rewards are higher. This contrasts with the biological evidence discussed in the

Make the link

...to the study of Economics, which often considers human behaviour as rational and based on choices.

Someone who has had a series of lazy boyfriends/girlfriends develops a lower comparison level to judge new ones by

Sampling: considering costs and rewards and comparing other potential relationships.
Bargaining: giving and receiving rewards, and considering whether deeper commitment is worthwhile.
Commitment: as intimacy increases, the relationship becomes more predictable and costs are lowered.
Institutionalisation: norms are established as the pattern of exchange within the relationship.

previous section, which suggests that brain chemistry involved in falling in love leads to obsessional thoughts about the partner.

There is mounting evidence that humans don't actually behave as rationally as the theory suggests. Miller (2005) states that it is unrealistic to reduce human relationships to a series of rational choices, while many aspects of attraction seem to be culturally universal and not due to conscious choice (Perrett *et al.*, 1994).

We tend to give more gifts at the start of a relationship

Evolutionary theory

According to the evolutionary approach, humans have a basic need to form social relationships of various kinds. To put it simply, we are social animals like other primates, and we have evolved a basic motivation to interact with others. Research into relationship universals supports this view.

The **evolutionary theory of relationships** states that human relationship behaviour has been shaped by Darwinian natural selection. A major aspect of this is that people will engage in behaviour to maximise their **reproductive success**. However, this can be a balance between producing a lot of offspring, or fewer offspring and caring for them well. Bowlby's theory of attachment is also influenced by evolutionary theory – it suggests that bonding with children is an innate strategy to boost the infant's chances of survival, just as baby birds open their beaks wide to be fed.

Bowlby's theory of attachment is influenced by evolutionary theory

Top tip

The theories of social exchange and evolution/parental investment contrast very clearly with each other. Try to think of examples of relationship behaviour and consider how these could be explained in terms of these theories.

Parental investment

One aspect of the theory is that for biological reasons, males and females invest different amounts of resources in having and raising children and that these differences have led the two sexes to evolve different behavioural strategies (Trivers, 1972). **Parental investment** means investing resources in raising offspring at a cost to the parent. Once a baby is born, both parents have a genetic stake in the child's survival, as every child gets exactly 50% of its genes from each parent. Indeed, parenthood in the whole animal kingdom can be seen as an evolved strategy to improve the survival chances of offspring. However, in the vast majority of species, fathers do no childrearing whatsoever. In contrast, Quinlan (2008) notes that in humans cross-culturally, the societies with the highest degree of relationship stability are the ones where males contribute approximately 50% of the resources needed to look after their children.

Even in societies that have relatively equal roles for males and females, females biologically put in more parental investment, as nine months of pregnancy is typically followed by a period of breastfeeding. This **differential investment** is increased if the mother is also the primary carer for her offspring. Another sex difference is that women can have fewer offspring over the lifespan than a man can, meaning that, theoretically, the best evolutionary strategy in terms of survival of her genes would be to look after the children well and seek a partner who is willing to provide support. Male reproduction is less constrained biologically and males could potentially have a large number of offspring with many women – but doing so might come at a cost in terms of a reduced ability to care for the children, thus not ensuring their survival.

Both parents have a genetic stake in a child's survival

The cost of parental investment also implies that in a long-term relationship, there will be an advantage to both partners to ensure that the other stays faithful. For a male, this is to ensure that any children have his genes, so he is not providing care for someone else's offspring. For a woman, this is because she would have to invest more in her children's care if their father didn't stay.

Dunbar's number

Dunbar's number – based on the work of researcher Robin Dunbar – is the idea that a human's friendship group is limited to around 150 individuals. People can have more contacts than that, but it is the upper limit for how many people we can maintain close contact with, including family members and friends (see the evolutionary approach, chapter 1).

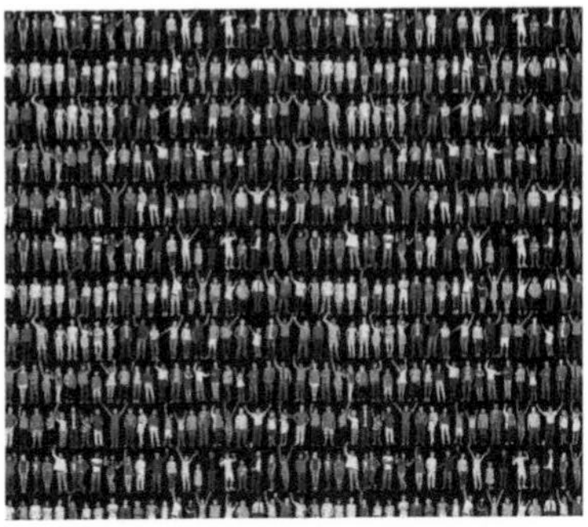

Dunbar's number is the idea that a human's friendship group is limited to around 150 individuals

Such a limit is thought to be based on the size of our brains. The **social brain hypothesis** states that the human brain evolved to be larger because people gained a survival advantage from keeping track of social relationships. This contrasts with previous researchers such as Morris (1967), who suggested that humans evolved large brains because of the challenges of surviving and hunting. Dunbar (1998) stated that the number is a trade-off between the benefits of a bigger group and the costs of a larger brain. Having a large brain is costly in energy but having a large group is beneficial for lots of reasons, including protection. At some point over the past 100,000 years, humans have evolved this biological upper limit. Beyond around 150, it is simply not possible for our brains to keep track of the relationships with others – and crucially, keep track of the relationships they have with each other.

Primates with larger social groups need larger brains in order to keep track of relationships

So is there any evidence that brain size links to group size? Dunbar (1992) studied the group size of a range of primates and found that the size of the neocortex in each species was correlated – the bigger the social group, the bigger the neocortex of the brain. As a comparison, chimpanzees have a maximum group size of 50, and around one-third of the neocortex size that humans do (Dunbar, 1992). In contrast, there was no clear relationship between brain size and the complexity of the environment where they obtained their food. This is strong evidence that primates with larger social groups need larger brains in order to keep track of relationships.

Dunbar's number has been supported by the finding that a group size of around 150 seems to be fairly typical in humans through history – from the settlements recorded in the Domesday Book, to the tribal groups in hunter-gatherer societies (Dunbar, 1993). In a neat application to the modern world, Hill and Dunbar (2003) looked at the size of networks to which people send Christmas cards. It fitted the theory – 153.5 was the mean total population of all households receiving cards from each individual. Although people often have a much larger group of contacts on social media, Gonçalves *et al.* (2011) found that the number of people we regularly contact through sites such as Twitter remains under 200.

A study found that people send Christmas cards to 153.5 people on average

? Discussion point

Do you have a social group of around 150?

Innate nature of attachments

Evolutionary approaches also imply that many aspects of human relationships are innate – designed by evolution to maximise the chances of surviving, reproducing and raising healthy offspring. According to this view, beauty is seen as pre-programmed preference for features that indicate health and fertility (Perrett *et al.*, 1998). This can include facial symmetry, which is thought to indicate health.

We may also be influenced by factors that we are unaware of, such as the **pheromones** – air-bound hormones the body can release – in another person's smell. Wedekind *et al.* (1995) conducted a study of the effects of pheromones on partner preference; 49 women were asked to rate the attractiveness of the odours of t-shirts that had been worn by men who either had a similar or dissimilar human leukocyte antigen (HLA) type. (From the point of view of the immune system of potential offspring, it is better if partners have a different HLA type.) Women rated the odour of the HLA-dissimilar men as more pleasant. This suggests that pheromones have an unconscious effect on attraction, prompting us to select partners who will improve the survival chances of potential offspring.

If relationship behaviour is innate, this helps to explain why certain aspects of maternal behaviour are universal. As Bowlby argued, social releasers improve a child's survival advantage. This contrasts with an older, behaviourist view that babies form an attachment based on the reward from being fed. Harlow (1959) tried to distinguish between these two ideas with an experiment on monkeys and found strong evidence that infants need physical contact with a parent, rather than simply desiring to be fed (see key study).

Pheromones have an unconscious effect on attraction

Key study: Love in infant monkeys: Harlow's (1959) experiments into attachment

Aim: *The dominant view at the time, from the behaviourist approach, was that infants form social bonds with their carers due to classical and operant conditioning. For example, Dollard and Miller (1950) believed that food is a primary reinforcer, something that is directly rewarding because of its importance to a species' survival. A carer who provides the food is a secondary reinforcer who becomes associated with a primary reinforcer, until their presence becomes rewarding. Harlow disagreed – he said that a baby has an innate need to bond with a parent and gets pleasure from contact/cuddling.*

Method: *Harlow conducted a study in which infant monkeys were taken away from their mother and placed in a cage containing a cold, wire mother-like figure with a feeding bottle, and a soft cloth mother figure that did not. If attachments are formed through association with feeding, then the infant monkeys should become attached to the wire 'mother'.*

Findings: *It was found that the infant only used the wire mother to feed. Rather than forming an attachment to the wire mother, the infant spent most of its time – around 23 hours per day – clinging to the cloth figure, even though it provided no food. It also ran to the cloth mother when frightened. This outcome suggests that rather than learning attachment through conditioning, monkeys, and perhaps humans as well, have an innate drive for 'contact comfort'.*

Evaluation: *Harlow's theory has had a huge influence and it has become widely accepted that some aspects of attachment bonding are innate, at least in infants. However, it has been criticised for being very cruel to the monkeys. There are also issues with external validity of his studies, that is, the findings from monkeys cannot be generalised to humans with any certainty.*

A photograph from the study

Evaluation

This theory of social relationships is based on the well-established theory of evolution by natural selection. Many people will not feel comfortable with the idea that their relationship behaviour is outside of their conscious control. However, it does help to explain relationships that do not seem to be based on rational choices, such as abuse victims and people who suffer from 'Stockholm syndrome' – the condition where hostages develop an attraction to their captors.

Nevertheless, the theory cannot easily explain **same-sex relationships**, because it states that relationships essentially exist to have children and pass on one's genes. It is therefore limited in how well it can explain all relationships. The concept of differential investment tends to ignore the broader social context (e.g. the role played by friends/family in a person's choice of partner).

This theory of social relationships cannot easily explain same-sex relationships

Another limitation of the evolutionary theory is that there are considerable cultural differences in what is considered attractive. If our relationship behaviour is innate and due to the evolutionary drive to pass on genes, it is hard to understand why it should be so easily influenced by culture, such as the trend for extreme thinness in women (which is not beneficial for childbearing).

Dunbar's number does seem to be applicable to a large number of situations, from hunter-gatherer tribes to Twitter engagement. However, it is based on correlational studies of brain size that do not prove cause-and-effect, while De Ruiter *et al.* (2011) have argued that although the neocortex plays an important role in social functioning, its size does not directly determine social skills.

Filter theory

Top tip

To help you remember the filters, write each one in your notes beside an example based on a real relationship, such as a celebrity couple.

Filter theory is another theory that focuses particularly on romantic relationships. It focuses on the thought processes and decisions that someone goes through as they narrow the **field of potential partners** from everyone they meet to the few people who are actually compatible for a long-term relationship (Kerckhoff & Davis, 1962).

The theory states that a person's choice of romantic partner goes through a series of psychological **filters**, each of which reduces the number of potential options available. It can therefore be linked to the 'sampling' stage in social exchange theory, and provides an alternative to some of the evolutionary aspects that affect attraction, such as youth, facial symmetry and pheromones.

Filter theory compares the relationship choices we make to the layers of a water filter

Imagine a water filter. It might have several layers: the first layers remove larger objects, but smaller ones get through. The lower layers are designed to filter out smaller objects. According to filter theory, our psychological filters work in a similar way – they begin by ruling out people who are highly incompatible, for example the wrong gender or sexual orientation for our preferences, or people who are already in a monogamous relationship with someone else. We then move on to filter according to a more detailed consideration.

There are several possible filters. Some of the most widely discussed are as follows:

Availability	Filter out anyone who is not eligible to be in a relationship at all. Someone who is married to another person might not be considered further.
Category	Filter by age and sexuality. People of an incompatible sexuality or very different age can be removed from consideration.
Attractiveness	Filter on the basis of physical looks. People who are not suitably physically attractive can be removed from consideration. This could include having a similar level of physical attractiveness to our own, i.e. matching.
Similarity	Filter on the basis of education, social background and interests. Consider whether the potential partner has a similar background to our own.
Complementarity	Filter on the basis of complementary views. Consider whether the potential partner has attitudes and traits that fit well with our own.
Proximity	Filter out people who do not live close by. Consider who lives close enough to be a practical option.

Evidence

There is some evidence that people do filter out potential romantic partners on the basis of these factors, and that some filters are used before others. Kerckhoff and Davis (1962) studied couples across the early stages of their relationships and concluded that similarity acted as a filter before **complementarity** of traits (which they found to be more important after a year or more). In other words, we may at first be attracted to someone similar to ourselves, but as time goes on we find out whether we are compatible. In some cases, this will mean having differences in our traits – for example, one person liking to drive and the other person preferring to sit in the passenger seat.

Proximity could affect a person's choice of partner

Similarity of couples across many different demographic factors can be studied using correlation; the closer a correlation comes to 1.0, the more the partners tend to be similar on a particular factor (see chapter 8). For example, married couples tend to have a correlation of 0.5 or higher in terms of number of years of schooling completed (Heath *et al.*, 1985). Evidence on the matching hypothesis (see previous section) supports the idea that looks can act as a filter.

Education level is a filter that affects choice of partner

There is cross-cultural support for this idea as well. In a study of multiple societies in East Africa, Brewer (1968) found three factors in particular affected choice of partner:

- education level
- proximity of where they lived
- perceived similarity.

Evaluation

Filter theory provides a useful explanation of the partner choice process. As noted earlier, it fits with the 'sampling' phase of social exchange theory. However, unlike that theory, it does not fully explain why different people have different priorities.

It is not clear from the theory which should take priority – for example, proximity of location, or similarity? Often these might conflict; a less similar potential partner might live closer. The entire concept of filtering out partners who don't live nearby may be increasingly outdated as it becomes easier to form and maintain relationships over the Internet (see final section of this chapter).

The theory fits with some aspects of the matching hypothesis. However, it also shares some of the same flaws – the supporting research is dated, and focuses too much on young heterosexual couples.

A strength of the theory is that it is able to accommodate some of the principles from evolutionary theories. For example, the attractiveness filter could be informed by research into facial symmetry.

While filters seem to make some basic sense, there is relatively little evidence that people actually make choices on this basis. The findings conflict with evolutionary evidence which suggests that some aspects of attraction operate on an automatic level. In addition, people do not always filter out potential partners on the basis of their marital status – attraction can form towards someone who is already in a marriage or other long-term relationship.

Overall, this is a simplistic and rather dated view of the partner choice process, but it makes a useful attempt to consider many of the factors that influence attraction, and to combine them into a theory.

Rusbult's investment theory

According to investment theory, having children or moving in together are forms of investment in a relationship which makes it likely to last longer

Like filter theory, Caryl Rusbult's **investment theory** of romantic relationships focuses on the relationship choices that people make, but it is more concerned with whether relationships are maintained or break up, rather than how they were formed. It draws heavily on the idea of investment – something that was previously described as a key factor in evolutionary theories of relationships (see above).

According to Rusbult (1980), whether someone stays in a relationship or not has less to do with their personality and more to do with prior circumstances. She argues that maintaining a relationship (rather than breaking up) depends on three key factors:

- Satisfaction level: how satisfied is the person at present with the state of the relationship? Are they having their needs and wants met, and do they feel fulfilled?
- Comparison with alternatives: if they were to leave, where would they go? A lack of options will motivate a person to stay in their current relationship; appealing alternatives will motivate them to consider leaving.
- Investment size: this refers to any time, effort, money or social commitments that have been made. Getting married is a form of investment, as is money and time spent on a partner, or shared children, friends and property.

Influences on satisfaction

Shared friendships or family networks add to relationship satisfaction, according to Rusbult

Rusbult also highlighted two aspects that increase or decrease the level of **satisfaction** in a relationship:

- Equity: this means fairness. Is what you put into a relationship proportional to what you get out? A lack of equity decreases satisfaction.
- Social network: relationships go beyond the couple; a relationship that comes with a strong network of friends or family increases satisfaction.

Role of investment and satisfaction

The first two factors of relationship commitment highlighted by Rusbult fit well with the idea of costs and benefits associated with social exchange theory, but the third factor adds an extra psychological dimension. It shows that even if we are dissatisfied and have good alternatives to a current relationship, we may still stick with what we have due to the large amount of time, money or effort expended so far.

This implies that the longer a relationship goes on, the more the investment factor is likely to outweigh the other two factors. A very new relationship may easily break up due to dissatisfaction, but the greater investment size in a long-term relationship may contribute to its continuation.

Rusbult's idea of investment fits with the economic idea of the sunk cost. On a rational level, money or an investment that has already been spent and can't be recovered should not make any difference to future decisions. However, economists have frequently noticed that despite this, people tend to continue with poor strategies, such as pouring money into a failing company. On a personal level, you may experience this if you have paid money to go to a club or event. If you are not enjoying a free event, you will leave, but if you have already paid to attend an event (i.e. made an investment), you tend to feel that you should stay longer to get your money's worth – even if you're having a bad time!

Make the link

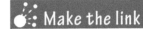

...with your studies of Economics.

Investment in harmful relationships

One of the key things that Rusbult's theory adds to our understanding of relationships is a clearer picture of why people stay in harmful relationships. While still recognising the role of costs and benefits, Rusbult's theory is more realistic in that it takes into account broader social factors that affect satisfaction, as well as the time and effort people have expended upon their relationship over the months or years.

Rusbult and Martz (1995) found support for the theory in a questionnaire study of women in abusive relationships. They found greater levels of relationship commitment among women who had fewer alternatives, reported relatively higher levels of satisfaction (i.e. the abuse was less severe) and who had already invested heavily in their relationships such as by getting married and having children.

Evaluation

Rusbult's theory does a better job of explaining why people stay in abusive relationships than does social exchange theory. According to social exchange theory, people may accept an abusive relationship because their comparison level is low, or because the costs of leaving are high. However, Rusbult's theory shows why tolerance of abuse may change over time.

Rusbult's model has also been successfully applied to homosexual relationships, giving it an advantage over evolutionary theories. And although it mainly focuses on romantic relationships, similar principles can be applied to friendships and family relationships, too.

Key concepts

- Social exchange theory
- Costs and benefits
- Comparison level
- Stages of a relationship
- Evolutionary theory of relationships
- Reproductive success
- Parental investment
- Differential investment
- Dunbar's number
- Social brain hypothesis
- Pheromones
- Same-sex relationships
- Filter theory
- Filters
- Field of potential partners
- Complementarity
- Investment theory
- Satisfaction

Questions

1. Give two examples of potential costs of a relationship.
2. What are the four stages in social exchange theory?
3. Does the matching hypothesis support social exchange theory?
4. What is a comparison level?
5. Give one example of how males and females may have different evolutionary strategies.
6. What is the maximum number of close relationships we can have, according to Dunbar?
7. What is meant by differential investment?
8. Explain how the studies of Harlow (1959) and Wedekind *et al.* (1995) supported the evolutionary theory of relationships.
9. Give an example of a filter, from the filter theory of romantic relationships.
10. What three factors did Rusbult consider to be key to relationship commitment?

Activities

1. Choose a short story, play or film that focuses on a romantic relationship. Now write a careful description in your notes about which of the four theories best explains the features of the relationship. Give examples.
2. Write a list of relationship behaviours – parenting, friendships and romantic relationships – that fit with evolutionary theory. Beside each one, note what advantage it would be in terms of passing on genes to future generations.

Virtual and parasocial relationships

Virtual relationships

Not all **social relationships** involve meeting in a face-to-face context. The Internet is increasingly a medium for all types of relationships to be maintained and developed, through social networking sites such as Facebook and Instagram, discussion forums, or sites associated with hobbies or gaming. These sites facilitate friendships primarily, but romantic relationships can also develop.

Internet dating, that is, meeting potential partners through a website, is a highly prevalent way of forming romantic relationships, with millions of people in the UK signed up to Internet dating sites. Typically, such sites allow people to browse profiles that include a photo and short description.

Not all social relationships involve meeting in a face-to-face context

As Internet dating has increased in popularity, psychologists have become interested to find out whether forming and maintaining relationships via the Internet shares the same characteristics as when people form relationships in a face-to-face context.

Gating features

A person forming a new relationship online is able to manipulate their image. If the initial contact is via text or on a site where they use an avatar to represent themselves, they may have the opportunity – unavailable in face-to-face communication – of presenting themselves without the risk of being judged by appearance.

This could have the benefit of overcoming shyness or other obstacles, phenomena known as **gating features**. The removal of these features – which could include disabilities as well as conditions such as stuttering, which make it harder to initiate a conversation with a stranger – has the potential to make it easier for people to initiate positive relationships and to present themselves the way they would like to be seen (McKenna *et al.*, 2002).

Internet-based friendships and romantic relationships may appeal to particular personality types. Tosun and Lajunen (2010) found that students who were high in extraversion (being very outgoing and talkative) tended to use the Internet to extend real-life relationships, whereas students who scored high on psychoticism (being moody, closed-minded and aggressive) tended to use the Internet as a substitute for face-to-face relationships, and found it easier to reveal their thoughts and feelings online.

While providing alternative options is largely a benefit of the Internet's role in social relationships, there are concerns that it makes it easier for people with extreme and harmful views to meet and communicate on a regular basis. Doing so can increase the strength of extreme views, through a process known as **group polarisation**.

> **Make the link**
>
> ...with the concept of personality, which plays a role in several other topics, for example Stress (see pages 156–157).

Walther's hyperpersonal theory

Joseph Walther explained that the differences in communication format and the ability to better manage how you present yourself online leads to two main differences in communication in an Internet-mediated relationship (Walther, 1996):

- A lesser amount of information is disclosed.
- Communications may be asynchronous, i.e. not take place at the same time.

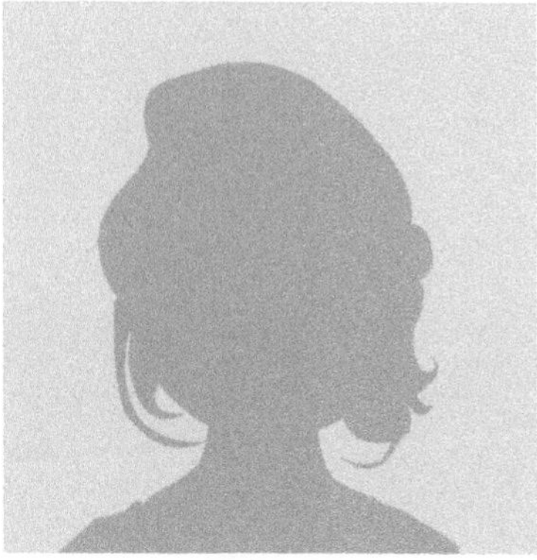

It is easier to control how you present yourself online than in face-to-face communication

Due to the slower nature of messaging and the ability to edit what information is released, people may be able to manage how they are perceived more easily online than in everyday life, taking time to think over their responses to messages in a way that would not be possible in face-to-face conversation. They can also manage what information is revealed and what is not, from personal details to photos. This leads to communication that is more intensely emotional and intimate, and '*where we may exceed what we may accomplish face-to-face, in terms of our impression-generating and relational goals.*' (Walther, 1996, p. 28). The concept of hyperpersonal communication forms the basis Walther's **hyperpersonal theory**.

The concept of hyperpersonal communication can be linked to the idea of self-schemas and to self-actualisation. Humanist psychologist Carl Rogers (1961) believed we have two conflicting versions of ourselves:

- our actual self: how we are at present
- our ideal self: how we would like to be.

According to this framework, the hyperpersonal nature of Internet communication may make it much easier for people to portray their ideal self than their actual self online. (At the same time, it needn't mean that we are getting any closer to that ideal self in reality!)

Make the link

...with the humanist approach to psychology, and to self-schemas in the topic of Depression.

Another line of evidence to suggest that **virtual relationships** may lead to more intimate communication than face-to-face interactions is Rubin's (1975) 'strangers on the train' study. This experiment found that people were more likely to reveal personal details about their lives to a stranger than to people they knew. The same may well hold on the Internet; the relative anonymity of some websites may facilitate greater sharing and earlier personal revelations than would be the case in face-to-face contexts.

Reduced cues theory

Online messages may suffer from reduced social cues to provide context

In contrast to the hyperpersonal theory, Sproull and Kiesler (1995) felt that people may avoid disclosing information via email and other online media. They studied the role of the Internet and email communication in the workplace and argued that without the social cues that accompany face-to-face conversation, people are more likely to be rude or aggressive in response to self-disclosures. Their **reduced cues theory** argued that this may lead people to be less willing to share their ideas, feelings or personal insights.

This idea is familiar today in the context of 'trolls' who deliberately post offensive messages online. One reason that people may be more aggressive online is that they don't fear the consequences of doing so, due to the (relative) anonymity they experience – a phenomenon called **deindividuation**. This concept is not unique to the Internet, and has been studied for many decades. According to Festinger *et al.*

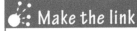

(1952), our sense of ourselves as individuals, along with how we are perceived on a personal level, motivates us to follow social norms such as politeness. When we are in a crowd or otherwise anonymous, such social norms no longer hold, and some of our more aggressive and selfish urges start to reveal themselves. In a similar vein, Zimbardo (1969) found that wearing a hood to conceal their identity led people to be more obedient in the Milgram electric shock paradigm (and therefore made them more likely to harm another person).

Sproull and Kiesler also highlighted the relative permanence of online communication compared to face-to-face conversation. For example, this makes it much easier for employees to be held accountable for comments posted online and may result in disciplinary action. An understanding that everything we post may be saved as a screenshot or on a computer server and judged at a later date might also contribute to people being less willing to disclose their feelings online. (Compare this idea with the key study.)

Overall, the reduced cues theory may be an over-simplification of virtual relationships, as the amount people reveal will depend on the context and the purpose of the communication. Gibbs *et al.* (2006) note that in the context of online dating, revealing information about yourself can help to avoid wasting time on potential partners who wouldn't be suitable in the long term (and therefore links to filters – see previous section).

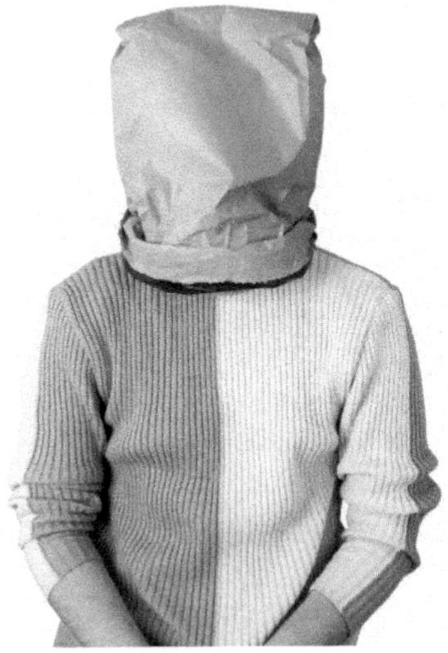

We may be less constrained by social norms when anonymous

Key study: Walther *et al.* (2018): the effect of message persistence and disclosure on liking

Aim: *The study primarily aimed to develop Walther's hyperpersonal theory. The researchers were also influenced by a classic psychological theory known as self-perception theory, with its counter-intuitive principle that observing our own behaviour can change our later attitudes (Bem, 1967). It is well known that personal self-disclosures in a relationship can increase liking, and the researchers believed that being able to see our own self-disclosure messages on screen would lead to our liking a communication partner better. If so, the ability to read our own chat messages could be a factor affecting the intimacy level of online communication.*

Method: *Participants were paired up for the task, with one asking questions and another answering questions via real-time online text chat. There were 136 pairs and all were undergraduate students. Questions included some 'intimate' topics, such as 'describe a time when you were in love with someone'. In the message persistence condition, a participant's own messages accumulated and scrolled across the screen so that the participant could see them (persistent condition), or else did not appear at all (invisible condition). The researchers also varied whether disclosures were reciprocated or not; in one condition, participants were asked to reciprocate by chatting about a similar thing that had happened to them, while in another condition they were told to 'deflect' by saying neutral things like 'okay' or 'I see what you are saying'. The dependent variable was liking for the partner in the*

Make the link

...with responsiveness as a factor affecting attraction, as discussed earlier in this chapter.

task, rated using a 13-item Likert scale, with items such as 'my partner is one of the most likeable people I know' (Rubin, 1970).

Findings: *in terms of the persistence of messages, the researchers didn't find that this had an overall effect, but they did find that it interacted with the other variables. The highest level of liking was found when persistent messages received reciprocal self-disclosures. The lowest level of liking was found when the invisible (non-persistent) messages were met with deflection. The researchers concluded that the visibility of one's own messages increases liking, but only with a reciprocating partner.*

The ability to re-read one's own messages boosts liking, but only when the communication has been reciprocated

Evaluation: *This study provided a useful new dimension to hyperpersonal theory. The theory focuses on what is missing from online communication; in contrast, the persistence of messages is something that is present online but absent in face-to-face interactions. A strength of the study is that the task had high mundane realism – making personal revelations about one's life via online chat is an authentic task. However, the realism is reduced slightly by the total invisibility of messages in one condition (which does not usually happen in real life), as well as the fact that participants were told whether to disclose or not, possibly leading to artificiality in their responses. Another limitation in the research was that the participants were all undergraduates, making it hard to generalise to older adults. Overall the study provided a useful advance to hyperpersonal theory with potential for applications to real-world settings.*

Maintenance of existing relationships

Of course, the Internet is not only used to form new relationships but plays a key role in maintaining existing relationships. Friends in different parts of the world can chat on a daily basis, while couples might find it easier to stay in touch when they are at school, college or work than was the case in the past, particularly if there are times when one partner needs to travel abroad.

There are pitfalls for couples, too. Clayton (2014) found that high levels of Twitter activity were correlated with couples breaking up, and suggested that disagreements over Twitter activities played a role in such conflicts.

There may be concerns of overuse of the Internet in lieu of real-world interactions, but for many, the Internet provides a non-threatening alternative to real-world networking. Campbell *et al.* (2006) found that the amount of time spent online was not associated with social anxiety, and there is evidence that people on the autism spectrum can find everyday communication easier through the forum of social media than on a face-to-face basis (Benford & Standen, 2009). While it may be possible to hide aspects of your identity online, Kim and Lee's (2011) study of Facebook posts found that greater honesty tended to lead to more happiness and to genuine social support.

Parasocial relationships

A parasocial relationship is a one-sided relationship between an ordinary individual and a celebrity or media personality. The person may be a fan but this relationship is stronger and more intense than the behaviour of a typical fan. It may be perceived by others to be a crush or obsession, while the celebrity in question generally has no knowledge of the person's feelings.

Individuals who are engaged in a parasocial relationship may feel that they know the celebrity, and often research them in great detail. In the case of TV or YouTube stars, they may watch every episode or broadcast and treat each one like a face-to-face encounter. They may discuss the latest broadcast in a very one-sided way, focusing entirely on the celebrity in question and ignoring other aspects of the content.

Parasocial relationships are more commonly, though not exclusively, found among adolescents. One reason for this could be that most adolescents have not yet developed a fully mature social network, and the parasocial relationship acts as a substitute for some aspects which will later be met by their social life as an adult.

Turner (1993) found that parasocial relationships are more likely to occur when the celebrity and their fan have similar attitudes and values, suggesting that filter theory might apply (see previous section). However, there was no matching of appearance, as occurs in face-to-face relationships.

? Discussion point

What sort of celebrity or media personality is most likely to be the object of a parasocial relationship? Do these people have anything in common, besides being famous?

Levels of parasocial relationships

Historically, parasocial relationships have tended to be viewed as problematic. They may be compared to cases of **stalking**, where a fan follows a celebrity around and may attempt to harm them.

West and Sweeting (2004) highlighted the dangers of teenagers trying to attain the body image of celebrities that they idolise, including the development of eating disorders or harm to the individual's developing self-esteem. Maltby *et al.* (2004) found a link between more intense parasocial relationships and poorer mental health.

However, parasocial relationships can also be seen in a more positive light. They may serve a useful function in adolescence by prompting young people to emulate creative or successful role models.

One way to distinguish problematic parasocial relationships from more positive ones is to use questionnaires to determine an individual's level of obsession, and identify any delusions that they might have. According to this line of research, parasocial relationships may occur on various levels, each with their own features and representing a particular dimension of thoughts, feelings and behaviour. Giles and Maltby (2006) identify three key levels:

- **Entertainment-social:** at this level, the fan enjoys finding out about the celebrity, keeping up with news and gossip about them, and discussing them with friends – or anyone else who will listen.
- **Intense-personal:** at this level, the fan has developed a level of obsession towards the celebrity. They are likely to agree with questionnaire items such as 'I consider this person to be my soul mate'. They may react emotionally to a problem experienced by the celebrity as strongly as if it had happened to them or to a family member.

> **? Discussion point**
> Are you aware of any cases of celebrity stalking?

> **? Discussion point**
> Do you agree that some celebrities might be positive role models during adolescence?

> **Top tip**
> If asked to analyse theories or explanations in this topic, identifying the aims of each theory, and comparing different theories to each other, can be a good source of marks.

Absorption means an extreme and effortless focus on the target celebrity

- **Borderline pathological:** at this level, the beliefs about the celebrity show clear signs of being out of touch with reality, and the emotions are at the extreme end of the scale. The fan may express a willingness to die for the celebrity.

These three levels range from mild to extreme but they could also reflect the personality of the fan. The levels mirror the three dimensions of Eysenck's personality theory – extraversion, neuroticism and psychoticism – and different people may therefore experience all of these levels to different degrees.

Further research by Sheridan *et al.* (2006) has suggested that a fourth level or dimension be added, covering active attempts by the fan to contact the celebrity by letter or email, accompanied by delusional beliefs that they have a real relationship with him or her or that they are destined to be together. According to some definitions, active attempts to contact the celebrity mean that it ceases to be a parasocial relationship and should instead be defined as stalking.

Attachment theory

As discussed earlier in this chapter, Ainsworth and colleagues presented three types of attachment in child–parent relationships: secure, insecure-avoidant and insecure-resistant. Hazan and Shaver (1987) linked this to romantic relationships and, in this context, an individual with insecure-resistant attachment can be excessively clingy and obsessive.

A very similar idea can be applied to parasocial relationships. Individuals with an insecure-resistant attachment type can be clingy, but also very vulnerable to being upset by rejection. For such people, a parasocial relationship provides a comforting alternative to the real thing – the celebrity can never reject them, and they can act in a clingy and obsessive way without needing to worry about how the other person will react.

The evidence for this idea is limited, but it does raise the possibility that a parasocial relationship could be connected to an individual's attachments to their friends or parents. Supporting this idea, Giles and Maltby (2004) found that an intense personal interest in celebrities was connected to low levels of closeness to parents, and they suggested that parasocial relationships are a problematic expression of a relatively normal developmental change: becoming more emotionally autonomous as you grow up.

The absorption–addiction model

McCutcheon *et al.* (2002) argue that individuals who engage in parasocial behaviours typically believe that they have a special connection with the star, and that this is supported by connecting with social networks of like-minded fans. They argue that this prompts a cognitive change in attention, which they describe as absorption – an extreme and largely effortless focus, which the researchers compare to classic ideas about hypnotism. This results in the celebrity coming before all else in the individual's thoughts. *'Absorption is achieved through an effortless focusing of attention rather than by determined concentration, and this results in a heightened sense of reality of the idolized celebrity'* (p. 81).

The researchers also note that obsessional focus on information about the celebrity may serve to fill emotional gaps in the life of the individual. However, in doing so, the pleasure the person gains from their obsessive behaviour may have an addictive quality. Like other addictions, the person may develop a level of tolerance, whereby they need an increasing 'dose' to satisfy their craving, helping to explain why some people progress to increasing levels of parasocial relationship. They may also experience psychological withdrawal if denied access to a means of following or finding out about the object of their obsession. Together, these concepts make up the **absorption–addiction** model.

? Discussion point

Could people who are not famous be the object of someone's parasocial attachment? For example, if someone follows you on Instagram or Twitter, is it possible that they might become obsessed with you?

Questions

1. Give one example of how a new social relationship can form online.
2. What are gating features, and how do virtual relationships affect them?
3. According to hyperpersonal theory, what two key things are different in online communication compared to face-to-face interaction?
4. How does deindividuation link to virtual relationships?
5. What was the key finding of Walther *et al.* (2018)?
6. Give an example of the type of person who might be the object of a parasocial relationship.
7. Are parasocial relationships always seen as a bad thing?
8. At which level of parasocial relationships would a person react to something bad happening to the celebrity as if it had happened to themselves?
9. Which of Ainsworth's attachment types can help to explain parasocial relationships?
10. Does the absorption–addiction model state that levels of obsession within parasocial relationships tend to remain constant?

Key concepts

- Virtual relationships
- Social media
- Gating features
- Hyperpersonal theory
- Deindividuation
- Reduced cues theory
- Parasocial relationships
- Entertainment-social
- Intense-personal
- Borderline pathological
- Stalking
- Absorption–addiction model
- Attachment theory

Activities

1. With a partner or group, discuss whether you feel you are more or less likely to disclose information about yourself online than in face-to-face communication. Does it depend on the website and who will be reading the information? Do your views fit better with the ideas of Walther or those of Sproull and Kiesler?
2. Look again at the three levels of parasocial relationships identified by Giles and Maltby. Would you be concerned if a friend was showing any of these behaviours? Write a fictional script or short story about a situation where this happens.
3. Read the article 'Praying at the altar of the stars' by Giles and Maltby (2006). It is available at https://thepsychologist.bps.org.uk/volume-19/edition-2/praying-altar-stars. Find one detail or research study mentioned in the article that you weren't previously aware of, and prepare to share your thoughts on it with the rest of the class.

End of topic project

In your class or another suitable group, conduct a simple observation study into relationships, as follows:

- First, identify a suitable piece of video footage. For ethical reasons, do not use footage of anyone you know. It is best to avoid any acted/scripted behaviour such as dramas/soap operas/music videos. Some better suggestions include:
  - an interview, e.g. of a famous couple
  - a piece of sports footage
  - a conversation during a reality TV show.
- Now prepare an observation schedule (see chapter 8). Brainstorm likely relationship behaviours. For this type of observation, a good choice would be to make a tally mark each time a behaviour occurs. Alternatively, you could write verbal descriptions at 30-second intervals.
- Draw conclusions.
- Prepare and deliver a short talk to your class on what you found and concluded from this observation. Refer to at least one relevant background research study – ideally including one that you have discovered for yourself outside of class!

End of topic specimen exam questions

1.	Explain the evolutionary theory of relationships.	12 marks
2.	Describe the methodology of one study relevant to a theory of romantic relationships.	4 marks
3.	Evaluate Walther's hyperpersonal theory, with reference to research.	8 marks
4.	Analyse two different explanations of parasocial relationships.	12 marks

14 Aggression

For the topic of Aggression, you should be able to explain:

- Biological influences on aggression.
- Social psychological explanations of aggression.
- Media influences on aggression.
- Relevant research evidence on aggression.

You need to develop the following skills:

- Explaining concepts relevant to aggression.
- Explaining and evaluating theories relevant to aggression.
- Using research evidence to back up factual statements and evaluation.
- Analysing research evidence relevant to aggression.

What is aggression?

Aggression clearly involves harmful or violent actions, but this can be defined quite broadly. For example, is shouting at someone an aggressive act? What about hacking their computer? Does the behaviour have to be illicit, or could a legal action – such as a prisoner being executed – count as aggression?

Aggression is a word that we all use in everyday speech but like everything in psychology, it's necessary to agree on an objective definition. Psychologists don't always agree on what aggression is or what causes it, but there is agreement that the definition must be applied to all situations, and not be limited to the forms of aggression of which we disapprove!

Aggression is usually defined behaviourally – that is, in terms of what we do, rather than in terms of the intention of the action. One possible definition would be to say 'any deliberately harmful act towards another member of the same species'. Such a definition excludes actions such as hunting or killing for food or pest control, but is otherwise quite broad, possibly including such actions as sacking an employee or sending a hurtful email.

In order to make the definition less broad, it might make sense to include the emotions behind aggression as part of our definition. After all, when we experience aggression, it is often associated with emotions such as fear and anger. However, it is not always possible to find out exactly what people are feeling when they are being aggressive, and it is nearly impossible to state with certainty what animals are feeling when they behave aggressively (and yet, we can still recognise

! Syllabus note

Aggression is a topic in the Social Behaviour unit in Higher Psychology. National 5 students should instead study the option topic Non-verbal communication (chapter 11).

animal aggression when we see it!). Furthermore, military action such as bombing another country might not be motivated by anger, but many people would still consider this to be aggressive.

Types of aggression

It is helpful to consider different forms of aggression that you might observe or read about:

- **Impulsive aggression:** here the aggressive act is spontaneous and focused on another individual, with the aim of harming them in some way. Such aggression may be a reaction, for example hitting someone after they insult you. This category includes physical and verbal attacks but could also include social forms of aggression such as gossiping about someone who annoys you.
- **Instrumental aggression:** here the aggression is a means to an end, or it aims to obtain a desired goal, for example to scare someone off or to steal something. Such aggression may occur through a third party, for example a crime boss dispatching thugs to coerce someone into paying money. It is associated with psychopathy and antisocial personality disorder (Coccaro *et al.*, 2015).
- **Sanctioned aggression:** here the aggression is of a form that is within the rules of a society or the international community, for example locking up a criminal. The extent to which some actions by a state's armed forces are legitimate may be disputed, but they may at least be legal within a particular set of laws. (Of course, they may not be legal – and national law may conflict with international law.)

Passive-aggressive behaviour includes not talking to someone

You may also have heard the term **passive-aggression**. Passive-aggressive behaviour can be defined as being deliberately uncooperative, while not doing anything overtly aggressive or breaking any rules. Examples include not talking to people, not replying to messages or slamming doors. The passive-aggressive person tends not to be upfront about the negative emotions they are feeling, saying *'I'm not upset/angry'* or *'that's fine/whatever'* when their behaviour, tone or body language indicate otherwise (Whitson, 2010). They may also procrastinate or deliberately do tasks badly, either at home or in the workplace. Although often harmless, passive aggression can form part of a pattern of abusive behaviour within some relationships.

You might want to think about these types of aggression as you work through this topic.

> **Top tip**
>
> Impulsive aggression is also called '**person-oriented**' or 'reactive' aggression, while instrumental aggression is also called 'premeditated' aggression.

Biological influences on aggression

Hormonal influences

It probably comes as little surprise to anyone that **hormones** can influence behaviour. But what is a hormone? It is a chemical messenger used by the body. Typically it is released by a gland and travels around the bloodstream, affecting organs or other parts of the body. For example, the hormone that causes the fight-or-flight response – adrenaline – is released by the adrenal glands and causes our heart rate to rise (see chapter 6).

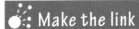

Testosterone is a hormone that plays a particular role in aggression. This is the same hormone that is associated with male sexual development – its levels greatly increase in boys when they approach puberty, and it is responsible for physical changes such as increased body hair, bone and muscle growth, and the production of sperm cells. It is also produced in women at much lower levels. Its role in increasing muscle and bone mass has led to it being used as an illegal drug by some athletes, such as boxers.

The behavioural effects of testosterone are linked to sex and relationships. Males with higher levels of testosterone have more sexual partners across the lifespan (Pollet *et al.*, 2011) and testosterone levels are associated with sexual arousal in both men and women. Interestingly, these links seem to work both ways – being single seems to boost testosterone levels in men, while engaging in a committed relationship has the opposite effect (McIntyre, *et al.*, 2006). Although there are also associations between women's testosterone level and dating behaviour, these are much weaker (Pollet *et al.*, 2011).

Testosterone is also strongly associated with competition and aggression. Higher levels of testosterone (or sensitivity to testosterone) is associated with increased fighting in many species. The challenge hypothesis suggests that the hormone's main function is to help species seek and fight for mates, see off challengers, and keep mates that they have already paired up with ('**mate-guarding**'). This has been shown in birds, who have also shown increased levels of testosterone while fighting for **territory**. Animals have also shown increased aggression when they are injected with testosterone.

However, findings linking aggression and testosterone in humans are less clear cut. On the one hand, testosterone is the male sex hormone, and men are responsible for many more violent crimes than women. On the other hand, most men don't commit violent crimes, while some women do. And given that behaviour such as committing to a relationship can reduce testosterone levels, there is probably not a simple cause-and-effect link between testosterone and aggression.

Neural influences

Certain areas of the brain play a key role in aggressive behaviour. In particular, scientists have focused their attention on a set of brain areas called the limbic system which are involved in a wide range of emotional processes. These areas are closely linked to the frontal lobe of the neocortex, a brain area that plays a key role in working memory and decision making.

Within the limbic system, an area called the **amygdala** is strongly associated with fear and aggression, and there have been cases where individuals with abnormalities in this brain area have shown aggressive behaviour. In the 1960s, an American named Charles Whitman, the 'Texas tower sniper', committed a mass shooting on a Texas university campus. He also shot his wife and mother and was eventually killed by police. An autopsy revealed that he had a tumour

Make the link

...with the Higher option topic of Stress.

adjacent to his amygdala. It was speculated that this may have prompted his aggressive impulses, although it is difficult to be sure.

The amygdala can also be stimulated experimentally. Brain areas tend to become more active when stimulated with electrodes, giving researchers a clue about their function. In one case, when a woman's amygdala was stimulated in this way, she became threatening and verbally abusive (King, 1961).

A limitation in such research is that cases of brain abnormalities are very unusual, while cases of electrical stimulation can't explain everyday aggression. However, the research does support the idea that the amygdala plays a key role in whether we act aggressively or not.

Researchers have also studied the role of neurotransmitters, in particular serotonin. This chemical is best known for its link to mood and is boosted by anti-depressants. Early studies showed that suicides via violent methods (such as gunshot) were often linked to particularly low levels of serotonin. A study by Brown *et al.* (1979) looked at serotonin levels among Navy recruits who were being evaluated for their fitness for duty. They found a significant negative correlation between serotonin levels and levels of aggressive and passive-aggressive behaviour. Coccaro *et al.* (2015, *p. 297)* concluded that *'there is considerable data to support the hypothesis that serotonin is involved in behaviors described as impulsive rather than premeditated'*.

Top tip

The Raine *et al.* (1997) study of brain abnormalities in murderers (see chapter 1) could also be used as research for neural explanations of aggression.

Make the link

...with the biological and evolutionary approaches to psychology.

Evolutionary influences

As mentioned in the introduction (chapter 1), evolutionary psychology is the application of Darwin's theory of natural selection as it applies to human behaviour. The **evolutionary approach** views aggression (and non-aggression) as based on strategies which helped our ancestors to survive, breed and raise offspring effectively (Cosmides & Tooby, 1997).

Some species may use aggression in order to win breeding rights

A major question for evolutionary psychologists is why aggression would have been useful for our ancestors. In considering this, it is useful to study our nearest relatives in the animal kingdom, other primate species.

- Some species, such as baboons, show high levels of aggression among males, with those who are victorious in fights becoming the dominant male, and having breeding rights with a group of females. In these species, males do little or no childcare, and there tends to be considerable **sexual dimorphism** (males and females are physically very different).
- Other species, such as marmosets, show much lower levels of aggression. In these species, males and females form long-term pair bonds, do very little fighting and are more equally involved in raising offspring. There is little sexual dimorphism (the two sexes look very similar and are of a similar size).

Make the link

...with evolutionary explanations of sleep.

Humans are a highly social species and our stressors are largely social (see chapter 6). This means that we might expect aggression to occur within social interactions such as gossip (Dunbar, 1996), something that we commonly observe, and a social context where people are constantly trying to establish a better place within a **social hierarchy**.

In contrast, some species show highly ritualised forms of aggression only at specific times of the year.

Genetic influences

A general principle of the evolutionary approach (see previous page) is that behaviours have evolved to serve a purpose that aids survival or reproduction. However, this doesn't help us to understand why some people are much more aggressive than others. It is of great social importance to know why some people become mass murderers while others go through life engaging in little or no aggression at all. One possible factor at play is individual genetic differences. Is aggression written in our genes?

Researchers have focused on one gene in particular – **monoamine oxidase A** (**MAOA**). There are different versions of this gene and one, called MAOA-L, affects the level of the neurotransmitter serotonin, with implications for aggression (see above).

A study by Caspi *et al.* (2002) looked at the role of MAOA-L in boys who had suffered abuse. They wanted to know why some men who have suffered abuse in childhood grow up to be antisocial and violent, while others do not. They believed that deficient MAOA activity caused by the MAOA-L ('L' standing for low) version of the gene may lead to a person being hyper-reactive to threats, and this could be particularly problematic in early childhood when resilience to demands and threats has not yet fully developed.

In their study, Caspi and colleagues found that the presence of the gene interacted with childhood abuse. Of the men in the study who had experienced abusive childhoods, around 12% had the MAOA-L gene, but these participants were responsible for almost half of the convictions for violent crimes among the sample. This supports the idea that some people are genetically more predisposed to aggression, but that adverse life events play a role too.

In recent years, it has been discovered that genes aren't a simple instruction book for the body and how they act depends on environmental circumstances – genes and the environment interact biologically, and genes can be switched off or on depending on life experiences and the environment. The study of this process is known as **epigenetics**. Epigenetics, along with other factors such as developmental age, affect whether a gene is expressed or not at any given time. Therefore, for identical twins with the same genes, some genes may not be active in one twin due to their life experience. This helps to explain why psychological traits and disorders are never 100% heritable.

Prenatal exposure to testosterone is one factor that could interact with genes. During pregnancy, women's levels of testosterone vary (for reasons that are not fully understood) and this can affect the baby. For example, males who were exposed to more testosterone as foetuses have relatively shorter index fingers compared to their ring fingers. Bailey and Hurd (2005) found a correlation between this physical difference among men and their responses to a physical aggression questionnaire as adults.

Make the link

...with the Depression topic, both in terms of the diathesis-stress model of psychopathology and the use of monoamine oxidase inhibitors (MAOIs) as an antidepressant.

Top tip

Low MAO levels increase the availability of the neurotransmitter serotonin. This is surprising given that low levels of serotonin also link to aggression. It seems that an imbalance in either direction can lead to impulsive behaviour.

Ethology

Ethology is similar in many respects to evolutionary psychology, but there are some key differences. While evolutionary psychology focuses on mating strategies and survival in humans, ethology places more of an emphasis on the natural habitat. It recognises that while behaviours have evolved and are caused by genes, most species also adapt to environmental circumstances and learn from experience. Ethology also places much more of an emphasis on animals rather than studying human societies and early human fossils, and makes greater use of experimental methodology. Two concepts from ethology that are important for the study of aggression include:

- A **fixed action pattern**. This is similar to an 'instinct', but ethologists are interested in how these actions can respond to circumstances and adapt to specific environmental contexts.
- A **releaser** (or 'releasing mechanism'). This is a social action or gesture that prompts another animal to perform a fixed action pattern. For example, a baby bird opening its beak prompts a parent bird to feed it.

Ethologist Karl von Frisch conducted groundbreaking research into the behaviour of honey bees

The field of ethology took off in the mid-twentieth century, led by three European researchers who jointly received a Nobel Prize for their work: Niko Tinbergen, Karl von Frisch, and Konrad Lorenz. The approach of all three differed from mainstream psychology at the time in that they mainly studied animals in natural settings (although they did also conduct lab-based work – see key study).

Tinbergen is known for his studies of aggression, mating and parenting in fish and birds. In particular, he was interested in how animals establish a territory, and show aggression when this is invaded by other individuals. His classic study of stickleback fish (see key study) demonstrated how fixed action patterns relating to mating and aggression are prompted by releasers which the experimenters were able to mimic.

Von Frisch is best known for his study of bees. He discovered that honey bees do a 'waggle dance' when they return to their hive after discovering flowers that contain nectar. In a series of experiments, von Frisch discovered that the figure-of-eight shaped dance informed the other bees of the distance, direction and quantity of the food – it was a form of communication. The dance alerts other bees to the presence of a food source, allowing them to help harvest it for the benefit of the hive.

Lorenz is best known for his work on imprinting. He found that newborn geese form a rapid and relatively permanent bond with their mother, but that this same 'imprinting' process could apply to another large, moving object near to where they hatch – even a person! Lorenz also published a book on the causes of aggression in the animal kingdom, in which he highlighted that most animals have innate releasers that bring to an end a fight, such as a dog rolling over onto its back. He suggested that humans may have lost this trait, leading to violence which doesn't stop. He also argued that the long-distance nature of violence with guns means that we don't get visual and auditory feedback about a victim's suffering – cues which might put a stop to violence among other animals.

Key study: Tinbergen's (1952) study of aggression in sticklebacks

Aim: *The study aimed to explore courtship and aggression in stickleback fish. At the time, ethologists were beginning to challenge an age-old idea that humans are rational while other species act on instincts. Tinbergen wanted to find commonalities across species, and map out the releasers in the environment and among social structures that prompt aggressive behaviour.*

Method: *At mating time, the male stickleback forms a territory from which he will attempt to drive out intruders. He builds a nest in the sand, and his scales change colour so that he has a bright red underside. The male courts the female with a zig-zag 'dance', until she swims towards him with her head up. He then swims into the nest, the female follows and lays her eggs, and the male fertilises the eggs.*

In a lab study, Tinbergen experimented with the releasers that would cause the male to react aggressively. He used model fish of various colours, testing the reactions of the male and female sticklebacks. He also observed the behaviour of two males that were placed very close together.

Sticklebacks engage in distinctive forms of aggression associated with courtship and mating

Findings: *Tinbergen found that a male stickleback would treat most model fish as if they were a rival male, but that the greatest levels of aggression were shown towards the models painted red. When rival (real) males were placed close together, they behaved in a hostile way but the researchers observed very little real fighting; the fish made jerky movements towards each other without actually touching. This fits with the ethological theory that releasers are used to prevent any serious harm being caused – aggression is largely a form of ritual.*

The research also found that a female will attempt to follow a red model fish even if there is no nest present and the model was simply stuck into the sand. However, this behaviour only occurred when the females were pregnant; otherwise they ignored the red model fish.

Overall, the behaviour of the fish showed what ethologists call fixed action patterns, and demonstrated that these are context-specific. The social group can include part of this context, and aggression which was observed was ritualistic rather than involving real fighting. The female fish did not show aggression.

Evaluation: *Tinbergen believed that the links between internal drives and external stimuli could apply to other species, including humans, as could concepts such as territory and ritualised aspects of fighting. However, it is far from clear whether aggression in fish can be generalised to humans. The study did provide some useful evidence that aggression is not purely due to biological drives such as hormones but that these interact with social stimuli and how we interpret them (such as whether someone perceives a stimulus as a threat or not). The study was well controlled, boosting the internal validity and reliability of its findings, though some of the experiments were rather cruel to the fish, raising ethical issues about animal experimentation.*

Key concepts

- Aggression
- Impulsive aggression
- Instrumental aggression
- Sanctioned aggression
- Testosterone
- Mate-guarding
- Amygdala
- Sexual dimorphism
- Social hierarchy
- Monoamine oxidase A (MAOA)
- Evolutionary approach
- Epigenetics
- Ethology
- Fixed action pattern
- Releaser
- Territory

Questions

1. Is aggression generally defined as harming members of one's own species or harming members of another species?
2. What type of aggression is involved when someone gets angry during a sports match and punches another player?
3. Which hormone is strongly associated with aggressive behaviour?
4. In which part of the brain is the amygdala?
5. Can cases of damage to the amygdala easily explain everyday aggression?
6. What term means genes being switched off or on depending on life experiences and the environment?
7. According to the evolutionary approach, why has aggression evolved?
8. Give two reasons why Lorenz thought that aggression is worse in humans than in other species.
9. What is a fixed action pattern?
10. Were Tinbergen's sticklebacks always aggressive towards other fish?

Activities

1. With a partner or group, discuss how you feel that aggression should be defined. Would you include harm to other species, such as hunting? What about harm that occurs within the remit of a person's job, such as giving someone a parking ticket or imprisoning someone?
2. Find out more about the functions of amygdala. To begin with, you could look at the research which suggests that it is involved in responding to aggressive body language in others, as discussed in chapter 11 of this book. See how many links you can make to other topics in psychology.
3. Find out about another experiment from the field of ethology – there are many to choose from. Report back your findings to the class. What do you think are the key principles of ethology, and does it have anything to offer psychology nowadays? How does it differ from behaviourism and the evolutionary approach?

Social explanations of aggression

While it is generally accepted that brain areas and hormones play a role in aggression, this is not the whole story. As the study of epigenetics suggests, it's important to understand the social context as well, as external factors could cause genes to be expressed or not, and may influence the release of hormones. Ethology also places a major emphasis on how the social context interacts with biological factors.

This section focuses on the social-psychological context of aggression and includes factors that lead to learning of aggression by children and the role of workplaces and institutions.

Social learning theory

Social learning theory (SLT) is based on the work of Albert Bandura. It owes a lot to the behaviourist approach to psychology as it, too, explains behaviour primarily in terms of learning through experience. However, SLT also shares some elements with the cognitive approach, as it recognises that people make mental models of actions and their results. These models can be influenced not just by what happens to you as an individual, but also by what happens to others around you. Bandura called this observational learning – learning from watching another person's behaviour experiences (see chapter 1 for further background to the theory).

Social learning theory tries to explain processes that lead to learning, maintaining and using new behavioural actions. Bandura and colleagues were particularly interested in how children learn aggression and violence. At the time – in the 1960s – television was becoming a mainstream fixture in American homes, and there was some concern about how much violence children were watching on their screens.

A key principle of the theory is that behaviour is imitated for a reason and is more likely if an observed behaviour is rewarded. According to this view, children are less likely to imitate the aggression of a TV or movie character that dies, but more likely to imitate the aggression of a heroic character who is rewarded and admired for their actions. However, this principle is vague, as it is difficult to establish objectively what constitutes a reward (except to say that it is anything that increases the level of a behaviour – a circular argument!). For example, a person who smiles and appears to have enjoyed themselves could be considered to have gained a reward.

> **? Discussion point**
>
> Can you think of examples from current movies where characters commit violent acts and are then rewarded?

Evidence

Bandura and his colleagues conducted a number of experiments to test whether children would imitate violence that they observed. Some of the key questions asked in this series of studies included:

- Would children imitate adult aggression that they witness?
- Does the sex of the adult make any difference?
- Does it matter if the violence is seen live or on a TV screen?
- Does it matter if the violence is realistic or not?
- If the adult uses a weapon, would the child do so as well?
- Would verbal aggression be imitated?

Images from the experiment

Their classic paradigm was to show an adult attacking a large inflatable toy doll, nicknamed a **Bobo doll**. The adult would kick or punch the doll, and in some conditions they would hit it with a mallet, or sit on it and repeatedly punch it in the face. Children would sit and watch this either live or via a recording on TV, and would then be given a chance to play in a room containing the doll and various other toys. Disturbingly, children showed a strong tendency to mimic the violence they had seen, with much larger rates of aggression compared to a control group who played in the same room without first witnessing the adult aggression. Boys showed more aggression overall but were more likely to mimic a same-sex role model, and both sexes were more likely to use a weapon if they had seen it being used by a role model. Girls also imitated verbal aggression more when they had witnessed it from a female role model (Bandura *et al.*, 1961).

The same effect was found when the violence had been on screen, and even when a 'cartoon' version was used, where the scene was made to look unrealistic and the adult was dressed up as a cat (see key study).

Key study: Bandura, Ross and Ross (1963): imitation of aggression

Aim: *The study aimed to explore the factors that would lead to children learning and repeating violence that they observed. It was based around the social learning theory framework, which suggests that we can learn things observationally. This contrasted with the mainstream behaviourist approach at the time, which stated that people learn from direct experience. The researchers wanted to know if TV and movie violence was potentially harmful to children by showing them aggressive actions which they would then learn and repeat.*

Method: *The experiment involved 96 preschool children. Their mean age was four years and four months. A questionnaire was given to the children's nursery to assess their everyday level of aggression. They were then divided between three experimental conditions and a control condition, with 24 participants in each, matched according to their aggression scores. It was a field experiment. The three experimental conditions were: an aggressive live model condition, an aggressive film condition, a cartoon-aggression film condition. One male and one female adult acted as role models for all of these conditions, and three observers were also used.*

In the aggressive live model condition, children were taken one at a time to a room that included a Bobo doll and other items, together with an adult role model. After one minute, the adult would attack the Bobo doll, punching him and hitting him with a mallet, and yelling things like 'sock him in the nose' and 'kick him'.

In the aggressive film condition, children were taken to a room to work on potato prints, and the same aggression as described above was shown to them on a colour movie recording.

In the cartoon-aggression film condition, the same model and aggression was shown again, except that this time the (female)

Top tip

The Bandura research is an example of a matched participants design.

Top tip

The Bandura research was a field experiment – it took place in Stanford University Nursery School.

model was dressed up in a cat costume, and the room's surroundings were depicted as a brightly-coloured fantasy land. In this condition, the verbal aggression was done in an unrealistic high-pitched voice, and the whole thing was introduced with music and a picture of a cat labelled 'Herman the cat'.

After this, all children (including the control group, who had not witnessed any aggression) were taken to another room where they started to play with attractive toys but then had them taken away from them – a procedure which was expected to cause what the researchers called 'mild aggression arousal'. Finally, the children were taken to a room that included both aggression-related and neutral toys, and were observed through a one-way mirror.

Findings: *The researchers looked for various types of aggression among the children – verbal and physical – as well as whether it was a direct imitation of the role model or another, unrelated type of aggression. They also divided results by the gender of both the role model and the child (allowing comparisons of same-sex versus opposite-sex models). They found that boys were more aggressive overall, and particularly so if the role model was male. Females imitated verbal aggression more from a female model than a male. Overall, there were more violent acts from participants following the live aggression condition than the other groups, but the difference was slight. The number of violent acts following video and cartoon conditions were both closer to the live aggression condition than they were to the control group. There were around three times as many violent acts from those in the cartoon condition than from those in the control group.*

The study suggests that witnessing violent acts can lead to repetition of those acts, even by young children, and even in unrealistic TV contexts. This is important when media violence is relatively commonplace. The study also has some implications for the concept of active learning. Typically, it is assumed that learners need to actively engage in a task in order to learn something, but in this study passive observation was enough to affect behaviour.

Evaluation: *The first thing that might occur to you is that this study wasn't very ethical! Young children were deliberately exposed to violence, simply to see what would happen, and those who did become more aggressive could well have harmed classmates or siblings. However, it could be argued that the level of play-aggression witnessed was little more than they would see on a regular basis on TV at home or in the playground. A strength of the study was its use of more than one observer. The researchers measured the level of inter-observer reliability (see page 208). In this study, ratings made by different observers were very strongly correlated, showing that the observations provided a reliable form of data. Overall it was a well-controlled study.*

Although the study can tell us about the effects of role models on children's aggression and how this operates through the media, it's not clear whether the experimental task caused aggression or just influenced the form that it took, as some of the control group children also showed high levels of aggressive play.

Top tip

A later study (Bandura, 1965) showed adult models being rewarded or punished, and found less imitation if the adult was punished. However, this difference disappeared if the child was given an incentive to copy the behaviour.

Some researchers have tried to tackle the question of what causes prison violence

Deprivation versus importation

In the mid-twentieth century, America experienced a major problem with violence committed by prison inmates, with rioting and attacks on prison guards being commonplace. This led to a series of fascinating research studies which have raised major questions about the entire nature of social behaviour. In particular, psychologists began to reject the traditional view that prisoners do bad things because they are inherently bad people, and instead focused on the situational pressures and social processes at play.

Sykes (1958) made an early contribution to this field, and one which focused on the conditions experienced by prisoners. He suggested that although American prison inmates were not subject to some of the cruel punishments of the past, they were deprived of key needs and wants in life. This led to frustration, and therefore to aggression. In particular, Sykes argued that the prisoners were deprived of the following five things:

1. **Liberty:** the men were not free to go where they pleased – they had been locked up and needed permission to wash or go to the toilet.
2. **Goods:** the men were not able to have the possessions they wanted, or to buy things that would make their lives more pleasant.
3. **Sexual relationships:** the men were not able to engage in (heterosexual) relationships while in prison.
4. **Autonomy:** the men couldn't do what they wanted or make choices about how to spend their time, as they had to follow prison timetables.
5. **Security:** although locked up, the men often didn't feel safe, and this led to stress and a sense of helplessness.

Sykes' idea is known as a **deprivation model** of aggression. It has certain strengths. It fits with a classic idea that frustration leads to aggression – the **frustration-aggression hypothesis**. According to Dollard *et al.* (1939), aggression is always preceded by frustration, and frustration always leads to aggression. It's easy to see why the forms of deprivation identified by Sykes would lead to frustration, and therefore (according to the hypothesis), to aggression. However, later researchers have argued that the frustration-aggression hypothesis is too simplistic – while frustration may trigger aggression, it can also be expressed in other ways.

Irwin and Cressey (1962) had a different explanation. They suggested that the reason prisoners are violent in prison is because they bring violent habits into the institution when they are imprisoned. Their **importation model** essentially argued that some prisoners are violent people outside, and they continue to be violent people inside.

However, rather than basing this argument on a criminal's personality or on biological factors, Irwin and Cressey (1962) thought that prisoners imported their outside **subculture** into prison life, and that this subculture may be influenced by gangs or other aggressive social norms. They felt that previous researchers had mistakenly focused on the function of prison violence inside the prison itself (such as getting what you want by fighting), and ignored *'the deviant cultures which exist outside any given prison'* (p. 145).

Irwin and Cressey focused their research on three key subcultures:

- **Thief subculture:** this is the dominant subculture for most criminals outside of prison. It is dominated by loyalty and secrecy, and a disregard for society's rules. Skill, loyalty and toughness are highly valued.
- **Convict subculture:** this is the dominant subculture within the prison. For prisoners who have been inside for a long time or who have grown up in institutions, it is necessary to be tough and manipulative in order to avoid being controlled by others. This subculture has similarities to gang culture on the outside of the institution, and Irwin and Cressey also link it to harder elements of lower class US culture.
- **Legitimate subculture:** this is the dominant subculture for people who have had little previous experience of criminality, such as first-time offenders. They show low levels of aggression at first, but this will increase if they adopt convict subculture.

Irwin and Cressey thought that people of all three types of subculture would behave differently in prison. The prisoner from the thief subculture is mainly interested in doing their time as quickly as possible and getting out, and will try to conduct profitable business while inside. The prisoner from the convict subculture, on the other hand, is motivated to gain status and control over other prisoners. Both will participate in riots but for different reasons: the thief out of a sense of loyalty to the group, and the convict because his desire for control has been frustrated.

Top tip

A social norm is a behaviour that is widely accepted in a particular group or culture, but which is not inevitable and may change over time.

? Discussion point

How many of Sykes' five deprivations can also be applied to the life of a school pupil?

Evidence

Most researchers agree that deprivation is not an absolute condition, but is relative to other people or groups, and relative to a person's expectations. According to Davies (1970), our expectations of how well we are going to do in the future is based on past or current experience. For example, if someone's conditions have been improving, they expect things to keep getting better. Anger and frustration can result from reality not meeting those expectations – even if people are better off in absolute terms than they were in the past. This is illustrated by the considerable hostility shown by white Americans towards black Americans after desegregation. Despite being objectively better off than blacks, whites tended to feel that they weren't as well off as they should be (Vanneman & Pettigrew, 1972).

A strength of the importation model is that it fits with what we know about conformity (see chapter 10). If someone is a lone conventional convict among a majority with criminal subcultures, the Asch research would suggest that they are likely to conform to the majority and adopt their behaviour, even when they know it is wrong. The theory also fits with the cognitive approach and its view of how beliefs and schemas affect behaviour.

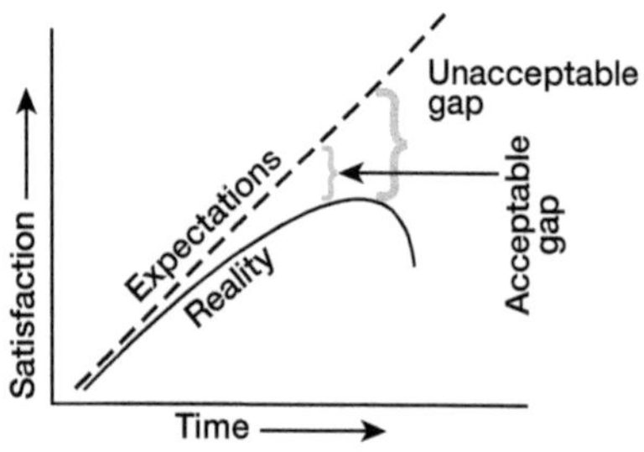

Attempts have been made to apply the concept of importation to reduce aggression, but a review by Gravel *et al.* (2013) found that attempts to control and separate gang members inside prison to minimise the effects of their subculture had met with variable success.

Ekland-Olson *et al.* (1983) found that the main factor affecting prison violence was the age of the prisoners, with younger prisoners committing more aggressive acts. This speaks against both theories, as prisoners of all ages face similar deprivations, and would theoretically import similar subcultures into prison. However, it could be argued that younger prisoners are more frustrated by deprivation than older prisoners.

Overall, although these theories helped to identify some major psychological issues affecting prisoner behaviour, neither fully explains why aggression occurs or why it varies from prison to prison within the same society.

Make the link

...between Sykes' deprivation model and Maslow's hierarchy of needs (see chapter 1).

Dysfunctional institutions

Another researcher whose work was stimulated by the state of America's prisons was Philip Zimbardo. According to Zimbardo, aggression has multiple causes, most of which relate to the social norms of the situation, rather than to the subculture or personality (i.e. the disposition) of the prison inmates, or to specific issues with their needs. Zimbardo also highlighted the high level of aggression shown by many prison guards of the time, despite not experiencing the deprivations identified by Sykes (see above). He focused on **dysfunctional institutions** – places separated from the outside world, with a harmful set of values and social norms that were difficult to scrutinise or challenge.

Zimbardo and colleagues conducted a study which became famous as much for its questionable ethics as for its results – the **Stanford prison experiment**. They converted the basement of Stanford University's psychology department into a mock prison, complete with prison cells as well as a cupboard that was available for solitary confinement of prisoners. They recruited student volunteers to fill their 'prison', and randomly allocated each of these participants to the role of prisoner or guard. The experiment was made highly realistic, with local police recruited to 'arrest' participants, authentic uniforms, and bread and water punishments for misbehaviour.

One of the key conclusions of the study was that 'guards' and 'prisoners' adapted to their assigned roles, with the guards becoming increasingly abusive and the prisoners cowed and submissive. Guards who didn't participate in abusive treatment of prisoners were forced into line by their peers, leading to social pressure to conform to aggressive norms. Essentially, there was no workable mechanism for questioning or changing the values of the institution. The prisoners were very distressed but seemed largely to accept their ordeal without demanding to be released from the study; as Zimbardo *et al.* (1973) put it *'the mind is a formidable jailor'*. The researchers argued that in the real world, prisoner and guard violence is not due to personality, subculture or deprivation but because they adopt the expectations of their social role (Haney *et al.*, 1973) – an idea known as **situational attribution**.

Later researchers have criticised the conclusions of the Stanford prison experiment. Haslam *et al.* (2018) accessed a recording from the study in which an experimenter can be heard saying to a reluctant guard, 'we need you to be tough'. They argue that the guards were instructed to behave harshly to prisoners and were following the researchers' lead, rather than automatically adopting a social role.

Another interesting and disturbing study of the effects of an institution on aggression was James Calhoun's rat city experiment. If you studied the Individual Behaviour topic of Stress, you may remember that Calhoun (1962) conducted an observational study into the effects of overcrowding on rats. He allowed rats to breed freely until there were 80 rats in a space that was only suitable for 48. Many rats became aggressive – some cannibalised or sexually assaulted other rats, or attacked them in gangs. The findings from the rat city are difficult to generalise to humans, but they are suggestive: could some of the violence that often plagues inner cities and prisons be due to dysfunctional, overcrowded conditions?

Make the link

...between the topics of Stress and Aggression.

Questions

1. Which technological development were Bandura and colleagues concerned about?
2. To which psychological approach is social learning theory strongly linked?
3. True or false: in the Bandura *et al.* research, girls imitated verbal aggression more if it was witnessed from a female role model rather than a male.
4. True or false: in the Bandura *et al.* research, boys showed more aggression overall.
5. What did Bandura and colleagues do to make the action less realistic in the cartoon-aggression film condition? Name three things.
6. Which subculture was most strongly associated with aggression, according to the importation model?
7. Name two of the things that prisoners are deprived of, according to Sykes (1958).
8. Name three things that Zimbardo and colleagues did to make the Stanford prison experiment more realistic.
9. Does everyone agree that aggression in the Stanford prison experiment was due to the guards adopting their social role?
10. What did Calhoun's 'rat city' study suggest about aggression?

Key concepts

- Social learning theory (SLT)
- Bobo doll
- Deprivation model
- Importation model
- Thief subculture
- Convict subculture
- Legitimate subculture
- Dysfunctional institutions
- Stanford prison experiment
- Situational attribution
- Frustration-aggression hypothesis

Activities

1. Draw a mind map showing each of the social-psychological explanations of aggression. The four main branches should be:
   - social learning theory
   - the deprivation model
   - the importation model
   - Zimbardo's theory of situational attribution/dysfunctional institutions.

   Then add further details, including concepts and research studies.
2. Find out about the BBC prison experiment – a follow-up study to the Stanford prison experiment (http://www.bbcprisonstudy.org). It was conducted by Haslam and Reicher in 2002. The findings and conclusions were notably different from those of Zimbardo and colleagues. Find out why, and report back your findings to the class. You can also read their critique of the Milgram and Zimbardo studies here: http://journals.plos.org/plosbiology/article?id=10.1371/journal.pbio.1001426.

Top tip

The media includes multiple different sources of information and entertainment, including TV, the internet, music videos, movies, games, newspapers, radio, and podcasts.

Observation of violence could prime later aggression in children, even if there is no immediate imitation

Aggression and the media

People are often concerned about whether the **media** has a harmful effect on people, and these concerns are nothing new. They informed Bandura's 1960s studies into the effect of TV role models on children (see above), and more recently attention has turned to the effects of violent video games and the Internet.

However, some researchers believe that these concerns are fuelled by moral panic, and that there is no real problem. Gauntlett (2005) argues that concerns about the effect of the media on violence are exaggerated, and that every generation has experienced changes and new technology that have initially caused concerns. Similarly, Pinker (2011) argues that, historically, levels of violence have decreased, despite the growing range of media influences we are exposed to.

Cognitive priming

Cognitive priming is the effect of prior exposure to a stimulus on later behaviour. For example, if you heard a song a few days ago and you hear it again today, the chances are that you will like it more than if you had never heard it before. The previous exposure to the stimulus has changed your later response – even if you don't remember hearing the song before!

Cognitive priming has also been used as an explanation for aggression. The media might not directly cause aggression in children but, it is argued, they may learn aggressive responses, which could affect the way they respond to a threatening or stressful situation in the future. Cognitively, priming could be establishing schemas (or 'scripts') for how to act in violent situations.

Evidence

In one experiment on priming, Bushman (1998) showed people 15-minute clips from two movies, one violent (*Karate Kid III*) and one non-violent (*Gorillas in the Mist*), and then gave them a word association task. Some of the words used in the task had more than one meaning, one linked to violence and one not – for example 'box'. After each prompt word, participants were told to think of as many word associations as they could, as quickly as possible, and the researchers analysed these associations. They found that people were more likely to make the association with the violent words after watching the violent clip.

If it's the case that such priming in the real-world causes people to behave more aggressively after watching TV or movies, then there should be evidence of society-wide increases in aggression as TV watching increases. However, such evidence is far from conclusive. Television was introduced to the island of St Helena, in the South Atlantic, in 1995. Researchers studied the behaviour of children on the island before and after this event, in a research project that began in 1993. Questionnaires were given to both teachers and parents, and observations made in school playgrounds. Ultimately, the researchers concluded that television had made very little difference to aggression (Charlton, 1998). There were very few behavioural problems on the island before the study, and this remained the case after the introduction of TV. However, it has been suggested that some of the more violent children's shows popular on the mainland were not broadcast on St. Helena.

A different finding emerged from a study by Williams (1986) in a mountainous region of Canada. She was able to study two towns which received a television signal for the first time – one of which received one channel, and one of which received multiple channels. A third town in the study had no TV reception, and acted as a control group. She found increased levels of aggression in the towns which received TV, as well as reduced child–adult interaction, more gender stereotypes, and decreased IQs and creativity scores among the children. One obvious difference in this study compared to Charlton's (1998) was that it studied regular mainland towns, whereas St. Helena (with a population of just over 4,000) is a tightly knit isolated community where there was a strong level of community support and oversight, minimising antisocial behaviour.

Top tip

The experiments of both Williams (1986) and Charlton (1998) are natural experiments. The researchers could not directly control the independent variable – it happened naturally, without their intervention.

More broadly, it's difficult to know how representative either of these studies are. Worldwide, IQ scores increased at a rate of around 3 points per decade throughout the period that TV became more widespread (Flynn, 1984), which conflicts with the findings in the Canadian study. In combination, the two studies do suggest that the effects of TV are likely to be context-specific, depending on what is watched and on the general culture, activity levels and family networks which the children experience.

Top tip

The Bandura *et al.* (1963) study relates to the effects of TV on aggression, making it a suitable key study when discussing media influences on aggression.

Computer games

Violent **computer games** have been the subject of research scrutiny for many years. Some school shootings and other violent incidents have been linked – at least by the media – to the perpetrators' use of violent games. Perhaps the best-known example is the Columbine school shooting, where the two teenage shooters were known to have been fans of the most popular first-person shooter game of the time, 'Doom'.

On the other hand, many children play these games, and most do not commit violent crimes. Non-experimental research tends to rely on correlations, and cause-and-effect can be hard to establish: if people who play violent video games show more aggression, is this because of the games, or could it be the case that people who are already aggressive are more drawn to violent games?

Evidence from social learning theory provides an initial rationale for the effects of a video game on real-world violence. According to this view, playing the game results in observational learning, where the violent actions of the game become part of a player's behavioural repertoire. In an active computer game (especially a first-person game), this effect may be stronger than simply watching violence passively on TV.

The evidence for an effect of violent video games on aggression is limited

Evidence

To date, the evidence linking computer games and violence is actually quite weak, and relies on laboratory studies where 'aggression' is tested by measures such as administering punishments during a game. In one such study, Anderson and Dill (2000) used a task where participants had the option of administering a punishment in the form of a loud noise to a (fictional) partner. Participants who had previously engaged in a violent video game were more likely to administer this punishment for longer (see key study).

However, critics have argued that such laboratory models of aggression lack external validity, and that the violent and non-violent games studied may differ on other variables such as difficulty or competitiveness, leading to confounding variables (Ferguson, 2014). In addition, many of the early studies which apparently demonstrated a connection between video games and aggression failed to replicate in later research (Ferguson, op cit.). Levels of violence across society have been dropping at the same time as computer games have become more popular – a scenario that is difficult to square with the hypothesis that video games make people more aggressive.

Some researchers have made the case that computer games can have positive psychological effects. For example, Durkin and Barber (2002) found that 16-year-olds who regularly played computer games were as well adjusted as their peers, and no more prone to engaging in risky behaviour. Gamers also scored more favourably on measures of family closeness, positive school engagement, mental health, substance use, and obedience to parents, when compared to those who never played computer games at all. It has also been argued that the cognitive demands of computer games can develop working memory (Johnson, 2005), as well as having educational potential. Cooperative games may boost altruistic behaviour.

There remains some concern about the specific case of highly violent games and this is reflected in the age limits which have been placed on some titles. However, an interesting development in recent years is that violent computer games are now most often played cooperatively, via the Internet, rather than individually. In a series of experiments, Velez *et al.* (2016) concluded that playing violent games cooperatively can offset the effects that they would otherwise have on players' aggression levels.

Key study: Anderson and Dill's (2000) study of violent video games

Aim: *The researchers wanted to test the effects of violent versus non-violent games. Studies of the effects of violent games are often non-experimental, making it hard to separate out confounding variables. If you compare gamers versus non-gamers in the real world, there may be some pre-existing differences between the groups – perhaps violent people are drawn to violent video games, rather than video games making people violent. Anderson and Dill aimed to avoid this confounding variable by randomly allocating students to violent or non-violent games in an experiment.*

Method: *The researchers allocated psychology students to either a violent video game ('Wolfenstein 3D') or a non-violent game (Myst) in a lab experiment. Overall, 210 students took part (106 male and 104 female). It was important to hide the aim from participants in order to avoid demand characteristics. The researchers therefore told participants that the study aimed to test how quickly they learned motor skills, and how this affected later tasks.*

Participants played the game for 30 minutes, stopping after 15 mins to complete a questionnaire provided by researchers. One week later, researchers invited participants back to play a competitive one-to-one reaction time game. The participants were led to believe they were playing against another participant in the next cubicle. In fact, they were alone, and the researchers had fixed the outcome so that they would win around half of the tasks. After each trial, they could 'punish' their opponent by playing a blast of noise in the neighbouring cubicle. Crucially, participants could pick the noise volume and duration.

Findings: *The key finding was that those who had previously played the violent game gave longer blasts of noise to their (fictional) opponents. Males generally show more violence throughout society and in other species (as we have seen throughout this chapter), but in this task, the reverse was found – women showed a greater degree of aggression by delivering longer blasts of noise than men did. The researchers concluded that violent video games can lead directly to long-term increases in violent behaviour due to cognitive priming. They also suggested that the sex difference may be due to women's greater dislike of the games during the experiment, as well as social norms which favour more subtle displays of aggression among women.*

Evaluation: *The study was a lab experiment, replicable and well controlled, and used a large sample. However, it had several limitations that should be considered. First, in so far as violent games have an effect on aggression, the observed effects could be reduced due to experience because, on average, men play video games more than women. Second, despite what they were told about the aim of the study, the participants were psychology students and may have guessed what the researchers were looking for. They may have altered their behaviour to fit expectations.*

Disinhibition due to anonymity can increase aggressive and antisocial actions

Third, although the differences in noise duration were statistically significant, they were rather small in real terms, with a mean of 6.81 seconds for the violent game condition versus 6.65 seconds for the non-violent game condition. Finally, the task is unrealistic and may lack external validity – showing aggression by playing loud noises is quite different from attacking someone in real life, and it's hard to be sure that the participants would be any more likely to stab or shoot someone. It might have been expected that more aggressive people would use louder blasts of noise but no differences were found in the choice of noise intensity.

Overall, it is an interesting study and contribution to the emerging picture of the role of computer games in violence.

Disinhibition

Often we are inhibited from acting in a particular way due to social norms or the potential consequences of our actions. It's possible that in computer games, or other online contexts, people feel disinhibited due to the buffer that exists between their actions and any potential harm that they may cause.

Disinhibition can also play a role in the real world. Mann (1981) has described the phenomenon of the baiting (deliberately taunting) crowd. He analysed newspaper reports of people committing suicide by jumping from buildings or bridges, and found that often a crowd had gathered and witnessed the act. Shockingly, in almost half of cases where there had been a crowd, some baiting (such as shouting 'jump') had occurred. Baiting was more likely to occur in large crowds and in conditions of darkness, suggesting that anonymity played a role in the behaviour.

According to Festinger *et al.* (1952), our sense of ourselves as individuals, along with how we are perceived on a personal level, motivates us to follow social norms such as politeness. When we are in a crowd or otherwise anonymous, such social norms no longer hold, and some of our more aggressive and selfish urges start to reveal themselves. In a similar vein, Zimbardo (1969) found that wearing a hood to conceal their identity led to people being more obedient in the Milgram electric shock paradigm (and therefore made them more likely to harm another person).

Online, this kind of dynamic can be seen in the context of 'trolls' who post deliberately offensive messages online. One reason that people may be more aggressive online is that they are disinhibited due to not fearing the consequences of their actions. Suler (2004) links this to several factors, most notably:

- Invisibility: the online trolls can't be seen or identified.
- Asynchronicity: there is often no immediate negative reaction to their behaviour, meaning that trolls don't get negative feedback as happens with offline rudeness or hurtful behaviour.

Make the link

...with obedience to commit aggressive acts in Milgram's experiments, and with the role of power, status and uniform in obedience.

- Dissociative imagination: the trolls often adopt an alternate identity online and are unconstrained by the norms of their offline persona.
- Lack of authority: in real life, authority figures display obvious trappings of status via uniforms or the way they dress. Online, the lack of such status markers makes it easier for anyone to become a target.

However, Suler also recognises that individual differences such as personality play a role, too – some online trolls are simply very unpleasant people.

Top tip

If asked to analyse media influences on aggression, comparing the different explanations can be a good source of marks. You could also identify the aims and principles of the explanations, and analyse the methodology of the supporting evidence.

Questions

1. What is meant by cognitive priming?
2. Which explanation, cognitive priming or disinhibition, suggests that people are more aggressive because they are less affected by the consequences of their actions?
3. What was the independent variable in Bushman (1998)'s study?
4. On which island was TV introduced for the first time in the 1990s, facilitating a natural experiment into the effects of TV violence?
5. If people who play violent video games also show more aggression, does that prove that video games cause aggression?
6. What was the dependent variable in Anderson & Dill's (2000) study?
7. Give an example of a possible confounding variable in studies of computer game violence.
8. State two positive characteristics that have been linked to playing video games.
9. What is meant by disinhibition?
10. Give one factor that affects the aggressive behaviour of online trolls.

Key concepts

- Media
- Computer games
- Cognitive priming
- Disinhibition

Activities

1. How many people in your class or year group play computer games, and what type do they play? Conduct a small-scale survey. Distinguish between violent and non-violent games, and you could also ask if people play cooperatively online or if they prefer to play solo games. If possible, try to find out if your findings are representative of society as a whole.
2. Stage a class debate about the role of violent media. One side should argue for and one side against the idea that violent TV, movies and computer games are harmful. If possible, try to combine this debate with a Media Studies or Sociology class.

End of topic project

In your class or another suitable group, conduct a simple observation study into aggression, as follows:

- First, identify a suitable piece of video footage of animal aggression. (For ethical reasons, as well as validity, do not use footage of human aggression; on TV, such behaviour is either scripted, or highly ritualised, e.g. boxing). A documentary showing animal fights within the same species, such as during mating season, would be a good choice.
- Now prepare an observation schedule (see chapter 8). Brainstorm likely aggressive behaviours. For this type of observation, a good choice would be to make a tally mark each time a behaviour occurs. Alternatively, you could write verbal descriptions at 30-second intervals.
- Draw conclusions.
- Prepare and deliver a short talk to your class on what you found and concluded from this observation. Do your findings fit with any of the theories discussed in this chapter? What can be generalised from animal to human aggression? Refer to at least one relevant background research study.

End of topic specimen exam questions

1.	Briefly explain two neural or hormonal factors affecting aggression.	4 marks
2.	Analyse the evolutionary explanation of aggression.	12 marks
3.	Explain the role of dysfunctional institutions in aggression, referring to research evidence.	6 marks
4.	Evaluate one research study into media influences on aggression.	8 marks
5.	Analyse the links between the media and aggressive behavior.	15 marks

Answers

Answers

Chapter 1: The biological approach (page 11)

1. *A neuron.*
2. *The central nervous system.*
3. *Broca's area.*
4. *Emotions.*
5. *Oxytocin.*
6. *Depression and eating disorders.*
7. *A gland.*
8. *A gene.*
9. *Environmental factors stop the gene from having an effect on the individual, i.e. it does not do anything.*
10. *'et al.' stands for 'et alii', which means 'and others' in Latin.*

Chapter 1: The psychoanalytic approach (page 19)

1. *The id.*
2. *An iceberg.*
3. *The anal stage.*
4. *A fear of horses.*
5. *Oedipus complex.*
6. *Denial.*
7. *Reaction formation.*
8. *Projection.*
9. *Free association.*
10. *One patient/longitudinal/lots of in-depth data/several techniques used/ideal for unusual cases.*

Chapter 1: The cognitive approach (page 25)

1. *A cognitive process – something that occurs between a stimulus and the behavioural response.*
2. *Computer.*
3. *He said that cognition is a meaningful process, and computers do not try to make sense of stimuli.*
4. *A schema is a set of ideas or a pattern of thought about a particular concept or situation.*
5. *A script is similar to a schema, but it concerns how to act in social situations.*
6. *Jean Piaget.*
7. *A child focusing on one aspect of a problem and ignoring other important aspects, such as the height or width of a water glass when judging volume.*
8. *Personalisation.*
9. *A distortion in thinking, where the person focuses on a small negative detail.*
10. *Cognitive behavioural therapy (CBT).*

Chapter 1: The behaviourist approach (page 32)

1. *False. It shows classical conditioning.*
2. *Classical conditioning.*
3. *Reinforcement.*
4. *Punishment. Negative reinforcement strengthens a behaviour.*
5. *Classical conditioning.*
6. *False.*
7. *True.*
8. *The Skinner box.*
9. *Social learning/social learning theory.*
10. *No. Other researchers such as Chomsky argued that it was over-simplistic and inaccurate.*

Chapter 1: The evolutionary approach (page 39)

1. *Charles Darwin.*
2. *Modern humans have existed for around 200,000 years but various other species of the genus 'Homo' for around 2 million years.*
3. *Yes, humans are classified as apes.*
4. *No, apes (like us) are generally larger and have certain key physical differences including no tail, opposable thumbs and brachiating arms (able to swing beneath branches).*
5. *Our ancestors probably lived in rainforests up to around 5 million years ago, but for the key period of human evolution – when we started walking, using language, using fire and making complex tools – we lived in an open savannah environment.*
6. *Approximately 12,000 years.*
7. *The environment of evolutionary adaptiveness.*

8. *A person who lives by foraging and hunting rather than farming.*
9. *150 individuals.*
10. *Fossil evidence is often incomplete, meaning we cannot know everything that happened during human evolution/sometimes evolution is used to justify sexism or immoral behaviour, but this is a case of the naturalistic fallacy/ humans are very different from other species, making comparisons with apes very limited.*

Chapter 2: The biology of sleep (page 52)

1. *Non-REM sleep/nREM sleep.*
2. *Circadian rhythms.*
3. *The brain's electrical activity/brain waves.*
4. *Five sleep stages, 4–5 times per night, so 20–25 stages in total.*
5. *Dreams.*
6. *'Time giver'.*
7. *The hypothalamus.*
8. *Melatonin.*
9. *Adenosine.*
10. *The late teens.*

Chapter 2: The restoration theory of sleep (page 59)

1. *To repair their bodies.*
2. *Sleep could reduce danger from predators/ sleep could reduce how much energy an animal uses when not finding food.*
3. *Repairing injuries/removal of waste chemicals/replenishing neurotransmitters.*
4. *Because it is physically inactive and therefore energy is not being used for other jobs.*
5. *Non-REM sleep.*
6. *A longer period of non-REM sleep.*
7. *They believed that REM sleep is essential for brain restoration and slow-wave sleep is essential for bodily restoration.*
8. *Hospital patients who had longer REM sleep after drug overdoses or spinal surgery/the level of neurotransmitters in the brain reduces during the day.*
9. *For the brain.*
10. *No. There are large variations, e.g. carnivores sleep more than herbivores.*

Chapter 2: Explanations of dreams (page 63)

1. *Latent content.*
2. *Giraffes.*
3. *Condensation.*
4. *It states that most dreams have an important hidden meaning, whereas the biological and cognitive approaches both assume that dream content is a by-product of other processes.*
5. *Activation-synthesis.*
6. *The idea that dream content will link to what we have been thinking about or doing during the day.*
7. *Cause it to be forgotten/deleted.*
8. *In order to make space and to avoid obsessions or hallucinations.*
9. *Neural network computer models of learning, in which reverse learning was shown to be useful.*
10. *No. Sleep is generally thought to be beneficial to memory, while a lack of sleep harms cognitive functioning.*

Chapter 2: Factors that affect sleep quality (page 71)

1. *Bad mood/reduced functioning/lack of alertness/depression/coronary heart disease/ digestive illnesses/reproductive problems, etc.*
2. *Hallucination of a suit of furry worms/a nurse dripping saliva/the scientist's tie jumping/ hotel drawer spurting flames.*
3. *Caffeine/amphetamines/alcohol/ anti-depressants.*
4. *Caffeine blocks adenosine receptors, meaning that we don't experience as much fatigue due to the build-up of adenosine in the brain.*
5. *The screen contains light and, in particular, a lot of blue wavelengths. These suppress melatonin release, delaying sleep and harming sleep quality.*
6. *Difficulty sleeping due to air travel to a different time zone.*
7. *Six days of 'nightshifts'.*
8. *Use of bright light as a zeitgeber to change circadian rhythms, combined with total darkness when sleeping.*
9. *A sleep problem or disorder relating to abnormal behaviours while sleeping rather than a problem with the amount of sleep.*
10. *They can treat people who have insomnia, jet lag or problems from shift work by promoting release of melatonin, and therefore sleepiness, on an appropriate regular 24-hour schedule.*

Chapter 3: What is a phobia? (page 78)

1. *The level of distress/the level of harm.*
2. *Anxiety disorders.*
3. *A person with a phobia may have had a bad or scary experience at some point, such as being harmed by the object of their fear.*

4. *It harms the person's ability to lead a healthy and fulfilled life.*
5. *A diagnostic system used to identify psychological problems in an objective way.*
6. *A strong and irrational fear of the particular stimulus or situation/avoidance of the stimulus or situation.*
7. *Avoidance.*
8. *Avoiding certain situations may make it harder for the person to lead an ordinary life and may conflict with their work life.*
9. *A very extreme anxiety response which tends to feature raised heart rate, sweating and nausea.*
10. *If they are unexpectedly exposed to the stimulus that they fear.*

Chapter 3: Types of phobias (page 82)

1. *A specific phobia.*
2. *Heights/water/enclosed spaces/weather.*
3. *They are common; over 6% of the population in Europe and North America suffers from a specific phobia severe enough to be diagnosed at any given time.*
4. *False. They are long lasting and can be lifelong.*
5. *Social anxiety disorder.*
6. *Public speaking/eating in public/socialising or hosting/meeting new people/speaking to an authority figure/etc.*
7. *The worry that the sufferer will try but fail to make a good impression.*
8. *They could experience extreme anxiety or have a panic attack.*
9. *No. Many can go outside in certain circumstances, e.g. when travelling by car.*
10. *Female.*

Chapter 3: Genetic explanations of phobias (page 85)

1. *The nature-nurture debate.*
2. *Identical (monozygotic/MZ) twins and non-identical (dizygotic/DZ) twins.*
3. *Medical, social anxiety and agoraphobia.*
4. *That genes play a significant but not overwhelming role.*
5. *We have a genetic tendency, meaning that we're more likely to learn that fear.*
6. *False.*
7. *No. It's not clear that they had any long-term fear.*
8. *They appeared to fear a smell which they had not previously experienced, but which their biological father had been taught to fear.*
9. *No. It went against the view that biological inheritance is a slow process, and that learning of new memories can only happen in an individual, and cannot be inherited.*
10. *It is difficult to generalise from mice to humans/it is difficult to generalise from a learned fear of a smell to the experience of phobias or social anxiety/human fears involve more thought processes/the researchers have not established a biological mechanism.*

Chapter 3: Behaviourist explanations of phobias (page 90)

1. *The behaviourist approach.*
2. *Classical conditioning.*
3. *Operant conditioning.*
4. *Little Albert, an 11-month-old boy.*
5. *Via an aversive experience where fear/pain are associated with a stimulus such as an animal.*
6. *Via operant conditioning. The avoidance behaviour takes the individual away from the feared stimulus, and this acts as a reward.*
7. *Negative reinforcement.*
8. *First the rats learned to fear the buzzer, then they learned to avoid it by jumping a barrier.*
9. *Seeing the parent experience an aversive experience could lead to observational learning.*
10. *They lack an explanation of the thought processes in phobias/the research is largely based on animals.*

Chapter 3: Therapies for phobias (page 94)

1. *A talking therapy, such as behavioural therapies or cognitive behavioural therapy (CBT).*
2. *Classical conditioning.*
3. *The therapy can be highly stressful to the individual, as it involves exposure to the feared stimulus.*
4. *A hierarchy of fears/anxiety hierarchy.*
5. *The least feared.*
6. *Cognitive behavioural therapy.*
7. *Both.*
8. *Social anxiety disorder/depression/autism/shyness.*
9. *Treatment involving chemicals such as anti-anxiety drugs.*
10. *These forms of therapy have a good rate of success/unlike drugs, there are no risky side effects/it costs money to see a therapist, although it may be free on the NHS or similar/these therapies may fail to tackle the root cause of the phobia/etc.*

Chapter 4: What is depression? (page 99)

1. *Such opinions are subjective and highly influenced by social norms.*
2. *Being unable to keep yourself clean and fed/ not having positive relationships/being unable to concentrate on everyday tasks/being unable to hold down a job/etc.*
3. *What symptoms are shown and how long they are shown for.*
4. *Mood disorders/eating disorders/sleep disorders (or anxiety disorders etc).*
5. *It has medicalised normal experiences/lack of validity/too many new disorders/accused of being too closely linked to drug companies.*
6. *20–30%.*
7. *True.*
8. *Two weeks.*
9. *No. The symptoms are the same but are shown over a longer time period.*
10. *The individual periodically experiences an episode of mania – with high, unrealistic moods and energetic behaviour.*

Chapter 4: Biological explanations of depression (page 105)

1. *Neurotransmitter imbalance theory.*
2. *Serotonin.*
3. *The thyroid hormones.*
4. *A predisposition in someone's biology or thought processes makes them more vulnerable to a psychological problem.*
5. *They found a 46% rate for identical twins, compared to 20% for non-identical twins.*
6. *This fails to take account of social processes/ leads to missed opportunities to intervene in social processes.*
7. *Treatment based on chemicals, i.e. drugs.*
8. *SSRIs and SNRIs.*
9. *They have fewer side effects and may be just as effective as SSRIs.*
10. *Memory loss.*

Chapter 4: Cognitive explanations of depression (page 112)

1. *Self, world and future.*
2. *I am useless/this problem is all my fault/I did this really badly.*
3. *No. Like any schema, they involve complex interconnected knowledge and feelings, and are difficult to change.*
4. *I must do well and win approval, or else I am a bad person/other people must behave well or else they deserve to be punished/my life must be easy, without any discomfort or danger, or else I can't enjoy life.*
5. *Cognitive behavioural therapy.*
6. *True.*
7. *Cognitive restructuring.*
8. *Both CBT and antidepressants were better than a placebo; drugs worked faster but CBT caught up and did not have negative side effects. A combination was best overall.*
9. *CBT or a combination of drugs and CBT.*
10. *No. Because someone could have negative thoughts because of their low mood rather than vice versa.*

Chapter 5: Memory stores (page 119)

1. *Encoding, storage and retrieval.*
2. *No. It is an active process, and it takes time and sleep for a memory to be consolidated.*
3. *Around half a second.*
4. *One for each sense.*
5. *Seven plus or minus two items.*
6. *It can hold a list lasting around one-and-a-half to two seconds, or 3–4 unrelated items.*
7. *Temporary.*
8. *No. It can also manipulate visual information.*
9. *Episodic LTM.*
10. *Make predictions/fill in gaps in knowledge/ distort information/help to interpret incoming information/play a role in solving problems.*

Chapter 5: The multi-store model (page 123)

1. *At least five.*
2. *Whether attention is paid to it.*
3. *Sensory memory, but most information fades from it rapidly.*
4. *The length of time it remains in working memory.*
5. *Maintenance rehearsal.*
6. *No.*
7. *The serial position effect.*
8. *It occurs because the first few items in the list have more opportunity to be rehearsed. This would be reduced if the list was presented very quickly.*
9. *Murdock (1962)/Glanzer & Cunitz (1966)/ Craik (1970).*
10. *Yes and no. They help to establish that WM and LTM are separate, but also show that it must be more complicated than is shown in the model.*

Chapter 5: The working memory model (page 127)

1. *Explain how we engage in everyday tasks and process information in WM.*
2. *The central executive.*
3. *Slave systems.*
4. *The word length effect.*
5. *multi-tasking*
6. *The phonological loop (or the phonological store/articulatory process).*
7. *True.*
8. *The episodic buffer.*
9. *The central executive (or: how it links to LTM).*
10. *Yes. For example, language learning and language disorders.*

Chapter 5: Forgetting (page 133)

1. *All three, but especially sensory memory and working memory.*
2. *Information doesn't disappear but just becomes less accessible.*
3. *Displacement.*
4. *Proactive interference.*
5. *State cues and context cues.*
6. *The frontal lobe.*
7. *LTM, particularly semantic and episodic LTM.*
8. *No.*
9. *Long-term potentiation.*
10. *No. First, it will be hard to transfer the information to a different context (the exam hall), and second, it is best to learn in multiple contexts.*

Chapter 6: The physiology of stress (page 142)

1. *Stress.*
2. *Short-term/immediate stress.*
3. *Running away (flight).*
4. *Sweating/tense muscles/increased blood clotting/release of glucose/slowed digestion/ heightened vision and awareness.*
5. *Long-term or repeated exposure to stress.*
6. *Having to give a speech/being attacked or threatened/a job interview/etc. Must be a short-term situation.*
7. *After 6–48 hours.*
8. *A general term for illnesses that occur due to changes in the exhaustion stage of general adaptation syndrome, and could include ulcers, heart disease and hypertension.*
9. *That all stressors have the same effect/ everyone reacts in the same way to stressors.*
10. *Yes. Animals were harmed in the research.*

Chapter 6: Stress and health (page 147)

1. *Prolonged stress/long-term stress.*
2. *Chronic stress.*
3. *Cortisol.*
4. *Anger and irritability/emotional outbursts/ difficulty concentrating.*
5. *Coronary heart disease.*
6. *Depression and eating disorders. (You could also mention panic disorder, schizophrenia, etc.)*
7. *Immunosuppression.*
8. *Killer T cells.*
9. *At exam time.*
10. *Fleshner (2000).*

Chapter 6: Sources of stress (page 152)

1. *Environmental/occupational/social.*
2. *Random, unpredictable noises.*
3. *Calhoun (1962).*
4. *Both experienced stress which depended on their place in the hierarchy, with the highest ranked individuals being less stressed.*
5. *Workload/exams/deadlines/meetings/ interaction with colleagues/low pay/ being fired.*
6. *An internal locus of control, i.e. feeling that you are in control of what happens.*
7. *Commitment, control and challenge.*
8. *Time urgency/competitiveness/doing several things at once/high alertness/hostility/etc.*
9. *Teenagers feel the effects of stressors more/ people of different ages experience different social and occupational stressors.*
10. *Males have a greater and more sustained release of adrenaline/females benefit more from a release of oxytocin during social support.*

Chapter 6: Coping strategies (page 159)

1. *Drugs.*
2. *Benzodiazepines.*
3. *They can make people sleep/they can be addictive.*

4. *Beta-blockers. No. They don't deal directly with the cause of stress.*
5. *Conceptualisation.*
6. *Using the techniques in real-life stressful situations, such as in the workplace.*
7. *The person may be taught skills/may practise skills/may use techniques such as role-playing and visualisation.*
8. *Instrumental social support.*
9. *Nuckolls et al. (1972).*
10. *Exercise.*

Chapter 8: The scientific method and the research process (page 184)

1. *They can disprove but not prove a theory.*
2. *An explanation of the available facts.*
3. *Because the scientific method requires all ideas to be supported by reliable research evidence.*
4. *Karl Popper.*
5. *Yes, though the criticism should be based on evidence.*
6. *Experiments, observations, surveys, interviews, case studies.*
7. *Gathering data.*
8. *Each study provides a single piece of evidence and our overall understanding builds up over time.*
9. *Yes, because it is important to check/confirm results.*
10. *There is no final stage, because it is a continual, cyclical process!*

Chapter 8: Populations and samples (page 188)

1. *The group of participants who are studied.*
2. *The target population.*
3. *There is no perfect size but the larger the better.*
4. *Findings from unrepresentative samples cannot always be generalised to the target population.*
5. *Random or systematic.*
6. *No, not always. It could be unrepresentative due to chance factors.*
7. *It should be unbiased, representative and large.*
8. *It is not susceptible to systematic bias.*
9. *Because it needs to be combined with another method of sampling, for example, opportunity.*
10. *Stratified.*

Chapter 8: Experimental methods (page 193)

1. *Lab experiments.*
2. *IV and DV.*
3. *Repeated measures.*
4. *Control over variables.*
5. *Cause and effect.*
6. *Artificiality/demand characteristics.*
7. *A field experiment is a true, controlled experiment whereas a natural experiment is not controlled by the researcher.*
8. *A quasi-experiment is controlled in most ways except that allocation to conditions/groups is non-random, while a natural experiment is uncontrolled.*
9. *5.*
10. *Noise, personality, ability.*

Chapter 8: Non-experimental methods (page 203)

1. *One with a fixed selection of answers.*
2. *Leading questions/loaded questions/jargon/ambiguity/bias.*
3. *Semi-structured.*
4. *It might be important to be able to explain the questions face-to-face.*
5. *Naturalistic.*
6. *Observer effect.*
7. *Obtains data on real behaviour as it happens.*
8. *Longitudinal, in-depth, individual case/small group.*
9. *Interviews, observations, brain scans, tests.*
10. *False. Studies often use a mixture of different methods.*

Chapter 8: General research issues (page 213)

1. *A prediction of expected results.*
2. *Yes. Variables in a hypothesis must be operationalised.*
3. *Internal validity.*
4. *Whether the findings of a study can be related to everyday situations.*
5. *No. Nobody would do that in everyday life.*
6. *Population validity.*
7. *No. A lab experiment involving a realistic, everyday task such as memorising a shopping list would have high mundane realism.*
8. *A set of ethical research standards published by an official research body or professional science organisation such as the British Psychological Society (BPS).*

9. *Confidentiality.*
10. *Yes, but parental consent is also needed.*

Chapter 8: Data and graphs (page 220)

1. *Mean, mode, median.*
2. *Bar graph, histogram, pie chart (or scattergram).*
3. *The median.*
4. *When there are extreme high or low scores.*
5. *The range.*
6. *The average amount by which the data deviate from the mean.*
7. *Often there is no mode – no score appears more than once – or more than one are equally common (multi-modal).*
8. *It includes every score in the calculation.*
9. *The bars of a histogram are continuous/joined together.*
10. *It standardises scores, making them easier to compare.*

Chapter 10: The nature of conformity (page 258)

1. *Normative.*
2. *Identification.*
3. *Dissent.*
4. *Beans.*
5. *75%.*
6. *Compliance.*
7. *Internalisation.*
8. *Minority influence.*
9. *Lab.*
10. *British engineering students.*

Chapter 10: Factors that affect conformity (page 263)

1. *The rise from two to three.*
2. *False.*
3. *True.*
4. *Three from: age, self-esteem, sex, thought processes, culture.*
5. *Santee and Maslach (1982).*
6. *Becoming more different from the majority rather than more similar.*
7. *Collectivist cultures.*
8. *They used filter sunglasses that resulted in people seeing different lengths of lines.*
9. *Male participants did not conform; having an 'ally' made very little difference.*
10. *104 Japanese university students.*

Chapter 10: Obedience (page 269)

1. *False.*
2. *Charismatic.*
3. *A hierarchy.*
4. *40.*
5. *26 of the participants (i.e. 65%).*
6. *Deception and stress to participants.*
7. *A hospital.*
8. *Peer (confederate teacher) giving the shock.*
9. *Agentic and autonomous state.*
10. *False. Authoritarian parenting does so, while democratic parenting encourages negotiation of reasonable boundaries.*

Chapter 11: Types of non-verbal communication (page 278)

1. *Posture and gesture.*
2. *Gesture.*
3. *Proximity.*
4. *As a sign that you are interested and paying attention/that you wish to communicate.*
5. *Difficult. It might be necessary to view a slow-motion recording.*
6. *They may provide some clues to emotions, but NVC is easily misinterpreted.*
7. *The mouth plus the eyes (Duchenne smile), or just the mouth.*
8. *A tribe in Papua New Guinea that had had very little contact with the outside world prior to Ekman and Friesen's (1971) study.*
9. *189 adults and 130 children.*
10. *Anger/disgust/contempt/surprise/fear/sadness.*

Chapter 11: Arguments for nature in NVC (page 284)

1. *The nature side.*
2. *The amygdala.*
3. *At six to eight weeks.*
4. *Before.*
5. *It would look more often/for longer at the 'normal' face.*
6. *Tongue out, pouting face, wiggling fingers, wide open mouth.*
7. *Each was shown four times for 15 seconds at a time.*
8. *Babies do this a lot anyway, in reaction to many situations, so it could have been unrelated to the stimulus.*
9. *There are several basic emotions that are fundamentally separate/facial expressions are the main way of conveying emotions/facial*

expressions are culturally universal/gestures are learned within a social group.

10. *Stroking the hand of ill relatives/hugging bereaved individuals/sitting in a 'vigil'/posture and proximity to the dying and deceased/ begging posture with outstretched hands.*

Chapter 11: Arguments for nurture in NVC (page 289)

1. *The nature–nurture debate.*
2. *Culture/parental upbringing/life experience.*
3. *Up to 50 cm.*
4. *It suggests a formal interaction suitable for work colleagues/it may convey a lack of warmth.*
5. *Cheeky/provocative/friendly/angry/defiant/ etc.*
6. *Observational learning.*
7. *Touching face and tapping foot.*
8. *Japanese (participants).*
9. *Men appear to prefer more personal space than women/women engage in more eye contact than men/women tend to speak in higher pitched tones.*
10. *The listener usually shows more gaze but if the person is dominant/powerful they make eye contact at the same time as speaking, and may show visual dominance behaviour when a less powerful person is speaking.*

Chapter 12: Prejudice and discrimination (page 296)

1. *To 'pre-judge', that is, to judge someone before knowing about them.*
2. *An out-group.*
3. *Any group about which people would use the word 'we'.*
4. *No. Some define it on the basis of feelings (affect), some include cognitive aspects such as beliefs, while others see it as a synonym of intergroup bias and also include behavioural aspects.*
5. *Behavioural.*
6. *No. Glick and Fiske (2001) found that positive sexism tended to correlate with harmful and violent sexism.*
7. *False. They were willing to admit more negative attitudes towards certain groups.*
8. *Groups based on race/sex/age/sexuality; for example Muslims, women, teenagers, gay people.*
9. *The Equality Act of 2010.*
10. *When a rule or law is unfair to a particular group.*

Chapter 12: Explanations of prejudice (page 301)

1. *Because cognitive resources such as attention are limited.*
2. *He stated that group categories are meaningful/useful/accurate.*
3. *The psychoanalytic approach.*
4. *Previous comments made by research participants.*
5. *Authoritarian aggression, authoritarian submission, conventionalism.*
6. *Social categorisation, social identification, social comparison and psychological distinctiveness.*
7. *Population validity, i.e. difficulty in generalising the results to older ages or to other groups in society.*
8. *This avoided pre-existing stereotypes playing a role in later attitudes.*
9. *Possible harm and distress/deception of both participants and their parents/etc.*
10. *Confirmation bias.*

Chapter 12: Reducing prejudice (page 314)

1. *An educational technique of promoting knowledge and understanding of an issue, for example prejudice and its effects.*
2. *Eye colour.*
3. *A specific education programme to tackle prejudice directly, particularly for people who have shown themselves to be bigots.*
4. *Minorities who are under-represented in a career or educational path.*
5. *No.*
6. *The contact hypothesis.*
7. *That each member of the group has to participate and communicate, because the task can't be completed without every part.*
8. *Self-esteem, liking for other children and academic performance.*
9. *It might affect their developing schemas of gender roles/they may be discouraged from pursuing certain careers.*
10. *Their perception of social norms.*

Chapter 13: The nature of relationships (page 321)

1. *No, not necessarily.*
2. *Affiliation*
3. *Maslow/Baumeister and Leary.*
4. *Using caregiver as a base, social releasers, develops schema for relationships, monotropy.*

5. *Less emphasis on parents/peers have a strong influence on personality development/ loneliness is more common.*
6. *The nucleus accumbens.*
7. *Insecure-resistant.*
8. *Rather than opposites, people who are similar tend to be attracted to each other.*
9. *Facial symmetry, responsiveness, similarity, familiarity.*
10. *Artificiality/superficial judgements/etc.*

Chapter 13: Theories of relationships (page 328)

1. *Money, time, etc.*
2. *Sampling, bargaining, commitment, institutionalisation.*
3. *To an extent – it implies a rational choice, but social exchange theory would predict that higher risk would lead to people choosing less attractive partners, which is not what was found by Berscheid* et al. *(1971).*
4. *A schema for relationships, which people use to judge current/potential new relationships.*
5. *Aim for different numbers of offspring or males aim for youthful partner/females aim for partner who can support them.*
6. *150.*
7. *Investment is the amount of costs incurred in looking after offspring. 'Differential' means that this is often unequal between the mother and father.*
8. *Harlow showed that relationships are partly innate, as infant monkeys bonded with their mothers due to an innate need for comfort. Wedekind* et al. *showed that romantic partner choices may be due to factors outside of our conscious awareness, such as pheromones, but in a way that gives a boost to our evolutionary fitness.*
9. *Availability/category/attractiveness/similarity/ complementarity/proximity.*
10. *Satisfaction, comparison to alternatives, investment size.*

Chapter 13: Virtual and parasocial relationships (page 339)

1. *Via online dating/a friendship formed via social media or a gaming website, etc.*
2. *Factors, such as shyness, that might make it harder for someone to initiate a face-to-face relationship; virtual relationships make it easier to present yourself however you like.*
3. *You can disclose less information, and communication can be asynchronous.*
4. *People may be less inhibited about being rude or aggressive online due to relative anonymity.*
5. *That the visibility of one's own messages increased liking for the other person, but only when there had been a high level of self-disclosure.*
6. *A TV star/YouTube star/musician/etc.*
7. *No. The celebrities can provide good role models and it can lead to social bonding among their fans.*
8. *The intense-personal level.*
9. *The insecure-resistant type.*
10. *No. It states that people tend to develop a tolerance and want an even greater 'fix' of information about the celebrity.*

Chapter 14: Biological influences on aggression (page 348)

1. *Harming members of one's own species.*
2. *Impulsive aggression.*
3. *Testosterone.*
4. *In the limbic system.*
5. *No. Because most aggression is carried out by people with healthy/normal brains.*
6. *Epigenetics.*
7. *In order to give people or animals an advantage in survival or reproduction.*
8. *He thought that we have lost the ability to show releasers which would stop aggression from progressing, and that the use of weapons limits the impact of visual and auditory feedback.*
9. *A set of actions which ethologists believe can respond to circumstances and adapt to specific environmental contexts.*
10. *No. Only the males were aggressive, only when another male came near their territory, and predominantly when the other fish or models were red-coloured. They also didn't engage in real fighting.*

Chapter 14: Social explanations of aggression (page 355)

1. *Television/movies.*
2. *The behaviourist approach.*
3. *True.*
4. *True.*

5. *Intro music/intro picture of 'Herman the cat'/ role mode in a cat costume/background shown as a fantasy land/verbal aggression in a high-pitched voice.*
6. *Convict subculture.*
7. *Two from: liberty/goods/sexual relationships/ autonomy/security.*
8. *Mocked up prison cells/local police recruited to 'arrest' participants/authentic uniforms/ bread and water punishments/etc.*
9. *No. Haslam and Reicher argue that the experimenters coerced the guards into acting aggressively.*
10. *That it could be due to overcrowding and bad living conditions.*

Chapter 14: Aggression and the media (page 362)

1. *Preparation for aggressive responses, where prior exposure to violence via the media makes later aggression more likely.*
2. *Disinhibition.*
3. *A violent v's non-violent movie.*
4. *St. Helena.*
5. *No, because this doesn't demonstrate cause and effect. It could be that aggressive people are more likely to choose the games.*
6. *Blasts of noise, supposedly played to a partner in a game.*
7. *A violent video game might be different in some other factor such as difficulty. Or video game players studied might different in some other way (besides their choice of game) such as their level of maturity or experience in playing computer games. Or similar.*
8. *Two from: better working memory/positive school engagement/better mental health/less substance use/more obedience to parents/ more educational potential/higher altriusm.*
9. *Being less constrained by social norms, e.g. when we feel anonymous.*
10. *One from: invisibility or anonymity/ asynchronicity of messages/dissociative imagination/lack of online authorities.*

Feedback

Feedback for Discussion point on page 16

This is short for 'et alii', which is Latin for 'and others'.

Feedback for Activity 1 on page 44

Australopithecus	*2–4 million years ago*
Homo erectus	*150,000–2 million years ago*
Start of agriculture	*12,000 years ago*
The first cities appeared	*5,000 years ago*
First modern humans	*300,000 years ago*
'Missing link' ancestor between humans and chimpanzees	*6–7 million years ago*
Beginning of the current ice age	*2.5 million years ago*
Neanderthals died out	*40,000 years ago.*

Feedback for Discussion point on page 129

Attention from the CE is limited, so you can only carry out several tasks if those tasks combined do not exceed the total attention available. If one task starts to take up most of your attention then it becomes much harder to do anything else and performance on that task (e.g. conversation while driving) may slow down or stop altogether. Tasks that are novel or complex require more attention, while routine tasks such as washing the dishes do not require much. If a task is automatic then it requires hardly any attention at all and it can be done without thinking about it.

Feedback for Discussion point on page 131

A model is simply a more detailed version of a theory. It sets out a possible structure for a process (e.g. memory) that can then be tested and changed.

Feedback for Discussion point on page 198

If the experimenter were to choose which participant went into which condition, this choice could be biased.

References

Abel, T., Havekes, R., Saletin, J.M. and Walker, M.P. (2013). Sleep, plasticity and memory from molecules review to whole-brain networks. *Current Biology, 23*, R774–R788.

Aboud, F.E. (2003). The formation of in-group favoritism and out-group prejudice in young children: Are they distinct attitudes? *Developmental Psychology, 39*, 48–60.

Abrams, D. and Houston, D.M. (2006). Equality, diversity and prejudice in Britain: results from the 2005 national survey. *Report for the Cabinet Office Equalities Review.* Kent: University of Kent Centre for the Study of Group Processes.

Abrams, D., Wetherell, M., Cochrane, S., Hogg, M.A. and Turner, J.C. (1990). Knowing what to think by knowing who you are: self-categorisation and the nature of norm formation. *British Journal of Social Psychology, 29*, 97–119.

Adam, K., & Oswald, I.A.N. (1983). Protein synthesis, bodily renewal and the sleep-wake cycle. *Clinical Science, 65*(6), 561–567.

Adolphs, R., Tranel, D. and Damasio, A.R. (1998). The human amygdala in social judgment. *Nature, 393*, 470–474.

Adorno, T.W., Frenkel-Brunswik, E., Levinson, D.J. and Sanford, R.N. (1950). *The Authoritarian Personality*. New York: Harper.

Ainsworth, M.D.S. and Bell, S.M. (1970). Attachment, exploration, and separation: Individual differences in strange-situation behavior of one-year-olds. *Child Development, 41*, 49–67.

Ainsworth, M.D.S., Bell, S.M. and Stayton, D.J. (1971). Individual differences in the strange-situation behaviour of one-year-olds. In H.R. Schaffer (Ed.), *The Origins of Human Social Relations*. New York: Academic Press, 17–52.

Allport, G. (1954). *The Nature of Prejudice*. New York: Double-Day Anchor.

Altemeyer, B. (1981). *Right-wing Authoritarianism*. Manitoba: University of Manitoba Press.

Altemeyer, B. (2006). *The Authoritarians*. Retrieved 28 July 2010 from http://home.cc.umanitoba.ca/~altemey/.

Altman, I. (1975). *The environment and social behaviour*. Monterey: Brooks/Cole.

Ambady, N. and Rosenthal, R. (1992). Thin slices of expressive behavior as predictors of interpersonal consequences: a meta-analysis. *Psychological bulletin, 111*, 256–274.

Ambady, N., Shih, M., Kim, A. and Pittinsky, T.L. (2001). Stereotype susceptibility in children: Effects of identity activation on quantitive performance. *Psychological Science, 12*, 385–390.

American Psychiatric Association (2013). *DSM-5*. Washington, D.C.: American Psychiatric Press.

Andersen, S.M. and Zimbardo, P.G. (1984). On resisting social influence. *Cultic Studies Journal, 1*, 196–219.

Anderson, C.A., & Dill, K. E. (2000). Video games and aggressive thoughts, feelings, and behavior in the laboratory and in life. *Journal of Personality and Social Psychology, 78*(4), 772–790.

Anderson, D.A. and Hamilton, M. (2005). Gender role stereotyping of parents in children's picture books: The invisible father. *Sex Roles, 52*, 145–151.

Anderson, I.M. (2000). Selective serotonin reuptake inhibitors versus tricyclic antidepressants: a meta-analysis of efficacy and tolerability. *Journal of Affective Disorders, 58*(1), 19–36.

Anderson, J.R., Gillies, A. and Lock, L.C. (2010). Pan thanatology. *Current Biology, 20*, R349–R351.

Anderson, R.C. (1984). Some reflections on the acquisition of knowledge. *Educational Researcher, 13*(9), 5–10.

Andrews, C. and Brewin, C.R. (2000). What did Freud get right? *The Psychologist, 13*, 605–607.

Angold, A., Costello, E.J., Erkanli, A. and Worthman, C.M. (1999). Pubertal changes in hormone levels and depression in girls. *Psychological Medicine, 29*, 1043–1053.

Anthony, A. (2009). Jane Elliott, the American schoolmarm who would rid us of our racism. *The Guardian*. Retrieved 26 January 2015 from http://www.theguardian.com/culture/2009/oct/18/racism-psychology-jane-elliott-4.

Argyle, M. and Cook, M. (1976). *Gaze and Mutual Gaze*. Cambridge: Cambridge University Press.

Aronson, E. and Bridgeman, D. (1979). Jigsaw groups and the desegregated classroom: in pursuit of common goals. In E. Aronson (Ed.), *Readings About the Social Animal* (6th edn). New York: W.H. Freeman.

Asch, S.E. (1956). Studies of independence and conformity: I. A minority of one against a unanimous majority. *Psychological Monographs: General and Applied, 70*(9), 1–70.

Asch, S.E. (1951). Effects of group pressure upon the modification and distortion of judgment. In H. Guetzkow (Ed.), *Groups, Leadership and Men*. Pittsburgh, PA: Carnegie Press.

Asch, S.E. (1955). Opinions and social pressure. *Scientific American, 193*, 31–35.

Atkinson, R.C. and Shiffrin, R.M. (1968). Human memory: a proposed system and its control processes. In K.W. Spence and J.T. Spence (Eds.), *The Psychology of Learning and Motivation*: Vol. 2. London: Academic Press.

Avigdor, R. (1951). *The Development of Stereotypes as a Result of Group Interaction, on file in the Library,* New York University. Cited by Sherif *et al.* (1954).

Baddeley, A.D. (1966). Short term memory for word sequences as a function of acoustic, semantic and formal similarity. *Quarterly Journal of Experimental Psychology, 18*, 362–365.

Baddeley, A.D. (2000). The episodic buffer: a new component of working memory? *Trends in Cognitive Sciences, 4*, 417–423.

Baddeley, A.D. (2012). Working memory: theories, models, and controversies. *Annual Review of Psychology, 63*, 1–29.

Baddeley, A.D., Grant, S., Wight, E. and Thomson, N. (1973). Imagery and visual working, In P.M.A. Rabbitt and S. Darnit (Eds.), *Attention and Performance: V*. London: Academic Press.

Baddeley, A.D. and Hitch, G. (1974). Working memory. In G.H. Bower (Ed.), *The Psychology of Learning and Motivation*: Vol. 8. London: Academic Press.

Baddeley, A.D., Thomson, N. and Buchanan, M. (1975). Word length and the structure of short-term memory. *Journal of Verbal Learning and Verbal Behaviour, 14*, 575–589.

Bailey, A. A., & Hurd, P. L. (2005). Finger length ratio predicts physical aggression in men but not women. *Biological Psychiatry, 68*, 215–222.

Bandura, A. (1965). Influence of models' reinforcement contingencies on the acquisition of imitative responses. *Journal of Personality and Social Psychology, 1*, 589–595.

Bandura, A., Ross, D., & Ross, S.A. (1961). Transmission of aggression through imitation of aggressive models. *Journal of Abnormal and Social Psychology, 63*(3), 575–582.

Bandura, A., Ross, D., & Ross, S.A. (1963). Imitation of film-mediated aggressive models. *Journal of Abnormal and Social Psychology,* 66(1), 3–11.

Bartlett, F.C. (1932). *Remembering: A Study in Experimental and Social Psychology*. Cambridge: Cambridge University Press.

Bailly, G., Raidt, S. and Elisei, F. (2010). Gaze, conversational agents and face-to-face communication. *Speech Communication, 52*, 598–612.

Banyard, P., & Grayson, L. (2000). *Introducing psychological research* (2nd Ed). London: Palgrave Macmillan.

Bargh, J.A. and Chartrand, T.L. (1999). The unbearable automaticity of being. *American Psychologist, 54*, 462.

Baron, R.A. and Byrne, D. (1997). *Social Psychology* (8th edn). London: Allyn and Bacon.

Bass, B.M. (1955). Authoritarianism or acquiescence? *Journal of Abnormal and Social Psychology, 51*, 616–623.

Baumeister, R.F. and Leary, M.R. (1995). The need to belong: Desire for interpersonal attachments as a fundamental human motivation. *Psychological Bulletin, 117*, 497–529.

BBC (2002). Bergkamp's fear revealed. *BBC Sport website*. Retrieved 19 May 2018 from http://news.bbc.co.uk/sport1/hi/football/eng_prem/2280779.stm.

Beck, A. (1976). *Cognitive therapy and the emotional disorders*. New York: International Universities Press.

Bell, V. (2014). The concept of stress, sponsored by Big Tobacco. *Mindhacks Blog*. Retrieved 1 December 2014 from http://mindhacks.com/2014/07/14/the-concept-of-stress-sponsored-by-big-tobacco/.

Benford, P., & Standen, P. (2009). The internet: a comfortable communication medium for people with Asperger syndrome (AS) and high functioning autism (HFA)?. Journal of Assistive Technologies, 3(2), 44–53.

Benington, J.H. and Heller, H.C. (1995). Restoration of brain energy metabolism as the function of sleep. *Progress in Neurobiology, 45*, 347–360.

Bennet-Levy, J., & Marteau, T. (1984). Fear of Animals: What is prepared? *British Journal of Psychology, 75*, 37–42.

Berscheid, E., Dion, K., Walster, E. and Walster, G.W. (1971). Physical attractiveness and dating choice: A test of the matching hypothesis. *Journal of Experimental Social Psychology, 7*, 173–189.

Bezrukova, K., Jehn, K.A. and Spell, C.S. (2012). Reviewing diversity training: where we have been and where we should go. *Academy of Management Learning and Education, 11*, 207–227.

Bickman, L. (1974). Clothes make the person. *Psychology Today, 8*, 48–51.

Bjork, R.A. (1994). Memory and metamemory considerations in the training of human beings. In J. Metcalfe and A. Shimamura, (Eds.), *Metacognition: Knowing about Knowing* (pp. 185–205). Cambridge, MA: MIT Press.

Boese, A. (2007). *Elephants on Acid: and Other Bizarre Experiments*. Orlando: Harvest Books.

Bower, G.H. (1972). Mental imagery and associative learning. In L.W. Gregg and G.H. Bower (Eds.), *Cognition in Learning and Memory*. New York: Wiley, 51–88.

Bowlby, J. (1958). The nature of the child's tie to his mother. *International Journal of Psychoanalysis, 39*, 350–373.

BPS (2014). BPS Code of Human Research Ethics (2nd Ed.). Retrieved 3 September 2018 from https://www.bps.org.uk/sites/bps.org.uk/files/Policy%20-%20Files/BPS%20Code%20of%20Human%20Research%20Ethics.pdf

Breazeal, C. and Scassellati, B. (2002). Robots that imitate humans. *Trends in Cognitive Sciences, 6*, 481–487.

Brewer, M.B. (1968). Determinants of social distance among East African tribal groups. *Journal of Personality and Social Psychology, 10*(3), 279–289.

Brewer, M.B. (1988). A dual process model of impression formation. In T.K. Srul & R.S. Wyer (Eds.) *Advances in social cognition. A dual process model of impression formation* (pp. 1–36). Hillsdale, NJ: Lawrence Erlbaum Associates.

Brewer, W.F. and Treyens, J.C. (1981). Role of schemata in memory for places. *Cognitive Psychology, 13*, 207–230.

British Psychological Society (2011). Response to the American Psychiatric Association: DSM-5 development. Retrieved 3 February 2015 from http://apps.bps.org.uk/_publicationfiles/consultation-responses/DSM-5%202011%20-%20BPS%20response.pdf.

British Psychological Society (2014). BPS code of human research ethics (2nd Ed). Retrieved 3 September 2018 from https://www.bps.org.uk/sites/bps.org.uk/files/Policy%20-%20Files/BPS%20Code%20of%20Human%20Research%20Ethics.pdf.

Brown, G.L., Goodwin, F.K., Ballenger, J.C., Goyer, P.F., Major L.F. (1979). Aggression in humans correlates with cerebrospinal fluid amine metabolites. *Psychiatry Research, 1*(2), 131–139.

Brown, G.W. and Harris, T.O. (1978). *Social Origins of Depression: A Study of Psychiatric Disorder in Women*. London: Tavistock Publications.

Brown, R. and McNeill, D. (1966). The 'tip-of-the-tongue' phenomenon. *Journal of Verbal Learning and Verbal Behaviour, 5*, 325–337.

Brown, R., & McNeill, D. (1966). The "tip of the tongue" phenomenon. *Journal of Verbal Learning and Verbal Behavior, 5*(4), 325–337.

Brown, R.J. and Turner, J.C. (1981). Interpersonal and intergroup behaviour. In J.C. Turner and H. Giles (Eds.), *Intergroup Behaviour*. Oxford: Basil Blackwell, 33–65.

Brown, R.P., Charnsangavej, T., Keough, K.A., Newman, M.L., & Rentfrow, P.J. (2000). Putting the" affirm" into affirmative action: Preferential selection and academic performance. *Journal of Personality and Social Psychology, 79*(5), 736–747.

Bruner, J. (1992). *Acts of Meaning*. Boston, MA: Harvard University Press.

Burger, J.M. (1992). *Desire for Control: Personality, Social and Clinical Perspectives*. New York: Plenum.

Bushman, B.J. (1998). Priming effects of media violence on the accessibility of aggressive constructs in memory. *Personality and Social Psychology Bulletin, 24*(5), 537–545.

Buss, D. (1989). Sex differences in human mate preferences: evolutionary hypotheses tested in

37 cultures. *Behavioural and Brain Sciences, 12*, 1–14.

Byrne, R.W. and Corp, N. (2004). Neocortex size predicts deception rate in primates. *Proceedings of the Royal Society of London B, 271*, 1693–1699.

Cacioppo, J.T. and Hawkley, L.C. (2009). Perceived social isolation and cognition. *Trends in Cognitive Science, 13*, 447–454.

Calhoun, J.B. (1962). Population density and social pathology. *Scientific American, 206*, 139–148.

Caldera, Y.M., Huston, A.C. and O'Brien, M. (1989). Social interactions and play patterns of parents and toddlers with feminine, masculine, and neutral toys. *Child Development, 60*, 70–76.

Campbell, A.J., Cumming, S.R., & Hughes, I. (2006). Internet use by the socially fearful: *Addiction or therapy?. CyberPsychology & Behavior, 9*(1), 69–81.

Cannon, W.B. (1927). The James-Lange theory of emotions: a critical examination and an alternative theory. *American Journal of Psychology, 39*, 106–124.

Carlson, N. (1998). *Physiology of Behaviour* (5th edn). Boston: Allyn and Bacon.

Caspi, A., McClay, J., Moffitt, T.E., Mill, J., Martin, J., Craig, I.W., ... & Poulton, R. (2002). Role of genotype in the cycle of violence in maltreated children. *Science, 297*(5582), 851–854.

Catania, A.C. (1992). *Learning* (3rd edn). Englewood Cliffs: Prentice Hall.

Cepeda, N.J., Vul, E., Rohrer, D., Wixted, J.T. and Pashler, H. (2008). Spacing effects in learning: a temporal ridgeline of optimal retention. *Psychological Science, 19*, 1095–1102.

Chang, A.M., Aeschbach, D., Duffy, J.F., & Czeisler, C. A. (2015). Evening use of light-emitting eReaders negatively affects sleep, circadian timing, and next-morning alertness. *Proceedings of the National Academy of Sciences, 112*(4), 1232–1237.

Charlton, T. (1998). Reproaching television for violence in society: Passing the buck? Interim results from a naturalistic study in St Helena, South Atlantic. *Journal of Clinical Forensic Medicine, 5*(4), 169–171.

Chartrand, T.L. and Bargh, J. (1999). The chameleon effect: The perception-behaviour link and social interaction. *Journal of Personality and Social Psychology, 76*, 893–910.

Chomsky, A.N. (1959). A review of Skinner's verbal behavior. *Language, 35*, 26–58.

Clayton, R.B. (2014). The third wheel: The impact of twitter use on relationship infidelity and divorce. *Cyberpsychology, Behavior, and Social Networking, 17*, 425–430.

Coccaro, E.F., Fanning, J.R., Phan, K.L., & Lee, R. (2015). Serotonin and impulsive aggression. *CNS Spectrums, 20*(3), 295–302.

Cohen, C.E. (1981). Person categories and social perception: testing some boundaries of the processing effects of prior knowledge. *Journal of Personality and Social Psychology, 40*, 441–452.

Cohen, F., Tyrrell, D.A.J. and Smith, A.P. (1991). Psychological stress and susceptibility to the common cold. *New England Journal of Medicine, 325*, 606–612.

Cohen, S., Evans, G.W., Krantz, D.S. and Stokols, D. (1980). Physiological, motivational, and cognitive effects of aircraft noise on children: moving from the laboratory to the field. *American Psychologist, 35*, 231.

Colman, A.M. (1987). *Facts, Fallacies and Frauds in Psychology*. London: Routledge.

Colten, M.E. and Gore, S. (1991). *Adolescent Stress: Causes and Consequences*. Piscataway: Transaction Publishing.

Conty, L., Gimmig, D., Belletier, C., George, N., & Huguet, P. (2010). The cost of being watched: Stroop interference increases under concomitant eye contact. *Cognition, 115*(1), 133–139.

Cook, M., & Mineka, S. (1989). Observational conditioning of fear to fear-relevant versus fear-irrelevant stimuli in rhesus monkeys. *Journal of Abnormal Psychology, 98*, 448–459.

Cook, M. (1978). *Perceiving Others*. London: Routledge.

Coren, S. (1998). Sleep deprivation, psychosis and mental efficiency. *Psychiatric Times, 15*, 1–3.

Cosmides, L., & Tooby, J. (1997). Evolutionary psychology: A primer. Retrieved 16 June 2018 from https://www.cep.ucsb.edu/primer.html

Cowan, N. (1988). Evolving conceptions of memory storage, selective attention, and their mutual constraints within the human information-processing system. *Psychological Bulletin, 104*(2), 163–191.

Cowan, N. (2017). The many faces of working memory and short-term storage. *Psychonomic Bulletin & Review, 24*(4), 1158–1170.

Cox, T. (1978). *Stress*. Macmillan: London.

Cutrona, C.E. (1996). *Social Support in Couples: Marriage as a Resource in Times of Stress*. Thousand Oaks: Sage Publications.

Craik, F.I.M. and Watkins, M.J. (1973). The role of rehearsal in short-term memory. *Journal of Verbal Learning and Verbal Behavior, 12*, 599–607.

Craik, F.I.M. and Tulving, E. (1975). Depth of processing and the retention of words in episodic memory. *Journal of Experimental Psychology: General, 104*, 268–294.

Crick, F. and Mitchison, G. (1983). The function of dream sleep. *Nature, 304*, 111–114.

Craik, F.I.M. (1970). The fate of primary memory items in free recall. *Journal of Verbal Learning and Verbal Behaviour, 9*, 143–148.

Czeisler, C., Johnson, M.P., Duffy, J.F., Brown, E.N., Ronda, J.M. and Kronauer, R.E. (1990). Exposure to bright light and darkness to treat physiologic maladaption to night work. *The New England Journal of Medicine, 322*, 1253–1259.

Dalal, P.K. and Sivakumar, T. (2009). Moving towards ICD-11 and DSM-V: concept and evolution of psychiatric classification. *Indian Journal of Psychiatry, 51*, 310.

Darley, C.F., Tinklenberg, J.R., Roth, W.T., Hollister, L. E., Atkinson, R. C. (1973). Influence of marihuana on storage and retrieval processes in memory. *Memory and Cognition, 1*, 196–200.

Dartnell, L. (2014). *The Knowledge*. London: Bodley Head.

Davies, J.C. (1970). "The j-curve of rising and declining satisfactions as a cause of some great revolutions and a contained rebellion," in H.D. Graham & T.R. Gurr (Eds.), *The History of Violence in America* (pp. 690–731). New York: Bantam Books.

De Gelder, B. (2006). Towards the neurobiology of emotional body language. *Nature Reviews Neuroscience, 7*, 242–249.

DeLongis, A., Coyne, J.C., Dakof, G., Folkman, S. and Lazarus, R.S. (1982). The impact of daily hassles, uplifts and major life events to health status. *Health Psychology, 1*, 119–136.

Dement, W. and Kleitman, N. (1957). The relation of eye movements during sleep to dream activity: an objective method for the study of dreaming. *Journal of Experimental Psychology, 53*, 339–346.

De Ruiter, J., Weston, G. and Lyon, S.M. (2011). Dunbar's number: group size and brain physiology in humans reexamined. *American Anthropologist, 113*, 557–568.

DeScioli, P. and Kurzban, R. (2009). The alliance hypothesis for human friendship. *PloS One, 4*, e5802.

DeSteno, D., Breazeal, C., Frank, R.H, Pizarro, D., Baumann, J., Dickens, L. and Lee, J.J. (2012). Detecting the trustworthiness of novel partners in economic exchange. *Psychological Science, 23*, 1549–1556.

Deutsch, M. and Gerrard, H.B. (1955). A study of normative and informational influence upon individual judgement. *Journal of Abnormal and Social Psychology, 51*, 629–636.

Dias, B.G., & Ressler, K.J. (2014). Parental olfactory experience influences behavior and neural structure in subsequent generations. *Nature Neuroscience, 17*(1), 89–96.

Di Gallo, A., & Parry-Jones, W.L. (1996). Psychological sequelae of road traffic accidents: an inadequately addressed problem. *British Journal of Psychiatry, 169*(4), 405–407.

Distel, M.A., Vink, J. M., Willemsen, G., Middeldorp, C.M., Merckelbach, H.L.G.J., & Boomsma, D.I. (2008). Heritability of self-reported phobic fear. *Behavioural Genetics, 38*, 24–33.

Doidge, N. (2007). *The Brain That Changes Itself.* New York: Viking.

Dollard, J. and Miller, N.E. (1950). *Personality and Psychotherapy.* New York: McGraw-Hill.

Dollard, J., Miller, N.E., Doob, L.W., Mowrer, O.H., & Sears, R. R. (1939). *Frustration and aggression*. New Haven, CT: Yale University Press.

Domhoff, G.W. (2005). The content of dreams: methodologic and theoretical implications. In M.H. Kryger, T. Roth and W.C. Dement (Eds.), *Principles and Practices of Sleep Medicine* (4th edn). Philadelphia: W.B. Saunders, 522–534.

Domhoff, G.W. (2011). Dreams are embodied simulations that dramatize conception and concerns: the continuity hypothesis in empirical, theoretical, and historical context. *International Journal of Dream Research, 4*, 50–62.

Domhoff, G.W., Meyer-Gomez, K. and Schredl, M. (2006). Dreams as the expression of conceptions and concerns: a comparison of German and American college students.

Imagination, Cognition and Personality, 25, 269–282.

Duggan, F., Lee, A.S. and Murray, R.M. (1990). Does personality predict long-term outcome in depression? *British Journal of Psychiatry, 157*, 19–24.

Dunbar, R.I.M. (1992). Neocortex size as a constraint on group size in primates. *Journal of Human Evolution, 22*, 469–493.

Dunbar, R.I.M. (1993). Coevolution of neocortical size, group size and language in humans. *Behavioural and Brain Sciences, 16*, 681–735.

Dunbar, R.I.M. (1996). *Grooming, Gossip and the Evolution of Language*. Cambridge: Harvard University Press.

Dunbar, R.I.M. (1998). The social brain hypothesis. *Brain, 9*, 178–190.

Duncan, J., Seitz., R.J., Kolodny, J., Bor, D., Herzog, H., Ahmed, A., Newell, F.N. and Emslie, H. (2000). A neural basis for general intelligence. *Science, 289*, 457–459.

Durkin, K., & Barber, B. (2002). Not so doomed: Computer game play and positive adolescent development. *Journal of Applied Developmental Psychology, 23*(4), 373–392.

Dutton, D.G. and Aron, A.P. (1974). Some evidence for heightened sexual attraction under conditions of high anxiety. *Journal of Personality and Social Psychology, 30*, 510–517.

Dweck, C.S. (2006). *Mindset: How You Can Fulfil Your Potential.* London: Robinson Books.

Eagly, A.H. (1987). *Sex Differences in Social Behaviour: A Social-Role Interpretation.* Hillsdale: Lawrence Erlbaum.

Efron, D. (1941). *Gesture, Race and Culture: A Tentative Study of the Spatio-temporal and 'Linguistic' Aspects of the Gestural Behavior of Eastern Jews and Southern Italians in New York City, Living under Similar as well as Different Environmental Conditions.* Morningside Heights, NY: King's Crown Press.

Ekirch, A.R. (2006). *At Day's Close: Night in Times Past.* New York: Norton.

Ekland-Olson, S., Barrick, D.M., & Cohen, L.E. (1983). Prison overcrowding and disciplinary problems: An analysis of the Texas prison system. *Journal of Applied Behavioral Science, 19*(2), 163–176.

Ekman, P. (1999). Basic Emotions. In T. Dalgleish and M. Power (Eds.), *Handbook of Cognition and Emotion*. Sussex: Wiley.

Ekman, P. (2009a). Lie catching and microexpressions. In C.W. Martin (Ed.), *The Philosophy of Deception*. New York: OUP USA, 118–133.

Ekman, P. (2009b). Darwin's contributions to our understanding of emotional expressions. *Philosophical Transactions of the Royal Society of London B – Biological Sciences, 364*, 3449–3451.

Ekman, P. and Friesen, W.V. (1971). Constants across cultures in the face and emotion. *Journal of Personality and Social Psychology, 17*, 124–129.

Elliott, J. (1977). The power and pathology of prejudice. In P.G. Zimbardo and F.L. Ruch (Eds.), *Psychology and Life* (9th edn). Glenview: Scott, Foresman.

Ellis, A. and Grieger, R. (1977). *Handbook of Rational-Emotive Therapy*. New York: Springer.

Ellis, A. (2003). Early theories and practices of rational emotive behavior therapy and how they have been augmented and revised during the last three decades. *Journal of Rational-Emotive and Cognitive-Behavior Therapy, 21*, 219–243.

Ellis, N.C. and Hennelly, R.A. (1980). A bilingual word-length effect: Implications for intelligence testing and the relative ease of mental calculation in Welsh and English. *British Journal of Psychology, 71*, 43–51.

Ericsson, K.A., & Kintsch, W. (1995). Long term working memory. *Psychological Review, 102*, 211–245.

Eriksson, P.S., Perfilieva, E., Björk-Eriksson, T., Alborn, A., Nordborg, C., Peterson, D.A. and Gage, F.H. (1998). Neurogenesis in the adult human hippocampus. *Nature Medicine, 4*, 1313–1317.

Evans, G. and Johnson, D. (2000). Stress and open-office noise. *Journal of Applied Psychology, 85*, 779–783.

Evans, G.W., Lercher, P., Meis, M., Ising, H. and Kofler, W.W. (2001). Community noise exposure and stress in children. *Journal of the Acoustical Society of America, 109*, 1023.

Eysenck, M.W. (1986). Working memory. In G. Cohen, M.W. Eysenck and M.A. Le Voi (Eds.), *Memory: A Cognitive Approach*. Milton Keynes: Open University Press.

Falconier, M. K., Nussbeck, F., Bodenmann, G., Schneider, H., & Bradbury, T. (2015). Stress from daily hassles in couples: Its effects on intradyadic stress, relationship satisfaction, and physical and psychological well-being. *Journal of Marital and Family Therapy, 41*(2), 221–235.

Fagan, J.F. (1976). Infants' recognition of invariant features of faces. *Child Development, 47*, 627–638.

Farroni, T., Csibra, G., Simion, F., & Johnson, M.H. (2002). Eye contact detection in humans from birth. *PNAS, 99*(14), 9602–9605.

Fayol, M. and Monteil, J. (1988). The notion of script: from general to developmental and social psychology. *Cahiers de Psychologie Cognitive/ Current Psychology of Cognition, 8*, 335–361.

Felipe, N.J. and Sommer, R. (1966). Invasions of personal space. *Social problems, 14*, 206–214.

Ferguson, C. J. (2014). Is video game violence bad? *The Psychologist, 27*(5), 324–327.

Festinger, L., Pepitone, A., & Newcomb, T. (1952). Some consequences of de-individuation in a group. *Journal of Abnormal and Social Psychology, 47*(2S), 382–389.

Fisher, S. and Greenberg, R.P. (1996). *Freud Scientifically Reappraised: Testing the Theories and the Therapy*. New York: Wiley.

Fišar, Z. (2016). Drugs related to monoamine oxidase activity. *Progress in Neuro-Psychopharmacology and Biological Psychiatry, 69*, 112–124.

Fiske, S.T., Cuddy, A.J. and Glick, P. (2007). Universal dimensions of social cognition: warmth and competence. *Trends in Cognitive Sciences, 11*, 77–83.

Fiske, S.T., Cuddy, A.J., & Glick, P. (2007). Universal dimensions of social cognition: Warmth and competence. *Trends in Cognitive Sciences, 11*(2), 77–83.

Fiske, S.T. and Taylor, S.E. (1991). *Social Cognition*. New York: McGraw-Hill.

Fleshner, M. (2000). Exercise and neuroendocrine regulation of antibody production: protective effect of physical activity on stress-induced suppression of the specific antibody response. *International Journal of Sports Medicine, 21*, 14–15.

Flynn, J.R. (1984). The mean IQ of Americans: massive gains 1932 to 1978. *Psychological Bulletin, 95*, 29–51.

Folkman, S., Lazarus, R.S., Dunkel-Schetter, C., DeLongis, A. and Gruen, R.J. (1986). Dynamics of a stressful encounter: cognitive appraisal, coping, and encounter outcomes. *Journal of Personality and Social Psychology, 50*, 992–1003.

Frankenhauser, M., Dunne, E. and Lundberg, U. (1976). Sex-differences in sympathetic-adrenal medullary reactions induced by different stressors. *Psychopharmacology, 47*, 1–5.

Freedman, J.L. (1975). *Crowding and Behavior*. San Francisco: Freeman.

Freud, S. (1900/1991). *The Interpretation of Dreams*. In *The Complete Psychological Works of Sigmund Freud*, Vol. 4. London: Penguin Books.

Freud, S. (1909/2002). Analysis of a phobia in a five year old boy. In *The 'Wolfman' and Other Cases* (Penguin Modern Classics). London: Penguin Books.

Freud, S. (1910). The origin and development of psychoanalysis. *American Journal of Psychology, 21*, 181–218.

Freud, S. (1933/1965). *New Introductory Lectures on Psychoanalysis*. Standard Edition. New York: Norton.

Friedman, M. and Rosenman, R.H. (1974). *Type A Behaviour and Your Heart*. New York: Harper Row.

Friedman, M., & Rosenman, R.H. (1959). Association of specific overt behavior pattern with blood and cardiovascular findings: blood cholesterol level, blood clotting time, incidence of arcus senilis, and clinical coronary artery disease. *Journal of the American Medical Association, 169*(12), 1286–1296.

Friesen, W.V. (1972). Cultural differences in facial expression in a social situation: An experimental test of the concept of display rules. *Unpublished doctoral dissertation*. University of California, San Francisco.

Furley, P. and Schweizer, G. (2014). The expression of victory and loss: estimating who's leading or trailing from nonverbal cues in sports. *Journal of Nonverbal Behavior, 38*, 13–29.

Fyock, J. and Stangor, C. (1994). The role of memory biases in stereotype maintenance. *British Journal of Social Psychology, 33*, 331–343.

Gathercole, S.E. and Baddeley, A.D. (1990). Phonological memory deficits in language disordered children: is there a causal connection? *Journal of Memory and Language, 29*, 336–360.

Gauntlett, D. (2005), *Moving experiences: Media effects and beyond* (2nd Ed.), London: John Libbey.

Gelder, M., Mayou, R., & Geddes, J. (2005). *Psychiatry* (3rd ed). New York: Oxford University Press.

Gibbs, J.L., Ellison, N.B., & Heino, R.D. (2006). Self-presentation in online personals: The role of anticipated future interaction, self-disclosure, and perceived success in Internet dating. *Communication Research, 33*(2), 152–177.

Giles, D.C., & Maltby, J. (2004). The role of media figures in adolescent development: Relations between autonomy, attachment, and interest in celebrities. *Personality and Individual Differences, 36*(4), 813–822.

Giles, D.C., & Maltby, J. (2006). Praying at the alter of the stars. *The Psychologist, 19*(5), 82–85.

Gladwell, M. (2010). *What the Dog Saw.* London: Penguin.

Glanzer, M. and Cunitz, A.R. (1966). Two storage mechanisms in free recall. *Journal of Verbal Learning and Verbal Behaviour, 5*, 351–360.

Glass, D.C., Singer, J.E. and Friedman, L.N. (1969). Psychic cost of adaptation to an environmental stressor. *Journal of Personality and Social Psychology, 12*, 200–210.

Glassman, W.E. (2000). *Approaches to Psychology* (3rd edn). Buckingham: Open University Press.

Glick, P. (2005). Choice of scapegoats. In J.F. Dovidio, P. Glick, & L. A. Rudman (Eds.). *On the nature of prejudice: Fifty years after Allport* (pp. 244–261). New York: Wiley.

Glick, P. and Fiske, S.T. (2001). An ambivalent alliance: Hostile and benevolent sexism as complementary justifications for gender inequality. *American Psychologist, 56*, 109–118.

Godden, D.R., & Baddeley, A.D. (1975). Context-dependent memory in two natural environments: On land and underwater. *British Journal of Psychology, 66*(3), 325–331.

Goldacre, B. (2012). *Bad Pharma.* London: Fourth Estate.

Goldstein, D.S. and Kopin, I.J. (2007). Evolution of concepts of stress. *Stress, 10*, 109–120.

Gonçalves, B., Perra, N. and Vespignani, A. (2011). Modeling users' activity on Twitter networks: validation of Dunbar's number. *PLoS One, 6*: e22656.

Goodwin, R. (1999). *Personal Relationships Across Cultures.* London: Routledge.

Gordon, I., Zagoory-Sharon, O., Leckman, J.F. and Feldman, R. (2010). Oxytocin and the development of parenting in humans. *Biological Psychiatry, 68*, 377–382.

Gujar, N., McDonald, S., Nishida, M. and Walker, M. (2010). A role for REM sleep in recalibrating the sensitivity of the human brain to specific emotions. *Cerebral Cortex, 21*, 115–123.

Guthrie, J.P., Ash, R.A., & Bendapudi, V. (1995). Additional validity evidence for a measure of morningness. *Journal of Applied Psychology, 80*(1), 186–190.

Halasz *et al.*, 1985, cited by Carlson, N. (1998). *Physiology of Behaviour* (5th edn). Boston: Allyn and Bacon.

Hall, E.T. (1966). *The hidden dimension.* New York: Doubleday.

Haney, C., Banks, W.C., & Zimbardo, P.G. (1973). A study of prisoners and guards in a simulated prison. *Naval Research Reviews, 9*, 1–17.

Harlow, H.F. (1959). Love in infant monkeys. *Scientific American, 200*, 688–674.

Haslam, A., Reicher, S.D., & Van Bavel, J.J. (2018). Rethinking the 'nature' of brutality: Uncovering the role of identity leadership in the Stanford Prison Experiment. (in press).

Haslam, S.A., Jetten, J., Postmes, T. and Haslam, C. (2009). Social identity, health and well-being: an emerging agenda for applied psychology. *Applied Psychology: An International Review, 58*, 1–23.

Hazan, C. and Shaver, P.R. (1987). Romantic love conceptualised as an attachment process. *Journal of Personality and Social Psychology, 52*, 511–524.

Hazan, C. and Zeifman, D. (1999). Pair bonds as attachments: evaluating the evidence. In J. Cassidy and P.R. Shaver (Eds.), *Handbook of Attachment: Theory, Research and Clinical Applications*, 336–354.

Hebb, D.O. (1949). *The Organization of Behavior.* New York: John Wiley and Sons.

Heath, A.C., Berg, K., Eaves, L.J., Solaas, M.H., Sundet, J., Nance, W.E., ... & Magnus, P. (1985). No decline in assortative mating for educational level. *Behavior Genetics, 15*(4), 349–369.

Herculano-Houzel, S. (2012). The remarkable, yet not extraordinary, human brain as a scaled-up primate brain and its associated cost.

Proceedings of the National Academy of Sciences, 109(Suppl. 1), 10661–10668.

Hewstone, M., Rubin, M. and Willis, H. (2002). Intergroup bias. *Annual Review of Psychology, 53*, 575–604.

Hill, R.A. and Dunbar, R.I. (2003). Social network size in humans. *Human Nature, 14*, 53–72.

Hobson, J.A. (2005). Sleep is of the brain, by the brain and for the brain. *Nature, 437*, 1254–1256.

Hobson, J.A. and McCarley, R.W. (1977). The brain as a dream state generator: an activation-synthesis hypothesis of the dream process. *The American Journal of Psychiatry, 134*, 1335–1348.

Hofling, C.K., Brotzman, E., Dalrymple, S., Graves, N. and Pierce, C.M. (1966). An experimental study in nurse-physician relationships. *Journal of Nervous and Mental Disease, 143*, 171–180.

Hogg, M.A. and Abrams, D. (1988). *Social Identifications: A Social Psychology of Intergroup Relations and Group Processes*. London: Routledge.

Hogg, M.A., & Vaughan, G.M. (1998). *Social psychology* (2nd). London: Pearson.

Holland, R.W., Roeder, U., van Baaren, R.B., Brandt, A.C. and Hannover, B. (2004). Don't stand so close to me: the effects of self-construal on interpersonal closeness. *Psychological Science, 15*, 237–242.

Holt-Lunstad, J., Smith, T.B. and Layton, J.B. (2010). Social relationships and mortality risk: a meta-analytic review. *PLoS Med, 7*: e1000316.

Holz, J., Piosczyk, H., Landmann, N., Feige, B., Spiegelhalder, K., Riemann, D., Nissen, C. and Voderholzer, U. (2012). The timing of learning before night-time sleep differentially affects declarative and procedural long-term memory consolidation in adolescents. *PLoS One, 7*, e40963.

Horne, J.A. (1978). A review of the biological effects of total sleep deprivation in man. *Biological Psychology, 7*, 55–102.

Horne, J.A. and Harley, L.J. (1988). Human SWS following selective head heating during wakefulness. In: J.A. Horne (Ed.), *Sleep '88*. Stuttgart: Fischer Verlag, 188–190.

Hornsey, M.J., Spears, R., Cremers, I. and Hogg, M.A. (2003). Relations between high and low power groups: the importance of legitimacy. *Personality and Social Psychology Bulletin, 29*, 216–227.

Horwitz, A. (2007). Transforming normality into pathology: the DSM and the outcomes of stressful social arrangements. *Journal of Health and Social Behavior, 48*, 211–222.

Howitt, D., Billig, M., Cramer, D. and Edwards, D. (1989). *Social Psychology: Conflicts and Continuities*. New York: McGraw-Hill International.

Irwin, J., & Cressey, D.R. (1962). Thieves, convicts and the inmate culture. *Social Problems, 10*(2), 142–155.

James, O. (2002). *They F*** You Up: How to Survive Family Life*. London: Bloomsbury.

Jenness, A. (1932). The role of discussion in changing opinion regarding matter of fact. *Journal of Abnormal and Social Psychology, 27*, 279–296.

Johansson, G., Aronsson, G. and Lindstrom, B.O. (1978). Social psychological and neuroendocrine stress reactions in highly mechanised work. *Ergonomics, 21*, 583–99.

Johnson, S. (2005). *Everything bad Is good for you: How today's popular culture is actually making us smarter*. London: Penguin.

Jones, F. and Bright, J. (2001). *Stress: Myth, Theory and Research*. Harlow: Pearson.

Jones, S.S. (2009). The development of imitation in infancy. *Philosophical Transactions of the Royal Society B: Biological Sciences, 364*, 2325–2335.

Joseph, J. (2012). The 'missing heritability' of psychiatric disorders: elusive genes or non-existent genes? *Applied Developmental Science, 16*, 65–83.

Judd, C.M. and Park, B. (1988). Out-group homogeneity: judgments of variability at the individual and group levels. *Journal of Personality and Social Psychology, 54*, 778–788.

Jung, C.G. (1961). *Freud and Psychoanalysis. Collected Works*, Vol. 4. New York: Pantheon.

Jung, C.G. (1964). *Man and his Symbols*. New York: Dell.

Kandel, E.R. and Hawkins, R.D. (1992). The biological basis of learning and individuality. *Scientific American 267*, 78–86.

Kanner, A.D., Coyne, J.C., Schaefer, C., & Lazarus, R.S. (1981). Comparison of two modes of stress measurement: Daily hassles and uplifts versus major life events. *Journal of Behavioral Medicine, 4*(1), 1–39.

Kapler, I.V., Weston, T. and Wiseheart, M. (2015). Spacing in a simulated undergraduate classroom: Long-term benefits for factual and higher-level learning. *Learning and Instruction, 36*, 38–45.

Karlins, M., Coffman, T.L. and Walters, G. (1969). On the fading of social stereotypes: Studies in three generations of college students. *Journal of Personality and Social Psychology, 13*, 1–16.

Kelman, H. (1958). Compliance, internalisation and identification: three processes of attitude change. *Journal of Conflict Resolution, 2*, 51–60.

Kendon, A. and Cook, M. (1969). The consistency of gaze patterns in social interaction. *British Journal of Psychology, 60*, 481–494.

Kerckhoff, A.C., & Davis, K.E. (1962). Value consensus and need complementarity in mate selection. *American Sociological Review, 27*, 295–303.

Kiecolt-Glaser, J.K., Garner, W., Speicher, C.E., Penn, G.M., Holliday, J. and Glaser, R. (1984). Psychosocial modifiers of immunocompetence in medical students. *Psychosomatic Medicine, 46*, 7–14.

Kiecolt-Glaser, J.K., Marucha, P.T., Malarkey, W.B., Mercado, A.M. and Glaser, R. (1995). Slowing of wound healing by psychological stress. *The Lancet, 346*, 1194–1196.

Kilham, W. and Mann, L. (1974). Level of destructive obedience as a function of transmitter and executant roles in the Milgram obedience paradigm. *Journal of Personality and Social Psychology, 29*(5), 696–702.

Kim, J., & Lee, J.E.R. (2011). The Facebook paths to happiness: Effects of the number of Facebook friends and self-presentation on subjective well-being. *CyberPsychology, Behavior, and Social Networking, 14*(6), 359–364.

King, H.E. (1961). Psychological effects of excitation in the limbic system. In D.E. Sheer (Ed.), *Electrical stimulation of the brain* (pp. 477–486). Austin: University of Texas Press.

Kobasa, S.C. (1979). Stressful life events, personality, and health: an inquiry into hardiness. *Journal of Personality and Social Psychology, 37*(1), 1–11.

Kohlberg, L. (1969). *Stages in the Development of Moral Thought and Action*. New York: Holt.

Koriat, A., Bjork, R.A., Sheffer, L., & Bar, S.K. (2004). Predicting one's own forgetting: the role of experience-based and theory-based processes. *Journal of Experimental Psychology: General, 133*(4), 643.

Krauss Whitbourne, S. (2011). The essential guide to defense mechanisms: can you spot your favorite form of self-deception? Retrieved 12 November 2014 from http://www.psychologytoday.com/blog/fulfillment-any-age/201110/the-essential-guide-defense-mechanisms.

Krauss Whitbourne, S. (2012). The ultimate guide to body language. *Psychology Today*. Retrieved 22 January 2015 from http://www.psychologytoday.com/blog/fulfillment-any-age/201206/the-ultimate-guide-body-language.

Kruijshaar, M.E., Barendregt, J., Vos, T., de Graaf, R., Spijker, J. and Andrews, G. (2005). Lifetime prevalence estimates of major depression: an indirect estimation method and a quantification of recall bias. *European Journal of Epidemiology, 20*, 103–111.

Kuzmanovic, B., Georgescu, A.L., Eickhoff, S.B., Shah, N.J., Bente, G., Fink, G.R., & Vogeley, K. (2009). Duration matters: dissociating neural correlates of detection and evaluation of social gaze. *Neuroimage, 46*(4), 1154–1163.

Laar, C.V., Levin, S., Sinclair, S. and Sidanius, J. (2005). The effect of university roommate contact on ethnic attitudes and behaviour. *Journal of Experimental and Social Psychology, 41*, 329–345.

Lang, P.J. and Lazovik, A.D. (1963). Experimental desensitisation of a phobia. *Journal of Abnormal and Social Psychology, 66*, 519–525.

Langlois, J.H. and Roggman, L.A. (1990). Attractive faces are only average. *Psychological Science, 1*, 115–121.

Lazarus, R.S. and Folkman, S. (1984). *Stress, Appraisal and Coping*. New York: Springer.

Lindzey, G., Hall, C.S. and Thompson, R.F. (1978). *Psychology* (2nd edn). New York: Worth Publishers.

Lømo, T. (2003). The discovery of long-term potentiation. *Philosophical Transactions of the Royal Society of London. Series B: Biological Sciences, 358*, 617–620.

Maltby, J., Day, L., McCutcheon, L.E., Gillett, R., Houran, J. & Ashe, D. (2004). Celebrity worship using an adaptational-continuum model of personality and coping. *British Journal of Psychology, 95*, 411–428.

McCutcheon, L.E., Lange, R., & Houran, J. (2002). Conceptualization and measurement of celebrity worship. *British Journal of Psychology, 93*(1), 67–87.

McDaniel, M.A., Roediger, H.L. and McDermott, K.B. (2007). Generalizing test-enhanced learning from the laboratory to the classroom. *Psychonomic Bulletin and Review, 14*, 200–206.

McEwen, B.S. and Sapolsky, R.M. (1995). Stress and cognitive function. *Current Opinion in Neurobiology, 5*, 205–216.

McGuffin, P., Katz, R., Rutherford, J. and Watkins, S. (1996). The heritability of DSM-IV unipolar depression: a hospital based twin register study. *Archives of General Psychiatry, 53*, 129–136.

McIntyre, M., Gangestad, S. W., Gray, P.B., Chapman, J.F., Burnham, T.C., O'rourke, M.T., & Thornhill, R. (2006). Romantic involvement often reduces men's testosterone levels - but not always: The moderating role of extrapair sexual interest. *Journal of Personality and Social Psychology, 91*(4), 642–651.

McKenna, K.Y., Green, A.S., & Gleason, M.E. (2002). Relationship formation on the Internet: What's the big attraction?. *Journal of Social Issues, 58*(1), 9–31.

McNeill, D. (1992). *Hand and Mind: What Gestures Reveal About Thought*. Chicago: University of Chicago Press.

Maguire, E.A., Gadian, D.G., Johnsrude, I.S., Good, C.D., Ashburner, J., Frackowiak, R.S.J. and Frith, C.D. (2000). Navigation-related structural change in the hippocampi of taxi drivers. *Proceedings of the National Academy of Sciences of the United States of America, 97*, 4398–4403.

Mann, L. (1981). The baiting crowd in episodes of threatened suicide. *Journal of Personality and Social Psychology, 41*(4), 703–709.

Marazziti, D. and Canale, D. (2004). Hormonal changes when falling in love. *Psychoneuroendocrinology, 29*, 931–936.

March, J.S., Silva, S., Petrycki, S., Curry, J., Wells, K., Fairbank, J., Burns, B., Domino, M., McNulty, S., Vitiello, B. and Severe, J. (2007). The treatment for adolescents with depression study (TADS): long-term effectiveness and safety outcomes. *Archives of General Psychiatry, 64*, 1132–1143.

Marmot, M.G., Bosma, H., Hemingway, H., Brunner, E. and Stansfeld, S. (1997). Contribution of job control and other risk factors to social variations in coronary heart disease incidence. *The Lancet, 350*, 235–239.

Marsh, R.L., Hicks, J.L. and Cook, G.I. (2005). On the relationship between effort toward an ongoing task and cue detection in event-based prospective memory. *Journal of Experimental Psychology: Learning, Memory, and Cognition, 31*, 68–75.

Maslow, A.H. (1943). A theory of human motivation. *Psychological Review, 50*, 370–396.

Matsumoto, D. (1989). Cultural differences of the perception of emotion. *Journal of Cross-Cultural Psychology, 20*, 92–105.

Mednick, S., Nakayama, K. and Stickgold, R. (2003). Sleep-dependent learning: a nap is as good as a night. *Nature Neuroscience, 6*, 697–698.

Meichenbaum, D. (2007). Stress inoculation training: a preventative and treatment approach. In P.M. Lehrer, R.L. Woolfolk and W.E. Sime (Eds.), *Principles and Practice of Stress Management* (3rd edn). New York: Guilford Press.

Meloen, J.D. (1993). The F scale as a predictor of fascism: an overview of 40 years of authoritarianism research. In W.F. Stone, G. Lederer and R. Christie (Eds.), *Strength and Weakness: The Authoritarian Personality Today*. New York: Springer-Verlag, 47–69.

Meltzoff, A.N. and Moore, M.K. (1977). Imitation of facial and manual gestures by human neonates. *Science, 198*, 75–78.

Messinger, D.S., Fogel, A. and Dickson, K. (2001). All smiles are positive, but some smiles are more positive than others. *Developmental Psychology, 37*, 642–653.

Middlemist, R.D., Knowles, E.S. and Matter, C.F. (1976). Personal space invasions in the lavatory: suggestive evidence for arousal. *Journal of Personality and Social Psychology, 33*, 541–546.

Milgram, S. (1963). Behavioural study of obedience. *Journal of Abnormal and Social Psychology, 67*, 371–378.

Milgram, S. (1974). *Obedience to Authority.* New York: Harper and Row.

Miller, G.A. (1956). The magical number seven, plus or minus two: Some limits on our capacity for processing information. *Psychological Review, 63*, 343–355.

Miller, K. (2005). *Communication Theories*. New York: McGraw Hill.

Milner, B. (1970). Memory and the medial temporal regions of the brain. *Biology of Memory, 23*, 31–59.

Mischel, W., Ebbeson, E.B. and Raskoff Zeiss, A. (1972). Cognitive and attentional mechanisms in delay of gratification. *Journal of Personality and Social Psychology, 21*, 204–218.

Mori, K. and Arai, M. (2010). No need to fake it: reproduction of the Asch experiment without confederates. *International Journal of Psychology, 45*, 390–397.

Morris, D. (1967). *The Naked Ape*. London: Jonathan Cape.

Moscovici, S. (1981). On social representations. In J.P. Forgas (Ed.), *Social Cognition: Perspectives in Everyday Understanding*. London: Academic Press.

Moscovici, S., Lage, E. and Naffrechoux, M. (1969). Influence of a consistent minority on the responses of a majority in a color perception task. *Sociometry, 32*, 365–380.

Mowrer, O.H. (1939). A stimulus-response analysis of anxiety and its role as a reinforcing agent. *Psychological Review, 46*(6), 553–565.

Mowrer, O.H. (1947). On the dual nature of learning—a re-interpretation of "conditioning" and "problem-solving." *Harvard Educational Review, 17*, 102–148.

Mowrer, O.H. (1960). *Learning theory and behavior*. Hoboken, NJ: John Wiley & Sons.

Moyer, M.W. (2016). Eye contact: How long is too long? *Scientific American: Mind*. Retrieved 24 May 2018 from https://www.scientificamerican.com/article/eye-contact-how-long-is-too-long/

Mumford, D.B., Whitehouse, A.M. and Plattes, M. (1991). Sociocultural correlates of eating disorders among Asian schoolgirls in Bradford. *British Journal of Psychiatry, 158*, 222–228.

Murdock Jr, B.B. (1962). The serial position effect of free recall. *Journal of Experimental Psychology, 64*(5), 482–488.

Murray, C.J. and Lopez, A.D. (1997). Alternative projections of mortality and disability by cause 1990–020: Global burden of disease study. *The Lancet, 349*, 1498–1504.

Murray, D.J. (1968). Articulation and acoustic confusability in short-term memory. *Journal of Experimental Psychology, 78*, 679–684.

Murstein, B.I. (1972). Physical attractiveness and marital choice. *Journal of Personality and Social Psychology, 22*, 8–12.

Nelson-Jones, R. (2000). *Six Key Approaches to Counselling and Therapy.* London: Continuum International.

NHS (2016). Beta blockers. *NHS Website*. Retrieved 3 September 2018 from https://www.nhs.uk/conditions/Beta-blockers/

NHS (2018). Antidepressants. *NHS website*. Retrieved 3 September 2018 from https://www.nhs.uk/conditions/antidepressants/

Norman, R.M., Sorrentino, R.M., Gawronski, B., Szeto, A.C., Ye, Y. and Windell, D. (2010). Attitudes and physical distance to an individual with schizophrenia: the moderating effect of self-transcendent values. *Social Psychiatry and Psychiatric Epidemiology, 45*, 751–758.

Nuckolls, K.B., Cassel, J. and Kaplan, B.H. (1972). Psychological Assets, life crisis and the prognosis of pregnancy. *American Journal of Epidemiology, 95*, 431–441.

Nutt, D. (2009). Equasy: an overlooked addiction. *Journal of Psychopharmacology, 23*, 3–5.

Orne, M.T. (1962). On the social psychology of the psychological experiment: With particular reference to demand characteristics and their implications. *American Psychologist, 17*, 776–783.

Orr-Andrawes, A. (1987). The case of Anna O.: a neuropsychiatric perspective. *Journal of the American Psychoanalytic Association, 35*, 387–419.

Oswald, I. (1966). *Sleep*. London: Penguin.

Otteson, J.P., & Otteson, C.R. (1980). Effect of teacher's gaze on children's story recall. *Perceptual and Motor Skills, 50*(1), 35-42.

Paivio, A. (1969). Mental imagery in associative learning and memory. *Psychological Review, 76*, 241–263.

Paluck, E.L. (2009). Reducing intergroup prejudice and conflict using the media: A field experiment in Rwanda. *Journal of Personality and Social Psychology, 96*(3), 574–587.

Papakostas, G.I., Thase, M.E., Fava, M., Nelson, J.C., & Shelton, R.C. (2007). Are antidepressant drugs that combine seratonergic and noradrenergic mechanisms of action more effective than selective seratonin reuptake inhibitors in treaating maajor depressive disorder? A meta-analysis of studies of newer agents. *Biological Psychiatry, 62*(11), 1217–27.

Patel, V. (2001). Cultural factors and international epidemiology: depression and public health. *British Medical Bulletin, 57*, 33–45.

Pearlstein, T., Howard, M., Salisbury, A., & Zlotnick, C. (2009). Postpartum depression. *American Journal of Obstetrics and Gynecology, 200*(4), 357–64.

Percy, J. (2014). David Elleray should face FA action for racist remarks to another official, says Lord Ouseley. *The Telegraph*. Retrieved 26 January 2015 from http://www.telegraph.co.uk/sport/football/news/10946451/David-Elleray-should-face-FA-action-for-racist-remarks-to-another-official-says-Lord-Ouseley.html.

Perrett, D.I., May, K.A. and Yoshikawa, S. (1994). Facial shape and judgments of female attractiveness. *Nature, 368*, 239–242.

Perrett, D.I., Lee, K.J., Penton-Voak, I., Rowland, D., Yoshikawa, S., Burt, D.M., Henzi, S.P., Castles, D.L. and Akamatsu, S. (1998). Effects of sexual dimorphism on facial attractiveness. *Nature, 394*, 884–887.

Perrin, S. and Spencer, C. (1981). Independence or conformity in the Asch experiment as a reflection of cultural and situational factors. *British Journal of Social Psychology, 20*, 205–209.

Perry, G. (2014). The view from the boys. *The Psychologist, 27*, 834–5.

Peterson, L.R. and Peterson, M.J. (1959). Short-term retention of individual verbal items. *Journal of Experimental Psychology, 58*, 193–198.

Pettigrew, T.F. (2017). Social psychological perspectives on Trump supporters. *Journal of Social and Political Psychology, 5*(1), 107–116.

Pettigrew, T.F., & Martin, J. (1987). Shaping the organizational context for Black American inclusion. *Journal of Social Issues, 43*(1), 41–78.

Pezdek, K., Whetstone, T., Reynolds, K., Askari, N. and Dougherty, T. (1989). Memory for real-world scenes: the role of consistency with schema expectation. *Journal of Experimental Psychology: Learning, Memory, and Cognition, 15*, 587–595.

Phillips, M.L. (2009). Circadian rhythms: of owls, larks and alarm clocks. *Nature, 458*, 142–144.

Piliavin, I.M., Rodin, J. and Piliavin, J.A. (1969). Good Samaritanism: an underground phenomenon? *Journal of Personality and Social Psychology, 13*, 289–299.

Pink, D. (2018). When: *The Scientific Secrets of Perfect Timing*. Edinburgh: Canongate Books.

Pinker, S. (2011). *The better angels of our nature: The decline of violence in history and its causes*. London: Penguin.

Pinker, S. (1994). *The Language Instinct*. London: Penguin Books.

Polikovsky, S., Kameda, Y. and Ohta, Y. (2009). Facial micro-expressions recognition using high speed camera and 3D-gradient descriptor. In *Imaging for Crime Detection and Prevention, Proceedings of 3rd International Conference*, 16, doi: 10.1049/ic.2009.0244.

Pollet, T. V., van der Meij, L., Cobey, K.D., & Buunk, A.P. (2011). Testosterone levels and their associations with lifetime number of opposite sex partners and remarriage in a large sample of American elderly men and women. *Hormones and Behavior, 60*(1), 72–77.

Premack, D. and Premack, A.J. (1983). *The Mind of an Ape*. New York: Norton.

Quinlan, R.J. (2008). Human pair-bonds: Evolutionary functions, ecological variation, and adaptive development. *Evolutionary Anthropology, 17*, 227–238.

Rahe, R.H., Mahan, J. and Arthur, R. (1970). Predictions of near-future health-change from subjects' preceding life changes. *Journal of Psychosomatic Research, 14*, 401–406.

Raine, A., Buchsbaum, M. and LaCasse, L. (1997). Brain abnormalities in murderers indicated by positron emission tomography. *Biological Psychiatry, 42*, 495–508.

Raj, A. and van Oudenaarden, A. (2008). Nature, nurture, or chance: stochastic gene expression and its consequences. *Cell, 135*, 216–226.

Rank, S.G. and Jacobson, C.K. (1977). Hospital nurses' compliance with medication overdose orders: a failure to replicate. *Journal of Health and Social Behavior, 18*, 188–193.

Rasch, B. and Born, J. (2013). About sleep's role in memory. *Physiological Review, 93*, 681–766.

Reynolds, K.J., Subašić, E. and Tindall, K. (2015). The problem of behaviour change: from social norms to an ingroup focus. *Social and Personality Psychology Compass, 9*, 45–56.

Riggle, E. D., Ellis, A. L., & Crawford, A. M. (1996). The impact of "media contact" on attitudes toward gay men. *Journal of Homosexuality, 31*(3), 55–69.

Roehrs, T. and Roth, T. (2001). Sleep, sleepiness, and alcohol use. *Alcohol Research and Health, 25*, 101–109.

Rogers, C. (1961). *On becoming a person: A therapist's view of psychotherapy*. London: Constable.

Rosenhan, D.L. (1973). On being sane in insane places. *Science, 179*, 250–258.

Rotter, J.B. (1966). Generalised expectancies for internal versus external control of reinforcement. *Psychological Monographs*, 80, 1–28.

Rowley-Conwy, P. (2001). Time, change and the archaeology of hunter-gatherers: how original is the 'original affluent society'? In C. Panter-Brick, R.H. Layton and P. Rowley-Conwy (Eds.), *Hunter-gatherers: An Interdisciplinary Perspective*. Cambridge: Cambridge University Press, 39–72.

Royal College of Psychiatrists (2018). Benzodiazepines. Retrieved 3 September 2018 from http://www.rcpsych.ac.uk/healthadvice/treatmentswellbeing/benzodiazepines.aspx.

Rubenstein, C., Shaver, P. and Peplau, L.A. (1979). Loneliness. *Human Nature, 2*, 58–65.

Rubin, M. and Hewstone, M. (1998). Social identity theory's self-esteem hypothesis: a review and some suggestions for clarification. *Personality and Social Psychology Review, 2*, 40–62.

Rubin, Z. (1970). Measurement of romantic love. *Journal of Personality and Social Psychology, 16*(2), 265–273.

Rubin, Z. (1973). *Liking and Loving: An Invitation to Social Psychology*. New York: Holt, Rinehart and Winston.

Rubin, Z. (1975). Disclosing oneself to a stranger: Reciprocity and its limits. *Journal of Experimental Social Psychology, 11*(3), 233–260.

Rusbult, C.E. (1980). Commitment and satisfaction in romantic associations: A test of the investment model. *Journal of Experimental Social Psychology, 16*(2), 172–186.

Rusbult, C.E., & Martz, J.M. (1995). Remaining in an abusive relationship: An investment model analysis of nonvoluntary dependence. *Personality and Social Psychology Bulletin, 21*(6), 558–571.

Rutland, A. (1999). The development of national prejudice, in-group favouritism and self-stereotypes in British children. *British Journal of Social Psychology, 38*, 55–70.

Sacks, O. (1998). *The Man who Mistook his Wife for a Hat and Other Clinical Tales*. London: Picador.

Santee, R.T. and Maslach, C. (1982). To agree or not to agree: personal dissent amid social pressure to conform. *Journal of Personality and Social Psychology, 42*, 690–700.

Santhi, N., Thorne, H.C., van der Veen, D.R., Johnsen, S., Mills, S.L., Hommes, V., Schlangen, L.J., Archer, S.N. and Dijk, D.J. (2012). The spectral composition of evening light and individual differences in the suppression of melatonin and delay of sleep in humans. *Journal of Pineal Research, 53*, 47–59.

Sapolsky, R.M. (1995). Social subordinance as a marker of hypercortisolism: Some unexpected subtleties. *Annals of the New York Academy of Sciences, 771*, 626–639.

Saunders, T., Driskell, J.E., Johnston, J.H. and Salas, E. (1996). The effect of stress inoculation training on anxiety and performance. *Journal of Occupational Health Psychology, 1*, 170–186.

Schachter, S. and Singer, J.E. (1962). Cognitive, social and physiological determinants of emotional state. *Psychological Review, 69*, 379–399.

Scheele, D., Striepens, N., Güntürkün, O., Deutschländer, S., Maier, W., Kendrick, K.M. and Hurlemann, R. (2012). Oxytocin modulates social distance between males and females. *Journal of Neuroscience, 32*, 16074–16079.

Schmidt, F.L. (1992). What do data really mean? Research findings, meta-analysis, and cumulative knowledge in psychology. *American Psychologist, 47*, 1173–1181.

Scoville, W.B. and Milner, B. (1957). Loss of recent memory after bilateral hippocampal lesions.

Journal of Neurology, Neurosurgery and Psychiatry, 20, 11–21.

Sears, D.O. (1986). College sophomores in the laboratory: influences of a narrow data base on psychology's view of human nature. *Journal of Personality and Social Psychology, 51*, 513–530.

Seehagen, S., Konrad, C., Herbert, J. S. and Schneider, S. (2015). Timely sleep facilitates declarative memory consolidation in infants. *Proceedings of the National Academy of Sciences, 112*, 1625–1629.

Seligman, M. (1971). *Phobias and preparedness. Behaviour Therapy, 2*, 307-320.

Selye, H. (1936). A syndrome produced by diverse nocuous agents. *Nature, 138*, 32.

Selye, H. (1956). *The Stress of Life*. New York: McGraw-Hill.

Shapiro, C.M., Bortz, R., Mitchell, D., Bartel, P. and Jooste, P. (1981) Slow-wave sleep: a recovery period after exercise. *Science, 214*, 1253–1254.

Sheffield, M.E.J. and Dombeck, D.A. (2015). Calcium transient prevalence across the dendritic arbour predicts place field properties. *Nature, 517*, 200–204.

Sheridan, L., Maltby, J., & Gillett, R. (2006). Pathological public figure preoccupation: Its relationship with dissociation and absorption. *Personality and Individual Differences, 41*(3), 525–535.

Sherif, M. (1935). A study of some factors in perception. *Archives of Psychology, 27*, 1–60.

Sherif, M. (1966). In common predicament: *Social psychology of intergroup conflict and cooperation*. Boston: Houghton Mifflin.

Sherif, M. (1977). Crisis in social psychology: some remarks towards breaking through the crisis. *Personality and Social Psychology Bulletin, 3*, 368–382.

Sherif, M., Harvey, O.J., White, B.J., Hood, W.R. and Sherif, C.W. (1954). *Experimental Study of Positive and Negative Intergroup Attitudes between Experimentally Produced Groups*. Oklahoma: University of Oklahoma Press.

Siegel, J.M. (2005). Clues to the functions of mammalian sleep. *Nature, 437*, 1264–1271.

Skinner, B.F. (1938). *The Behavior of Organisms: An Experimental Analysis.* New York: Appleton-Century.

Skinner, B.F. (1957). *Verbal Behavior.* Acton: Copley Publishing.

Smith, P.B. and Bond, M.H. (1993). *Social Psychology Across Cultures: Analysis and Perspectives.* Hemel Hempstead: Harvester Wheatsheaf.

Smith, S.M., & Rothkopf, E.Z. (1984). Contextual enrichment and distribution of practice in the classroom. *Cognition and Instruction, 1*, 341–358.

Smithsonian National Museum of Natural History (2015). Homo erectus. *Human Origins.* Retrieved 3 September 2018 from http://humanorigins.si.edu/evidence/human-fossils/species/homo-erectus.

Spencer, S.J., Steele, C.M. and Quinn, D.M. (1999). Stereotype threat and women's math performance. *Journal of Experimental Social Psychology, 35*, 4–28.

Sperling, G. (1960). The information available in brief visual presentations. *Psychological Monographs, 74*, 1–29.

Sproull, L., & Kiesler, S. (1986). Reducing social context cues: Electronic mail in organizational communication. *Management Science, 32*(11), 1492–1512.

Squire, L.R. (2004). Minireview – memory systems of the brain: a brief history and current perspective. *Neurobiology of Learning and Memory, 82*, 171–177.

Statland, B.E. and Demas, T.J. (1980). Serum caffeine half-lives: Healthy subjects vs. patients having alcoholic hepatic disease. *American Journal of Clinical Pathology, 73*, 390–393.

Stein, M.B., Walker, J.R. and Forde, D.R. (1994). Setting diagnostic thresholds for social phobia: considerations from a community survey of social anxiety. *American Journal of Psychiatry, 151*, 408–412.

Steinberg, L. and Monahan, K.C. (2007). Age differences in resistance to peer influence. *Developmental Psychology, 43*, 1531–1543.

Stickgold, R. (2009). How do I remember? Let me count the ways. *Sleep Medicine Reviews, 13*: 305–308.

Stoet, G., O'Connor, D.B., Conner, M. and Laws, K.R. (2013). Are women better than men at multi-tasking? *BioMed Central Psychology, 1*, 18.

Stroop, J.R. (1935). Studies of interference in serial verbal reactions. *Journal of Experimental Psychology, 18*, 643.

Suler, J. (2004). The online disinhibition effect. *Cyberpsychology & Behavior, 7*(3), 321–326.

Sykes, G.M. (1958). *The society of captives: A study of a maximum security prison*. New York: Princeton University Press.

Tajfel, H. (1970). Experiments in intergroup discrimination. *Scientific American, 223*, 96–105.

Tajfel, H. (1982). Social psychology of intergroup relations. *Annual Review of Psychology, 33*, 1–39.

Tajfel, H. and Turner, J.C. (1979). An integrative theory of intergroup conflict. In W.G. Austin and S. Worchel (Eds.), *The Social Psychology of Intergroup Relations*. Monterey: Brooks/Cole.

Taylor, S.E., Klein, L.C., Lewis, B.P., Gruenewald, T.L., Gurung, R.A.R. and Updegraff, J.A. (2000). Biobehavioural responses to stress in females: tend-and-befriend, not fight-or-flight. *Psychological Review, 107*, 411–429.

Tellegen, A., Lykken, D.T., Bouchard, T.J., Wilcox, K.J., Segal, N.L. and Rich, S. (1988). Personality similarity in twins reared apart and together. *Journal of Personality and Social Psychology, 54*, 1031–1039.

Thibaut, J.W. and Kelley, H.H. (1959). *The Social Psychology of Groups*. New York: Wiley.

Thigpen, C. and Cleckley, H. (1954). A case of multiple personality disorder. *Journal of Abnormal and Social Psychology, 49*, 135–151.

Tinbergen, N. (1952). The curious behavior of the stickleback. *Scientific American, 187*(6), 22–27.

Tosun, L.P., & Lajunen, T. (2010). Does Internet use reflect your personality? Relationship between Eysenck's personality dimensions and Internet use. *Computers in Human Behavior, 26*(2), 162–167.

Trivers, R.L. (1972). Parental investment and sexual selection. In B. Campbell (Ed.), *Sexual Selection and the Descent of Man*. Chicago: Adeline, 136–179.

Turner, J.R. (1993). Interpersonal and psychological predictors of parasocial interaction with different television performers. *Communication Quarterly, 41*(4), 443–453.

Tversky, A. and Kahneman, D. (1974). Judgment under uncertainty: heuristics and biases. *Science, 185*, 1124–1131.

Van Dongen, H.P.A., Vitellaro, K.M. and Dinges, D.F. (2005). Individual differences in adult human sleep and wakefulness: Leitmotif for a research agenda. *Sleep, 28*, 479–496.

van Ijzendoorn, M.H. (1989). Moral judgment, authoritarianism, and ethnocentrism. *Journal of Social Psychology, 129*, 37–45.

van Ijzendoorn, M.H. and Kroonenberg, P.M. (1988). Cross-cultural patterns of attachment: a meta-analysis of the strange situation. *Child Development, 59*, 147–156.

Vanneman, R. D., & Pettigrew, T. F. (1972). Race and relative deprivation in the urban United States. *Race, 13*(4), 461–486.

Velez, J.A., Greitemeyer, T., Whitaker, J. L., Ewoldsen, D. R., & Bushman, B. J. (2016). Violent video games and reciprocity: The attenuating effects of cooperative game play on subsequent aggression. *Communication Research, 43*(4), 447–467.

Wagner, D.R. (1999). Circadian rhythm sleep disorders. *Current Treatment Options in Neurology, 1*, 299–308.

Walker, M.P., Brakefield, T., Hobson, J.A. and Stickgold, R. (2003). Dissociable stages of human memory consolidation and reconsolidation. *Nature, 425*, 616–620.

Walker, R.S., Hill, K.R., Flinn, M.V. and Ellsworth, R.M. (2011). Evolutionary history of hunter-gatherer marriage practices. *PLoS One, 6*, e19066.

Walster, E., Aronson, V., Abrahams, D. and Rottman, L. (1966). Importance of physical attractiveness in dating behavior. *Journal of Personality and Social Psychology, 4*, 508–516.

Walther, J.B. (1996). Computer-mediated communication: Impersonal, interpersonal, and hyperpersonal interaction. *Communication Research, 23*(1), 3–43.

Watson, J.B. (1913). Psychology as the behaviourist views it. *Psychological Review, 20*, 158–177.

Watson, J.B. and Rayner, R. (1920). Conditioned emotional reactions. *Journal of Experimental Psychology, 3*, 1–14.

Waugh, N.C. and Norman, D.A. (1965). Primary memory. *Psychological Review, 72*, 89–104.

Wedekind, C., Seebeck, T., Bettens, F. and Paepke, A.J. (1995). MHC-dependent mate preferences in humans. *Proceedings of the Royal Society of London. Series B: Biological Sciences, 260*, 245–249.

Wehr, T.A. (1992). In short photoperiods, human sleep is biphasic. *Journal of Sleep Research, 1*, 103–107.

West, P., & Sweeting, H. (2004). *Evidence on equalisation in health in youth from the West of Scotland. Social Science & Medicine, 59*(1), 13–27.

Whitson, S. (2010). 10 things passive aggressive people say: your early-warning system for hidden hostility. *Psychology Today*. Retrieved 3 September 2018 from https://www.psychologytoday.com/blog/passive-aggressive-diaries/201011/10-things-passive-aggressive-people-say.

Williams, T.M. (1986). *The impact of television: A natural experiment in three communities*. New York: Academic Press.

Wilson, S. and Nutt, D.J. (2013). *Sleep Disorders*. Oxford: Oxford University Press.

Wiseman, R. (2014). *Night School: The Life-Changing Science of Sleep*. London: Macmillan.

Wlazlo, Z., Schroeder-Hartwig, K., Hand, I., Kaiser, G., & Münchau, N. (1990). Exposure in vivo vs social skills training for social phobia: Long-term outcomes and differential effects. *Behaviour Research & Therapy, 28*(3), 181–193.

Wolfson, A.R. and Carskadon, M.A. (1998). Sleep schedules and daytime functioning in adolescents. *Child Development, 69*, 875–887.

Wolpe, J. (1958). *Psychotherapy by reciprocal inhibition*. Stanford, CA: Stanford University Press.

Yuki, M., Maddux, W.W. & Masuda, T. (2007). Cultural differences in using the eyes and mouth as cues to recognize emotions in Japan and the United States. *Journal of Experimental Social Psychology, 43*(2), 303–311.

Zajonc, R.B. (1968). Attitudinal effects of mere exposure. *Journal of Personality and Social Psychology, 9*: 1–27.

Zajonc, R.B. (1985). Emotion and facial efference: A theory reclaimed. *Science, 228*, 15–21.

Zimbardo, P. G. (1969). The human choice: Individuation, reason, and order vs. deindividuation, impulse, and chaos. In W.J. Arnold & D. Levine (Eds.), *Nebraska Symposium on Motivation* (pp. 237–307). Lincoln: University of Nebraska Press.

Zimbardo, P.G., Banks, P.G., Haney, C. and Jaffe, D. (1973). Pirandellian prison: the mind is a formidable jailor. *New York Times Magazine*, 38–60.

Zubin, J. and Spring, B. (1977). Vulnerability: a new view of schizophrenia. *Journal of Abnormal Psychology, 86*, 103–126.

Index

001/06022019

10 9 8 7 6 5 4 3

ISBN 9780008282240

Published byLeckie & Leckie Ltd
An imprint of HarperCollinsPublishers
Westerhill Road, Bishopbriggs, Glasgow, G64 2QT
T: 0844 576 8126 F: 0844 576 8131
leckieandleckie@harpercollins.co.uk
www.leckieandleckie.co.uk

Printed and bound by CPI Group (UK) Ltd, Croydon, CR0 4YY

A CIP Catalogue record for this book is available from the British Library.

Acknowledgements
P12 (bottom) © Apic/Hulton Archive/Getty Images; P13 (bottom left) © rook76 / Shutterstock.com; P14 © Paul Harris/Hulton Archive/Getty Images; P19 © ullstein bild/Getty Images; P21 (top) © De Agostini Picture Library/De Agostini/Getty Images; P21 (bottom) © magno/Hulton Archive/Getty Images; P27 (left) © Reg Burkett/Hulton Archive/Getty Images; P27 (right) (top left) Hans-Werner / licensed under the Creative Commons Attribution-Share Alike 3.0 Unported license; P28 © AFP/Getty Images;P32 © Hulton Archive/Archive Photos/Getty Images; P33 © Sovfoto/Universal Images Group/Getty Images; P34 (top) "Little-albert" by John B Watson - Akron psychology archives. Licensed under Public Domain via Wikimedia Commons - https://commons.wikimedia.org/wiki/File:Little-albert.jpg#/media/File:Little-albert.jpg; P34 (bottom) © Nina Leen/The LIFE Picture Collection/Getty Images; P35 (top) © Jon Brenneis/The LIFE Images Collection/Getty Images; P36 (bottom) © ullstein bild/Getty Images; P38 © ullstein bild/Getty Images; P40 (bottom) Reconstruction by John Gurche; photographed by Tim Evanson. Licensed under the Creative Commons Attribution-Share Alike 2.0 Generic license; P42 (bottom) © Gil.K / Shutterstock.com; P43 © Kenneth Garrett/National Geographic/Getty Images; P45 Albert Einstein 1947 by Photograph by Oren Jack Turner, Princeton, N.J. - The Library of Congress. Licensed under Public Domain via Wikimedia Commons - https://commons.wikimedia.org/wiki/File:Albert_Einstein_1947.jpg#/media/File:Albert_Einstein_1947.jpg; P48 (top) © Iakov Filimonov / Shutterstock.com; P53 © BSIP/Universal Images Group/Getty Images; P66 (top) © Central Press/Hulton Archive/Getty Images; P68 (top) © AFP/Getty Images; P71 © Ted Russell/The LIFE Images Collection/Getty Images; P74 (bottom) © Boston Globe/Getty Images; P95 (bottom) © Boston Globe/Getty Images; P101 (top) © Christophe Michot / Shutterstock.com; P106 (bottom) © Leonard Zhukovsky / Shutterstock.com; P107 (right) © National Public Radio;P113 © Martin Good / Shutterstock.com; P139 (bottom) Henry Molaison in 1986, aged 60, enjoying an unmemorable memory experiment at Massachusetts Institute of Technology. Photo by Jenni Ogden, author of Trouble In Mind: Stories from a neuropsychologist's casebook. OUP, New York, 2012;P128 (bottom) © The Washington Post/Getty Images; P144 (middle) © erichon / Shutterstock.com; P153 (top) © EQRoy / Shutterstock.com; P144 (bottom) © Toronto Star Archives/Toronto Star/Getty Images; P210 © Archive Photos/Moviepix/Getty Images; P239 (middle) Mond-vergleich. Licensed under Public Domain via Wikimedia Commons - https://commons.wikimedia.org/wiki/File:Mond-vergleich.svg#/media/File:Mond-vergleich.svg; P260 (middle) Asch conformity 1955 by Source (WP:NFCC#4). Licensed under Fair use via Wikipedia - https://en.wikipedia.org/wiki/File:Asch_conformity_1955.jpg#/media/File:Asch_conformity_1955.jpg; P261 Asch experiment by Fred the Oyster. Licensed under GFDL via Wikimedia Commons - https://commons.wikimedia.org/wiki/File:Asch_experiment.svg#/media/File:Asch_experiment.svg; P266 (top) © Lisa Maree Williams/Getty Images News; P293 © Apic/Getty Images; P297 (bottom Terrence Spencer/The LIFE Picture Collection/Getty Images; P298 (top) © David M. Benett/Getty Images Entertainment/Getty Images; P298 (middle) © NICHOLAS KAMM/AFP/Getty Images; P298 (bottom) © Christian Marquardt/Getty Images News; P299 (bottom) © Matt Cardy/Getty Images News; P302 (top) FOX/FOX Image Collection/Getty Images; P304 © Becker/Hulton Archive/Getty Images; P305 (bottom) © Photo 12/Universal Images Group/Getty Images; P307 (top) "Henri Tajfel" by European Association of Social Psychologie - www.easp.eu/_img/pics/persons/tajfel.jpg. Licensed under CC BY 3.0 via Wikimedia Commons - https://commons.wikimedia.org/wiki/File:Henri_Tajfel.jpg#/media/File:Henri_Tajfel.jpg; P307 (middle) © DEA / G. NIMATALLAH/De Agostini/Getty Images; P307 (bottom) © DEA / E. LESSING/De Agostini/Getty Images; P308 (top) © Matt Cardy/Getty Images; P308 (bottom) © Aspen Photo / Shutterstock.com; P310 (bottom) © ullstein bild/Getty Images; P315 (top) © Paul Schutzer/The LIFE Premium Collection/Getty Images; P333 (top) © Nina Leen/The LIFE Picture Collection/Getty Images; P358 © Chronicle / Alamy Stock Photo

All other images © Shutterstock.com or public domain.

Whilst every effort has been made to trace the copyright holders, in cases where this has been unsuccessful, or if any have inadvertently been overlooked, the Publishers would gladly receive any information enabling them to rectify any error or omission at the first opportunity.